Canadian-American
Summit Diplomacy
1923-1973

Selected Speeches and Documents

edited and with an introduction by
Roger Frank Swanson

The Carleton Library No. 81
McClelland and Stewart Limited

In debating the means we must not lose sight of the common ends.

R.B. Bennett
April 25, 1933

I am going to keep alongside you, as good neighbours.

W.L. Mackenzie King
June 12, 1947

Together, the United States and Canada prove to the world that a great power and a lesser power can work in harmony without the smaller being submerged by his bigger neighbour.

Louis S. St. Laurent
November 13, 1953.

I come into your country. You come into mine. . . . We get together. We discuss. We are not at all afraid.

John G. Diefenbaker
June 3, 1960

. . . if, for Canada I can drink Vodka with Khrushchev, for Canada I could eat hominy grits with Johnson.

Lester B. Pearson
January 20, 1965

Have the Americans stopped loving us?

Pierre E. Trudeau
December 7, 1971

Contents

Preface

This volume identifies and documents the summit meetings between Canadian Prime Ministers and U.S. Presidents from 1923 to 1973. The speeches and documents in this volume are virtually all first person Prime Ministerial or Presidential sources. Editorial notes at the beginning of the chapters briefly summarize each meeting the Prime Minister had with a U.S. President, with references to the materials documented. Of a total of 61 Canadian-American summit meetings in the past half century, 42 are documented, although all are discussed in the editorial notes. A summit meeting is simply defined as a personal interaction between a Prime Minister and a President, or a series of such personal interactions, unbroken by either of the two leaders returning to their respective countries.

There has been an attempt to include in this volume as full a range of significant first person sources as possible, and to present them with a minimum of editing. Thus, the value of this volume is that the leaders are left to recreate their own periods. Further compression of documentation would have the unfortunate result of distorting precisely that which the documents are attempting to present. This attempt at comprehensiveness is especially important with respect to both the substance and the rhetoric of Canadian-American summit meetings. It is the juxtaposition of differences and similarities, divergence and convergence, that provides the conceptual key to understanding both the dynamics of this summitry, and the Canada-United States relationship itself.

This volume does not constitute a definitive collection. In view of the 50-year period surveyed, and the wide contextual variety of these meetings especially in the multilateral sphere (e.g., a bilateral talk at a United Nations session), an absolutely exhaustive listing is neither possible, given reasonable resources, nor useful. Moreover, the full import of the majority of those meetings identified is still shrouded in bureaucratic secrecy. Thus, not only may many of the meetings appear substantively vague about the issues discussed, but a meeting that now appears unimportant might with the declassification of files be found to be of significance. Nonetheless, it is felt that the public record is sufficiently extensive, and revealing, to warrant this volume. Certainly the editor hopes that it will be of some use in illuminating a dimension of the Canada-United States relationship, and this notwithstanding those inadequacies in compiling and excerpting that he might have passed on to the reader.

This sequence of Canadian-American summit meetings was identified by surveying primary sources (e.g., government publications, documents, and memoirs) and secondary sources (e.g., yearbooks, histories, and very importantly, 50 years of both the Toronto *Globe and Mail* and the *New York Times*). The criterion of selection of the meetings documented in this volume was, quite simply, their relative importance in the context of Canada-United States relations, both overall and according to specific issue areas. In selecting the materials to be documented, the guideline used was the extent to which they shed light on the substance and the rhetoric of the relationship, as well as on the attitudes and styles of the respective leaders. These materials take three forms: (1) singular (e.g., Prime Ministerial or Presidential speech), (2) interactive (e.g., exchange of remarks or toasts), and (3) convergent (e.g., Joint Statements issued during or after a meeting). Agreements signed during the meetings, such as the Columbia River Treaty, are not included because they are available in other sources. However, the agreement is included if it constituted a Joint Statement emanating from the meeting, for example, the Ogdensburg Agreement.

The year 1923 was chosen as the starting point in this summit sequence for three reasons. This year marks the first time a United States President travelled to Canada during his incumbency, when President Warren G. Harding visited Vancouver, British Columbia. More importantly, the year 1923 can be viewed as one of the key dates in the evolution of Canadian autonomy. In this year, the Canadian Minister of Justice signed the Halibut Treaty with the United States, marking the first time a Canadian official signed an international treaty alone. Thereafter, British representatives neither partook in the negotiations on treaties affecting Canada nor did they sign treaties on Canada's behalf. In addition, there was the Imperial Conference in 1923, at which it was agreed in principle that each member of the Commonwealth had the authority to negotiate its own international treaties, resulting in the presumption that each Dominion had full control of its own foreign policy. Thus, by 1923, Canada had to be regarded as something more than a component of the British Empire. The stage was therefore set for Canadian-American summit diplomacy.

Acknowledgements

For their permission to use the material which constitutes the documentation in this book I am grateful to the following sources:

To the Honourable J.W. Pickersgill for permission to use a portion of the typescript *King Diaries* included here as document 1, Section A of the Introduction, and to Mr. Pickersgill and the University of Toronto Press for permission to use portions of *The MacKenzie King Record* included here as the first documents in Sections E, F, G, and H of Chapter II, the first documents of Sections A, B, and D, and the third documents of Sections C and F of Chapter III. To *The Globe*, Toronto for permission to use material from an article by William Marchington on November 12, 1935, as document 2, Section A, Chapter II; and to *The Globe and Mail*, Toronto for an article on August 19, 1938, cited here as document 3, Section C, Chapter II. To *The New York Times* for copyright 1936, 1938, 1947 by the New York Times Company, reprinted by permission and cited as documents 1 and 2 of Sections B and D of Chapter II and document 3 in Section E of Chapter III. To *The Canadian Forum*, Toronto, for material in the September, 1973 edition cited as documents 1 and 2 of Section C of Chapter VI. To the Herbert Hoover Presidential Library in West Branch, Iowa, for permission to use the two documents from Mr. Hoover's papers cited in Section A of Chapter I. To Random House, Inc., for material from Volumes II and IV of *The Public Papers and Addresses of Franklin D. Roosevelt*, Samuel Rosenman, editor, which are included as documents 2 and 4 of Section B, Chapter I; and documents 1, 3, and 4 of Section A, Chapter II. To Macmillan Publishing Co., Inc., and the Franklin D. Roosevelt Memorial Library for permission to use material from the 1938 and 1940 Volumes of *The Public Papers and Addresses of Franklin D. Roosevelt*, edited by Samuel Rosenman, which are included as documents 1 and 2 of Section C, and document 2 of Section F, both in Chapter II. To Harper & Rowe Publishers, Inc., for Volumes 1941 and 1943 of *The Public Papers and Addresses of Franklin D. Roosevelt*, edited by Samuel Rosenman, parts of which are cited as document 2, Section G, and document 1, Section I, both of Chapter II. To the National Archives and Records Service of the General Services Administration for materials in *The Public Papers of the Presidents of the United States: Harry S. Truman, Dwight D. Eisenhower, John F. Kennedy,* and *Lyndon B. Johnson:* Volumes 1945, 1947, 1949, 1951; 1953, 1956, 1958, 1960-61; 1961, 1963; 1963-64 Book I, 1963-64 Book II, 1965, 1966, 1967; which are cited in the book as pp/President's Name. To the Lyndon B. Johnson Library at Austin, Texas, to include a transcript of a press conference cited as document 1, Section E, Chapter VI. And to the White House Press Office for a press statement issued during Mr. Nixon's term of office included here as document 1 Section A, Chapter VII.

I am also grateful to the Clerk of the House of Commons for material taken from the sessional bound volumes of the Debates of the House of Commons, Canada, cited as CHCD. For papers and speeches of Canadian Prime Ministers other than those in the House of Commons, I am grateful to Dr. Gertrude Gunn, Head Librarian of the Harriet Irving Library, University of New Brunswick, for permission to use items from the Bennett papers included as documents 1, 3, and 5, Section B of Chapter I; and to the Prime Minister's Office for materials included as document 3, Section A, Chapter IV; document 5, Section B and document 1, Section G, both of Chapter VI; and, document 2, Section B of Chapter VII (as recorded by ACE-Federal Reporters, Inc., of Washington, D.C.).

Also my gratitude to Information Canada for permission to quote material from *External Affairs* included as document 4, Section A of Chapter V and document 2, Section A, Chapter VII; and from *Statements and Speeches* included as document 3, Section B and document 1, Section F, both in Chapter V. And to the U.S. Department of State for material contained in *Foreign Relations of the United States* cited as documents 1 and 2, Section C, Chapter III; in the *Department of State Bulletin* included as document 2, Section F, Chapter V, and in the United States Information Agency's publication *Visit to Canada of the President* for document 3, Section C, Chapter VII. Finally to the National Press Club of Washington, D.C., for transcripts of speeches included as document 1, Section C, Chapter IV, and document 3, Section A, Chapter VII; to the Alumni Office of the College of William and Mary, Williamsburg, Virginia, for material printed originally in *The Alumni Gazette of the College of William and Mary in Virginia* which is cited as documents 1 and 2, Section F, Chapter III; and to the General Alumni Association of Temple University in Philadelphia, Pennsylvania, for Mr. Pearson's speech included as document 1, Section F, Chapter VI.

*   *   *

For their secretarial assistance, special appreciation is extended to Mesdames Micheline Thibaud and Elaine Ferat, and to Ms. Linda Ross. The editor is indebted to those colleagues who have commented on this volume. He is also indebted to those Canadian and American graduate students who have worked with him on it—Messrs. Larry Kohler and John Kirton, Ms. Eleanore Wellwood, and especially Mr. Robert Simmons. Given the personal commitment of these students to their respective nations, and their academic commitment to studying relations between Canada and the United States, this volume must necessarily be dedicated to them, and students like them. It is done so, respectfully.

R.F.S.
Mosherville, Pennsylvania

Abbreviations for Main Sources

CHCD   *Canada, House of Commons Debates*

S/S   *Statements and Speeches*, published by the Department of External Affairs

Ext/Aff   *External Affairs*, monthly journal published by the Department of External Affairs.

PAC   *Public Archives of Canada*, Ottawa

PMO   Prime Minister's Office

King Record   *The Mackenzie King Record*, 4 volumes, J.W. Pickersgill and D.F. Forster, Toronto: University of Toronto Press

TGM   Toronto *Globe And Mail* (Prior to November 1936, *The Globe*)

WHPS   White House Press Secretary (Office of), Washington, D.C.

DSB   *The Department of State Bulletin*, weekly publication of the Department of State

For/Rel   *Foreign Relations of The United States.* Collections of foreign policy documents compiled by the Department of State

PP/U.S. Presidents. Public Papers (Of United States Presidents)
   (The papers of Presidents from Harry S. Truman to Richard M. Nixon are published by the United States Government Printing Office, under the series *Public Papers of the Presidents of the United States.* The papers of Franklin D. Roosevelt are published by three Houses; 1928-1936—Random House; 1937-1940—Macmillan; 1941-1945—Russell & Russell under the title *The Public Papers and Addresses of Franklin Delano Roosevelt.*)

NYT   *New York Times*

List of Tables

Introduction

Canadian-American summitry is less a continuum than a kaleidoscope. Indeed, it might be considered, to quote George Bain, "a diplomatic adaptation of the old New England custom of bundling" which he defined as "an exercise in familiarization at close quarters with consequences hard to predict."[1] Notwithstanding the substantive and rhetorical haze surrounding these meetings from King and Coolidge to Trudeau and Nixon, they constitute an important dimension of the Canada-United States relationship. Cloaked in a rhetoric all their own, these summit meetings have performed several useful functions, in varying degrees substantive. The overall utility of Canadian-American summitry lies more in the atmospherics it generates than in any definitive accomplishments. Each meeting is a snapshot—freezing rhetoric and issues which become, at the summit, a microcosm of the Canadian-United States relationship. Issues briefly flick up to the summit level—the St. Lawrence Seaway proposal flicked for over thirty years—where they sometimes receive an impetus for resolution. But just as often they are benignly exorcised in a communiqué, after which they are again taken up by sub-summit officials and processed through routine decisional channels.

Summit diplomacy, defined generally as a meeting at the chief of state or head of government level, is as old as is the debate about its merits.[2] From the 1280 B.C. negotiations of Ramses II of Egypt, the historical record is replete with examples of monarchs and chiefs of

---

[1]George Bain, "Meeting By Pearson, Kennedy Is Diplomatic-Style Bundling," TGM (May 8, 1963). (Mr. Bain was referring specifically to the May 1963 Hyannis Port meeting.)

[2]This is but one facet of a conventional definition: "the determination and publicizing of foreign policy and the management of foreign affairs at the chief of state or head of government level." This ranges from foreign policy determination at this level, to personal communications, to personal representatives, to visits and summit conferences. (See Elmer Plischke, *Summit Diplomacy: Personal Diplomacy of the President of the United States*, (College Park, Maryland: Bureau of Governmental Research, College of Business and Public Administration, University of Maryland, 1958), p. 5.)

state or heads of government conducting personal diplomacy. However, recent history has witnessed "the intensification of its use, the development of new forms, and popularization in the public consciousness."[3] Also of recent origin is the term itself. It is appropriate that one of the first times the word "summit" was used was in August of 1943 at the first Quebec Conference which included Franklin D. Roosevelt, Winston Churchill, and W.L. Mackenzie King. The Roosevelt-Churchill Joint Statement issued at the end of the Conference declared: "Considering that these (American and British) forces are intermingled in continuous action against the enemy in several quarters of the globe, it is indispensable that entire unity of aim and method should be maintained *at the summit* of the war direction." It was not until the middle and late 1950s that the press began to use the expression "summit conference," generally referring to meetings of the great powers.[4] Canadian Prime Ministers and U.S. Presidents have not perceived themselves as conducting "summit" meetings. Their public statements abound with references to "informal" meetings but not to summitry, even when describing state visits. Likewise, references to Canadian-American "summit meetings" by the press are also lacking, but with some recent exceptions. For example, the word "summit" was used by the *Globe and Mail* in describing the Trudeau-Nixon December 1971 Washington meeting, and their April 1972 Ottawa meeting.[5]

Tables I and II list Canadian Prime Ministers, American Presidents, and their Secretaries and Ambassadors from 1923 to 1973. During this time span, every Canadian Prime Minister has, during his term of office, travelled to the United States at least twice to meet with a President. The first summit meeting in this volume was between Prime Minister W.L. Mackenzie King and President Calvin Coolidge. Noteworthy for its formality, according to King's Diary account, this meeting took place in Washington in November of 1927. (For documentation, see Section A following this Introduction.) The trip enabled King to visit several old friends and inspect the newly established Canadian Legation in Washington. At a White House luncheon in his honour hosted by President Coolidge, the two leaders informally discussed such subjects as the St. Lawrence Seaway, broadcasting, and the U.S. Legation in Ottawa.[6]

---

[3]*Ibid.*, p. 3.

[4]*Ibid.*, p. 4.

[5]"PM's Meeting with Nixon," TGM (December 7, 1971), and "A Modest Little Summit," TGM (April 17, 1972), p. 6.

[6]See "Premier King Arrives in Washington on Visit," NYT (November 23, 1927), p. 3; "Canadian Premier Guest of Coolidge," TGM (November 24, 1927), p. 3; and "Canadian Premier To Be Honor Guest At Washington Fete," TGM (November 21, 1927), p. 1.

TABLE I

CANADIAN PRIME MINISTERS, THEIR SECRETARIES OF STATE
FOR EXTERNAL AFFAIRS, AND AMBASSADORS
TO THE UNITED STATES 1923-1973*

Prime Minister	Secretaries of State for External Affairs	Ambassadors to the United States
W. L. M. King (1921-1926)	W. L. M. King (1921-1926)	— — — — —
A. Meighen (1926)	A. Meighen (1926)	
W. L. M. King (1926-1930)	W. L. M. King (1926-1930)	— — — — —
R. B. Bennett (1930-1935)	R. B. Bennett (1930-1935)	V. M. Massey (1927-1930)
W. L. M. King (1935-1948)	W. L. M. King (1935-1946)	W. D. Herridge (1931-1935)
		H. M. Marler (1936-1939)
		L. C. Christie (1939-1941)
		L. G. McCarthy (1941-1944)
		L. B. Pearson (1944-1946)
	L. S. St. Laurent (1946-1948)	H. H. Wrong (1946-1948)
L. S. St. Laurent (1948-1957)	L. B. Pearson (1948-1957)	H. H. Wrong (1948-1953)
		A. D. P. Heeney (1953-1957)
J. G. Diefenbaker (1957-1963)	J. G. Diefenbaker (1957)	N. R. Robertson (1957-1958)
	S. J. Smith (1957-1959)	
	H. C. Green (1959-1963)	A. D. P. Heeney (1959-1962)
		C. S. A. Ritchie (1962-1963)
L. B. Pearson (1963-1968)	P. Martin (1963-1968)	C. S. A. Ritchie (1963-1966)
		A. E. Ritchie (1966-1968)
P. E. Trudeau (1968-)	M. W. Sharp (1968-)	A. E. Ritchie (1968-1970)
		M. Cadieux (1970-)

* Legations were established in Ottawa and Washington in 1923, and were elevated to embassies in 1943, thereby elevating the Ministers to Ambassadors.

The historical antecedents of Canadian Prime Ministerial visits to the United States to meet with Presidents are both elusive and beyond the time span of this volume. The origins of Canadian-American summitry can be found in the pre-twentieth century visits of Prime Ministers to Washington, not to meet with Presidents, but as members of British delegations. An example would be that of Sir John A. Macdonald in March of 1871 when he came to Washington as the British-appointed Canadian Commissioner of the Anglo-American Joint High Commission, which deliberated such issues as the Alabama claims and Canadian fisheries. Examples of pre-1923 Prime Ministerial-Presidential meetings in the United States would include an October 1899 Chicago meeting between President McKinley, Prime Minister Laurier, and Mexico's Vice President Mariseal, representing President Diaz; a January 1918 Borden-Wilson meeting; and a July 1922 King-Harding meeting—the latter two occurring in Washington.[7]

[7]See respectively, "Views English Relations," NYT (March 1, 1871), p. 8; "The President Has A Busy Day," NYT (October 10, 1899); "Canada A Partner Now, Borden's View," NYT (March 2, 1918), p. 2; and "Canada for Treaty Making Permanent Peace on Frontier," NYT (July 13, 1922), pp. 1, 4.

TABLE II

U.S. PRESIDENTS, THEIR SECRETARIES OF STATE, AND
AMBASSADORS TO CANADA, 1923-1973

President	Secretary of State	Ministers and Ambassadors To Canada
W. G. Harding (1921-1923)	C. E. Hughes (1921-1923)	— — — — —
C. Coolidge (1923-1929)	F. B. Kellogg (1925-1929)	W. Phillips (1927-1929)
H. C. Hoover (1929-1933)	H. L. Stimson (1929-1933)	W. Phillips (1929)
		A. MacNider (1930-1932)
F. D. Roosevelt (1933-1945)	C. Hull (1933-1944)	W. D. Robbins (1933-1935)
		N. Armour (1935-1938)
		D. C. Roper (1939)
		J. H. R. Cromwell (1940)
		J. P. Moffat (1940-1943)
	E. R. Stettinius (1944)	R. Atherton (1943-1945)
H. S. Truman (1945-1953)	E. R. Stettinius (1944-1945)	R. Atherton (1945-1948)
	J. F. Byrnes (1945-1947)	
	G. C. Marshall (1947-1949)	
		L. A. Steinhardt (1948-1950)
	D. G. Acheson (1949-1953)	
		S. Woodward (1950-1953)
D. D. Eisenhower (1953-1961)	J. F. Dulles (1953-1959)	R. D. Stuart (1953-1956)
		L. T. Merchant (1956-1958)
		R. B. Wigglesworth (1958-1960)
	C. A. Herter (1959-1961)	
J. F. Kennedy (1961-1963)	D. Rusk (1961-1963)	L. T. Merchant (1961-1962)
		W. W. Butterworth (1962-1963)
L. B. Johnson (1963-1969)	D. Rusk (1963-1969)	W. W. Butterworth (1963-1968)
		H. F. Linder (1968-1969)
R. M. Nixon (1969-1974)	W. P. Rogers (1969-1973)	H. F. Linder (1969)
	H. D. Kissinger (1973-)	A. W. Schmidt (1969-1973)*

*William J. Porter was appointed Ambassador to Canada but did not assume his
duties until 1974.

To turn to U.S. Presidents visiting Canada for summit consultations,
it will quickly become apparent that these visits—although very much
taken for granted today—are a rather recent phenomenon, with the first
Presidential summit visit occurring in July 1936. The first President to
visit Canada during his term of office was Warren G. Harding during a
July 1923 trip to British Columbia, although he did not meet with a
Canadian Prime Minister.[8] The President had been on a tour of the
United States, and it was while returning from Alaska that Harding
stopped off at Vancouver.[9] (See Appendix A.) President Franklin D.

---

[8]This was an historical visit not just from the standpoint of Canada-U.S.
relations, for President Harding was also the fourth President to leave the
territory of the U.S. during his incumbency. Theodore Roosevelt was the first
President to break the tradition by visiting Panama in November of 1906;
William Taft was the second by visiting Mexico in October of 1909 as part of an

Roosevelt was the second President to visit Canada, after Mr. Harding, but was the first President to meet with a Canadian Prime Minister on Canadian soil. This was during his July 1936 visit to Quebec. Mr. Roosevelt was also the first President to visit Ottawa, and the first President to address Members of the Canadian Parliament and public, both of which occurred in the same visit on August 25, 1943.

Since Roosevelt, every President has visited Canada. Also since Roosevelt, every President has visited Ottawa and addressed Parliament, with the exception of Lyndon B. Johnson. Dwight D. Eisenhower is the only President to have done so twice—in November of 1953 during the tenure of Mr. St. Laurent, and in July of 1958 during Mr. Diefenbaker's Government. The other Presidents visiting Ottawa were Mr. Truman in June of 1947 during the tenure of Mr. King; John F. Kennedy in May of 1961 during the Government of Mr. Diefenbaker; and Richard M. Nixon in April of 1972 during Pierre E. Trudeau's incumbency. In contrast, no Canadian Prime Minister has addressed the U.S. Congress, although two Governors General have done so—Lord Tweedsmuir in April of 1937 and the Honourable Vincent Massey in May of 1954. Canadian Prime Ministers have apparently been satisfied with speeches before the National Press Club of Washington (St. Laurent and Trudeau) or more frequently, press conferences. However, given the frequency of Prime Ministerial-Presidential meetings in the United States, and since other heads of government have addressed the Congress, that Canadian Prime Ministers have never done so is somewhat puzzling.[10]

It is therefore interesting to speculate whether Canada has had a "special relationship" with the United States in the overall context of U.S. summit diplomacy. Although there is no sufficiently reliable comparative data from which to draw definitive conclusions, a listing provided by the U.S. Department of State would appear to suggest that

---

exchange with President Diaz; and Woodrow Wilson was the third when he headed the U.S. delegation to the Paris Peace Conference at the end of World War I. Every U.S. President since Wilson has left the territory of the U.S. while in office. (See Elmer Plischke, *Conduct of American Diplomacy* (Princeton, N.J.: D. Van Nostrand, Inc., 1961), p. 49.)

[9]See "Canadians Cheer Harding Assurance of Friendship," NYT (July 27, 1923), pp. 1, 2.

[10]For example, Australia's Prime Minister Robert Gordon Menzies addressed the Senate and the House twice (in 1950 and 1955) and the former Premier of South Africa Jan Smuts addressed the Senate once (1930). Moreover, the U.S. Senate and/or House has received such U.K. Prime Ministers as Churchill (in 1941, 1943, and 1952), Harold Macmillan (1958, 1960), Ramsay Macdonald (1939), and Anthony Eden (1958). Other heads of governments addressing the Senate and/or the House include the Prime Ministers of such countries as Afghanistan, Ghana, Italy, India, Japan, Burma and Pakistan.

no such "special" Canada-United States summit relationship exists.[11] In the first place, U.S. Presidents have met most frequently with the Prime Ministers of the United Kingdom, closely followed by the Prime Ministers of Canada. The totals of both nations are substantially higher than those of all other countries. Secondly, U.S. Presidents have received the British Prime Minister almost as often as the Canadian Prime Minister. And thirdly, Presidents have travelled to the United Kingdom and its possessions most often, with Canada in second place. Thus, in terms of all three categories, it would appear that Canada has no more of a "special" summit relationship with the United States than does the United Kingdom. Of special interest is the parallel nature of U.S. Presidential visits to Canada and Mexico. American Presidents have travelled to Mexico about as often as they have to Canada. Indeed, U.S. Presidents from Truman through Nixon have travelled to Canada and Mexico an equal number of times: Truman once to Canada and once to Mexico; Eisenhower three times to each country; Kennedy once to each country; Johnson three times to each country; and Nixon twice to each country. It would appear therefore that in terms of U.S. Presidential summit visits to other countries, there is a North American and Anglo-American "special relationship," rather than just a Canadian-United States one.

The Significance of Canadian-American Summitry

Prime Ministerial-Presidential summit meetings are rather an enigmatic phenomenon. The questions dealt with at the summit level over the past half century have been those which have in many respects defined the Canada-U.S. relationship: 1935 Trade Agreement, 1940 Ogdensburg Agreement, 1941 Hyde Park Declaration, 1959 St. Lawrence Seaway Project, 1963 Nuclear Weapons Controversy, 1964 Seaborn Vietnam Missions, 1964 Columbia River Treaty, 1965 Auto Pact, and the 1972 Great Lakes Water Quality Agreement. This prominent listing, however, should not obscure the fact that summit issues have varied markedly in volume, focus, and subject matter. This variability is hardly surprising. Canadian-American summitry occurs both in a bilateral context, and as part of multilateral gatherings of several heads of government. Moreover, those events which occasion summitry range from purely ceremonial events to the review of, and actual agreement on, issues.

Table III provides a simplified checklist of the nature of Canadian-

---

[11]These figures refer to heads of government meetings up to 1971. Given differences in reliability and definitional criteria, these figures are not the same as those used elsewhere in this volume. The breakout of Presidential visits to Mexico and Canada from Truman to Nixon is up to 1972 instead of 1971.

American summitry during the last fifty years. By presenting a capsule description of the salient features of each meeting, this table may serve to familiarize the reader with these meetings by highlighting their widely different character and importance. Thus, Table III first lists the two leaders at the meeting, its date and location. The next column points out whether the meeting took place in a bilateral or multilateral context. That is, in addition to strictly bilateral meetings, the chart indicates those times Canadian and U.S. leaders have met in the context of such international meetings as a NATO, UN or Pacific War Council conference, or when their talks took place during a tripartite gathering, as illustrated by the Roosevelt, Churchill, and King meetings.

As Table III also indicates, Canadian-American summitry can be ceremonial, substantive, or both. A ceremonial meeting refers to multilateral or bilateral gatherings whose purpose is to acknowledge a meaningful event. Multilaterally this would include, for example, commemoration of such achievements as the establishment of the United Nations. On the bilateral level, ceremonial meetings can take three forms: (1) the signing or proclamation of treaties (e.g., the September 1964 Pearson-Johnson proclamation of the Columbia River Treaty during their meeting in British Columbia); (2) the celebration of joint accomplishments such as the construction of bridges and power projects, or the establishment of an international park (e.g., the June 1959 Queen Elizabeth-Diefenbaker-Eisenhower opening of the St. Lawrence Seaway); and (3) the joint recognition of national events, such as funerals of national leaders and national celebrations (e.g., the Pearson November 1963 attendance at the funeral of President Kennedy).

As Table III further indicates, a substantive meeting is one which consists of a review of issues, an agreement on issues, or both. Issue review refers to those meetings during which there is: (1) a survey of current issues or exchange of ideas (e.g., the Bennett-Hoover January 1931 meeting during which they compared notes on the St. Lawrence Seaway Project); and (2) the reporting of one leader to the other (e.g., King reporting to Truman on the Gouzenko spy case during their September 1945 meeting). Thus, with issue review, the two leaders take due notice of each other's position, but without conclusive results. Issue review allows the two leaders to make known to each other their positions on bilateral and multilateral matters. This is especially important for Canadian Prime Ministers because Canada is the less powerful country, and the very size of the United States, with its multilateral preoccupations, can result in action which disadvantages Canada. For example, St. Laurent met with Eisenhower in May of 1953 and registered Canadian concern about U.S. trade policies.

The second dimension of a substantive meeting is significant issue agreement. This refers to those meetings from which something con-

TABLE III

CHECKLIST OF CANADIAN-AMERICAN SUMMIT MEETINGS 1923-1973

LEADERS	DATE	LOCATION	CONTEXT		CERE-MONIAL	SUBSTAN-TIVE		COMMENTS
			BILAT	MULTI		REVIEW	AGRMT	
King/Coolidge	Nov., 1927	Washington	X			X		St. Lawrence Seaway talks
Bennett/Hoover	Jan., 1931	Washington	X			X		"Unofficial" Seaway talks
Bennett/Roosevelt	Apr., 1933	Washington		X		X		Economic Problems and Freer Trade
King/Roosevelt	Nov., 1935	Washington	X				X	Joint Trade Agreement Negotiated
	Nov., 1935	Washington	X		X			Joint Trade Agreement Signed
	July, 1936	Quebec City	X		X			To Call on the Governor General
	March, 1937	Washington	X			X		Issue Survey before Imperial Conference
	Aug., 1938	Kingston, Ivy Lea, Ontario	X		X		X	Roosevelt Defence Pledge and Bridge Dedication
	Nov., 1938	Washington	X		X		X	Trade Agreement Extension
	June, 1939	Washington and Hyde Park, N.Y.	X		X			Royal Tour of King George VI
	Apr., 1940	Warm Springs, Ga. and Washington	X			X		First Wartime Meeting
	Aug., 1940	Ogdensburg, N.Y.	X				X	Ogdensburg Agreement on Defence Cooperation
	Apr., 1941	Washington and Hyde Park, N.Y.	X				X	Hyde Park Declaration on Defence Production
	Nov., 1941	Hyde Park, N.Y.	X			X		Personal Talks

Leader	Date	Location			Event
	Dec., 1941	Washington		X	St. Pierre and Miquelon Question with Churchill
	Apr., 1942	Washington		X	Pacific War Council
	June, 1942	Washington		X	Pacific War Council with Churchill
	Dec., 1942	Washington	X		General War Discussions
	May, 1943	Washington		X	Churchill, the Pacific War Council and bilateral matters
	Aug., 1943	Quebec City / Ottawa	X	X	First Quebec Conference and First Summit in Ottawa
	Sept., 1944	Quebec City		X	Second Quebec Conference
	March, 1945	Washington	X		In Retrospect
King/Truman	Apr., 1945	Hyde Park, N.Y.	X	X	Roosevelt Burial
	June, 1945	San Francisco	X	X	United Nations Founding Conference
	Sept., 1945	Washington	X	X	Gouzenko Spy Case Report
	Nov., 1945	Washington		X	U.S. - U.K. - Canada Atomic Energy Declaration
	Oct., 1946	New York City, Washington	X	X	U.N. Meeting and Concurrence on Joint Defence
	Apr., 1947	Washington		X	Cordial Issue Survey
	June, 1947	Ottawa	X	X	To call on Governor General and "To Solidify the Friendship"
St. Laurent/Truman	Apr., 1948	Williamsburg, Va.	X	X	Canadian-American Day College of William and Mary
	Feb., 1949	Washington	X		Getting Acquainted and the St. Lawrence Seaway Question
	Sept., 1951	Washington	X		Canada to build Seaway alone

St. Laurent/ Eisenhower	May, 1953	Washington	X		Multi-Issue "Goodwill" Call
	Nov., 1953	Ottawa	X		"The Threat is Present" for North America
	March, 1956	White Sulphur Springs, W. Va.	X		Canada-U.S.-Mexico "neighbourly chat"
	Dec., 1956	Augusta, Ga.	X		Golf Cart Diplomacy
Diefenbaker/ Eisenhower	Oct., 1957	Washington	X	X	Royal Tour of Queen Elizabeth II
	Dec., 1957	Paris	X		NATO Heads of Government Meeting
	July, 1958	Ottawa	X	X	Joint Defence Committee Created
	June, 1959	Montreal	X	X	St. Lawrence Seaway Opening with Queen Elizabeth II
	June, 1960	Washington	X		Following U-2 Incident
	Sept., 1960	New York City	X		Met During U.N. Session
	Jan., 1961	Washington	X	X	Columbia River Treaty Signed
Diefenbaker/ Kennedy	Feb., 1961	Washington	X		To Establish "acquaintanceship"
	May, 1961	Ottawa	X		The "things to push for" meeting
	Dec., 1962	Nassau, Bahamas	X		U.S.-U.K. Nuclear Discussions
Pearson/Kennedy	May, 1963	Hyannis Port, Mass.	X	X	Nuclear Warheads Settlement and General Normalization
Pearson/Johnson	Nov., 1963	Washington	X	X	Kennedy Funeral
	Jan., 1964	Washington	X	X	Columbia River and Campobello Park Signing

Date	Location				Event
Feb., 1964	New York City	X	X		Speeches at Kennedy Foundation
May, 1964	New York City	X		X	Seaborn's Intermediary Hanoi Missions
Sept., 1964	Washington State British Columbia	X	X	X	Columbia River Treaty Proclamation
Jan., 1965	LBJ Ranch	X	X	X	Auto Pact Signing
Apr., 1965	Camp David, Md.	X	X		After Pearson's Bombing Halt Speech
Aug., 1966	Campobello Is.	X	X	X	Campobello Park Dedication
May, 1967	Harrington Lake, Quebec	X	X		After EXPO '67 Visit
Trudeau/Nixon					
March, 1969	Washington	X	X	X	Trudeau's "Sleeping with the elephant"
March, 1969	Washington	X	X		Eisenhower Funeral
June, 1969	Massena, N.Y. Montreal	X	X		St. Lawrence Seaway Tenth Anniversary
Dec., 1971	Washington	X	X		Post Surcharge "fantastic assurances"
Apr., 1972	Ottawa	X	X	X	Great Lakes Water Quality Agreement Signing

clusive results. This can take two forms: (1) a formal agreement or accord embodied in a treaty or joint statement (e.g., the Pearson-Johnson January 1964 signing of the Columbia River Treaty); and (2) an agreement-in-principle which defines the boundaries within which significant issues will be dealt with by lower-level officials (e.g.,the May 1963 Pearson-Kennedy Hyannis Port meeting which broke the deadlock on Canadian acquisition of nuclear weapons).

Apart from the ceremonial and substantive dimensions, the role of Canadian-American summit diplomacy is too diverse to be incorporated in the simplified chart contained in this section. Thus, although not presented on Table III, some further interrelated functions might be noted. A summit meeting can have the effect of generating domestic support for joint Canada-U.S. measures, in that these measures symbolically receive the highest type of endorsement through the action of the President and the Prime Minister. For example, the January 1965 Pearson-Johnson signing of the Auto Pact unequivocally registered President Johnson's support of the Pact to the U.S. Congress.

In addition, Canadian-American summitry can service the internal political processes of the two nations, and especially Canada, by demonstrating to an audience of constituents and colleagues a leader's effectiveness in handling the bilateral relationship. For example, Opposition charges that a Prime Minister has either allowed relations with the United States to deteriorate, or that he has not fully utilized the Canadian-American relationship to Canada's advantage, can result in serious political damage to a Government. Such charges, to cite just three examples, were levelled against Prime Ministers Bennett, Diefenbaker, and Trudeau. To cite the latest case, Prime Minister Trudeau in his December 1971 visit to Washington was quite frank in noting in his press conference that "there was a motion of lack of confidence moved in Canada against the government because it had not established good relations with the Americans." Thus, the avowed purpose of his Washington meeting was, to quote the Prime Minister, to see "if there was any fence-mending needed." Indeed, there is evidence to suggest that these Canadian-American summit meetings service the Canadian political function of widening a Prime Minister's domestic limits of action, by illustrating to the Opposition and the public that bilateral relations are in good order, and that a proposed Canadian action will not unduly disrupt the relationship. For example, this appears to have constituted at least part of the rationale for Prime Minister St. Laurent's September 1951 summit visit to Washington concerning the proposed Canadian decision to "go it alone" with the St. Lawrence Seaway.

The intended audience may not be simply a domestic one. It is possible that Canadian-American summitry can provide Canada with an international prestige, and even influence in the world at large. For example, Prime Minister King rather candidly thanked Roosevelt and Churchill for putting "our country onto the map of the world" at the conclusion of the August 1943 First Quebec Conference which he had hosted. Finally, there may be no audience at all in Canadian-American summitry. This refers to the social dimension, whereby the two leaders meet for the purpose of informal companionship as well as issue review. Although oftentimes a public posture assumed to cover very serious negotiations, usefulness of the social dimension should not be underestimated to the extent that the affability of leaders can be utilized to national advantage. In the Canadian-U.S. context, the model of personal comradeship is, of course, King and Roosevelt. Albeit somewhat exaggerated, and used as an electoral technique by King, there is no doubt but that there was a "special" personal relationship, one which other Prime Ministers and Presidents tried to replicate but could not.

Perhaps the most fundamental and elusive function of Canadian-American summitry lies in an even wider context. The profoundly disparate and interdependent Canada-U.S. relationship necessitates continual reassurances at the summit level that the relationship will, in fact, continue in a manner satisfactory to both parties. And these reassurances are more important to Canada because of the bilateral disparity. More specifically, these reassurances are threefold: (1) that each party will maintain its special access to the other concerning issues important to it; (2) that the benefits accruing from the relationship will continue; and (3) that the political, economic and strategic integrity of each party is not violated in the relationship. The deeds and words of Canadian-American summitry are therefore especially noteworthy. The deeds are provided by the very meetings of Prime Ministers and Presidents, notwithstanding their substantive outcomes; the words by a special set of rhetoric applicable only to the Canada-United States relationship. Hence, the meetings occur with a seemingly irrevocable cadence, and oftentimes appear to be ephemeral. The rhetoric is not new, and oftentimes appears to be somewhat less than elevating. But both the meetings and rhetoric are important.

These Canadian-American summit meetings have therefore become an integral part of the symbolic and decisional processes of the Canada-United States relationship. Within this context, these meetings appear to be propelled by a set of forces which contain their own logic and dynamics. Indeed, there is a certain perceived necessity about Prime Ministers and Presidents meeting periodically. Should this necessity be violated—should this momentum of Canadian-American summitry be disturbed—the symbolic vacuum would be filled with Canadian and American, but especially Canadian, doubts and questioning about their counterparts' most basic attitudes towards the bilateral relationship. Paradoxically, the very recurrence of this summitry and its accompanying rhetoric about the security of "friendship and neigh-bourliness" itself suggests a profound sense of insecurity. That is, these assurances have not been transferable from generation to genera-tion, nor even from leader to leader, nor, for that matter, from year to year as witnessed recently by Prime Minister Trudeau's exchanges with President Nixon. What is interesting—and perhaps disconcerting—is the extent to which these summit assurances are becoming increasingly primordial. It was sufficient for President Eisenhower during his November 1953 visit to Ottawa to assure Canadians of U.S. respect for Canadian sovereignty in the light of joint defence cooperation. How-ever, conditions had sufficiently changed by the early 1970s that President Nixon felt it necessary during his April 1972 visit to Ottawa to reassure Canadians that the U.S. would also respect the economic and political intregrity of Canada, a reassurance which virtually consti-tuted a U.S. declaration of Canadian independence. This illustrates both shifts in issue priority, and the continuity of fundamental tensions generated by the disparate relationship.

It must be noted that Canadian-American summitry is not without its disadvantages. Confidential issue resolution tends to be difficult in view of the publicity usually given these meetings. But even if substan-tive bargaining does occur, there is the twofold danger that the leaders might not have sufficient expertise to pursue detailed discussions satisfactorily, and that agreements concluded might be arrived at too hastily. For example, Prime Minister King had the habit of going to Washington accompanied only by his Private Secretary and one or two advisors, whereupon he would engage in extremely important discus-sions with President Roosevelt on a wide range of matters within a relatively short time. And of course, if an impasse is reached in summit negotiations, there is no higher political authority to invoke, and because the two leaders are themselves negotiating, they might lock themselves into positions they later regret.[12]

The disadvantages of summitry relate to not only substantive negoti-ations, but also the rhetorical dimension. In a summit meeting with all the attendant publicity, there is a temptation, difficult to resist, to join in a rhetorical embrace that can return to haunt—if not compromise—the two participants. It is not so much that commitments are not kept, for specific commitments are generally not made. But the sometimes promiscuous rhetoric of bilateral togetherness, or even the simple fact that the two leaders are meeting, can beget public and official expecta-tions that subsequently are not or cannot be met. For example, the first Diefenbaker-Kennedy meeting and the first Trudeau-Nixon meeting were, in varying degrees, both hailed as new eras of consultation. The question was, of course, how could the progenitors deliver on this

---

[12]See Plischke's *Summit Diplomacy*, *op. cit.*, pp. 119-23.

—either to each other or to their respective constituencies—given basic disagreement on such issues as the Canadian acquisition of nuclear weapons and the surcharge.

Finally, the personal contact between leaders at summit meetings can have a negative effect by aggravating genuine divergences over issues. Instead of decreasing chances of misunderstanding and disagreement, summitry can increase and exacerbate them by personalizing what sometimes might better be left an impersonal process. For example, the personal rapport between Diefenbaker and Kennedy was somewhat less than warm, and as it evolved did not materially contribute to the resolution of issues. And of course the Pearson-Johnson April 1965 meeting, after the Prime Minister's Temple University bombing halt speech on Vietnam, was one of the more abrasive Canadian-American summit meetings.

Moreover, in addition to the personal dimension, the derivative international prestige resulting from Canadian-U.S. summitry can have a negative impact. For example, after the May 1967 Pearson-Johnson meeting during which they quietly discussed the impending Middle Eastern crisis, President Nasser denounced Pearson for what Nasser saw as Pearson's resulting pro-Israeli stance.

Placing summit diplomacy in a wider perspective than the Canadian-American context, writers and practitioners have expressed their reservations about its utility from Philippe de Comines in the 15th century to Sir Harold Nicolson in the 1940s. More recently, Lester B. Pearson had his own reservations about summitry in general, characterized by his statement that "prize fighters also have very close personal contacts."[13] And former U.S. Secretary of State Dean Rusk could conclude in 1960 that "summit diplomacy is to be approached with the wariness with which a prudent physician prescribes a habit-forming drug—a technique to be employed rarely and under the most exceptional circumstances with rigorous safeguards against its becoming a debilitating or dangerous habit."[14] If summit diplomacy is a drug, Canadian and U.S. leaders are addicted.

A Tabular Overview of Canadian-American Summitry

Canadian Prime Ministers and U.S. Presidents have met 61 times in the past half century. In view of both the King-Roosevelt relationship and the war years, it is not surprising that the decade having the greatest number of Canadian-American summit meetings was the 1940s—with

---

[13]Lester B. Pearson, *Diplomacy in the Nuclear Age* (Westport, Connecticut: Greenwood Press, Publishers), p. 9.

[14]Dean Rusk, "The President," *Foreign Affairs*, Vol. 38, No. 3 (April, 1960), p. 361.

a total of 21 from 1940-49.[15] Of special interest is the relatively low number of meetings in the 1950s, which had the same number of meetings as the decade of the 1930s. There were nine meetings from 1950-59, and nine meetings from 1930-39. The decade of the 1960s witnessed the resurgence of Canadian-U.S. summitry almost to the 1940s level, with a total of nineteen meetings from 1960-69. There was one meeting from 1923-29, and up to the end of 1973, there were two meetings. The shortest period between meetings was six days (King-Roosevelt, from November 7-9 to November 15 1935). The longest period between meetings was three years, two months (King-Coolidge from November 1927 to Bennett-Hoover in January 1931); the second longest was three years (St. Laurent-Eisenhower from November 1953 to December 1956); and the third longest was two years, five months (Trudeau-Nixon from June 1969 to December 1971).

This section attempts to answer three basic questions. How many times have individual Canadian Prime Ministers and U.S. Presidents met, and what is the total number of meetings by pairs of leaders? Secondly, what is the average number of summit meetings per years in office both of individual Prime Ministers and Presidents, and of Prime Ministers/Presidents serving concurrently? Thirdly, how many times have Canadian Prime Ministers travelled to the United States to meet with Presidents (and the converse), what is the geographical location of these meetings, how reciprocal have these summit visits been, and how soon have they occurred after the advent of new leaders? It should be noted that all of these tabulations, while helpful in the aggregate, are misleading in suggesting that the meetings were of equal significance. To be fully meaningful, these meetings would have to be weighted according to outcome.

Given the total of 61 Canadian-U.S. summit meetings from 1923 to 1973, Table IV indicates the number of meetings for each Prime Minister and for each President both as individual leaders and as pairs of leaders. On the Canadian side, Prime Minister King leads the list in number of meetings, followed in decreasing order by Diefenbaker and Pearson, St. Laurent, Trudeau (to 1973), and Bennett. On the U.S. side, President Roosevelt has had the greatest number of meetings with Canadian Prime Ministers, followed again in decreasing order, by Eisenhower, Truman, Johnson, Nixon (to 1973), Kennedy, and

---

[15] As stated in the preface; a meeting is simply defined as a personal interaction between a Prime Minister and a President, or a series of such personal interactions, unbroken by either of the two leaders returning to their respective countries. For example, the King-Roosevelt November 7-9 and November 15, 1935 Washington interactions are regarded as two meetings because Mr. King returned to Ottawa during the interval between them. However, the Roosevelt-King April 1941 interactions at Washington and Hyde Park are regarded as one meeting because Mr. King did not return to Canada.

Coolidge and Hoover. Of special interest are the pairs of Prime Ministerial-Presidential relationships. As the table also indicates, from 1923 to the present, there is a total of twelve pairs of Canadian-U.S. leaders who have met at least once. The pair involved in the greatest number of meetings is overwhelmingly King/Roosevelt, followed in decreasing order by Pearson/Johnson, King/Truman, Diefenbaker/Eisenhower, Trudeau/Nixon, St. Laurent/Eisenhower, Diefenbaker/Kennedy, St. Laurent/Truman—with King/Coolidge, Bennett/Hoover, Bennett/Roosevelt, and Pearson/Kennedy all tieing for last place.

A more meaningful set of figures than the number of times each Prime Minister and President met is a comparison between the number of meetings and the number of years the respective leaders held office. This "summit ratio" therefore represents the average number of Prime Ministerial and Presidential meetings expressed per year but computed on a quarter yearly basis. Table v indicates the summit ratios for

TABLE IV
SUMMIT MEETINGS BETWEEN CANADIAN
PRIME MINISTERS AND
U.S. PRESIDENTS 1923-1973

PRESIDENTS / PRIME MINISTERS	Total Meetings	C. Coolidge	H. Hoover	F. D. Roosevelt	H. S. Truman	D. D. Eisenhower	J. F. Kennedy	L. B. Johnson	R. M. Nixon
Total Meetings	61	1	1	20	10	11	4	9	5
R. B. Bennett	2		1	1					
W. L. M. King	28	1		19	8				
L. S. St. Laurent	6				2	4			
J. G. Diefenbaker	10					7	3		
L. B. Pearson	10						1	9	
P. E. Trudeau	5								5

TOTAL MEETINGS BY PAIRS OF LEADERS

individual Canadian Prime Ministers and U.S. Presidents, and for the twelve pairs of Canadian-U.S. leaders who have met at least once. Somewhat surprisingly, rather than King, Pearson leads the list in summit ratios on the Canadian side followed in decreasing order by Diefenbaker, King, Trudeau, St.Laurent, and Bennett.[16] On the U.S. side, Johnson leads the list followed in decreasing order by Roosevelt, Kennedy, Eisenhower, Truman, Nixon, Hoover, and Coolidge. Finally, and again somewhat surprisingly, the summit ratios for the pairs of leaders are as follows: in first place is King/Truman, followed closely by the pairs of King/Roosevelt, Diefenbaker/Eisenhower, Pearson/Kennedy, and Pearson/Johnson. The Diefenbaker/Kennedy pair ranks third, followed in decreasing order by Trudeau/Nixon, St. Laurent/Eisenhower, St.Laurent/Truman, with Bennett/Roosevelt and King/Coolidge having the same number, and ending with Bennett/Hoover. It is apparent that the King/Roosevelt, King/Truman, Diefenbaker/Eisenhower, Pearson/Kennedy, and Pearson/Johnson pairs were all remarkably consistent in the frequency with which they held meetings.

TABLE V
SUMMIT RATIOS BETWEEN CANADIAN PRIME MINISTERS AND U.S. PRESIDENTS 1923-1973
(Meetings per year)

PRIME MINISTERS / PRESIDENTS	Summit Ratios of Cdn. Leaders	C. Coolidge	H. Hoover	F. D. Roosevelt	H. S. Truman	D. D. Eisenhower	J. F. Kennedy	L. B. Johnson	R. M. Nixon
Summit Ratios of U.S. Leaders		.17	.25	1.67	1.29	1.38	1.45	1.71	1.00
R. B. Bennett	.40		.36	.40					
W. L. M. King	1.30	.40		2.00	2.13				
L. S. St. Laurent	.71				.47	.89			
J. G. Diefenbaker	1.74					2.00	1.33		
L. B. Pearson	2.00						2.00	2.00	
P. E. Trudeau	.86								1.00

[16]However, if King's ratio is calculated from 1935 onward, it becomes 2.07 providing him with a comfortable lead over all others. With regard to Presidents, it might be noted that Roosevelt and Kennedy did not complete their terms of office.

There remains the question concerning Prime Ministerial and Presidential summit travels to the United States and Canada respectively. Forty-eight summit meetings occurred in the United States, fourteen in Canada, and two elsewhere, in Nassau and Paris.[17] Table VI indicates the number of Prime Ministerial summit visits to the United States. It can readily be seen that King leads the list, followed in decreasing order by Pearson, St. Laurent and Diefenbaker, Trudeau, and Bennett. From the standpoint of geographical distribution, approximately 70 per cent of these meetings on U.S. soil occurred in Washington, D.C., alone, or Washington in combination with another city. Over 14 per cent of these meetings occurred in New York State alone. The remaining 16 per cent of the meetings took place in the states of California, Virginia, West Virginia, Georgia, Massachusetts, Texas, and Washington. Only two Canadian Prime Ministers (King and Pearson) have met with Presidents in the U.S. West. From the standpoint of geography, the most diverse Canadian Prime Minister is Pearson —who met with Presidents twice in Washington, twice in New York, and once in Massachusetts, Washington State, Texas, and Maryland.

Table VII indicates the number of Presidential summit visits to Canada. Roosevelt leads the list, followed in decreasing order by Eisenhower, Johnson, Nixon, Truman, and Kennedy. From the standpoint of geographical distribution of Canadian-U.S. summit meetings on Canadian soil—President Johnson leads the listing of U.S. Presidents—having met in British Columbia, Ontario, Quebec and New Brunswick. Indeed, Johnson is the only President to have met with a Prime Minister in the Canadian West. The usual pattern appears to be that if a President visits Canada once to meet with a Prime Minister, it is to Ottawa (Truman and Kennedy). If he visits twice, it is to Ottawa and Montreal (President Eisenhower visited Ottawa twice and Montreal once; Nixon visited Montreal and Ottawa once each).

Finally, there has been a notable lack of reciprocity in the number of visits exchanged between Canadian and U.S. leaders, as Table VIII indicates. Overall, Prime Ministers have visited the United States 48 times, and received Presidents in Canada only 14 times. The Prime Minister most successful in achieving reciprocity in summit visits was Diefenbaker, followed by Trudeau, Pearson, King, and St. Laurent. Those Presidents most willing to partake in such reciprocity were Kennedy and Nixon, closely followed by Johnson and Eisenhower,

[17]The breakout exceeds the overall total of 61 by 3. This is because three meetings took place in Canada and the U.S., and are counted twice—the August 1938 King-Roosevelt dedication of the Thousand Islands Bridge in Ontario and New York; the September 1964 Pearson-Johnson ceremonial proclamation of the Columbia River Treaty in British Columbia and Washington; and the June 1969 Trudeau-Nixon tenth anniversary celebration of the St. Lawrence Seaway in New York and Quebec.

TABLE VI
PRIME MINISTERIAL SUMMIT VISITS TO THE U.S. 1923-1973

PRIME MINISTERS	Total Summit Visits to U.S.	C. Coolidge	H. Hoover	F. D. Roosevelt	H. S. Truman	D. D. Eisenhower	J. F. Kennedy	L. B. Johnson	R. M. Nixon
	48		MEETINGS PER PRESIDENT						
R. B. Bennett	2		1	1					
W. L. M. King	24	1		16	7				
L. S. St. Laurent	5				2	3			
J. G. Diefenbaker	5					4	1		
L. B. Pearson	8						1	7	
P. E. Trudeau	4								4

TABLE VII

PRESIDENTIAL SUMMIT VISITS TO CANADA 1923-1973

PRIME MINISTERS		C. Coolidge	H. Hoover	F. D. Roosevelt	H. S. Truman	D. D. Eisenhower	J. F. Kennedy	L. B. Johnson	R. M. Nixon
Total Summit Visits to Canada	14			4	1	3	1	3	2
R. B. Bennett									
W. L. M. King	MEETINGS PER PRIME MINISTER			4	1				
L. S. St. Laurent						1			
J. G. Diefenbaker						2	1		
L. B. Pearson								3	
P. E. Trudeau									2

with Roosevelt and Truman far behind. The only balanced pair was that of Diefenbaker/Kennedy, each of whom paid a single visit to each other. Despite large imbalances in the early periods, since the Eisenhower and Diefenbaker administrations, Canadian leaders have paid approximately two visits for every one received, a ratio which mirrors the disparity in size and influence of the two nations.[18]

TABLE VIII

RECIPROCITY OF SUMMIT VISITS 1923-1973

PRESIDENTS PRIME MINISTERS	Visits received: Visits given	C. Coolidge	H. Hoover	F. D. Roosevelt	H. S. Truman	D. D. Eisenhower	J. F. Kennedy	L. B. Johnson	R. M. Nixon
Visits given: Visits received	48: 14	1:0	1:0	17:4	9:1	7:3	2:1	7:3	4:2
R. B. Bennett	2:0		1:0	1:0					
W. L. M. King	24:5	1:0		16:4	7:1				
L. S. St. Laurent	5:1				2:0	3:1			
J. G. Diefenbaker	5:3					4:2	1:1		
L. B. Pearson	8:3						1:0	7:3	
P. E. Trudeau	4:2								4:2

Considerations of disparity and influence are also relevant in considering how quickly summit meetings take place after the advent of new Canadian and U.S. leaders. As Table IX indicates, there is a remarkable consistency in the speed with which new leaders upon taking office have met with their counterparts. Excluding the earliest pair (King and Coolidge) and the two pairs of leaders who never met during their common terms (King and Hoover, Trudeau and Johnson), all leaders have met within five months after a change of leadership on either side. Indeed, over half of the new leaders have met within one month. This apparent desire to establish personal rapport is therefore quite pro-

---

[18]For analytically related discussions see Steven J. Brams, "The Structure of Influence Relationships in the International System," in James N. Rosenau, *International Politics and Foreign Policy* (New York: The Free Press, 1969), pp. 583-99; and George Modelski, "The World's Foreign Ministers: A Political Elite," *Journal of Conflict Resolution*, Vol. XIV, No. 2 (June 1970), pp. 135-75.

nounced. Some indication of the source of this desire may be surmised from the fact that all such "first" visits, without exception, have taken the form of Canadian Prime Ministers travelling to the United States. Thus, this pattern well reflects not only the disparity between the two nations, but also the consistent need for Canadian reassurance, access, and influence to which disparity gives rise.

TABLE IX

LENGTH OF TIME BEFORE FIRST MEETINGS OF PAIRS OF LEADERS 1923-1973

Leader Pair	First Date of Common Term	First Date of Pair Meeting	Interval Between First Date of Common Term and First Meeting
King/Coolidge	Sept., 1926	Nov., 1927	14 months
King/Hoover	March, 1929	—	—
Bennett/Hoover	Aug., 1930	Jan., 1931	5 months
Bennett Roosevelt	March, 1933	April, 1933	1 month
King/Roosevelt	Oct., 1935	Nov., 1935	1 month
King/Truman	April, 1945	April, 1945	less than 1 month
St. Laurent/Truman	Nov., 1948	Feb., 1949	3 months
St. Laurent/Eisenhower	Jan., 1953	May, 1953	4 months
Diefenbaker/Eisenhower	June, 1957	Oct., 1957	4 months
Diefenbaker/Kennedy	Jan., 1961	Feb., 1961	1 month
Pearson/Kennedy	April, 1963	May, 1963	1 month
Pearson/Johnson	Nov., 1963	Nov., 1963	less than 1 month
Trudeau/Johnson	April, 1968	—	—
Trudeau/Nixon	Jan., 1969	March, 1969	2 months

A. President Calvin Coolidge and Prime Minister W.L. Mackenzie King, Washington, D.C., November 22-24, 1927

1. Prime Minister King's Account of Meeting (PAC King Diaries— Typescript, MG 26, J 13, Vol. 41, 1927, pp.246-49)

. . . At 5 we called at White House. Was rec'd by an A.D.C. (?) in full uniform & Mr. Castle, 1st Secretary, then taken to an audience with the Presdt., was introduced as P.M. of Canada accompanied by Can. Minister. Mr. Coolidge stood motionless in black morning coat. Asked when I arrived & left, if snow in Ottawa. Spoke of troops & their visit to White House very cordially & of cross at Arlington. Asked how long I was staying. When I sd it depended on Mr. Massey's keeping me, he sd to come & stay at White House if Massey did not want to keep me. Was glad to see me here, very pleased to have Phillips at Ottawa, & Massey made his own friends etc. He talked more than I had expected he would, seemed brighter a [one word illegible] & a smile (?). We bowed again as we left room. It was the most formal ceremony I have ever been thro'. Next I left cards on the vice-Predt. & on Taft. . . .

At 1.30 Vincent & I went to the White House for luncheon. We were met at the front door by the A.D.C.'s in full uniform, a representative of the Army, etc. One by one the other guests arrived & assembled in the blue room opposite the main entrance. Secretary of State Kellog, ... of Army, Davis of Trade & Commerce, Hoover, Mr. Cassell of State Dept., a representative of the Navy & one or two others. When we were assembled the President came in & shook hands with each in turn, indicated to me to walk with him to the dining room. A band was located in the hall which played as we walked in & during luncheon. At the table I was given the place of honour to the President's right with Mr. Cassell to my right. Vincent was to the left of the president.

Throughout the luncheon Mr. Coolidge conversed quite freely. He was very quiet & self-contained, only spoke when he clearly wanted to. He spoke about my visit at the legation, asked me if I was still welcome there, or words to that effect recalling yesterday's conversation.

He [Coolidge] brought up during lunch the St. Lawrence Waterways & the Chicago Diversion, regarding the former he said, they appreciated our difficulties & the political considerat'ns of which we had to take account. That the U.S. were not anxious to press us in the matter, they felt a canal to the sea would be a help to the West of both countries. He told deputations that came to him about the canal, they should help to get public opinion in Canada in favour of it,—Boards of Trade, etc. etc., to go to them rather than to him. I spoke of the situation being parallel to that of Reciprocity & that every evidence of eagerness from the side of the U.S. was certain to make our path more difficult. This he recognized very clearly & said so. He mentioned they were being pressed to construct an all-American canal to the Hudson—he felt this wd be a great expense & hoped it would not be necessary. They were not considering it at present, tho' it might in time come to be a factor. I explained that we had also the constitn'l question to get out of the way. He was familiar with that, said a similar question was up with them in the West. As to the Chicago Diversion he said he supposed it wd have [to] be met by works which would serve to raise the level of the lakes, compensating works at the end of the lakes rather than stopping the diversion. I intimated we saw difficulties in stopping diversion entirely & wished to be reasonable, but the position was a serious one. I told of how largely our harbours etc. had been affected.

We spoke of broadcasting, (television) etc. The Presdt. said no man could stand the campaigning of the kind Roosevelt did, that broadcasting was helpful in preventing press from misquoting addressing or publishing only in part. I urged what it meant in requiring an appeal to the nation as a whole.

He spoke of the time he was sworn in by his father & asked about the members present. He said there were only four or five, but he was uncertain about the oath to be taken—how many etc. that Massachusetts had two oaths, that this had occasioned uncertainty as to time of swearing in. He seemed to feel deeply the significance of his father having administered the oath.

He spoke about intention of U.S. to have legation at Ottawa,—of his holiday being no holiday—office 16 miles from his home, in summer—that "Presidents & Prime Ministers" had no holiday.—

He invited me after lunch to walk with him to the verandah of the White House looking towards the Potomac, told me it used to come near a present fountain, that Adams used to go in bathing there before breakfast & that once a woman reporter held him up for an interview while he was in the water. He said if I had been Adams I should have got out & put on my clothes and told her to make a story out of that.

He spoke about our parties in Canada. When I told of our policy in lowering tariff on agriculturenps [sic] [agricultural implements] etc. He remarked on everything the farmers want, the tariff has already come almost to the free list. He did not believe in subsidies for the farmers.

All through our conversation I felt the president was a man of much clearer vision & thought than I had believed, a man very well informed, very careful in all his utterances, & exceedingly astute. He looks the pink of perfection in dress, is quite [quiet] & composed beyond words. Speaks when he wants to & is silent when he wants to be silent. The impression I have formed of him is much more favourable than I had supposed it would be. I regard him as anything but a silent man only.

The whole proceedings of the luncheon were carried out with great dignity. There was evidence of sincere respect for the President on the part of his colleagues.

After the President came back to the diningroom he shook hands with us all in turn & went off to his office. There were then several photographs taken on the steps of the White House, with Secy of State Kellogg, Davis, Hoover, Vincent Massey & myself. . . .

I. Prime Minister R.B. Bennett (August 1930-October 1935) (Presidents Herbert C. Hoover and Franklin D. Roosevelt)

Prime Minister R.B. Bennett assumed office in August of 1930 and served until October, 1935. During this time he had two meetings, both in Washington, with U.S. Presidents, Herbert C. Hoover in 1931 and Franklin D. Roosevelt in 1933. Mr. Hoover was President of the United States from March, 1929 to March, 1933, and this is the only known meeting he had with a Canadian Prime Minister. Roosevelt was President from March, 1933 to April, 1945, and while he was to have a total of twenty meetings with Canadian Prime Ministers—all but the one covered in this chapter with Mr. Bennett were with William Lyon Mackenzie King.

Bennett and Hoover's January 30 to February 1, 1931 Washington meeting resulted in nothing more than a vague statement about the proposed St. Lawrence Seaway.[1] (See Section A.) The purported reason for this "unofficial" visit was the Prime Minister's desire to inspect the Canadian Legation in Washington. For this meeting, the President was armed with a briefing paper on the Prime Minister prepared by the U.S. Assistant Secretary of State. This paper noted in part "The Conservative Party in Canada while not actively anti-American, is less friendly disposed to the United States than the Liberal Party. For political reasons, therefore, Mr. Bennett frequently finds it advisable to criticize us despite the fact that he personally is friendly to this country."[2] During the meeting, Prime Minister Bennett showed

---

[1] See "Bennett and Hoover To Take Up Problems," NYT (February 1, 1931), p. 1.

[2] Herbert Hoover Presidential Library, West Branch, Iowa, Paper No. 48B, Letter from Assistant Secretary of State William R. Castle to President Hoover, January 28, 1931.

marked restraint in being publicly associated with the President, refus-
ing to be photographed with him, as was traditional, on the White
House Lawn. However, the Prime Minister met with several United
States' officials and according to the United States Assistant Secretary
of State "talked over all sorts of questions informally."[3] In addition to
the Seaway issue, press questions to Mr. Bennett reflected concerns on
bilateral issues such as wheat, finances, prohibition and the recent
capture of the Canadian ship, *Josephine K*.[4] The documentation for this
meeting includes a statement of President Hoover issued after the
meeting, and a follow up letter from Hoover to his Secretary of State
Henry Stimson.

Bennett's second meeting with a President, and Roosevelt's first
meeting with a Canadian Prime Minister, occurred from April 24 to 29,
1933. (See Section B.) This visit took place in the context of the
multilateral "Washington Conversations" hosted by President
Roosevelt in preparation for the World Economic Conference
scheduled to resolve the international economic crisis. In these discussions Mr. Roosevelt conferred with Representatives of Great Britain,
France, Italy, Germany, Japan, China, Argentina, Brazil, Chilie, Mexico and Canada. Although the meetings with British Prime Minister
Ramsay MacDonald, former French Premier Edouard Herriot, and Mr.
Bennett overlapped, there was always the presumption of bilateral talks
with the U.S., and no multilateral session officially occurred for the
three visitors.[5] The purpose of these conversations was "the discussion
of fundamental problems before the International Economic Conference, in an effort to secure some general understanding in advance of its
convocation . . . and to educate public opinion."[6] Of greater significance to Prime Minister Bennett were economic issues between Canada
and the United States. Specifically, Bennett hoped for a trade arrangement with the United States that would give freer access to the U.S.
market for Canadian natural resource and agricultural products.[7] The
Prime Minister stayed at the White House from April 26 to 29 and
held conversations with the President on the morning of April 27

---

[3]"Bennett Departs, Silent To Trip," NYT (February 2, 1931).

[4]*Idem.*

[5]*The Canadian Annual Review of Public Affairs 1933* (Toronto: The Canadian Review Company Limited, 1934), p. 499.

[6]University of New Brunswick, Bennett Papers, #181596, Telegram from
Canadian Minister in Washington to Secretary of State for External Affairs,
Ottawa, April 8, 1933.

[7]See V.M. Kipp, "Dominion Premier Has Critical Task," NYT (April 23,
1933), Section 4, p. 1, and "Bennett Stresses Trade Mutuality," NYT (April 26,
1933), p. 1.

and the afternoon of April 28. No specific results were forthcoming from these meetings, or indeed the entire trip. Documentation for the visit includes a formal statement by the Prime Minister upon his arrival at the Canadian Legation, Joint Statements made by the President and Prime Minister after their meetings on April 27, and at the end of the visit on April 29, and two radio addresses made by the Canadian Prime Minister to the people of the United States on April 28 and 29.

A. President Herbert C. Hoover and Prime Minister R.B. Bennett, Washington, D.C., January 30-February 1, 1931

1. Remarks of President Hoover Following Discussions with Prime Minister Bennett, January 30, 1931

(Paper No. 48B, Herbert Hoover Presidential Library, West Branch, Iowa)

I have been very glad to welcome today the Canadian Premier upon his informal visit to Washington. We have no formal matters under discussion. We are mutually interested in the common welfare of our peoples. Informal conversations on problems of the future always lead to better understanding. I consider it a great compliment that Mr. Bennet has found it possible to come to Washington.

2. Follow-up Letter from President Hoover to U.S. Secretary of State Henry Stimson, March 18, 1931

(*Ibid.*, Paper No. 156)

My dear Mr. Secretary:

You will recollect that when Premier Bennett was here we had a somewhat indefinite discussion along the line that a preliminary commission should be set up to determine the principles on which a treaty could be negotiated for construction of the St. Lawrence Waterway. I was under the distinct impression that the matter would be taken up at once upon his return and that we would have some results.

Nothing has happened and I am wondering if it would not be desirable to take it up with our Minister and see if we cannot get the Canadians to take some sort of constructive action.

Yours faithfully,

B. President Franklin D. Roosevelt and Prime Minister R.B. Bennett, Washington, D.C., April 24-29, 1933

1. Formal Press Statement of Prime Minister Bennett Made at Canadian Legation, April 25, 1933

(Bennett Papers, Fredricton, New Brunswick, L-524, Vol. I, Nos. 11684-85)

The President of the United States has done a great and helpful thing in asking the representatives of the nations to meet him in Washington. I hope and believe that from the discussions there will emerge a united plan of action. The International Monetary and Economic Conference should in consequence be enabled to reach agreements which will ensure the enjoyment by mankind of prosperity and happiness. Individual nations and groups of nations have already achieved some progress in defeating the depression. But we have reached a point where it is certain that nothing but united action can avert world disaster. The forthcoming International Conference makes world action possible. The duty of every country is to make it certain.

There never has been a time when the difficulties were not enormous, and there never will be. Immediate action is imperative. The world is in tragic trouble and distress. If we do not soon defeat the forces of disruption and discord, they will defeat us. We must act boldly and unselfishly. The good will and good faith which the nations of the world have so often proclaimed must be translated into action. It may be our last chance. In the main, our economic system has served us well. It does not work with its old-time efficiency. It must be carefully examined and adjusted to new conditions. We must not seek excuses for inaction. We must not pause to balance too carefully each item of national profit and loss. In debating the means we must not lose sight of the common ends. Otherwise we will be certain witnesses of the wreck of our civilization.

Canada has a great stake in the success of the International Conference, as great as that of any other country of the world. Though her population is but ten millions, her area and natural resources are those of a great nation; so also is her international commerce. In trade Canada has attained the fifth place, exceeded only by the United States, Great Britain, France, and Germany. The Government of Canada will sincerely co-operate in the work of achieving world recovery by international action.

2. Joint Statement of President Roosevelt and Prime Minister Bennett Following Discussions, April 27, 1933

(PP/Franklin D. Roosevelt, Random House, Vol. 2, 1933, No. 45, pp. 149-50)

The Prime Minister of Canada and the President have discussed further the program of the World Economic Conference and related questions of trade policy in which these two neighboring Governments have an important and immediate concern.

They have found this exchange of views very helpful.

Present also were the Canadian Minister, the Secretary of State and Assistant Secretary of State Raymond Moley.

3. NBC Radio Address of Prime Minister Bennett to the American People, April 28, 1933

(Bennett Papers, Fredricton, New Brunswick, C-524, Vol. I, Nos. 117055-56)

I am grateful for this opportunity to discuss for a few minutes the problems that face your country and mine. In the peculiar relations of intimacy and yet of rivalry between Canada and the United States we have an international situation without parallel in history. We have to a great extent the same historical background. Our institutions of Government express the combined genius of Roman and Anglo Saxon for the preservation of constitutional liberty.

Our individual relationships touch at every point across an immense international boundary line. Many Canadians have settled in your country, and have contributed to its upbuilding. Among the items in our international balances are to be highly valued the great number of your countrymen who have taken up permanent residence in Canada. You have expressed your confidence in our national future by the investment in Canadian securities and enterprises of more than Four Thousand Millions of Dollars. This sum constitutes more than one-quarter of your total investments abroad.

In the past 20 years we have witnessed world changes, the magnitude of which no one can at the moment appraise. The world today is in the difficult position of being recast into a new economic mold. The business structure of this continent has been so shaken by world events as to require a reorientation of North American policies. Our countries have enjoyed throughout their respective histories the greatest measure of international trade of any neighbouring countries in the world. The amount of this trade has vastly increased since the Great War. During the period of the war Canada became a great industrial country while you, already one, accelerated your production in a degree that out-stripped all previous records. All this productive enterprise, of course was not directed into what could be called normal consumptive chan-nels, and the war ended with these huge producing machines en-deavouring to operate without customers able to buy their products. We have witnessed the unsuccessful efforts to adjust these tremendous implements of production to the modest purchasing power of today. As North American nations, we are most vitally interested in the restora-tion of the world to healthy normal conditions. In the capital city of this great nation representatives of the countries of the world are frankly seeking a solution of these great questions.

There are, of course, great monetary and economic problems which can only be successfully solved by co-operative action on the part of practically all countries of the world. Foremost among those is the paramount need of establishing some universal yardstick by which international balances and payments can be measured and settled. There is the immediate need of raising, by co-operative efforts, com-modity prices, and of expanding credit so as to stimulate industrial enterprise, increase employment, and enhance purchasing power. There is no agency more sensitive to psychological and political influ-ences than our banking and monetary institutions. Fears and alarms, wars and rumours of wars, the courage and optimism of nations and their leaders, are reflected daily in trading transactions. The extent to which this sensitive agency is serving our growing and varied needs, we may be inclined to undervalue. It has served us well, but it must be adjusted to meet the changed conditions of today and tomorrow. We must see to it that it is so adjusted as to serve effectively human interests and human needs. As we travel across this continent, we cannot but observe factories, terminals, rolling stock, harbours, and buildings in need of replacement, renovation and repair. We see millions of people eager to begin the work that has to be done. Capital and credit are available; confidence is lacking. So long as this situation persists, it is our business to compel such changes as are necessary to employ the riches and resources of our respective countries.

May I now touch briefly on some matters of more particular impor-tance to ourselves as neighbors. As I stated, there are no two neighbor-ing nations in the world enjoying so great a measure of international trade as Canada and the United States. You have an especially impor-tant stake in Canadian prosperity. For many years Canada has bought from the United States goods greatly exceeding in value those which it has sold to the United States, and has borrowed large sums of money in the United States to meet these unfavourable trade balances. Since 1929 our position has been very difficult. In that year we bought from other countries of the world more than we sold, although for some years previously we had been selling more than we bought. In 1931 Canada faced a serious financial crisis. We could not further borrow abroad. Our purchases were exceeding our sales. Canada was still confronted with a heavy unfavourable trade balance with the United States, which had averaged 225 million dollars a year over a period of 12 years. In spite of this, in your national interest, you further restricted the sale in your country of our goods. We were then left with two alternative courses; one was to default in paying our obligations in the terms of our promises, and the other was to sell more and purchase less abroad. Your tourist traffic contributed to our assistance. The visitor from the United States, though he may not realize it, as soon as he crosses the border into Canada, in the eyes of the economists dons a cloak of darkness and becomes "an invisible import." This welcome traffic, together with our increasing annual gold production, has enabled us to meet our obligations in this country and elsewhere.

But we are still purchasers of your goods of the first importance. In 1929 we bought $868,000,000 of United States goods; that meant that every Canadian man, woman, and child, spent on the average $87 in that year for products of the United States. In the same year the people of the United States bought $500,000,000 of Canadian goods, or just over $4 worth a head. These figures have shrunk sadly since then, but still your interest in the Canadian market is very great. In fact it might be said that each country has been substantially the other's best customer; but, though you have been a good customer of ours, we in Canada have been a still better customer of yours. Our two countries are happily free from those international political problems which have their roots in fear and jealousy. Our mutual problems are great, but they are essentially economic in character—to make easier an exchange of goods and services and to promote a freer movement of capital.

I am deeply grateful to your President for affording me the opportunity of discussing intimately with him both the vital problems with which all the countries of the world will soon be grappling at the International Monetary and Economic Conference in London, and the special questions which concern our two nations. I shall leave Washington greatly impressed by his earnestness and sincerity in seeking means to promote the welfare and happiness of mankind.

4. Second Joint Statement of President Roosevelt and Prime Minister Bennett Following Discussions, April 29, 1933

(PP/FDR, *op. cit.*, No. 45A. p. 150)

Our conversations have been eminently satisfactory in establishing a common ground of approach to the principal problems of the World Monetary and Economic Conference. We are agreed that our primary need is to insure an increase in the general level of commodity prices.

To this end simultaneous action must be taken both in the economic and in the monetary fields. Economic and monetary policies must be adjusted to permit a freer international exchange of commodities.

It is recognized that as soon as practicable an international monetary standard must be restored, with arrangements that will insure a more satisfactory operation of international monetary relationships. We have examined a series of proposals for the more effective employment of silver.

No one of these problems can be profitably dealt with in isolation from the others, nor can any single country accomplish a satisfactory solution. We therefore recognize the vital importance to mankind of the World Economic Conference, and the necessity of reaching, in the weeks which remain before it is convened, as great a measure of mutual understanding as possible.

We have also discussed the problems peculiar to the United States and Canada. We have agreed to begin a search for means to increase the exchange of commodities between our two countries, and thereby promote not only economic betterment on the North American continent, but also the general improvement of world conditions.

5. CBS Farewell Radio Address of Prime Minister Bennett to the American People, April 29, 1933

(Bennett Papers, Fredricton, New Brunswick, c-524, Vol. 1, Nos. 116875-78)

I have come to speak a few words of farewell this afternoon before I return to Canada.

We Canadians do not feel that we are strangers in your hospitable country, nor, I hope, do the people of the United States feel themselves to be strangers when they come as welcome visitors to Canada. We are friendly neighbors and speak to one another as such. This is natural and proper.

But I am nevertheless deeply impressed with the warm welcome and generous hospitality which I have received from your President, your Secretary of State and his assistants, and from all those with whom I have come in contact. I will carry with me many pleasant memories which I shall long cherish.

I am gratified to have had an opportunity of meeting in Washington my friend Mr. Ramsey MacDonald; I regret that his pressing duties prevented his visiting Canada, where he is always welcome. It has also been a pleasure to renew my acquaintance with Mr. Herriot.

I have been discussing in Washington matters of the most vital importance not only to the United States and Canada but, indeed, to all the countries of the world. Until recently the ordinary man regarded the quotations of foreign exchanges as a matter of no personal interest to himself. They were merely a dull row of scarcely intelligible figures of the financial page of his newspaper.

It is now being painfully impressed on the consciousness of mankind that these figures may have a profound bearing on the welfare of every one. The Saskatchewan wheat farmer, the Florida orange-grower, the Lancashire weaver, the Chinese coolie, the Chilean copper-miner —they all are finding that their lives are affected in no considerable measure by the fluctuations from day to day in the relative values of currencies as recorded by that row of figures.

Perhaps the greatest of the important objectives before the economic conference soon to meet in London is to restrict so far as possible those violent fluctuations and restore an effective and stable international measure of exchange values. All countries realize how important this is, but there is as yet no general agreement on the means by which it is to be achieved.

Your President is seeking to prepare for such a general agreement at the conference by undertaking intimate conversations with representatives of the nations of the world. He is not seeking agreements but the bases of understandings on which agreements may be made.

We are vitally interested in the success of those deliberations and in the solution of our special North American problem.

In this time of stress and trial, when we are girding ourselves for the task of vanquishing adversity, when we are resolved to put an end to the sorrow and hardship of the past few years, it is natural and right that we should carefully examine the assets and attributes upon which we may rely to support us in this task.

I look about me for assurance that we would not fall and seize upon, above all else, the basic characteristics of our people; that fortitude which braves misfortune, that patience which waits for better times, that steadfastness and optimism which are the certain harbingers of a new and greater prosperity, that belief in the wise purpose of an ever-present God who doeth all things well.

And to those of us who are called upon to guide the fortunes of our countries in these days it is an inspiration to know that, behind the effort of governments, lies a hope and confidence which these sad times have been powerless to impair.

In my country I have been heartened by what I have seen in every section of unselfishness and patience, self-sacrifice which ennobles poverty and explain anew the uses of adversity. I know that if I traveled in this great Republic I would find your people minded with our own. So to each and all of them I offer my tribute of praise and genuine admiration.

They do not say that trouble disproves the claim that our institutions are sound. They do not ask that we abandon them; rather have they proclaimed again their steadfast belief that, with care and skill, they will continue to serve us in full measure in the new conditions in which this world now finds itself.

Then we have a still further assurance of success in the undisputed fact that there has arisen among the nations a new will for cooperation. We have come definitely and universally to the view that each of us must contribute to a new scheme of international action.

The World Conference manifests our common consciousness of the need to get together. The action of your great President in asking us to meet him here not only supports the common view but translates our hopes into immediate action.

I for one am satisfied that through these conversations has been advanced in an immeasurable degree the prospect of achieving that concerted front before which adversity must give way.

Acknowledging your President's wide vision, unselfish purpose, his steady courage, and sincerity, his rare patience, and determination, I promise that Canada will play its part in the task of seeking world recovery through cooperation with the United States and all the other nations of the world.

II. Prime Minister W.L. Mackenzie King (October 1935-November 1948) (President Franklin D. Roosevelt)

During his first term of office Prime Minister King had a November, 1927 meeting with President Calvin Coolidge, as documented in Section B of the Introduction. King again held office from October 1935 to November 1948, during which time he had a total of 27 meetings with United States Presidents. Nineteen of these meetings were with President Roosevelt, who held office from March 1933 to April 1945. Eight of the meetings, which are discussed in the next chapter, were with Harry S. Truman who as Vice President, became President on Roosevelt's death. Of the nineteen King-Roosevelt meetings, ten are documented in this chapter.

The first two King-Roosevelt meetings occurred in the month of November 1935. (See Section A for documentation of both meetings.) While en route to a holiday in the Southern U.S., King visited Washington from November 7-10; rather than continuing South after the meeting he returned to Ottawa to consult with his colleagues and again returned to Washington on the 15th. Although King had characterized his meeting as a "courtesy call" noting that "I am simply here on holiday,"[1] he and President Roosevelt managed to negotiate a reciprocal trade agreement which placed Canadian-United States trade relations on a basis of mutual consent for the first time since 1866.[2]

---

[1] "Canada's Premier Arrives in Capital," NYT (November 8, 1935), p. 11.

[2] The President's authority to conclude the 1935 agreement with Canada stemmed from a 1934 act by which he was empowered to, first, negotiate reciprocal trade agreements with other countries; and second, raise or lower United States tariff rates by 50 per cent as a negotiating tool. Although other agreements had been concluded under this act, the Canada-United States pact was to that date by far the most significant. The fullest account of Canadian-

Negotiations by Prime Minister Bennett were called off during the Canadian General Elections that spring of 1935. King assumed office on October 23, and immediately notified the United States Minister to Canada of his desire to resume on a new basis discussions leading to a trade pact. The negotiations were resumed at the working level and within two weeks the Prime Minister, with a single advisor, was in Washington, where he met with President Roosevelt for six hours during November 8-9.[3] Having successfully concluded his negotiations, King returned to Ottawa on the 10th, and met with his Cabinet the following day. After a telephone conversation with the President, King issued a public announcement simultaneously with the President that agreement had been reached. This agreement constituted the origins of the contemporary Canadian-United States economic interaction. It granted mutual tariff concessions on commodities representing a large part of the bilateral trade. In addition to the trade agreement, the two November 1935 meetings are significant in that they established the basis of a King-Roosevelt rapport and working relationship that was to last until the President's death in 1945. It is no accident that during the ceremonies in the signing of the agreement, reporters detected a notable informality. The documentation for these two November 1935 meetings includes the following: the King-Roosevelt Joint Statement following their talks; King's announcement of the trade agreement from Ottawa; Roosevelt's announcement of the agreement during a speech at Arlington National Cemetery; and the exchange of remarks between the two leaders made when King returned to Washington on the 15th to sign the agreement.

The third King-Roosevelt meeting, on July 31, 1936, is historically important in that it was the first time a U.S. President met with a Canadian Prime Minister in Canada. (See Section B.) Entirely ceremonial in nature, Roosevelt spent eight hours in Quebec City in order to pay an official call on the Governor General, Lord Tweedsmuir.[4] The rationale for such a Presidential visit was stated by King in a letter to Roosevelt dated April 19, 1936, marked "Personal," noting that such a visit would "not only mean very much to our respective countries, and to relations which were never more friendly, but might have a quieting effect upon the situation in Europe, where international friend-

---

American trade negotiations in the 1930's is to be found in Kottman, R.N., *Reciprocity and the North Atlantic Triangle, 1932-1938*, Ithaca: Cornell University Press, 1968.

[3]See Turner Carledge, "President Joins Premier to Speed Canadian Treaty," NYT (November 9, 1935), p. 1; "Sees 'Economic Unity'," NYT (November 14, 1935), p. 8; and "Prime Minister King and Secretary of State Hull Sign," TGM (November 16, 1935), p. 2.

[4]See Charles W. Hurd, "Roosevelt Lauds Ties," NYT (August 1, 1936), p. 1; and "The President's Visit," TGM (August 1, 1936), p. 4.

liness and good will seem to have lost their footing altogether.''[5] The documentation for this meeting includes the addresses by Messrs. King and Roosevelt, with King emphasizing the "unfortified frontier" and the message of peace "which today the New World sends to the Old," and Roosevelt sounding the theme that Americans and Canadians are not "foreigners."

The fourth King-Roosevelt meeting, which is not documented, occurred in March of 1937 at the White House where King was an overnight guest. The two leaders discussed such issues as the St. Lawrence Seaway, the European situation and neutrality, with King noting that "There was nothing that committed anybody to anything."[6] King's rationale for the meeting was explicitly stated when he later noted: "It was obvious that before I go to the Imperial Conference I should ascertain the views of the President on the problems confronting the world and with which the conference will have to deal."[7]

King and Roosevelt met for the fifth time on August 18, 1938 at Kingston, Ontario, and at the Thousand Islands Bridge near Clayton, New York, and Ivy Lea, Ontario. (See Section c.) Ceremonial in nature, this was Roosevelt's second official trip to Canada. The purpose was twofold—to accept an honourary degree at Queen's University, Kingston, Ontario, and to dedicate the opening of the Thousand Islands Bridge. Especially important is the President's Kingston address which committed the United States to defend Canada against encroachment by the troops of any foreign power. This speech, coupled with King's reciprocal pledge made two days later that Canada would not permit itself to be used as a base against the United States by foreign powers, constitutes the core of contemporary Canadian-United States strategic obligations.[8] The President's speech at Ivy Lea is also important historically in that Roosevelt came forward with a strong call for the joint development of projects on the St. Lawrence. The documentation for this meeting includes the President's addresses at Queen's University and at the dedication of the Thousand Islands Bridge, and Prime Minister King's dedicatory address at the Bridge.

The sixth King-Roosevelt meeting took place in Washington from

[5]April 4, 1936, Personal letter from Prime Minister King to President Roosevelt, E.B. Nixon (ed.), *FDR and Foreign Affairs*, Vol. III, September 1935-January 1937, pp. 281-82.

[6]"King Back in Canada," NYT (March 21, 1937), p. 36.

[7]"World Issues Stand Voiced By President," TGM (March 8, 1937), p. 17; (The Imperial Conference was scheduled in May, after the coronation of King George VI).

[8]For a summary statement of the pledges, see Section F, Entry 3. For press accounts of the Roosevelt visit to Canada, see TGM (August 19, 1938), pp. 1, 6; "Britain is Cordial to Roosevelt Talk," NYT (August 19, 1938), p. 3.

November 17-19, 1938, during which the Canadian-United States trade agreement was reaffirmed and extended.[9] (See Section D.) Under the authority of the 1934 United States Trade Agreements Act which gave the President the authority to reduce tariffs on a reciprocal basis, Secretary of State Cordell Hull had negotiated eighteen such agreements including the earlier one with Canada in 1935. Negotiations with the United Kingdom were both important and complex due to the extent of United States trade with the United Kingdom, and also because of the United Kingdom's extensive trade arrangements with its colonies and dominions. It was decided in the Spring of 1938 that Canada should be brought in on the negotiations, as any agreement with the United States and Britain would require extensive adjustments on the part of both nations with Canada because of the Imperial Trade Agreements of 1932 and the Canadian-United States Trade Agreement of 1935. The agreements were ready by mid-November 1938, and President Roosevelt had invited Prime Minister King to Washington with an eye to having him present for their formal signing and for further consultations. Among those present for the ceremonies were Roosevelt, King, Secretary of State Hull, and the British Ambassador. The two documents signed at the White House were official executive agreements between the United States and Canada, and the United States and the United Kingdom for itself, Newfoundland and the over 50 non-self-governing colonies in the British Empire. Officials noted that this new agreement between the United States and Canada was "a more comprehensive agreement than the one it replaced and one which provides wider and more favorable export opportunities for both Canada and the United States."[10] After the signing, King remained at the White House as an overnight guest. No statement was issued concerning matters covered in their conversations, but the President indicated to newsmen that King had agreed to further negotiations for the improvement of the St. Lawrence River as a seaway to the Great Lakes. The documentation for this meeting includes the remarks of Roosevelt and King upon the signing of the Reciprocal Trade Agreements.

Subsequent to the November 1938 King-Roosevelt Washington meeting, the two leaders met in June of 1939 at Washington and Hyde Park. The 1939 meeting, which is not documented, involved the visit of King George VI to the United States accompanied by Prime Minister King as his Minister-In-Attendance. King's involvement was entirely ceremonial; indeed, four years later, during an August 1943 dinner toast at the First Quebec Conference, President Roosevelt himself

---

[9]See Harold Dingman, "Pact With U.S. Made Broader, Premier Says," TGM (November 12, 1938), p. 3; Bertram D. Hulen, "Hull Signs Trade Treaties," NYT (November 18, 1938), pp. 1, 12; and NYT (November 21, 1938), p. 8.
[10]NYT (November 19, 1938), p. 13.

claimed credit for arranging King's accompaniment of Their Majesties.[11]

The two leaders next met in April of 1940 while King was on holiday in the United States.[12] (See Section E.) Roosevelt invited him to Warm Springs, Georgia, on April 23-24, and the two leaders met again on April 29 in Washington while King was en route back to Canada. While in Washington, King also met with several U.S. officials. This "wholly informal personal visit," to quote King, was his first wartime meeting with Roosevelt.[13] According to the King Diary, his talks with the President covered the German occupation of Denmark and the implications for Greenland, the possibility of sending United States defence materials and destroyers to assist Great Britain, the St. Law-rence Seaway, a successor to the United States Minister to Canada, and the possibility of a Presidential visit to Canada. The documentation for this meeting consists of King's account in his Diary.

The ninth King-Roosevelt meeting, at Ogdensburg, New York, on August 17-18, 1940, is one of the most important meetings, for it marks the origins of the Canadian-United States defence interaction and the establishment of the Permanent Joint Board on Defence.[14] (See Section F.) In response to an earlier King suggestion, President Roosevelt telephoned on the afternoon of August 16, inviting the Prime Minister to join him in his private railroad car in Ogdensburg, New York to view Army maneuvers. After a military review and memorial service, the two leaders returned to the Presidential train and drafted the Joint Statement. The documentation of this meeting is especially com-prehensive, including King's account of the meeting in his Diary, the Joint Statement known as the "Ogdensburg Agreement," and King's interpretation of the agreement to the House of Commons. King's explanation to the Commons is significant in that it illustrates his triangular conceptualization of the Canada-United States-United King-dom relationship, including his assertion of Canada's "manifest destiny."

The tenth King-Roosevelt meeting, which occurred in Washington (April 16-17) and Hyde Park, New York (April 20, 1941), is also one of the more important meetings, for from a Joint Statement known as the "Hyde Park Declaration," Canada and the United States embarked on a course of coordinated defence production which continues to this

[11]J. W. Pickersgill, *The Mackenzie King Record*, Vol. I, 1939-44 (Toronto: University of Toronto Press, 1960), p. 549.

[12]See "Premier and President Meet," TGM (April 24, 1940); and Felix Belair, Jr., "President Has Mackenzie King as Guest," NYT (April 24, 1940), pp. 1, 5.

[13]Pickersgill, *op. cit.*, p. 106.

[14]See Charles Hurd, "Roosevelt Puts Canada Pact First," NYT (August 20, 1940), p. 1, 10; "Washington Hails New Defence Plan," NYT (August 19, 1940), p. 8.

day.[15] (See Section G.) While the United States was still officially neutral in the war, this summit meeting rationalized arrangements for wartime production between the United States and Canada, both to the advantage of Canada itself and in its role as conduit of war manufactures to the allies. The agreement alleviated pressure on the Canadian trade deficit and was seen as helping to speed war production. This particular meeting occurred in two stages—King briefly met with Roosevelt in Washington, from where he went to Virginia Beach for a holiday. Roosevelt went to his home at Hyde Park, where King joined him on the 20th. It was here that the Joint Statement was issued. The documentation for this meeting is comprehensive, including King's own account of the meeting, their Joint Statement, and King's interpretation of the declaration to the Canadian House of Commons.

After the Hyde Park meeting, King and Roosevelt held five meetings between April 1941 and May 1943, none of which is documented. Three of these five meetings took place in the wider context of wartime gatherings. In November 1941, King and Roosevelt met at the President's Hyde Park home, a meeting which King's biographer cites as "the least interesting and important of his visits to Roosevelt."[16] However, it is of interest that within a week of the meeting, Roosevelt wrote King a letter in which he extolled the advantages of their personal relationship. To quote the President's letter: "Sometimes I indulge in the thoroughly sanctimonious and pharisaical thought, which I hope that you are also occasionally guilty of, that it is a grand and glorious thing for Canada and the United States to have the team of Mackenzie and Roosevelt at the helm in days like these! Probably both nations could get along without us, but I think we may be pardoned for our thoughts, especially in view of the fact that our association so far has brought some proven benefits to both nations."[17] The second undocumented meeting took place in December 1941 and included Prime Minister Winston Churchill. Although of interest because the Free French seizure of St. Pierre and Miquelon was discussed, the import of the meeting stems from Churchill's wartime presence rather than from its bilateral Canadian-U.S. significance. Indeed, prior to the meeting, King expressed some concern "with the possibility of not being invited

---

[15]See "Premier King Pays Visit to Roosevelt," NYT (April 17, 1941), p. 10; Frank L. Kluckhohn, "U.S., Canada Join For War Output," NYT (April 21, 1941), p. 1; and "Mr. King Leaves for Session with Roosevelt," TGM (April 16, 1941), p. 13.

[16]J.W. Pickersgill, op. cit., p. 275.

[17]F.D.R. To Mackenzie King In Ottawa, The White House, November 5, 1941, in Elliot Roosevelt (ed.) Assisted by Joseph P. Lash; F.D.R.: His Personal Letters 1928-1945, Volume II (New York: Duell, Slone and Pearce, 1950), pp. 1232-33.

to be present.''[18] King noted that his interest was not personal and that he appreciated the problems involved in Canada being represented while the other Dominions were not. However, given ''the tactics my opponents were adopting,'' King feared they would suggest ''that all that had been said about my being a link between the two (Churchill and Roosevelt) amounted in reality to nothing.''[19]

The third undocumented meeting in this five-visit sequence was in April of 1942, and occurred in the multilateral context of the Pacific War Council which was a series of Presidential meetings with representatives of such countries as Australia, New Zealand, the United Kingdom and China. King was preoccupied with two issues: that Canada should have a place on the Munitions Assignment Board established by the U.S. and U.K., a position with which Roosevelt was sympathetic and said he would pursue. Secondly, it was agreed to issue an invitation to those Allied countries having air training programmes in North America (e.g. the Commonwealth and Norway had an air training school in Canada, China in the U.S.) for purposes of coordination and increased efficiency. King observed after his meeting with the President that ''I can talk with him as freely as I would with one of my own colleagues.''[20] Another undocumented meeting took place in June 1942 in Washington, also in the context of the Pacific War Council during which Churchill was present. General wartime developments were reviewed, first at a meeting of representatives of the British Dominions chaired by Churchill, and at a meeting of the Pacific War Council with Roosevelt presiding. The last undocumented meeting in this five-visit sequence took place in Washington in December of 1942. King spent the weekend at the White House during which he and Roosevelt had several discussions about the war, all of a general nature. King regarded this meeting as being a ''most restful and most helpful'' visit ''with an old friend in his own home.''[21] However, in the same month, King recorded in his Diary his suspicions of his American comrades with respect to a proposed joint study concerning the Alaskan Highway. King told his War Committee of ''the efforts that would be made by the Americans to control developments in our country after the war, and to bring Canada out of the orbit of the British Commonwealth of Nations into their own orbit.''[22]

The sixteenth King-Roosevelt meeting took place from May 18-21, 1943, in Washington, again in the context of the Pacific War Council

[18]J.W. Pickersgill, op. cit., p. 317.

[19]Idem.

[20]C.R. Blackburn, ''Allied Air Conference Will Be Held in Ottawa,'' TGM (April 18, 1942), p. 1.

[21]''Visit To FDR 'Most Helpful','' TGM (December 8, 1942), p. 15.

[22]J.W. Pickersgill, op. cit., p. 436.

and again including Churchill. Because of the bilateral Canadian-U.S. implications of the issues discussed, this meeting is documented. (See Section H.) Of interest in the documentation is the leaders' discussions of post-war international organization, their conceptions of their own international roles, the desirability of raising the Canadian Legation in Washington to the status of an Embassy, Canada's role in the Western Hemisphere, a Stalin-Roosevelt meeting in Alaska excluding King and Churchill, a Presidential visit to Ottawa, and a King-Roosevelt discussion of a possible fishing trip. The documentation for this meeting consists of King's account in his Diary. It is interesting to note that King later registered pique to his War Committee that Canada and the Dominions had not been given greater recognition for their war efforts: "It was perfectly clear to me that, so far as Britain and the U.S. were concerned, there was little thought of giving credit except in very general terms to what was being done by Canada."[23]

The seventeenth meeting between Messrs. King and Roosevelt occurred at Quebec City (August 17-24, 1943) after which the President went to Ottawa on August 25th. (See Section I.) This was the First Quebec Conference during which King hosted a meeting between Roosevelt and Churchill. In his only private meeting with the two principal leaders during the Conference, King records that there was discussion of the organization of the post-war world and the place of the government of China in it, as well as the recognition of de Gaulle's French National Committee by the allies.[24] Notwithstanding the international significance of this First Quebec Conference, the month of August 1943 is especially significant in the context of Canadian-United States relations because it marks the first official visit of a United States President to the capital city of Ottawa. Prime Minister King left Quebec City ahead of the President to oversee final arrangements in Ottawa. After a formal welcoming at Ottawa's Union Station, the President and the official party proceeded to Parliament Hill where a crowd of over 30,000, led by Canadian Parliamentarians, was waiting. Although Parliament was not in session, Members had been invited to Ottawa to replicate the custom of having honored guests address the Houses of Parliament. The documentation for this meeting includes the Joint Press Conference of Roosevelt, Churchill, and King at the conclusion of the First Quebec Conference; King's introduction of President Roosevelt in Ottawa; and the President's address on Parliament Hill.

After this August 1943 meeting, King and Roosevelt met two more times before the President's death in April of 1945. Neither meeting is

---

[23]*Ibid.*, p. 506.

[24]J.W. Pickersgill, *op. cit.*, p. 548; See Kenneth C. Cragg, "President Is Cheered in Ottawa," TGM (August 26, 1943), pp. 1, 2; and "Friendly Relations Cemented," TGM (August 26, 1943), pp. 1, 3.

documented. The second Quebec Conference was held in September of 1944, during which King again served as a host for Roosevelt and Churchill. It was at this conference that the two leaders, accompanied by numerous advisors, discussed final plans for conducting the war in Europe and the Pacific, and addressed themselves to such post-war problems as the occupation of Germany. At the conclusion of the Conference a Joint Press Conference was held, during which Prime Minister King noted "how honored the people of Canada feel that Quebec has again been chosen as the center for the Conference" and that at any time "Canada can afford to be host at a conference for those who are seeking to bring together the Nations of the world in bonds of friendship and peace." Canadians "will do so with the greatest pride and pleasure."[25]

The nineteenth and last King-Roosevelt meeting, which is not documented, took place in early March of 1945. King had been on holiday in Williamsburg, Virginia, and, en route back to Canada, stopped by to see the President. This meeting was a social event in which a host of subjects were discussed, but only in general. Indeed, at the conclusion of the meeting, President Roosevelt, almost as a benedictum on the King-Roosevelt years, called in reporters and with King at his side, made a brief statement. Roosevelt noted that he and Prime Minister King "are very, very old friends—personal friends . . . But since he has been Prime Minister, we have developed that friendship into a practical way of handling common problems between the Dominion and the United States."[26] Citing such accomplishments as the Ogdensburg and Hyde Park Declarations, the President referred to the "past ten years" in Canadian-United States relations as an "outstanding example of that spirit with which two countries that are neighbors and cousins, you might say, can get along, to their mutual benefit."[27] Nor was this "outstanding example" without its benefit to Mr. King given his election that Spring, which the Prime Minister duly noted in his Diary: "All this will be helpful in reviving in Canada the close relationship I have had with him and Churchill during the war."[28] Within a month, President Roosevelt was dead.

---

[25]PP/Franklin D. Roosevelt, Vol. 1944-45, No. 70, p. 268.

[26]PP/Franklin D. Roosevelt, *op. cit.*, No. 140, p. 589.

[27]*Ibid.*, pp. 589-90.

[28]J.W. Pickersgill and D.F. Forster, *The Mackenzie King Record*, Volume II, 1944-45 (Toronto: University of Toronto Press, 1968), p. 332.

A. President Franklin D. Roosevelt and Prime Minister W.L. Mackenzie King, Washington, D.C., November 7-10, 1935 and November 15, 1935

1. Joint Statement of President Roosevelt and Prime Minister King on Trade Relations, Washington, D.C., November 9, 1935

(PP/Franklin D. Roosevelt, Random House, Vol. 4, 1935, No. 157, p. 441)

The President of the United States and the Prime Minister of Canada have considered the question of increased trade which has been discussed for some time by representatives of the two nations. There is complete agreement on the objective of a greatly increased flow of trade for the benefit of both countries and substantial progress has been made toward this end. It is recognized that such an increase would be beneficially felt in all activities, because trade is but another word for increased employment, transportation and consumption.

2. Prime Minister King's Announcement of Trade Agreement, Press Statement, Ottawa

(TGM, November 12, 1935, p. 2. (Quoted in article by William Marchington, entitled "Text Effective When Ratified")

I am glad, on this Armistice Day, to be able to inform you that the Governments of Canada and the United States have reached a definite trade agreement. The terms of the agreement were approved by the Government of Canada at a meeting held this morning, prior to the proceedings on Parliament Hill. The formal text is now being prepared for signature. The agreement will be made public simultaneously in Canada and in the United States on the date of signature. It is expected that it will be possible to have the agreement in readiness for signature in the course of a few days.

3. President Roosevelt's Announcement of Trade Agreement, Armistice Day Address at Arlington National Cemetery, Washington, D.C., November 11, 1935

(PP/Franklin D. Roosevelt, *op. cit.*, No. 158, pp. 443-44)

. . . In many other fields, by word and by deed, we are giving example to the world by removing or lowering barriers which impede friendly intercourse. Our soldier and sailor dead call to us across the years to make our lives effective in building constructively for peace. It is fitting that on this Armistice Day, seventeen years later, I am privileged to tell you that between us and a great neighbor another act cementing our historic friendship has been agreed upon and is being consummated. Between Canada and the United States exists a neighborliness, a genuine friendship which for over a century has dispelled every passing rift.

Our two peoples, each independent, are closely knit by ties of blood and a common heritage; our standards of life are substantially the same; our commerce and our economic conditions rest upon the same foundations. Between two such peoples, if we would build constructively for peace and progress, the flow of intercourse should be mutually beneficial and not unduly hampered. Each has much to gain by material profit, by spiritual profit, by increased employment through the means of enlarged trade, one with the other.

I am, therefore, happy to be able to tell you almost in celebration of this Armistice Day that the Canadian Prime Minister and I, after thoughtful discussion of our national problems, have reached a definite agreement which will eliminate disagreements and unreasonable restrictions, and thus work to the advantage of both Canada and the United States.

I hope that this good example will reach around the world some day, for the power of good example is the strongest force in the world. It surpasses preachments; it excels good resolutions; it is far better than agreements unfulfilled. . . .

4. Exchange of Remarks Between President Roosevelt and Prime Minister King on Signing the Trade Agreement, Washington, D.C., November 15, 1935

(*Ibid.*, No. 168, pp. 460-61)

THE PRESIDENT: The Trade Agreement which has just been signed between the United States and Canada places the trade relations between the two countries on a basis of mutual agreement for the first time since 1866. I am happy to have a part in removing this anomaly in the relations between two countries which are united by so many bonds of friendship and common heritage.

The signing of this Agreement marks the reversal of the trend of the last two decades toward undue and unnecessary trade barriers between our two countries. I am confident that this constructive step will contribute greatly to the economic recovery of both the United States and Canada.

THE PRIME MINISTER: The kindly words and sentiments to which you, Mr. President, have just given expression, will be warmly welcomed by His Majesty the King in whose name I have had the honor to sign the Trade Treaty which has just been concluded between the United States and Canada.

They will, I know, be deeply appreciated by the people of Canada.

May I say, Mr. Secretary, that I very cordially endorse all that you have said of the mutual advantages likely to flow to our respective countries from the terms of the Treaty?

On behalf of Canada, I heartily reciprocate the sentiments of international good-will you have so generously expressed.

I believe with you that the signature of this Agreement is witness of the joint intention of the Governments of the United States and Canada to give rapid effect to our policies in a practical manner. At last our formal trade relations have been brought into harmony with the underlying realities of public and private friendship between our two peoples. The Agreement will, I am confident, confer substantial benefits alike on the producers and consumers of both countries, while safeguarding with great care every essential interest. I feel sure that its value will be shown beyond question by a marked increase in commerce within the next few months. This undoubtedly will help both countries to make more rapid progress toward complete economic recovery.

Nor will this agreement benefit North America alone. All the world will gain from greater trade on this continent.

Nor will its benefits be confined to trade. To an anxious and troubled world we hope that there will be opened to the Nations, by the force of our example, vistas of a surer path to progress and a more lasting road to peace.

B. Prime Minister W.L. Mackenzie King and President Franklin D. Roosevelt, Quebec City, P.Q., July 31, 1936

1. Address of Prime Minister King, July 31, 1936

(NYT, August 1, 1936, p. 5)

. . . On either side of that line which spreads its way across rivers and lakes, valleys and hills, mountains and plains, there is not to be and there has not been for over a century, save as a relic of the past, a fort or a fortification worthy of the name.

The place of armaments on land and water has been taken by international parks and bridges, expressive not of fear, suspicion or hate, but of international peace, friendship and good-will.

This is the joint achievement, not of two races, but of two peoples, the men and women of the United States and the men and women of Canada. Like the shaft to the memory of Wolfe Montcalm, this unfortified frontier speaks to the world not of differences, but of what is held in common, not of the passions of nations, but of their virtues; not of the devastation and desolation of war, but of the beauty and blessings of peace.

Today we are indebted to your visit for yet another symbol of international peace, friendship and good-will. In the three centuries and more of Canadian history, this ancient capital has known but two flags, the French and the British. Today, Mr. President, in your honor and in honor of our great and friendly neighbor, the flag of the United States is flying over the citadel of old Québec.

It is, I believe, something more than a coincidence that in this very week when the President of the Republic of France and His Majesty the King should have been standing side by side on a bit of Canadian soil in the Old World the President of the Republic of the United States of America and the representative of His Majesty should be exchanging greetings on Canadian soil in the New World.

I may perhaps be pardoned if I say this is an expression for the world of the friendship which Canada enjoys with all countries, but which for reasons that are obvious she has been privileged to share more intimately for a longer time with the two republics.

We who enjoy this friendship in so marked a way bear an inheritance of mind and heart to which all have contributed and which all cherish. We, like you, are dedicated to the cause of peace. I hold it true that the world must come to see whether it be within or beyond the confines of States. We are all members one of another; that over all nations is humanity, and that the only security of countries, as well as of individuals, lies in the well-being of mankind throughout the world. That great end can be effected through understanding and friendship; it can never be accomplished by force.

So long as nations strive to advance their separate aims by force, rather than their common ends by reason and cooperation, so long will war be inevitable and the fear of war continue to make science and industry a vast machine to further the destruction of humanity. They were meant to be God's given instruments for its progress and relief.

In these times when armaments are growing apace, when faith everywhere is being supplanted by fear, when dread and uncertainty overcrowd the skies, when the cry of humanity is increasingly for peace, the single shaft, the unfortified frontier, the century of peace have surely a message for the world.

It is a message of understanding and friendship between men and between nations which your visit to Canada, Mr. President, inspires in our hearts anew. It is a message which today the New World sends to the Old. What to the United States and Canada has become the priceless possession of this continent, we, like you, wish to see a part of the common heritage of mankind. . . .

2. Address of President Roosevelt, July 31, 1936

(Idem.)

From the moment I received the hospitable invitation of your Governor General I have been filled with the most happy anticipation of this all too brief visit. Canada and its people have always had a very real hold on my affections. I am happy again to be able to assure you of this fact in person and to express my grateful appreciation of the warmth of your welcome.

That I am not a stranger may be illustrated by the fact that since the age of 2, I have spent the majority of my Summers in the Province of New Brunswick, and by my recent most refreshing cruise along the beautiful shores of the Maritime Provinces, where once more I have found friendship, relaxation and deep contentment.

Nor am I ignorant or unmindful of the charms of other sections of this great Dominion—Ontario and that great empire which extends west of it to the Pacific.

But to many of my countrymen, and I am no exception to this rule, Quebec has a fascination all its own. The Plains of Abraham and the cliffs which lead to them are eternal memorials to brave French, to brave British and to brave American colonists who have fallen in battle, be it in victory or in defeat.

Yet there is a nobler monument; for on these fields of battle was born the living miracle which we are privileged to see today—two great racial stocks residing side by side in peace and friendship, each contributing its particular genius in the molding of a nation. This is a monument worthy of those who gave their lives; this is an example from which all thinking men draw deep satisfaction and inspiration.

While I was on my cruise I read in a newspaper that I was to be received with all the honors customarily rendered to a foreign ruler. Your Excellency, I am grateful for the honors: but something within me rebelled at that word "foreign". I say this because when I have been in Canada I have never heard a Canadian refer to an American as a "foreigner." He is just an "American." And, in the same way, in the United States, Canadians are not "foreigners," they are "Canadians."

That simple little distinction illustrates to me better than anything else the relationship between our two countries.

On both sides of the line we are so accustomed to an undefended boundary 3,000 miles long that we are inclined perhaps to minimize its vast importance, not only to our own continuing relations but also to the example which it sets to the other nations of the world.

Canadians and Americans visit each other each year by the hundreds of thousands—but, more important, they visit each other without the use of passports.

And within recent months, another significant action speaks louder than words, for the trade agreement which I had the privilege of signing with your Prime Minister last Autumn is tangible evidence of the desire of the people of both countries to practice what they preach when they speak of the good neighbor.

In the solution of the grave problems that face the world today, frank dealing, cooperation and a spirit of give and take between nations is more important than ever before.

The United States and Canada, and, indeed, all parts of the British Empire, share a democratic form of government which comes to us from common sources. We have adapted these institutions to our own needs and our own special conditions, but fundamentally they are the same.

The natural sympathy and understanding that exist between us was, I feel, demonstrated in the universal feeling of grief when the news of the death of the late King George was received in the United States. We felt not only that the head of a friendly nation had been removed but that a friend whose voice had penetrated into almost every home in the United States had been taken from us—a great King and a great gentleman.

It has also been my privilege to know His Majesty King Edward, and we look forward to the day when, finding it possible to come again to the Dominion, he may also visit with his nieghbors in the United States.

Mr. Prime Minister of Quebec, Mr. Mayor:

The words of kindness which you have addressed to me in the name of your great Province and of your beautiful City and which you address through me to the people of the United States touch me deeply; and I beg you to believe that I am deeply sensible of the warmth of your welcome . . . in us; what illustrious names are associated with this noble rock!

It is to pay homage to those heroes that thousands of my compatriots come every year to Quebec. Here they prolong their stay, lured by the great beauty of this site, by the soft charm of your countryside and by the hospitable greeting of your inhabitants. This Canadian hospitality, so simple and so open, has become a tradition in my country.

It is by these exchange of visits, by these continuous contacts between Canadians and Americans that we shall come to tighten the close bonds which already unite our two peoples.

And Mr. Mackenzie King, you already know the path to Washington. I hope that you will come and visit me and revisit me again.

And Your Excellency, we are looking forward, as you know, to a visit from you and her Excellency to Mrs. Roosevelt and myself at the White House as soon as it may be convenient for you. May we speed the day when the heads of the Canadian and American Nations will see more of each other, not as foreigners, but as neighbors and friends.

C. Prime Minister W. L. Mackenzie King and President Franklin D. Roosevelt, Kingston, Ontario and Thousand Islands Bridge, Clayton, New York and Ivy Lea, Ontario, August 18, 1938

1. Address of President Roosevelt at Queen's University, Kingston, Ontario, August 18, 1938

(PP/Franklin D. Roosevelt, Macmillan, Vol. 1938, No. 105, pp. 491-94)

To the pleasure of being once more on Canadian soil where I have passed so many happy hours of my life, there is added today a very warm sense of gratitude for being admitted to the fellowship of this ancient and famous University. I am glad to join the brotherhood which Queen's has contributed and is contributing not only to the spiritual leadership for which the college was established, but also to the social and public leadership in the civilized life of Canada.

An American President is precluded by our Constitution from accepting any title from a foreign Prince, potentate or power. Queen's University is not a Prince or a potentate but, assuredly, it is a power. Yet I can say, without constitutional reserve, that the acceptance of the title which you confer on me today would raise no qualms in the august breast of our own Supreme Court.

Civilization, after all, is not national—it is international—even though that observation, trite as it is to most of us, seems to be challenged in some parts of the world today. Ideas are not limited by territorial borders; they are the common inheritance of all free people. Thought is not anchored in any land; and the profit of education redounds to the equal benefit of the whole world. That is one form of free trade to which the leaders of every opposing political party can subscribe.

In a large sense we in the Americas stand charged today with the maintaining of that tradition. When, speaking a little over a year ago in a similar vein in the Republic of Brazil, I included the Dominion of Canada in the fellowship of the Americas, our South American neighbors gave hearty acclaim. We in all the Americas know the sorrow and the wreckage which may follow if the ability of men to understand each other is rooted out from among the nations.

Many of us here today know from experience that of all the devastations of war none is more tragic than the destruction which it brings to the processes of men's minds. Truth is denied because emotion pushes it aside. Forbearance is succeeded by bitterness. In that atmosphere human thought cannot advance.

It is impossible not to remember that for years when Canadians and Americans have met they have lightheartedly saluted as North American friends with little thought of dangers from overseas. Yet we are awake to the knowledge that the casual assumption of our greetings in earlier times, today must become a matter for serious thought.

A few days ago a whisper, fortunately untrue, raced 'round the world that armies standing over against each other in unhappy array were about to be set in motion. In a few short hours the effect of that whisper had been registered in Montreal and New York, in Ottawa and in Washington, in Toronto and in Chicago, in Vancouver and in San Francisco. Your businessmen and ours felt it alike; your farmers and ours heard it alike; your young men and ours wondered what effect this might have on their lives.

We in the Americas are no longer a far away continent, to which the eddies of controversies beyond the seas could bring no interest or no harm. Instead, we in the Americas have become a consideration to every propaganda office and to every general staff beyond the seas. The vast amount of our resources, the vigor of our commerce and the strength of our men have made us vital factors in world peace whether we choose it or not.

Happily, you and we, in friendship and in entire understanding, can look clear-eyed at these possibilities, resolving to leave no pathway unexplored, no technique undeveloped which may, if our hopes are realized, contribute to the peace of the world. Even if those hopes are disappointed, we can assure each other that this hemisphere at least shall remain a strong citadel wherein civilization can flourish unimpaired.

The Dominion of Canada is part of the sisterhood of the British Empire. I give to you assurance that the people of the United States will not stand idly by if domination of Canadian soil is threatened by any other Empire.

We as good neighbors are true friends because we maintain our own rights with frankness, because we refuse to accept the twists of secret diplomacy, because we settle our disputes by consultation and because we discuss our problems in the spirit of the common good. We seek to be scrupulously fair and helpful, not only in our relations with each other, but each of us at home in our relations with our own people.

But there is one process which we certainly cannot change and probably ought not to change. This is the feeling which ordinary men and women have about events which they can understand. We cannot prevent our people on either side of the border from having an opinion in regard to wanton brutality, in regard to undemocratic regimentation, in regard to misery inflicted on helpless peoples, or in regard to violations of accepted individual rights. All that any government, constituted as is yours and mine, can possibly undertake is to help make sure that the facts are known and fairly stated. No country where thought is free can prevent every fireside and home within its borders from considering the evidence for itself and rendering its own verdict; and the sum total of these conclusions of educated men and women will, in the long run, rightly become the national verdict.

That is what we mean when we say that public opinion ultimately governs policy. It is right and just that this should be the case.

Many of our ancestors, your ancestors and mine, and, by the way, I have loyalist blood in my veins too, came to Canada and the United States because they wished to break away from systems which forbade them to think freely, and their descendants have insisted on the right to know the truth—to argue their problems to a majority decision, and, if they remained unconvinced, to disagree in peace. As a tribute to our likeness in that respect, I note that the Bill of Rights in your country and in mine is substantially the same.

Mr. Chancellor, you of Canada who respect the educational tradition of our democratic continent will ever maintain good neighborship in ideas as we in the public service hope and propose to maintain it in the field of government and of foreign relations. My good friend, the Governor General of Canada, in receiving an honorary degree in June at that University at Cambridge, Massachusetts, to which Mackenzie King and I both belong, suggested that we cultivate three qualities to keep our foothold in the shifting sands of the present—humility, humanity and humor. I have been thinking in terms of a bridge which is to be dedicated this afternoon and so I could not help coming to the conclusion that all of these three qualities imbedded in education, build new spans to reestablish free intercourse throughout the world and bring forth an order in which free nations can live in peace.

2. *Address of President Roosevelt Dedicating International Bridge, Thousand Islands Bridge, August 18, 1938*

(*Ibid.*, No. 106, pp. 495-99)

My fellow bridge builder, Mr. Mackenzie King, and you who are here today representing millions of other bridge builders on both sides of the international line:

It has always seemed to me that the best symbol of common sense was a bridge. Common sense is sometimes slow in getting into action, and perhaps that is why we took so long to build this one.

It is a particular pleasure to me to meet you here, where a boundary is a gateway and not a wall. Between these islands an international gap, never wide, has been spanned, as gaps usually are, by the exercise of ability, guided by cooperative common sense. I hope that all my countrymen will use it freely. I know that they will find, as I have done today and on many other occasions, a happy welcome on the Canadian shore, and forthright fellowship with neighbors who are also friends.

The St. Lawrence River is more than a cartographic line between our two countries. God so formed North Ameria that the waters of an inland empire drain into the Great Lakes Basin. The rain that falls in this vast area finds outlet through this single natural funnel, close to which we now stand.

Events of history have made that river a boundary, and as a result the flow of these waters can be used only by joint agreement between our two governments. Between us, therefore, we stand as trustees for two countries of one of the richest natural assets provided anywhere in the world. The water that runs underneath this bridge spells unlimited power; permits access to raw materials both from this continent and from beyond the seas, and enhances commerce and production.

When a resource of this kind is placed at our very doors, I think the plain people of both countries agree that it is ordinary common sense to make use of it. Yet up to now the liquid wealth, which flowing water is, has run in large part unused to the sea. I really think that this situation suggests that we can agree upon some better arrangement than merely letting this water contribute a microscopic fraction to the level of the North Atlantic Ocean. The bridge which we here dedicate is a tangible proof that administration by two neighbors of a job to be done in common offers no difficulty. Obviously the same process applied on the larger scale to the resource of full sea-going navigation and of complete power development offered by the St. Lawrence River can build and maintain the necessary facilities to employ its magnificent possibilities.

I suppose it is true, as it has been true of all natural resources, that a good many people would like to have the job—and the profits—of developing it for themselves. In this case, however, the river happens to be placed in the hands of our two governments, and the responsibility for getting the results lies plainly at our doors.

At various times both the people of Canada and the people of the United States have dreamed of the St. Lawrence and Great Lakes development. They have translated those ideas into plans which with modern engineering skill can easily be carried out. While there has been no difference between us as to the object itself, history compels me to say that we have not been able to arrange matters so that both peoples have had the same idea at the same time. I offer a suggestion. How would it do for a change, if, instead of each of us having the idea at alternate intervals, we should get the idea simultaneously? And I am very much inclined to believe that we are rapidly approaching that happy and desirable event.

There are many prophets of evil. There always have been before anything was done. I am very clear that prophets of trouble are wrong when they express the fear that the St. Lawrence Waterway will handicap our railroad systems on both sides of the border. We know now that the effect of a waterway in most cases is not to take traffic away from railroad lines. Actually, it creates new possibilities, new business and new activity. Such a waterway generates more railroad traffic than it takes away.

There is today, a fourteen foot channel carrying traffic from the Great Lakes through the St. Lawrence River into the Atlantic Ocean. If this channel were improved and deepened to twenty-seven or thirty feet, every city in both nations on the Great Lakes and on the whole course of navigation from the sea to the Lakes would become an ocean port. The banks of the St. Lawrence Valley would become one of the great gateways of the world and would benefit accordingly. Here all that is needed is cooperative exercise of technical skill by joint use of the imagination and the vision which we know both our countries have. Can anyone doubt that, when this is done, the interests of both countries will be greatly advanced? Do we need to delay, do we need to deprive our peoples of the immediate employment and profit, or prevent our generation from reaping the harvest that awaits us?

Now let me make an unusual statement. I am sure that on neither side of the line will you misunderstand me. I consider that I have, myself, a particular interest in the St. Lawrence, dating back to my earliest days in the Legislature of the State of New York in 1911. I have a particular duty as President in connection with the development of the St. Lawrence, both for navigation and for power. The almost unparalleled opportunity which the river affords has not gone unnoticed by some of my friends on the American side of the border. A conception has been emerging in the United States which is not without a certain magnificence. This is no less than the conviction that if a private group could control the outlet of the Great Lakes Basin on both sides of the border, that group would have a monopoly in the development of a territory larger than many of the great empires in history.

If you were to search the records with which my Government is familiar, you would discover that literally every development of electric power, save only the Ontario-Hydro, is allied to, if not controlled by, a single American group, with, of course, the usual surrounding penumbra of allies, affiliates, subsidiaries and satellites. In earlier stages of development of natural resources on this continent, this was normal and usual. In recent decades we have come to realize the implications to the public—to the individual men and women, to businessmen, big and little, and even to government itself, resulting from the ownership by any group of the right to dispose of wealth which was granted to us collectively by nature herself.

The development of natural resources, and the proper handling of their fruits, is a major problem of government. Naturally, no solution would be acceptable to either nation which does not leave its government entirely master in its own house.

To put it bluntly, a group of American interests is here gradually putting itself into a position where, unless caution is exercised, they may in time be able to determine the economic and the social fate of a large area, both in Canada and the United States.

Now it is axiomatic in Canadian-American relations that both of us scrupulously respect the right of each of us to determine its own affairs. For that reason, when I know that the operation of uncontrolled American economic forces is slowly producing a result on the Canadian side of the border, which I know very well must eventually give American groups a great influence over Canadian development, I consider it the part of a good neighbor to discuss the question frankly with my Canadian neighbors. The least I can do is to call attention to the situation as I see it.

Our mutual friendship suggests this course in a matter of development as great and as crucial as that of the St. Lawrence River and the basin tributary to it. Fortunately among friendly nations today this is increasingly being done. Frank discussion among friends and neighbors is useful and essential. It is obvious today that some economic problems are international, if only because of the sheer weight which the solutions have on the lives of people outside, as well as inside any one country. To my mind, the development of St. Lawrence navigation and power is such a problem.

I look forward to the day when a Canadian Prime Minister and an American President can meet to dedicate, not a bridge across this water, but the very water itself, to the lasting and productive use of their respective peoples. Until that day comes, and I hope it may be soon, this bridge stands as an open door. There will be no challenge at the border and no guard to ask a countersign. Where the boundary is crossed the only word must be, "Pass, friend."

3. Address of Prime Minister King Dedicating International Bridge,
Thousand Islands Bridge, August 18, 1938

(TGM, August 19, 1938, p. 3)

I . . . have been privileged to enjoy a friendship with President Roosevelt which extends now over many years. Like him, I have sought, whenever and wherever the opportunity has presented itself, to further and cement ties of international friendship and good-will, not alone between the English-speaking countries of the world but between all countries.

It is a joy to me to be able to join with the President this afternoon in drawing to the attention of the citizens of other lands, as well as our own, the wide significance of today's proceedings, and much that is symbolized by the new structure, the dedication of which to public use is the occasion of this vast international gathering.

On behalf of the Government and people of Canada, I should like to say to President Roosevelt how pleased and honored we all feel that he should have found it possible, today, to pay our country another visit and to accept an honorary degree from one of its leading universities. . . .

Personal and official visits alike remind us how near to the heart of the President—and I might add, to the hearts of us all—is his policy of the good neighbor. For the many expressions of international friendship and goodwill toward our country by the Chief Executive of the United States, the government and people of Canada are profoundly grateful. It is a gratitude which may well be shared by an anxious world.

In honoring the Chief Executive of the United States, Queen's University has this morning been able also to pay a tribute of esteem and of enduring friendship to the people of the United States. . . .

It may, at this time, be not inappropriate to remark that the interchange of professors and students between our universities in their country has contributed richly to both. I hope that a continuance of this fraternity of learning may serve to deepen the channels of understanding between our respective countries.

I may be pardoned, perhaps, if I mention that this morning's ceremony vividly recalled to me my own indebtedness to the universities of the United States for opportunities for post-graduate study and research.

The passing years have served to increase, rather than to diminish, the sense of obligation I feel for the opportunities thus enjoyed. Particularly is it a pleasure to me to remember, at this time, my own academic connections with Harvard University; to recall that Harvard was the

President's alma mater, and that it was at Harvard, on an occasion not dissimilar to that of this morning, I first had the pleasure of meeting Mr. Roosevelt and of forming a friendship, which in years to come was not to be without its associations with the public life of our respective countries.

May I turn now to the particular ceremony of this afternoon and its significance. There is always a satisfaction in seeing the completion of an important public undertaking. I should like to join with others present in extending heartiest congratulations to all who have had to do with the conception, construction and completion of the Thousand Islands International Bridge. . . .

Upon a bridge, itself a symbol of international friendship and good will, we are celebrating once again a century and more of peace between the United States and Canada. When we reflect upon the disputed frontiers which threaten peace in other quarters of the globe, we cannot but feel that the ceremony in which we are participating has in it something of significance to the world.

It may be thought that we owe our achievement to a common background; or that it is due to chance that our frontiers differ so greatly from the frontiers or States on other continents. It is true that we can claim to share the culture of two Old World civilizations.

The names of Champlain and Frontenac, Marquette and La Salle belong scarcely less to you than to us, and no historian has recounted their exploits more vividly than your own Francis Parkman. Likewise, until 1776 the history and heritage of the British Commonwealth to which I referred a moment ago, belonged as much to the thirteen colonies as it does to us.

This common background, however, was not sufficient to ensure our peace. The Seven Years War, the War of the American Revolution, the War of 1812, the Canadian Rebellion of 1837-38, all turned the St. Lawrence and the Great Lakes into an area of significant conflict.

The descendants of those today are here assembled to rejoice that another link has been forged which serves to further their common interest, and to cement their friendship which was, in those turbulent periods of our history, at enmity one with the other in either civil or international strife.

Human nature is much the same wherever it exists. Our populations, after all, do not, in origin, differ greatly from those of Europe. Indeed, the European countries have contributed most to their composition. Each of our countries has its problems of race and creed and class; each has its full measure of political controversy. Nevertheless, we seem to have found the better way to secure and maintain our peace.

This international highway speaks of that better way. In itself it is one vast undertaking, but it is made up of pieces of solid ground and a series of bridges. Where solid ground has been lacking, and the way in consequence, made impassable, bridges have been built. Imposing structures they are, ingeniously combining utility and beauty.

In the realm of international relations we, too, have learned to bridge our differences.

We have practiced the art of building bridges. There is indeed no more striking symbol of unity, of intercourse and of friendship than a bridge. From antiquity to the present, bridges have been built to span the spaces of separation.

Their very appearance suggests the surmounting of difficulties, the overcoming of barriers, the broadening of the path of progress and peace. The people of this continent, whether concerned with steel and stone, or with the invisible realities of mind and spirit, have, for the most part, been bridge-builders worthy of the name.

In politics, as in road-making, it is a great thing, Mr. President, to know how to build bridges. In the art of international bridge-building there are two structures, each with its association with the St. Lawrence and the Great Lakes, of which I should like to say just a word. They stand out as monuments of international cooperation and good will. Each has its message for the world of today.

The one is the Rush-Bagot agreement of 1817, the other, the International Joint Commission created in 1909. Before the War of 1812 and while it was being waged, citadel and arsenals came into being. Naval yards were set up and armed craft appeared on the waters of the St. Lawrence and the lakes. Hostile forts frowned on each other from opposite shores.

An armament race had begun; and had it been permitted to continue, we should have been looking back on a century of suspicion, enmity and hatred, instead of rejoicing, as we are, in a century of peace.

In the course of the War of 1812, as many as twenty armed vessels were constructed in the naval yards at Kingston. One of these, the *St. Lawrence,* was actually larger in size, and carried more guns, than Nelson's *Victory* at the battle of Trafalgar.

Within three years of the conclusion of the war, we, happily, had determined to place our reliance upon reason instead of upon force, and to substitute for any surviving ill will such a measure of solid good will as should bridge succeeding years. By the Rush-Bagot agreement the total armament on the Great Lakes and the St. Lawrence, as well as Lake Champlain, was not to exceed six armed vessels weighing not more than 100 tons and mounting one eighteen-pounder apiece.

On the first of this month I had the honor of reopening at Kingston the large fort which has recently been restored. Its name is Fort Henry. It, too, owed much of its size and strength to the War of 1812 and to fears

of possible future invasion of Canada by her powerful neighbor. Fort
Henry has been reconstructed to attract, not repel, possible invasions
from the United States.

The Rush-Bagot agreement was a self-denying ordinance. As such it
provided a means of escape from competitive arming. It was limited in
its application to the St. Lawrence and the lakes. In fact, it served to end
all armaments on an international frontier extending from the Atlantic
Ocean to the Pacific.

This significant document has served as the most effective instrument in promoting, between our neighboring countries, an enduring
peace.

The decision never to arm against each other was taken, as I have
indicated, over a century ago. In our own time we have crowned that
decision by the construction of other bridges of international friendship
and understanding. By far the most important of them is the International Joint Commission. It was created to adjudicate all questions of
difference arising along our four thousand miles of frontier.

In the quarter of a century of its existence, by substituting investigation for dictation and conciliation for coercion, in the adjustment of
international disputes, the commission has solved many questions
likely to lead to serious controversy.

This bridge of peace has been the more significant in that while
countries on the continents of Europe and Asia have been increasing
their frontier armaments, the United States and Canada have settled all
their boundary differences by the method and processes of reasoned
discussion.

A word in conclusion: the international bridge building of which I
have been speaking, and of which our international bridges are fitting
symbols, has grown naturally out of our common needs and our
common will to live together as good friends and neighbors. All stand
as acts of faith in human intelligence and good will.

They mean for us a precious cultural and constitutional heritage,
which it is our joint purpose to foster and maintain.

It will be at once obvious that the challenges to an international
order, founded upon the rule of law, are many and dangerous. No one
who looks at the distracted and disordered state of the world today can
fail to be impressed by the extent to which the forces of international
anarchy are seeking to prevail, and to subvert those standards of human
conduct which we have come to regard as essential attributes of our
civilization. The task of the bridge builder remains.

I think I speak the mind of both countries when I say that, not only are
we determined to preserve the neighborly relations, and the free ways
of life, which are our priceless heritage, but that we earnestly wish to
see they become a part of the common heritage of mankind. To that

end, we are prepared to go on building bridges, to throw the span of friendship and of freedom across the troubled waters of our time.

D. President Franklin D. Roosevelt and Prime Minister W.L. Mackenzie King, Washington, D.C., November 17-19, 1938

1. Remarks of President Roosevelt Upon Signing the Anglo-American and Canadian-American Reciprocal Trade Agreements, November 17, 1938

(NYT, November 18, 1938, p. 12)

This is the third anniversary of the signing of the first great trade treaty between this country and Canada. We believed at that time it would be a success and result in increased trade both ways. At the same time we hoped to extend the principle to other parts of the empire and Great Britain itself. I am happy to find the representative of the King himself and Mr. Mackenzie King here.

A large number of people have been working on this trade treaty. The negotiations have been going on for many, many months. They have been carried on not by those sitting at the table here but by patriotic citizens of the three countries. So may we extend our thanks to the staffs of the three countries. They are not any of them forgotten.

2. Remarks of Prime Minister King Upon Signing the Anglo-American and Canadian-American Reciprocal Trade Agreements, November 17, 1938

(Idem)

Mr. President, I need scarcely say how pleased I am to have the honor of participating today in a ceremony similar to the one of three years ago. At that time I was privileged to take, with Mr. Secretary Hull, a part identical with that performed today. We had just affixed our signatures to an agreement between the United States and Canada, the value of which we hoped and believed would be shown beyond question by a marked increase in commerce between our two countries. The confidence which we felt on that occasion has been amply justified by experience.

The present agreement cannot be said to be in the nature of an untried experiment. Apart from all else it marks the fulfillment of expectations which were cherished at the time the agreement of 1935 was entered into and, therefore, carries with it the assurance of benefits mutually advantageous through years to come.

When our first agreement was signed I expressed to you, Mr. President, the hope that in time it would be possible to broaden its basis and enlarge its scope. A like expectation, if I am not mistaken, was held by Mr. Secretary Hull and yourself. It is, naturally, a great satisfaction to realize today the hopes which we then entertained. I should like to add that, as respects the relations between our two countries, the fair and friendly manner of the negotiation of both agreements has been hardly less important than their positive content.

On the earlier occasion, I also expressed the view that the benefits of our agreement would not be confined to trade. They have not been so confined. It is no exaggeration, but the simple truth, to say that the relations between the United States and Canada have never been happier than in the three years that have elapsed since November, 1935.

Today's ceremony has, fortunately, an even broader significance than that of three years ago. We have also just witnessed the conclusion of a far reaching agreement between the United States and the United Kingdom. There will be in Canada genuine satisfaction that in facing the problems of today, the two countries, with whose fortunes those of Canada are so closely linked, have effectively strengthened the friendly relations which have long prevailed between them. It must be increasingly apparent that the stability of the civilization we cherish depends more than ever on the friendly association of the great English-speaking nations of the Old World and the new.

We cannot but be impressed by the fact that the occasion of our coming together today has been, in part at least, determined by the willingness of the sister nations of the British Commonwealth to facilitate a Trade Agreement between the United Kingdom and the United States.

Our satisfaction at the conclusion of these long and arduous negotiations is all the greater because the agreements which have been reached are in no sense exclusive. Indeed, their effects will be to remove many obstacles from channels of world trade. Their benefits will extend far beyond the limits of the three countries immediately concerned.

We cannot too earnestly hope that they will provide to other countries an example of the mutual advantages which flow from the broadening of trade relations, not only in the realm of material well-being, but in the wider sphere of human understanding and goodwill. . . .

E.   President Franklin D. Roosevelt and Prime Minister W.L. Mackenzie King, Warm Springs, Georgia, and Washington, D.C., April 23-24, and 29, 1940

1. Prime Minister King's Account of Meeting

(Mackenzie King Record, University of Toronto Press, Vol. I, pp. 106-8, 110-11, 114-15)

[WARM SPRINGS]

   Most of their talk was about the war and there was "of course no question about his sympathies. He [Roosevelt] and everyone around him are all strongly for the Allies. . . .He was anxious to avoid recognizing a state of war between Germany and Norway [the German invasion of Norway and Denmark had begun on April 9] so that he would not have to issue a proclamation of neutrality but would continue to supply Norway with aeroplanes, ammunition, etc." When word came during the morning that both Norway and Denmark were represented at the Supreme Allied Council, and were thus probably formal belligerents, Roosevelt told the State Department "to take another day to find out whether they were official representatives or merely observers. He recalled how he had waited a week and 'phoned me before declaring Canada was at war." Indeed, at every stage in the conversation Roosevelt indicated he was stretching his powers to the limit to help the Allies.

   The German occupation of Denmark had raised difficulties about the status of Greenland, where the Aluminum Company of Canada owned cryolite mines which were providing essential supplies. Before Mackenzie King had left Ottawa, the Government had been considering what should be done to provide for the security of these mines. Roosevelt showed Mackenzie King a letter he had received from Cordell Hull indicating that "the Americans were anxious that Canada should not undertake anything in particular. I told the President we had received from the owners of the cryolite mines requests to protect them and had undertaken, in correspondence with Britain, to see that men were supplied who could be of service about the mine in protective ways. That we would expect, however, the British fleet to do what was needed on the Atlantic; also that we had sent up each year a ship to Baffinland which brought supplies to Greenland. That this ship would be taking more in the way of supplies this year than previously." Roosevelt indicated that the Americans would also send a supply ship and that the masters of the two ships should meet before they started out and have an understanding between them as to the best way of proceeding, but that "if a real danger arose, he would have to leave it to the

British to deal with submarines, etc. at sea. He thought no effort should be made, either by the United States or Canada, to get possession of Greenland, that whatever was done should be done subject to Greenland managing her own affairs." Mackenzie King discussed the question of Greenland further with Cordell Hull when he visited Washington on his return trip to Canada.

At one stage, Roosevelt told Mackenzie King to tell Norman Rogers that there was some defence equipment belonging to the United States Navy which might be useful on the east coast and in Newfoundland, and that "he could arrange to let us have at a nominal figure. That it was not new. A great deal of it left over from the last war, but quite serviceable enough for the purpose that would be required . . . That the navy always wanted new things. That he might supply his own people with new material and let us have his old material."

Mackenzie King asked Roosevelt "whether there were difficulties between England and the United States that Canada could be of any assistance" in overcoming, and Roosevelt replied that there had been "a couple of occasions when I thought I would pick up the telephone to speak to you. But those had passed." He did express the wish that the British would act more rapidly to build up their strength.

Roosevelt also "spoke of possibly finding it necessary to send destroyers and cruisers to assist the British" and Mackenzie King "could see he was quite concerned about the inadequacy of the defence of Canada both on the Atlantic and the Pacific" as presenting "a real danger to the United States." During their conversations, Mackenzie King had shown Roosevelt a reference in a speech he had made before the war when introducing Cordell Hull in Toronto in which he had spoken of a moral embargo of aggressor nations and he noted that Roosevelt was greatly interested and had "the moral embargo idea very strongly in mind" in the rest of their talks. Mackenzie King added that he himself believed "this is the method by which America will render its greatest assistance to the Allies particularly if Germany begins bombing unfortified cities in Britain"; he resolved to impress this on Cordell Hull when he saw him in Washington. . . .

Shortly before leaving Warm Springs, Mackenzie King raised the question of the St. Lawrence Waterway. Roosevelt asked how far they had got along in reaching a settlement and Mackenzie King replied "that I would like to say to him quite frankly that so far as we were concerned, except for the interest that we knew he had in the matter and for the promise I had given to have it further discussed if we once reached an agreement with our own provinces concerning it, I would not bring the matter up. That I thought, as a Federal Government, we felt there was not any great demand for the waterways at this time." Mackenzie King had promised Roosevelt in 1938 that as soon as the Governments of Ontario and Quebec withdrew their objections,

Canada would resume discussions with the United States, and he now told Roosevelt that since the Premier of Ontario was now favourable to the project he felt it was his duty to agree to go ahead if Roosevelt wished to do so. He added that Ralston did not want to proceed and felt, if they did go ahead, tolls should be charged on all vessels except those of the United States, Britain and Canada.

Mackenzie King found that Roosevelt "was all for paying project by tolls if that were possible. He then said he thought the best thing to do would be to have matters proceeded with up to the point of readiness to make a treaty, but not attempt the treaty itself until after the Presidential election." Roosevelt asked Mackenzie King "to tell Cordell Hull that this was his view. He thought the matter should stand over until after the elections and then, if thought advisable, a treaty concluded and put through at the first session of new Congress."

For Mackenzie King, the suggested postponement to 1941 was a "great relief."

They also discussed a successor as American Minister to Canada for James Cromwell who wanted to retire to become a candidate for the United States Senate. Mackenzie King recommended "someone of a thoughtful type of mind and as good a man as he could get. Just now, with world situation as it was, Ottawa was a very important centre even as between Britain and the United States. That much could be done there by conference in different ways that would be helpful in furthering mutual interests." Roosevelt indicated that the "man he had in mind was Moffat who had been an assistant to Sumner Welles [in the State Department] and was one of the best of the career men."

Before he left Warm Springs, Mackenzie King spoke to Roosevelt "about his paying us a visit in the summer, coming to Ottawa while Lord Athlone and the Princess were there. He said he would be glad, indeed, to consider this and would try to arrange it to come about the end of June."

Mackenzie King "found it exceedingly easy to talk with the President, and those around him tell me that he feels it the same with me. That he has looked forward to my coming as a rest. He certainly gave up all his time to me and took the greater part of both days as a complete holiday for a real chance to share a sense of genuine companionship." . . .

[WASHINGTON]

While at lunch at the British Embassy, Mackenzie King received word that the President, who had now returned from Georgia, would like to see him on his way to the station. When he called at the White House, in company with Loring Christie, Roosevelt said to him: "I did not carry out your advice, Mackenzie, to stay on another day or two, which I would have liked to have done. From the reports received about what was happening, I began to get rather jittery, so could not, of course, enjoy any rest in those circumstances and came back." The President was referring here to the suspicious activities of Italy. He told Mackenzie King what he was trying to do to dissuade Mussolini from going to war and Mackenzie King in turn repeated his suggestion about the possibility of a moral embargo.

At the close of their talk, the President said to Mackenzie King: " 'Well, Mackenzie, if there is more trouble you will not mind if I ring you up.' He turned to Christie and said: 'You will not mind if I go over your head and talk straight across the phone to Mr. King.' Christie said no; on the contrary he would be very much relieved. I said to the President that I would welcome a word from him at any time, to count on me for any help I could be in any way. We then exchanged a word or two about the very happy days we had together at Warm Springs and said goodbye."

Mackenzie King recognized there was no hope at this time of direct American intervention in the war. "The only possibility I see," he wrote on April 29, "is an amendment to the Neutrality Act." He added that "no man ever received a more wholehearted or brotherly welcome than I did from everyone in connection with the Administration with whom I came in contact."

F. President Franklin D. Roosevelt and Prime Minister W. L. Mackenzie King, Ogdensburg, New York, August 17-18, 1940

1. Prime Minister King's Account of Meeting

(Mackenzie King Record, University of Toronto Press, Vol. 1, pp. 131-35)

. . . During their talk after dinner, Roosevelt and Mackenzie King quickly agreed in principle on the establishment of a joint board composed of an equal number of representatives of both countries to study their common problems of defence and to make recommendations to the two Governments. After that, the President read over all the messages that Churchill had sent him regarding the destroyers and Atlantic bases. Mackenzie King had received copies of most of them from Churchill. In one message, Churchill had used the expression that the destroyers would be as precious to the British as rubies. When he came to the end of a despatch referring to the role of Canada, the President said: "This is where you come in." Mackenzie King replied "that Churchill had already communicated with me and that I had sent word to him that we were wholly agreeable to the United States being given bases on the islands of the Atlantic and that, as he knew, I had put this forward to Churchill some time ago. As to Newfoundland, I said both the British and our Government would probably have to do with that matter as well as the United States." Mackenzie King added that Power had left for Newfoundland that very day and that Canada was about to spend a million on facilities at Gander airport.

Mackenzie King observed that the President seemed "most anxious to meet the British and to get a *quid pro quo* for giving destroyers without consulting Congress, which public opinion would accept as fair. He said to me that up to the last few days, he had almost despaired of being able to meet the British on this request. That the United States itself had become so alarmed after French collapse, they did not wish to part with any of their own security." Roosevelt's decision not to put the question to Congress was, he told Mackenzie King, based on the advice of Senators and Congressmen who "had said to him: 'For God's sake don't put this question to Congress or you will have a few months' debate on it. Find some other way to deal with the matter!' "

Roosevelt said that only legal technicalities were holding up the transfer of the vessels, and he expected them to be overcome in the following week. He said Mackenzie King "could tell Churchill that that was all that was holding matters up at present. He then went on to say that I could advise him [Churchill] to begin to get the crews across at once unless we had crews ourselves that we could send. He thought it desirable that the men who manned the destroyers should be the ones to remain permanently on them, as crossing the ocean would give them that much in the way of extra experience." Roosevelt also told him of other ships, aircraft, and equipment he planned to make available to Britain.

"As we talked matters over," Mackenzie King continued, "the President made the remark that he did not like having conferences between the two countries on these matters carried on in secret. While that had been necessary to begin with, he felt that way about it. I said I was exactly of his mind. That it was a tremendous relief to have everything worked out in the open, apart from the effect that the Joint Board itself would have. Mr. Stimson spoke about what neutrality had cost the smaller countries. That part of the viciousness of Germany had been taking advantage of their good faith in seeking to preserve their neutrality and attack them unprepared as a consequence. Germany's action in that regard had justified neutral countries taking no chances of that kind of thing repeating itself on this side."

Before the breaking up on Saturday night, Roosevelt and Mackenzie King decided to give the press next day a joint statement they would prepare beforehand, and tentatively discussed the working of it.

On Sunday morning, Mackenzie King noted, "nothing was said of the previous night's conversations until we were coming back from the

Service, when I said to the President I wanted to be sure about one or two things I was free to say to Mr. Churchill.'' When they got back into the train, Mackenzie King took from his pocket ''the paper with a few questions I had noted down in the morning in order to get exact particulars for reply, to be sure I had all of last night's points carefully in mind.

''I then said to the President I disliked taking advantage of all he had done and was doing to proffer a further request, but that I had promised our own boys that I would, if possible, bring to his attention something further in the way of military equipment and supplies that we, in Canada, were most anxious to have. I then gave him the memo Ralston had given to me, adding to it what Angus Macdonald had requested. The President and Mr. Stimson were very nice about the way they received what I gave them and each remarked that they would have a great deal of difficulty. I explained that, as the President was aware, some of our permanent staff had been talking with Mr. Morgenthau. . . . That our men did not wish us to go over Morgenthau's head to the President until we were sure Morgenthau was agreeable to what was being presented. I explained that, by coincidence, word had come on Saturday morning that Morgenthau was quite prepared to have us go ahead. Both Stimson and the President laughed, saying that the difficulty was not with Morgenthau. It was with the defence services.'' Stimson explained how short the United States was of many of the items on the list and the President promised that he and Mr. Stimson would look over the list carefully together.

Mackenzie King added that while he and Stimson were looking at the list on the sofa, the President began to draft the statement for the press which they were to give jointly. ''He did this on a sheet of paper which he took from the basket and with a pencil in his hand, read aloud the draft he had prepared. It was clearly and concisely worded. Spoke of a Joint Commission. When he had finished the reading of the draft, I asked him whether he thought the word 'Commission' was as good as 'Board' or 'Committee.' Said the word 'Board' had been used the night before in conversation. Mr. Stimson agreed that Board would perhaps be better and the President also did. I pointed out that Commission suggested the necessity of formal appointments by Governments. I then questioned him as to the significance of the use of the word 'Permanent.' He said at once that he attached much importance to it. I said I was not questioning the wisdom of it but was anxious to get what he had in mind.'' Roosevelt felt the Board should not be designed ''to meet alone this particular situation but to help secure the continent for the future,'' and Mackenzie King concurred. The title agreed on was the Canada-United States Permanent Joint Board on Defence.

When they came to the question of numbers, the President spoke of four or five, at least one to be a layman. Mackenzie King ''asked how soon the Board would meet and where. The President added a sentence to say that the Board would meet shortly. I said I thought it might be well to have them meet this coming week and asked if he had any preference as to where they should meet. As he did not express a preference, I suggested it might be well for them to meet in Ottawa." Mackenzie King felt "it would be logical in that we had been working on the problems and the first thing would be for their men to become familiar with what we already knew. Power, for instance, today was in Newfoundland. He would be back and could state the situation as he found it there. The President said that that would be first rate. His idea was after a meeting in Ottawa, they might all wish to go to Newfoundland or to the Maritimes generally with a view to viewing matters concretely.

"The President read the statement a second time. I approved it in its entirety. Mr. Stimson thought it was all right." The statement was then given to the press.

In his diary for Sunday, Mackenzie King added that "on Saturday night, when we were thinking out loud the phraseology of a statement, the President said something about the Western Hemisphere. Mr. Stimson used the word: northern half of the Western Hemisphere. [The scope of the Board was confined to North America.] The President frequently said to me he assumed that, as regards the colonial possessions and Newfoundland, he would take that phase up direct with Churchill. I said that was right, but I thought, as we had undertaken protection of Newfoundland and were spending money there, the British Government would probably want our Government to cooperate in that part.

"During the evening, I had explained that we would not wish to sell or lease any sites in Canada but would be ready to work out matters of facilities. The President said he had mostly in mind the need, if Canada were invaded, for getting troops quickly into Canada. . . . That similarly if the U.S. should engage in a conflict in the South or around the Panama Canal, and had its men concentrated there, that it might help for us to be able to move men immediately through Maine to Portland, for example, which was the terminus of the old Grand Trunk and present Canadian National Railways. He thought we might have to arrange for annual manoeuvres of troops on our respective soils. I agreed that that would be all right. . . ."

2. *Joint Statement of President Roosevelt and Prime Minister King, August 18, 1940 (Known as the "Ogdensburg Agreement")*

(PP/Franklin D. Roosevelt, Macmillan, Vol. 1940, No. 80, p. 331)

The Prime Minister of Canada and the President have discussed the mutual problems of defense in relation to the safety of Canada and the United States.

It has been agreed that a Permanent Joint Board on Defense shall be set up at once by the two countries.

This Permanent Joint Board on Defense shall commence immediate studies relating to sea, land and air problems including personnel and matériel.

It will consider in the broad sense the defense of the north half of the Western Hemisphere.

The Permanent Joint Board on Defense will consist of four or five members from each country, most of them from the services. It will meet shortly.

3. Prime Minister King's Interpretation of the Ogdensburg Agreement to the Canadian House of Commons, November 12, 1940

(CHCD, November 12, 1940, pp. 55-60)

Now for a word as to the conversations which preceded the Ogdensburg agreement. The agreement itself was not due to any sudden or precipitate action. It was the outcome of several conversations between the president and myself with respect to coastal defence on both the Atlantic and the Pacific, in which the mutual interests of Canada and the United States were discussed. It has seemed to me that I should reserve for parliament such statement as it might be advisable to make with reference to those conversations which, in their nature, necessarily were highly confidential. I might say I have received the president's permission to refer to them publicly.

In the matter of time and significance, the conversations between president Roosevelt and myself on matters pertaining to the common interest of our two countries in the defence of their coasts, divide themselves naturally into two groups: the conversations which took place prior to the commencement of the war, and those which have taken place since.

The first conversation was on the occasion of a visit I paid the president at the White House, as long ago as March, 1937. At that time the discussion had reference to the position on the Pacific as well as on the Atlantic coasts. It was then agreed that, at some time in the future, meetings might be arranged between the staff officers of both countries to discuss problems of common defence.

On September 30 of that year, the President paid a visit to Victoria, British Columbia, crossing on a United States destroyer from Seattle. This visit led to arrangements for talks between staff officers regarding

Pacific coast problems, which took place in Washington in January, 1938.

I think I may say that on every occasion on which I have visited the president in the United States, or on which I have met the president on his visit to Canada, matters pertaining to the defence of this continent have been a subject of conversation between us.

The defences on the Atlantic were referred to particularly in our conversations in August, 1938, in the course of the president's visit to Kingston, and the opening of the Thousand Islands bridge at Ivy Lea. At that time, it will be recalled, the president made the open declaration that the people of the United States would not stand idly by if domination of Canadian soil were threatened by any other empire. To this declaration I replied at Woodbridge, Ontario, two days later, that we too had our obligations as a good, friendly neighbour.

Our common problems of defence were discussed at length and in a more concrete and definite way when I visited Washington in November, 1938, to sign the new Canadian-United States trade agreement.

In the summer of 1939, the president paid a visit to Canadian waters off the Atlantic coast. He subsequently told me that this visit, like his similar visit to Victoria two years earlier, had been occasioned by his concern with the problem of coastal defence.

With the outbreak of war, the question of coast defences became of vital importance. At the same time, the fact that Canada was a belligerent and the United States a neutral complicated the problem of pursuing the discussions. In the face of the European menace it was obviously desirable to give expression to the needs of joint defence. To the means, however, of effecting this end, the most careful consideration had to be given in order that there might be no grounds for the belief that there was any attempt on Canada's part to influence the policies or to interfere in the domestic affairs of a neutral country. Had there not been, between the president and myself, complete confidence in each other's purpose and motives, I question if the situation could have been met without occasioning genuine embarrassment to one side or the other, if not indeed to both. Fortunately, in the light of our previous conversations, there was no danger of the position being misunderstood, and my visit with the president at Warm Springs, in April of the present year, afforded an exceptional opportunity for a careful review of the whole situation.

This is perhaps an appropriate place for me to say that, from the beginning, and at the time of each conversation, the president made it perfectly clear that his primary interest in the subject was the defence of the United States. I was equally frank in making it clear that my concern was the effective defence of Canada, and the defence of the British commonwealth of nations as a whole.

If one thing above another became increasingly evident in the course of our conversations, it was that our respective countries had a common interest in the matter of the defence of this continent. Since this was the case, everything pointed to the wisdom of planning carefully in advance for whatever contingency might arise.

The conversations begun between the president and myself before the war, in the direct manner I have described, and at Warm Springs taken up anew after Canada had entered the war, were supplemented as the weeks went by, by conversations conducted through diplomatic channels. Staff conversations followed in due course.

I should perhaps say that I gave to my colleagues who were members of the war committee of the cabinet my entire confidence with respect to the conversations I had had with the president, and subsequent steps were taken with their knowledge and full approval. I should also like to say that the British government was kept duly informed of what was taking place. The Canadian government likewise was kept informed of the defence matters directly discussed between the British government and the United States. The discussions naturally included questions pertaining to the leasing of air and naval bases on the Atlantic.

As I have already mentioned, the president had announced the day before our meeting at Ogdensburg that conversations had been taking place between the two governments. The Ogdensburg agreement formally confirmed what the previous conversations and planning had initiated. It made known to the world that plans of joint defence were being studied and worked out between the two countries. It did one thing more: It made clear that the board which was being established to make studies and recommendations was not being formed for a single occasion to meet a particular situation, but was intended to deal with a continuing problem. The board on joint defence was, therefore, declared to be permanent.

By a minute of council approved by His Excellency the Governor General on August 21, the establishment of the Permanent Joint Board on Defence was formally ratified and confirmed. . . .

The permanent Joint Board on Defence might well be considered a logical development from the declarations made by President Roosevelt and myself in August, 1938. Let me recall these declarations to the minds of hon. members. The vital passage in Mr. Roosevelt's declaration at Kingston on August 18 reads:

> The Dominion of Canada is part of the sisterhood of the British empire. I give to you assurance that the people of the United States will not stand idly by if domination of Canadian soil is threatened by any other empire.

My acknowledgment of Mr. Roosevelt's Kingston declaration at

Woodbridge, Ontario, on August 21, 1938, contained these words:

> We, too, have our obligations as a good friendly neighbour, and
> one of them is to see that, at our own instance, our country is made
> as immune from attack or possible invasion as we can reasonably
> be expected to make it, and that, should the occasion ever arise,
> enemy forces should not be able to pursue their way, either by
> land, sea, or air to the United States, across Canadian territory.

These declarations marked the first public recognition by both countries of their reciprocity in defence.

I should be the last to claim that the Ogdensburg agreement was due
wholly to the conversations between the president and myself, or to our
reciprocal declarations in 1938. I am happy to know that, in a moment
of crisis, personal friendship and mutual confidence, shared over many
years between Mr. Roosevelt and myself, made it so easy for us to
conclude the agreement reached at Ogdensburg. In reality the agreement marks the full blossoming of a long association in harmony
between the people of Canada and the people of the United States, to
which, I hope and believe, the President and I have also in some
measure contributed. The link forged by the Canada-United States
defence agreement is no temporary axis. It was not formed by nations
whose common tie is a mutual desire for the destruction of their
neighbours. It is part of the enduring foundation of a new world order,
based on friendship and good will. In the furtherance of this new world
order, Canada, in liaison between the British commonwealth and the
United States, is fulfilling a manifest destiny.

It cannot be assumed that our common background would, of itself,
have produced harmonious relations between the two countries, much
as that background has helped to make possible a close understanding
between us. The understanding which exists owes its vitality to positive
and far-sighted statesmanship over more than a century.

May I recall in this connection the words I used at the opening of the
Thousand Islands bridge on August 18, 1938:

> . . . In the art of international bridge-building there are two
> structures, each with its association with the St. Lawrence and the
> Great Lakes, of which I should like to say just a word. They stand
> out as monuments of international cooperation and good will.
> Each has its message for the world of to-day. The one is the
> Rush-Bagot agreement of 1817: the other, the International Joint
> Commission created in 1909.

The Rush-Bagot agreement is a self-denying ordinance of mutual
disarmament. The International Joint Commission is an instrument for

the peaceful adjustment of differences. The permanent joint board is a mutual arrangement for common defence. All three may appear an inevitable progress dictated by ordinary common sense. But we need only to pause for a moment's reflection to realize that, in the madness of the world to-day, common sense is the highest statesmanship.

I doubt if any act by a Canadian government, and certainly no development in our internatioinal relations, has ever received such unanimous acclaim in this country. So far as I have been able to ascertain, not a single newspaper from coast to coast uttered a syllable of disapproval of the Ogdensburg agreement itself. Though estimates of its importance and of the contribution made by myself may have varied, almost no voice was raised to decry its significance. . . .

Although the presidential campaign was already in progress in the United States, and some effort to make political capital might perhaps have been expected, an examination of American press comment reveals a similar unanimous approval of the Ogdensburg agreement. . . .

The realization, both in Canada and in the United States, that each nation is obliged to assist in the defence of its neighbour because that is its own best defence, has grown in the two years which elapsed between the Kingston and Woodbridge declarations and the Ogdensburg agreement.

The events of those two momentous years have served, as well, to allay the fears of those in Canada who felt that closer relations with the United States would weaken Canada's ties with Britain. Throughout my public life, I have consistently maintained the view that the friendliest relations between Canada and the United States, far from weakening the bonds between the nations of the British commonwealth, would, at all times, prove a source of strength. Moreover, I have always held that in the promotion of Anglo-American friendship, Canada has a very special role to play. This belief, I am happy to say, is shared, in all three countries, by those who have worked for closer relations between the English-speaking communities. It is shared in fullest measure by the present Prime Minister of Great Britain. More than ten years ago, at a time when he himself was holding no public office, Mr. Churchill expressed this belief in terms which I should like to quote from an article of his which appeared in the *Saturday Evening Post* of February 15, 1930.

The words gain a prophetic significance in the light of all subsequent developments and of none more than those of the present day. I quote:

> Great Britain herself has for centuries been the proved and accepted champion of European freedom. She is the centre and head of the British commonwealth of nations. She is an equal partner in the English-speaking world.

It is at this point that the significance of Canada appears. Canada, which is linked to the British empire, first by the growing importance of her own nationhood, and secondly, by many ancient and sentimental ties precious to young and strong communities, is at the same time intimately associated with the United States.

The long, unguarded frontier, the habits and intercourse of daily life, the fruitful and profitable connections of business, the sympathies and even the antipathies of honest neighbourliness, make Canada a binder-together of the English-speaking peoples. She is a magnet exercising a double attraction, drawing both Great Britain and the United States towards herself and thus drawing them closer to each other. She is the only surviving bond which stretches from Europe across the Atlantic ocean. In fact, no state, no country, no band of men can more truly be described as the linchpin of peace and world progress.

It is a happy coincidence that the soundness of this view of Canada's position as a link between the British and American peoples should have been so amply demonstrated at a moment when the one who shared it so completely, and who expressed it in such eloquent terms, has come to hold the office of Prime Minister of Great Britain.

In an editorial comment which appeared in the London *Times* on August 22 of this year, the significance of the Ogdensburg agreement in the wider-relations between the English-speaking people was recognized in terms reminiscent of Mr. Churchill's utterance of ten years ago.

"The two countries" said the *Times* "will henceforward have closer ties than they have ever had in the past, and Canada more than ever before will be the linchpin of Anglo-American relations." . . .

The present war has, as I have shown, enlarged the opportunities and the solemn responsibility of Canada to serve as a vital link between the United States and the British commonwealth. This role is, however, not the only one which Canada is uniquely equipped to play in international relations. There is a third great nation with whom our ties are close. I have spoken of Canada's place as an interpreter of the English-speaking peoples. Canada, however, is not merely an English-speaking nation but is also a French-speaking nation. It is, indeed, the second French-speaking nation of the world.

The agony of France has thrown upon Canada a great responsibility and a great mission. As I pointed out at the moment of the collapse of France, "the tragic fate of France leaves to French Canada the duty of upholding the traditions of French culture and civilization, and the French passion for liberty in the world. This new responsibility will, I believe, be accepted proudly."

Events are throwing upon Canada not only the mission of upholding the traditions of French culture and civilization, but also the duty of helping to keep alive in the hearts of Frenchmen, all but prostrate to-day before a brutal conqueror, their devotion to liberty and their hopes of its ultimate triumph. . . .

G. President Franklin D. Roosevelt and Prime Minister W.L. Mackenzie King, Washington, D.C., April 16-17, 1941, and Hyde Park, New York, April 20, 1941

1. Prime Minister King's Account of Hyde Park Meeting

(Mackenzie King Record, University of Toronto Press, Vol. I, pp. 197-202)

. . . The three of them later drove to the house of one of the President's relatives for tea. ''On the way,'' Mackenzie King wrote, ''we talked a little about some of the defence measures, but more particularly of the talk I had had with Mr. Morgenthau. The President told me that Morgenthau had seen him, after talking with me, and had explained the situation to him. He thought perhaps it might be going a little too far to have something manufactured in Canada for the U.S. to Lease-Lend to England.''

Hopkins told Mackenzie King ''he had had a very satisfactory and nice talk with Mr. Howe and liked Howe very much. We spoke of different things that could be manufactured in Canada for the U.S.: aluminum, different kinds of ships, gun barrels, explosives, small ammunition, clothing.'' Mackenzie King explained that the list of supplies Canada could manufacture which Morgenthau had asked for had now been prepared and Hopkins ''said he thought it should be arranged that all their orders should be placed through Mr. Howe rather than a lot of contractors coming to Washington lobbying for contracts. I said I believed that would prove to be the best. He said perhaps I would tell Howe to let them know as soon as possible of any factories or other industrial establishments manufacturing for the U.S. and that they would send their men immediately, to view the premises and report upon them prior to the placing of contracts. Either the President or Mr. Hopkins spoke of our doing a good deal in the way of assembling for them.

''It was while we were driving together that I said to the President that, when I talked over the whole matter with Mr. Morgenthau, the latter had said to me he would like me to meet him on Monday, and that we would go together to the President and get his approval of what we had worked out together. That, during the week-end, officials were at work getting things in readiness for us. That I felt a little embarrassed about not carrying out this arrangement with Mr. Morgenthau and had really intended not to discuss it at all with him (the President) until Mr. Morgenthau and I had completed our part. That I wondered whether it would be necessary for me to go back to Washington to see Mr. Morgenthau or whether he would fully understand my having taken up the matter with him, the President.

"The President at once said that he did not think it would be necessary for me to go back. That Morgenthau, as a matter of fact, was nearby, and we could have a word with him when he got back to Hyde Park and straighten out matters here. I said that was splendid; that in the hope or anticipation of some possibility of the kind, I had drafted, before coming, a statement which I thought was of the kind to which Mr. Morgenthau would agree and which would cover the ground pretty well. That perhaps we could use that statement as a basis for further consideration of the matter. The President said that would be first rate. We can take that up after we get back to the house. . . .When the President said he would take up the statement himself I felt an immense relief off my mind, and that the object of the whole mission would thereby be fully achieved." . . .

"When the President had signed in his own hand the statement, he gave it to me and I thanked him warmly. Told him how very much I had enjoyed the visit and said good-bye, and expressed the hope that God would bless him and give him strength. He then said: now we will each go our own way for the present; you, to Canada in your car and I, to Washington in mine. We will pass each other on the way. He remained seated in his chair among his papers, looking very happy. I really think the day turned out to be a real rest and enjoyment to him, and that he got a great kick out of our having worked out this Agreement together without any Ministers or advisers or secretaries around, but as something on our own. He feels very strongly, as I do, about this perpetual circumventing of effort by others and the assumption that only those in specialized positions have any brains or judgment. To my mind, there never was stronger evidence of Divine guidance and answer to prayer on that score, more completely evidenced than in this transaction." . . .

2. *Joint Statement of President Roosevelt and Prime Minister King, Hyde Park, New York, April 20, 1941 (Known as the "Hyde Park Declaration")*

(PP/Franklin D. Roosevelt, Russell and Russell, Vol. 1941, pp. 582-83)

Among other important matters, the President and the Prime Minister discussed measures by which the most prompt and effective utilization might be made of the productive facilities of North America for the purposes both of local and hemisphere defense and of the assistance which in addition to their own programs both Canada and the United States are rendering to Great Britain and the other democracies.

It was agreed as a general principle that in mobilizing the resources of this continent each country should provide the other with the defense articles which it is best able to produce, and, above all, produce quickly, and that production programs should be coordinated to this end.

While Canada has expanded its productive capacity many-fold since the beginnning of the war, there are still numerous defense articles which it must obtain in the United States, and purchases of this character by Canada will be even greater in the coming year than in the past. On the other hand, there is existing and potential capacity in Canada for the speedy production of certain kinds of munitions, strategic materials, aluminum, and ships, which are urgently required by the United States for its own purposes.

While exact estimates cannot yet be made, it is hoped that during the next twelve months Canada can supply the United States with between $200,000,000 and $300,000,000 worth of such defense articles. This sum is a small fraction of the total defense program of the United States, but many of the articles to be provided are of vital importance. In addition, it is of great importance to the economic and financial relations between the two countries that payment by the United States for these supplies will materially assist Canada in meeting part of the cost of Canadian defense purchases in the United States.

Insofar as Canada's defense purchases in the United States consist of component parts to be used in equipment and munitions which Canada is producing for Great Britain, it was also agreed that Great Britain will obtain these parts under the Lend-Lease Act and forward them to Canada for inclusion in the finished article.

The technical and financial details will be worked out as soon as possible in accordance with the general principles which have been agreed upon between the President and the Prime Minister.

3. Prime Minister King's Interpretation of the Hyde Park Declaration to the Canadian House of Commons, April 28, 1941

(CHCD, April 28, 1941, pp. 2286-89)

I should like now to proceed with the statement I wish to make in regard to the so-called Hyde Park declaration.

On March 12, I described the United States lease-lend act as one of the milestones of freedom, pointing the way to ultimate and certain victory. The lease-lend act settled the principle of United States assistance to Britain and the other democracies. It did not, however, solve all of the complex economic problems involved in the mobilization of the resources of the United States and Canada in order to render to Britain, in the speediest manner, the most effective assistance and support.

One of the reasons for my recent visit to the United States and my conferences with the president, was the urgent need for Canada to find an immediate solution of some of the problems involved in our war-time economic relations with the United States and with the United Kingdom. Before indicating the extent to which a solution has been found in the Hyde Park declaration, I shall outline briefly the problems themselves.

It will be readily recognized that we, in Canada, could not possibly have embarked upon our existing programme of war production if we had not lived side by side with the greatest industrial nation in the world. Without ready access to the industrial production of the United States, and particularly the machine tools and other specialized equipment so necessary in producing the complex instruments of modern war, Canada's war effort would have been seriously retarded. We would have been forced to embark upon the production of many articles which, because of limited demand, could only have been produced at high cost, and over a considerable period of time. Canada also lacks certain essential raw materials which must be procured from the United States. Since the outbreak of war, we have steadily expanded our purchases in the United States of these essential tools, machines and materials which were required both for our own Canadian war effort, and in the production of war supplies for Britain.

Even in normal times Canada purchases much more from the United States than we sell to our neighbours. In peace time we were able to make up the deficit by converting into United States dollars the surplus sterling we received as a result of the sale of goods to Britain. But from the outset of war, this has been impossible. The government realized at once that Canada would be faced with a growing shortage of United States dollars to pay for our essential war purchases. To conserve the necessary exchange the foreign exchange control board was established on September 15, 1939. As the need has grown, increasingly stringent measures have been adapted to reduce the unessential demands for United States dollars in order to conserve sufficient funds to make our payments for essential weapons and supplies of war. These war purchases could not be reduced without a corresponding, or perhaps an even more serious, reduction in our war effort. Despite the drastic measures taken to conserve exchange, the lack of United States dollars was becoming, as one writer expressed it, one of the most serious "bottlenecks" in Canada's war effort.

The problem of exchange was the most urgent problem we faced in our economic relations with the United States. But we also realized a growing danger of possible unnecessary duplication of production facilities on the North American continent, with consequent undue pressure on scarce labour and materials if Canada and the United States each tried to make itself wholly self-sufficient in the field of war supplies. We felt it imperative to avoid such waste, which might well have had the most serious consequences. The experience of the Department of Munitions and Supply, and the studies of the permanent joint board on defence, both suggested the same solution. That solution was the co-ordination of the production of war materials of Canada and the United States. This was in reality a simple and logical extension, to the economic sphere, of the Ogdensburg agreement.

The practical experience of a year and a half of organizing and developing war production in Canada revealed that many of the essentials of war could be made in the comparatively small quantities required by Canada only at a prohibitive cost. They could, however, be produced economically in the United States where the demand was large enough to result in the economies of large-scale production. On the other hand, the production of other weapons and materials had been developed in Canada to the point where output could be expanded more quickly, and probably more economically, than new production facilities could be organized in the United States. It was, therefore, only common sense to extend to the production of war materials the same reciprocity in which at Ogdensburg, in August last, our two countries had permanently placed their defence.

During my Easter visit, I had the opportunity of preliminary discussions with the Secretary of State, Mr. Cordell Hull, and the Secretary of the Treasury, Mr. Morgenthau, at Washington. I also, later, had an opportunity of conferring with Mr. Harry Hopkins, who has been entrusted with immediate direction and supervision of the measures to be taken under the lease-lend act. On Sunday, April 20, I spent the day with the president at Hyde Park. At the close of the visit, I gave to the press a statement of the understanding which the president and I had reached regarding the problems I have mentioned. That statement it is proposed to call the Hyde Park declaration. (See previous entry.)

The immediate purpose of the joint declaration is set out in its first paragraph, which might be described as the preamble. It states that the president and I discussed measures by which the most prompt and effective utilization might be made of the productive facilities of North America. Let me emphasize the two words: prompt and effective. They indicate that while recognizing the short-run necessity of speed, the vital importance of the time factor, we have not lost sight of the longrun necessity of the utmost efficiency in the organization of our war production.

The preamble goes on to recognize a two-fold object in ensuring this prompt and effective utilization of the productive facilities of both countries. Not only does it envisage the extension of the scope of our joint defence arrangements to the economic sphere, but it recognizes the advantages of coordinating the use of the resources of both countries as a means of speeding up and increasing the volume of aid to Britain from this continent.

Let me state this in another way. The Hyde Park declaration is more than an extension of the Ogdensburg agreement for hemispheric defence. It is also a joint agreement between Canada and the United States for aid to Britain.

The basic principle underlying the agreement is set out in the second paragraph. It is a recognition of the fact that each country has special advantages for the production of certain war materials which are lacking in the other, and that both countries will benefit by each producing for the other, as well as for itself, the defence articles which it is best able to produce. It constitutes an acceptance of the economic inter-dependence of Canada and the United States as the foundation of the programme of war production in both countries. It represents the application to war production of the principle, recognized by Canada and the United States in the trade agreements of peace time, that the exchange of goods is of mutual benefit. . . .

Its most immediate significance is that, through the coordination of war production in both countries, it will result in the speeding up of aid to Britain by the United States and Canada. As a result of the better integration of North American industry, the proposed arrangement will, through increasing total production, have the further effect of increasing the total volume of aid to Britain. It will have a corresponding effect upon Canada's war effort. Full utilization of the production facilities we have built up, and specialization on those things which we are best fitted to produce, will increase both our national income and our own armed strength, as well as increasing our capacity to aid Britain.

As I have already said, the agreement will go a long way towards the solution of the exchange problem and, in this way, will remove one of the financial obstacles to the maximum war production programme of Canada and the United States. We, in Canada, have reason to be gratified at the understanding shown by the president and by the secretary of the treasury, of Canada's difficult exchange problem. We may, I am sure, feel an equal confidence that in the working out of the detailed technical and financial arrangements, Canadian officials will find the same generous measure of understanding and the same spirit of cooperation.

I have spoken thus far of the immediate significance of the declaration, of the effect it will have in speeding up aid to Britain in the critical months ahead, and of its importance in assisting us to meet our exchange problem. But beyond its immediate significance the Hyde Park declaration will have a permanent significance in the relations between Canada and the United States. It involves nothing less than a common plan of the economic defence of the western hemisphere. When we pause to reflect upon the consequences, in Europe, of the failure of the peace-loving nations to plan in concert their common defence, while yet there was time, we gain a new appreciation of the significance for the future of both Canada and the United States of the Ogdensburg agreement and of this new declaration which might well be called the economic corollary of Ogdensburg.

For Canada, the significance of the Hyde Park declaration may be summarized briefly as follows: first, it will help both Canada and the United States to provide maximum aid to Britain and to all the defenders of democracy; second, it will increase the effectiveness of Canada's direct war effort; and finally, through the increased industrial efficiency which will result, it will increase our own security and the security of North America.

It is appropriate at this point to emphasize the fact that, while the agreement will increase the effectiveness of our war effort and our assistance to Britain, the self-imposed burden upon the Canadian people will nevertheless remain as great as ever. The sacrifices which we are called upon to make will not be reduced by the Hyde Park declaration, but the results achieved by our sacrifices will, we believe, be considerably greater. At the same time, the risks of delays and breakdowns will be materially reduced. The utmost effort of the Canadian people is more than ever needed in the present phase of this terrible struggle; but in making that effort we shall have, as the result of the agreement, the added satisfaction of knowing that we are making a greater contribution than otherwise would be possible to the cause of freedom.

In referring to the passage of the lease-lend act, I expressed in this house the view that "Canada's example, as a nation of the new world, actively participating to the utmost limit in the present struggle, has also had its influence in arousing the people of the United States to their present realization that freedom itself is a stake in this war."

Unhesitatingly, to-day, I would go one step farther and would say that the example given by Canada has, I believe, aroused the admiration of our neighbours and made them ready to accept this new partnership.

Last November, I said to hon. members of this house that the link forged by the Ogdensburg agreement was no temporary axis, formed by nations whose common tie was a mutual desire for the destruction of their neighbours. The Hyde Park declaration is, I believe, a further convincing demonstration that Canada and the United States are indeed laying the enduring foundations of a new world order, an order based on international understanding, on mutual aid, on friendship and good will.

H. President Franklin D. Roosevelt and Prime Minister W.L. Mackenzie King, Washington, D.C., May 18-21, 1943, also with Prime Minister Winston Churchill

1. Prime Minister King's Account of Meeting

(Mackenzie King Record, University of Toronto Press, Vol. I, pp. 510-14)

Mackenzie King spent a good deal of time with both Churchill and Roosevelt during his stay at the White House. He dined with both of them and with several other guests on the day Churchill spoke to the Congress. There was nothing very notable in the conversation until the other guests left and Mackenzie King was alone with the President. Roosevelt then outlined some of his ideas about peace-making and post-war international organization. Roosevelt felt there would have to be a Supreme Council representing all the United Nations, and he stressed particularly the need of "someone who could fill the position of Moderator—someone who would keep his eye on the different countries to see that they were complying with the agreements made in connection with the peace, for example, limitation of armaments. . . .

"It would be the Moderator's duty possibly to warn in advance and, if necessary, to have the Council meet to take such action as might be necessary. He said, of course, the difficulty would be to find the man for that position. He would have to be someone who would have the confidence of all the nations. Smuts would be an ideal man for that position, but when the time came, he would be too old. The President then said, referring to himself, I could myself fill that position. I would have the confidence of the countries. I have forgotten just what reason he gave for doubting whether he could take it on. It may have had reference to his being required for further services in the office he is now holding."

After the meeting of the Pacific Council the next morning, Mackenzie King had lunch with Roosevelt, Churchill, and Harry Hopkins. Hopkins left right after lunch and the other three talked for some time. Roosevelt referred again to his idea of a world "Moderator," and after again dismissing Smuts because of his age, Roosevelt said to Churchill "Mackenzie would be accepted by the entire world. All countries have confidence in him. I simply laughed and said it was very nice of him to speak in that way but he must not be extravagant in what he was saying or words to that effect.

"Churchill then said: 'Is it not a fact that we three men who are at this table now, have had more experience in government than any other men in the world today.' The President said he agreed in that. I said there is no doubt in my mind that, but for you two men, the free countries of the world would have lost their freedom and these other powers would be in control. Churchill said: 'there was nothing truer than that.' The President, too, agreed that if they had not combined, and each played the part they had—combined together the strength that now exists—the whole situation would have been different. . . .

"They then, however, came back to the position that I held as between Britain and the United States; I understood both of them, and had their confidence as no other man. Roosevelt referred to our association going back to Harvard days, and Churchill to the beginning of 1900, and spoke of that period of time during which I had known each of them. The President then repeated what he had said about my holding a position which any country would recognize, and they both remarked that it was true that the three of us . . . at that table at that time had a place in government and experience that no other three men in the world had today."

They also discussed the question of raising the Canadian Legation in Washington to an Embassy. Roosevelt pointed out that the Latin American countries had all done so and that "Canada was the only country on the continent that had not an Embassy. I said that I had not favoured an Embassy up to the present out of sense of proportion. . . . Felt that we should take matters a step at a time, and added that I was thinking of having the Legation changed into an Embassy. I asked Churchill what he thought about it, how they would feel in England if that were done. Churchill's reply was that he thought Canada should be as strong in every way as she could be. That she should have as strong a position on this continent as she could possibly have. That he favoured her being given all the recognition possible and making her position felt. He said he did not know how the Foreign Office would view the matter. I pointed out it was for us to make our own decision. He agreed entirely with that."

When the President referred to the need of the consent of the King of England to the change, "Churchill at once said: 'No. He is the King of Canada just as much as he is the King of England. Canada has complete control of her own affairs. Mackenzie has just as much say in regard to what Canada is to do as I have in regard to Britain,' or words to that effect. I said we have a perfect equality of status, not stature but status, in all that pertains to our domestic and external affairs. Something was said about foreign policy. Churchill said that it was not an easy matter to reconcile all views but that we [members of Commonwealth], of course, would keep each other informed but that we [Canada] decided our own."

Churchill added that "Canada should be just as strong an American Western Hemisphere country as she could be. Equally she should hold as strong a place as she could within the British Empire. That that was all to the good for both. He went on to say that Canada could not be too strong as a North American country. He hoped that there would always be the closest relationship between different parts of the Empire. A great thing had been built up—this collection of peoples united as they were with common aims. That so far as this continent was concerned he would be glad to see Canada represent more and more the British in relation to the United States. He then spoke out quite strongly about Canada and her exceptional position in interpreting the two countries to each other.

"Both he and the President made some reference to my own part in that connection. This then led Churchill to speak quite passionately and strongly to the President, using the words: 'I am saying this in the presence of Canada's Prime Minister, deliberately to you, Mr. President. I beg of you not to keep aloof from the European situation, once this war is over, or in arranging for a final settlement of the war. And once the war is over, there will have to be a Council of Europe, a Council of Asia, and a Council of the Americas. Over all will be a World Council in which there will be a final appeal. You, Mr. President, should be on all three Councils. We should be perhaps on all three Councils, though I should be glad to have Canada represent the British as well as their own interests on the Council of the Americas.'

"The President indicated that he was not too sure how far America should go in being on a European Council. This caused Churchill to say quite earnestly: 'You are needed there as much as ever in your own interest. We have had two wars into which you have been drawn, and which are costing America a lot. Neither of them originated here. They both originated in Europe, and they will arise there again unless some of these countries can be kept in proper control by the rest of the world.' " . . .

Roosevelt had told Mackenzie King in an earlier conversation that he had sent a message to Moscow that he "wanted to see Stalin himself; he was a little concerned as to how he could tell Winston." At Mackenzie King's farewell talk with the President on May 21, Roosevelt returned to his message and to his concern about Churchill's reaction. "Mackenzie, I want to tell you what was in my letter to Stalin. I have told him—and here he was repeating what he had told me the night before last. I feel that he and I ought to meet and have a talk together, but I feel embarrassed as to how Winston might feel. What I should say to him. I have a hunch that Stalin does not want to see the two of us together, at least at the outset, and that he would like to talk with me alone but just how to say that to Winston, I am not sure. I replied that I thought Winston would thoroughly understand. That he, Winston, had been in Russia and has seen Stalin there. They had talked together alone, and particularly if he, the President, were going to see Stalin where he had indicated (he had told me this before), Winston would see that it would seem perfectly reasonable for him, the President, to see Stalin at that place by himself. He told me that what he had in mind was seeing him in Alaska, possibly at Nome. . . . Bering Sea was exactly the same distance from Washington as it was from Moscow. Stalin could make the journey easily in two days each way.

''He then said to me: what I was going to propose, Mackenzie, is that I come to Ottawa and spend a day with you there, and that we then go on together to see the Alcan Highway, He repeated the word 'Alcan.' I said I hope he will use the words 'Alaska Highway'—nobody likes 'Alcan.' I said in Parliament I never used the name but have emphasized the other.'' Roosevelt continued: ''After we had gone over the Highway, I could go on to Alaska and you could take another route. He thought the time might be August. I said I would be delighted to go with him as suggested. Was particularly anxious to have him in Ottawa to speak on Parliament Hill. . . . I said: 'You would have a tremendous demonstration on Parliament Hill.' People would come from B.C. and the Maritime Provinces, from all over in fact, to express their feeling toward him.

''He then said: If, by any chance, something should prevent Stalin making the trip, what I would like to do is to come to Ottawa just the same though perhaps this might be in July. I would have my revenue cutter on the Great Lakes. We could get aboard there and take a trip through the Great Lakes up to the Georgian Bay, and have a week's rest and fishing together there. He asked me about fishing, I said I did not know just what it was like in the Georgian Bay, but I would have inquiries made in the meantime. He said: you and I could have just a quiet time and rest there. I told him that idea also was excellent. He then said to keep this in mind but very secret.''

I. Prime Minister W.L. Mackenzie King and President Franklin D. Roosevelt, Quebec City, P.Q., also with Prime Minister Winston Churchill, August 17-24, 1943 (First Quebec Conference), and Ottawa, Ontario, August 25, 1943

1. Joint Press Conference of President Roosevelt and Prime Ministers Churchill and King, Quebec City, P. Q., August 24, 1943

(PP/Franklin D. Roosevelt, Russell and Russell, Vol. XII, 1943, No. 92, pp. 363-65)

THE PRESIDENT: (continuing) We have come here to Quebec, and we have appreciated the wonderful hospitality of Mr. King—

PRIME MINISTER CHURCHILL: (interjecting) Hear—hear.

THE PRESIDENT: (continuing) —and of the Canadian people, because he speaks for them.

I don't think we could find a more delightful spot than here, with its great historic background. I, like Mr. Churchill, wish we had had more time to get about and see things, and do things. I will say that I shall never forget the very excellent eating qualities of Quebec trout. That is something that I shall long remember. All in all, it has been a tremendous success.

We wanted last night to give out some kind of statement that would be—what shall I call it?—a bit exciting. Well, a statement has been prepared. I don't believe there's a "cough in a carload" in it.

In the statement we were compelled, Mr. Churchill and I, to speak of the "fleets, armies, and air forces of the two Nations." The reason for that is that this is a staff conference between the British and American staffs; but I want to point out that it is only because of that restriction that we did not speak of the splendid forces of the Dominion of Canada. They are at the front, as we all know, working with the British and the Americans; and I don't want anybody to think, anywhere in the world, that we have forgotten them—what the Canadians have been doing in this war.

Well, I think that's about all that I can say.

And I merely want once more to thank Mr. King and the people of the Dominion for all that they have done to make this a very busy, but a very happy ten days since we came here.

THE PRESS: Thank you, sir.

PRIME MINISTER MACKENZIE KING: Gentlemen, just one word before you part. I would like to say in your presence to the President and to the

Prime Minister of Great Britain, how greatly honored the people of Canada have felt that they should have agreed to hold the meeting which they have just been holding in Canada, and particularly in this historic old city of Quebec.

My colleagues and I were very proud indeed when we received word from Mr. Roosevelt and Mr. Churchill that they were agreed upon meeting in this city, in our country. I wish to thank them most warmly for having come here and spent the time that they have spent with us. We all wish that it might be longer. We all wish that there might have been a greater opportunity for our people to have the privilege of seeing them more, as they did yesterday in the city for the Prime Minister, and also for the President. But we realized that this is a very serious Conference, and that the matters being discussed here are the most important of any that can be discussed in the world at this time, that every moment and hour has been precious.

It has been my privilege to know something of what has been done behind the scenes, and I would just like to assure all of you ladies and gentlemen of the press that there hasn't been a moment in which the thoughts and the minds of these gentlemen and their military advisers have not been directed to the supreme purpose for which they have met and gathered together here.

I am delighted, Mr. President and Mr. Churchill, that you have both found it possible not only to see each other but to see just a bit of the immediate environs of the city, and to carry away many happy memories of the few days that we have had the privilege of having you in our midst.

May I say to you ladies and gentlemen of the press, on behalf of the Government, how deeply we appreciate—the Government of Canada—how deeply we appreciate the very helpful cooperation that you have given to all of us during the period of the Conference. And I want to thank you on behalf of what you have sent out to the world as the picture and background in which the Conference is being held, in which you have given the atmosphere in which these deliberations have taken place, and for what you have been able to give of all the proceedings.

You have helped to put our country onto the map of the world, at this time of greatest importance in the history of the world. I thank you for having done it, and for the manner in which you have done it.

2. Prime Minister King's Introduction of President Roosevelt to Members of the Canadian Senate, House of Commons, and the General Public, Ottawa, August 25, 1943

(CHCD, January 26, 1944, pp. 5435-38)

To-day will be for all time a memorable day for Canada. I need not remind you, Mr. President, how often I have expressed the desire that you might visit Ottawa during your term of office as President of the United States. We have hoped that on such a visit you would speak to the members of the Senate and the House of Commons, either within or without the walls of our Houses of Parliament. You know, too, how frequently His Excellency the Governor General and Her Royal Highness the Princess Alice have expressed the wish that they might have the honour of a visit from Mrs. Roosevelt and yourself at some time during His Excellency's term of office as the representative in Canada of His Majesty the King.

Perhaps I may be allowed also to mention how greatly, for personal reasons, I have looked forward to the plesasure of welcoming to the seat of government and to my own home one whose friendship, in ever closer association, I have been privileged to enjoy over many years. To-day all these hopes and wishes, so warmly cherished by the people of Canada, by their representatives in parliament, by His Excellency and Her Royal Highness and by myself, are being happily realized.

On behalf of all Canada I extend to you to-day, Mr. President, the warmest of welcomes to the capital of our country. I thank you for having honoured our capital city by your presence at a time which is without parallel in the history of human affairs.

The Canadian people will, I know, wish me to express to you the admiration which they feel for you and for your great career. We recognize in you one who has always had a deep concern for the wellbeing of his fellow men. We have long known that your services to the cause of freedom far exceed limits of race and bounds of nationality. We honour you as an undaunted champion of the rights of free men and a mighty leader of the forces of freedom in a world at war. We feel, too, a special affection for a lifelong friend of our country.

This is the first occasion on which a President of the United States has visited Canada's capital. It is particularly pleasing to us that this visit should have its association with your momentous meeting in the ancient capital of Canada with the Prime Minister of Great Britain. Over the past two years your meetings with Mr. Churchill have been the signal for great events. The conference at Quebec just concluded will, I am confident, mark a further advance towards final victory.

The City of Quebec is the birthplace of Canada. Beneath its cliffs, in 1608, Champlain founded a settlement and established a seat of government: upon its height is erected a monument commemorating in a single shaft the chivalry of Wolfe and Montcalm in the decisive battle of 1759. It is the city in which, in 1864, the fathers of the Canadian confederation assembled in conference to fashion the Canada that was to be. We were indeed delighted when we learned that Quebec had been selected as the place of meeting between Mr. Churchill and yourself.

We rejoice, Mr. President, that your visit to Ottawa comes at a moment when for the first time in our long history as close neighbours, soldiers of Canada and the United States have fought side by side. Combined British, United States and Canadian forces have just completed the occupation of Sicily as a first step in the liberation of Europe. Combined United States and Canadian forces have just occupied the last Japanese outpost in the western hemisphere.

The rapidity with which the American people gathered their strength, and the momentum and magnitude of their war effort, have filled the world with amazement. All Canada joins in admiration for the efficiency and heroism of the men of the fighting forces of the United States. In the southwest Pacific, in the Aleutians, in North Africa, in Sicily, in the skies over every battle-front and on all the oceans of the world, their deeds are recording a glorious chapter in the history of freedom.

In the combined efforts of the military forces and the peoples of the United States and the British empire, joined with those of the heroic peoples of Russia and China and of the other united nations, lies the certainty of complete victory over the forces of tyranny which have sought the domination of the world.

Canada counts it a high privilege to have the opportunity of drawing into relations of closer friendship, understanding, and good will, the United States and the nations of the British commonwealth. We are firmly convinced that in the continued close association of the British commonwealth of nations and the United States of America lies the surest guarantee of international peace, and of the furtherance of the well-being of mankind throughout the world.

Mr. President, once more, and using this time the other official language of our country, I wish to extend to you the most cordial welcome on behalf of all Canada.

3. Address of President Roosevelt to Members of the Canadian Senate, House of Commons, and the General Public, Ottawa, August 25, 1943

(*Ibid.*, pp. 5436-38)

It was exactly five years ago last Wednesday that I came to Canada to receive the high honour of a degree at Queen's university. On that occasion—one year before the invasion of Poland, three years before Pearl Harbor—I said:

> We in the Americas are no longer a far-away continent, to which the eddies of controversies beyond the seas could bring no interest or no harm. Instead, we in the Americas have become a consideration to every propaganda office and to every general staff beyond the seas. The vast amount of our resources, the vigour of our commerce, and the strength of our men have made us vital factors in world peace whether we choose it or not.

We did not choose this war—and that "we" includes each and every one of the united nations. War was violently forced upon us by criminal aggressors who measure their standards of morality by the extent of the death and the destruction that they can inflict upon their neighbours.

In this war, Canadians and Americans have fought shoulder to shoulder—as our men and our women and our children have worked together and played together in happier times of peace.

To-day, in devout gratitude, we are celebrating a brilliant victory won by British, Canadian and American fighting men in Sicily.

To-day, we rejoice also in another event for which we need not apologize. A year ago Japan occupied several of the Aleutian islands on our side of the ocean and made a great "to-do" about the invasion of the continent of North America. I regret to say that some Americans and some Canadians wished our governments to withdraw from the Atlantic and the Mediterranean campaigns and divert all our vast strength to the removal of the Japs from a few rocky specks in the north Pacific.

To-day, our wiser councils have maintained our efforts in the Atlantic and the Mediterranean and the China seas and the southwest Pacific with ever-growing contributions; and in the northwest Pacific a relatively small campaign has been assisted by the Japs themselves in the elimination of the last Jap from Attu and Kiska. We have been told that Japs never surrender; their headlong retreat satisfies us just as well.

Great councils are being held here on the free and honoured soil of Canada—councils which look to the future conduct of this war and to the years of building a new progress for mankind. To these councils Canadians and Americans alike again welcome that wise and good and gallant gentleman, the Prime Minister of Great Britain.

Mr. King, my old friend, may I through you thank the people of Canada for their hospitality to all of us. Your course and mine have run so closely and affectionately during these many long years that this meeting adds another link to that chain. I have always felt at home in Canada, and you, I think, have always felt at home in the United States.

During the past few days in Quebec, the combined staffs have been sitting around a table—which is a good custom—talking things over, discussing ways and means, in the manner of friends, in the manner of partners, and may I even say, in the manner of members of the same family.

We have talked constructively of our common purposes in this war—of our determination to achieve victory in the shortest possible time—of our essential cooperation with our great and brave fighting allies. And we have arrived, harmoniously, at certain definite conclusions. Of course, I am not at liberty to disclose just what these conclusions are. But, in due time, we shall communicate the secret information of the Quebec conference to Germany, Italy and Japan. We shall communicate this information to our enemies in the only language their twisted minds seem capable of understanding.

Sometimes I wish that that great master of intuition, the nazi leader, could have been present in spirit at the Quebec conference—I am thoroughly glad he was not there in person. If he and his generals had known our plans they would have realized that discretion is still the better part of valour and that surrender would pay them better now than later.

The evil characteristic that makes a nazi a nazi is his utter inability to understand and therefore to respect the qualities or the rights of his fellow-men. His only method of dealing with his neighbour is first to delude him with lies, then to attack him treacherously, then beat him down and step on him, and then either kill him or enslave him. And the same thing is true of the fanatical militarists of Japan.

Because their own instincts and impulses are essentially inhuman, our enemies simply cannot comprehend how it is that decent, sensible individual human beings manage to get along together and live together as neighbours. That is why our enemies are doing their desperate best to misrepresent the purposes and the results of this Quebec conference. They still seek to divide and conquer allies who refuse to be divided just as cheerfully as they refuse to be conquered.

We spend our energies and our resources and the very lives of our sons and daughters because a band of gangsters in the community of nations declines to recognize the fundamentals of decent, human conduct.

We have been forced to call out what we in the United States would call the sheriff's posse to break up the gang in order that gangsterism may be eliminated in the community of nations.

We are making sure—absolutely, irrevocably sure—that this time the lesson is driven home to them once and for all. Yes, we are going to be rid of outlaws this time.

Every one of the united nations believes that only a real and lasting peace can justify the sacrifices we are making, and our unanimity gives us confidence in seeking that goal.

It is no secret that at Quebec there was much talk of the post-war world. That discussion was doubtless duplicated simultaneously in dozens of nations and hundreds of cities and among millions of people.

There is a longing in the air. It is not a longing to go back to what they call "the good old days." I have distinct reservations as to how good "the good old days" were. I would rather believe that we can achieve new and better days.

Absolute victory in this war will give greater opportunities for the world because the winning of the war in itself is proving, certainly proving to all of us here, that concerted action can accomplish things. Surely we can make strides towards a greater freedom from want than the world has yet enjoyed. Surely by unanimous action in driving out the outlaws and keeping them under heel for ever, we can attain a freedom from fear of violence.

I am everlastingly angry only at those who assert vociferously that the Four Freedoms and the Atlantic charter are nonsense because they are unattainable. If they had lived a century and a half ago they would have sneered and said that the Declaration of Independence was utter piffle. If they had lived nearly a thousand years ago they would have laughed uproariously at the ideals of Magna Charta. And if they had lived several thousand years ago they would have derided Moses when he came from the mountain with the Ten Commandments.

We concede that these great teachings are not perfectly lived up to to-day, and we concede that the good old world cannot arrive at utopia overnight. But I would rather be a builder than a wrecker, hoping always that the structure of life is growing—not dying.

May the destroyers who still persist in our midst decrease. They, like some of our enemies, have a long road to travel before they accept the ethics of humanity.

Some day, in the distant future perhaps—but some day with certainty—all of them will remember with the Master—"Thou shalt love they neighbour as thyself."

Mr. Prime Minister, my visit to the old city of Quebec has recalled vividly to my mind that Canada is a nation founded on a union of two great races. The harmony of their equal partnership is an example to all mankind—an example everywhere in the world.

III. Prime Minister W. L. Mackenzie King (October 1935-November 1948) (President Harry S. Truman)

President Truman assumed office with the April, 1945, death of Franklin Roosevelt, and was reelected to a full term served from January 1949, to January 1953. While serving out Mr. Roosevelt's term, he met eight times with Prime Minister King of which six are documented. These eight meetings were the last of twenty-eight that Prime Minister King had with Presidents of the United States starting with Calvin Coolidge: President Truman subsequently had two meetings with Prime Minister St. Laurent during the term of office to which he was elected in 1948, as discussed in the next chapter.

Although not documented, President Truman and Prime Minister King were first together during their incumbencies when both leaders attended the April, 1945, Hyde Park burial of Roosevelt. Their second meeting, also not documented, took place at the San Francisco Conference on the United Nations Organization in June of 1945, when Mr. Truman met ceremonially with the foreign leaders who were delegates to the Conference.

Although Truman had hoped for an early meeting with King after coming into office, the two leaders did not meet until September 30, 1945, in Washington. (See Section A.) Even this third meeting was rushed and had been arranged on short notice, as Truman was leaving for Missouri and King for an Imperial Conference in London. The sole purpose of the meeting was to permit King to report to the President on developments in the Gouzenko spy case, which had arisen when a cipher clerk at the Soviet Embassy in Ottawa defected and gave Canadian authorities information on Soviet espionage activities.[1] Documentation for the meeting consists of King's account in his Diary.

---

[1]See C. B. Blackburn, "King At White House," TGM (October 1, 1945), pp. 1, 2.

While in Great Britain after this September meeting, Prime Minister King and the Prime Minister of the United Kingdom, Clement Attlee, received an invitation from President Truman to have a tripartite summit meeting.on the problems of nuclear weapons from November 10-15, 1945. (See Section B.) In an October 3, 1945 message to Congress President Truman had stated the purpose of the meeting: "I therefore propose to initiate discussions, first with our associates in this discovery, Great Britain and Canada, and then with other nations in an effort to effect agreement on the condition under which cooperation might replace rivalry in the field of atomic power."[2] Both Attlee and King arrived in Washington on November 10. The questions for the meeting were essentially what should be done with the "know-how" and the capacity for the production of atomic bombs. There was also some discussion of the difficulties in Palestine, but in this, as indeed for the discussion of the atomic bomb, attention was clearly focussed on the position of Britain more than that of Canada. The chief result of the meeting was the Joint Declaration on Atomic Energy. The documentation for this meeting consists of King's account and the Declaration.

King and Truman met for a fifth time in New York and Washington. At the United Nations General Assembly meeting in Flushing Meadows, New York, in October of 1946, Truman and King met at a reception, attended by the visiting leaders. This New York part of the meeting is not documented in that the two leaders only exchanged a few words and agreed to Mr. Truman's suggestion to meet over the weekend in Washington. Prime Minister King then trained to Washington on Sunday, October 27, 1946, holding discussions with Mr. Truman the next day at the White House.[3] (See Section C.) The President conducted the fifty minute meeting from a memorandum which reflected his interest in escalating joint defence discussions from the working level to "the highest authorities of both governments." The importance of this meeting lay in its role as a precursor of the host of subsequent Canadian-United States defence arrangements concluded through the Cold War. In February following this meeting, a Joint Statement on Defense Cooperation was issued by the two governments extending the principles of the Ogdensburg and Hyde Park declarations into post-war cooperation. Documentation includes the memorandum which President Truman used at the meeting, the United States account

---

[2]CHCD, December 17, 1945, p. 3635; for account of meeting, see Bertram D. Hulen, "Atom Bomb Policy Mapped as Truman, Attlee Open Talks," NYT (November 11, 1945), pp. 1, 3, and "The Atomic Agreement," NYT (November 16, 1945), p. 18.

[3]See "Truman Sees Mackenzie King," NYT (October 29, 1946), p. 7, and "King in Washington as Guest of Truman," TGM (October 28, 1946), p. 10.

of the meeting which is noteworthy in that it is based on Canadian governmental sources,[4] and King's account from his Diary.

The sixth meeting between President Truman and Prime Minister King took place on April 23, 1947, when Mr. King stopped off in Washington to see the President after spending some time in Virginia recovering from an illness. (See Section D.) Issues covered by the two leaders included Canada having "her rightful place in making the peace," Canadian membership in the Pan American Union, trade and defence matters, and the upcoming Presidential visit to Ottawa.[5] The documentation for this meeting consists of the King account in his Diary.

On June 10-12, 1947, Harry Truman paid the first State Visit of a President of the United States to the Canadian capital, making this King's seventh meeting with Truman. (See Section E.) The purpose of the meeting was to reciprocate the visit of the Canadian Governor General, Viscount Alexander of Tunis, to Washington. In the President's words, it was "just a friendly visit."[6] Ceremonial in nature, the trip followed the President's State Visit to Mexico, and there are no indications that substantive issues were discussed. Indeed, it was said that the Parliamentary Press Gallery had been cautioned to avoid, at the President's press conference, "any questions bearing on current issues in the United States and in Canada."[7] Despite the unsubstantive nature of the meeting, its symbolic value in declaring North American solidarity was evidently effective. For example, the *New York Times* reported that "Moscow radio told its Russian listeners today that President Truman's visit to Canada was part of a carefully designed plot to take the Dominion away from Britain."[8] Documenta-

---

[4]Subsequent to the summit meeting, King recounted it to Canadian Ambassador Designate Hume Wrong. Wrong sent a telegram summarizing the meeting to Lester Pearson, Under-Secretary of State for External Affairs in Ottawa. Pearson then recounted the Truman-King meeting in detail in a conversation in Ottawa with U.S. Ambassador Ray Atherton. Atherton then reported its content in a dispatch to J. Graham Parsons, Assistant Chief of the State Department's Division of Commonwealth Affairs, who recorded it in a "Top Secret" Memorandum. This Memorandum, which is documented in Section C, then served as the State Department's record of the King-Truman meeting, a record the Department obtained exclusively from Canadian sources.

[5]See NYT (April 22, 1947).

[6]PP/Harry S. Truman, Volume 1947, No. 46, p. 159.

[7]Teletype, Confidential, From the Canadian Ambassador to the United States to the Secretary of State for External Affairs, Canada, May 15, 1947, Public Archives of Canada, R67, 627, Vol. 39; see Harold B. Hinton, "Truman in Ottawa," NYT (June 11, 1947), pp. 1, 9, and "Mr. Truman's Call to Action," TGM (June 13, 1947), p. 6.

[8]"Truman Visit Plot, Says Soviet," NYT (June 14, 1947), p. 7.

tion for the visit covers the Prime Minister's introduction of President Truman to the Canadian Parliament, Mr. Truman's speech, the President's toast at a luncheon which reflects his distinctive style, and a joint press conference.

Mr. King's eighth meeting with President Truman, and his last meeting with a President of the United States, took place at a convocation at the College of William and Mary in Williamsburg, Virginia, on April 2, 1948.[9] (See Section F.) The College, in honour of Canadian-American Day, awarded the honourary degrees to King and Truman along with the Governor General of Canada and the Governor of Virginia. Although ceremonial in nature, Mr. King did have the opportunity of a brief conversation with President Truman in which they discussed the Soviet blockade of West Berlin. Documentation of the meeting includes the speeches of King and Truman at the Convocation, and King's account of the meeting from his Diary. The documentation is useful in setting forth the Cold War attitudes of the two leaders.

A. President Harry S. Truman and Prime Minister W.L. Mackenzie King, Washington, D.C., September 29-30, 1945

1. Prime Minister King's Account of Meeting

(Mackenzie King Record, University of Toronto Press, Vol. III, pp. 37-42)

Mackenzie King made a detailed record of his conversations with President Truman in his secret diary. "My decision to see the President before leaving for Europe was the outcome of my feeling that we owed it to the United States as well as to the United Kingdom to let those highest in authority in these two countries know all that we possessed in the way of information regarding R.E. [Russian espionage].

"There were other reasons which made it obviously desirable in the national interest that I should see the President before going abroad so that the country might know of my acceptance of his invitation. Just how matters were finally arranged I do not know and Robertson did not seem himself to clearly recollect whether the invitation which the President had renewed on Wednesday or Thursday last to stay at the White House, was the result of the President's initiative or of some word sent through Atherton that I would like to see him before going abroad. However, my position is that I was accepting the President's invitation. While it could not be for an overnight visit, it was wise to

---

[9]See Anthony Levierd, "Good Neighbor Plan Offered by President to Whole World," NYT (April 3, 1948), pp. 1, 8.

have at least a conversation before going abroad. Arrangements were made through Atherton.

"In conversation with Atherton toward the last, in his way of speaking, one might have thought that the going to Washington was rather something for which I was asking rather than something which I felt was in part acceptance of the President's invitation and in part obligation which Canada owed to an ally. I personally do not like that kind of effort to gain a certain position for the other party, either in conversation or in posture when talking to another. I am open and above board in everything, not attaching importance to individual words or gestures but in the open between individuals as far as that is possible in matters that have to be concealed from the public. . . .

"Robertson brought with him on the plane in a green folder—No. 10—a copy of the statement prepared by our police of the statements of information secured from examination of CORBY [Igor Gouzenko] and other sources. I spent the time on the 'plane between Ottawa and Washington re-reading much of this material. I continued re-reading some of it on Sunday morning at the Embassy immediately after breakfast before going to see the President. Robertson suggested I take the book with me which I did, in an ordinary brown envelope, under my arm. Was photographed at the entrance of the White House with this document under my arm. . . .

"Mr. Truman extended a cordial welcome. Said he was glad to see me and he hoped relations between us might be the same as they had been between President Roosevelt and myself. That he would welcome that sort of relationship. Was sorry that it had not been possible to have an earlier interview. He hoped I would come to stay after my return. He made some reference about our meeting at San Francisco and I then said I was sorry I could not accept the invitation for Friday night. That I had to be in Parliament until expressions of confidence on the Speech from the Throne were over. Told him what the divisions were. He turned to Acheson and said he wished he could be sure of twenty-seven of a majority over all."

After a few more social preliminaries, Mackenzie King "then said to the President that he would know something of what I was anxious to give him particulars of. He said that Acheson had given him some information. I then said I had felt it my duty to see that he was fully informed and that he was given the same information as I wished to give to the British Government. That I felt we were all equally concerned. I then said perhaps it would be better if I were to run over the whole business from the start; as I had learned of it at different stages. The President said that would be best and I then began with Robertson and Wrong coming to see me in my office at 11, on the day of the Opening of Parliament. Narrated the incidents regarding Corby. What had subsequently been obtained in the way of information. Told them of the extent of espionage in Canada. What we had learned about espionage in the United States. Mentioned particularly request as to information as to United States troops, etc., shipping to Russia; of information regarding the atomic bomb. The visit of a courier to the United States by one who turned out to be Inspector of the Red Army and of his having sized up the espionage system in the United States. Had sent out his report from Ottawa. Spoke of the Consul at New York who apparently had charge of the espionage business in the United States. Of the connection of that office with the organization in Switzerland; of large sums of money having gone from that office to Switzerland, etc.

"While proceeding with the discussion and speaking of our view of being careful not to disclose anything until the situation had been worked out, the President of his own volition said he felt every care must be taken to get full information before anything at all was disclosed. He said he assumed there must be similar penetration by the Russians into the conditions in the United States and that he would want to have this gone into very fully before any action was taken. The President also volunteered the statement that he thought the matter should be discussed between Attlee, himself and myself. That we should all be agreed on the course that was to be taken. Two or three times he repeated his view that nothing should be done without agreement between the three and above all nothing should be done which might result in premature action in any direction. He also said two or three times that he was particularly interested in anything I could tell him of what had happened in the United States or would give evidence of espionage there. I then said perhaps it would be best were I to read from the report I had with me; give him from the document I had with me the information I had. If he were agreeable, I would read it aloud. This the President said he would be pleased to have me do.

"I then read the preliminary statement concerning the espionage system in Russia. Read early portions about the system as it worked at the Embassy. Read about Primrose and others in key positions. Went particularly to the passages concerning the Russian Consulate in New York. The statements re the atomic bomb; information gained from the United States. What was thought to have gone from Chicago. Also the statement that an assistant secretary of the Secretary of State's Department was supposed to be implicated though I made perfectly clear this was only what Corby had said but I had no information to back it up. The President did not seem surprised. He turned to Acheson and said something to the effect that it would not be surprising. Acheson then said that they had thought the report had reference to an assistant to an assistant secretary. I said of course I knew nothing but what was in the statement as recorded there. Probably he was right and there might even be no foundation.

"I felt the reading was rather long and two or three times suggested abbreviations. The President said he was most interested. Finally I felt I had covered main points and put the book back into the envelope. I had kept emphasizing I was using the book because I wanted to give exactly the same information to Attlee. I told the President of my mission to England at the instance of Theodore Roosevelt in regard to Japan; of my having seized passports in Vancouver; of Edward Grey's passing on to Komura, information, etc. I told him I thought there was a possibility if Russians were confronted in a similar way with known facts that it might help to steady things and that might be a means of meeting the situation. How much farther we should go would depend on consultation. The President agreed with this and I said to him I thought we should relate the information we have to the question of the veto on the Security Council of the U.N. Organization. If at all possible, we should get the Russians to realize there must be confidence all in all or not at all and that their insistence on agreement on the part of the Great Powers to any action or use of force, was creating suspicion in itself. That they should be willing to do in the matter of the action to be taken, what the other four Great Powers were prepared to do. One must know the kind of a world we wanted to live in and be assured they were prepared to help to co-operate in furthering a similar kind of world. . . . He said something about Attlee coming out to have a talk with him. I was careful to explain about my going to England and its relation to conference with the British Government and about this coming up after I had first declined to go for purposes of consultation merely before Parliament met.

"As it got on toward 12, I felt I should not detain the President longer and said that I knew his time was very precious and I thought I should not press him longer. This was the second or third time I had said this and the President then seemed to acquiesce so I rose at once. When I saw Acheson there, I had mentioned that Robertson and Pearson could come over if the President wished it. He and Acheson spoke between themselves as to whether it was desirable or not without being committal. I saw apparently they preferred the three of us might speak first. I said we might leave that until after if it was desirable to have them come. Before we left the circular room, the President again repeated what he had said about hoping I would come and see him when I got back and that we might have the same kind of relationship that had been shared between President Roosevelt and myself. I was sorry not to have had a chance to talk with him quite alone as I had meant to say something about the impressions he himself had made in the handling of affairs; also a word about Canadian-U.S. relations.". . .

B.   President Harry S. Truman, Prime Minister W.L. Mackenzie King, and Prime Minister C.R. Attlee, Washington, D.C., November 10-15, 1945

1. Prime Minister King's Account of Meeting

(Mackenzie King Record, University of Toronto Press, Vol. III, pp. 97-98)[1]

The following morning the British delegation prepared a paper for circulation and consideration. That evening, the Secretary of State, James Byrnes, entertained Attlee and Mackenzie King and their parties to dinner. After the dinner, Pearson, Hume Wrong and Norman Robertson exchanged views with the Under Secretary of State, Dean Acheson, and subsequently prepared a Canadian draft of a joint statement which was submitted to Mackenzie King on Tuesday morning, November 13. Discussions between the President and the two prime ministers were resumed that afternoon. At this meeting, Byrnes produced a draft statement which did not prove to be entirely suitable and the Canadian group drew up a re-draft of the Byrnes statement on Wednesday morning. A second United States draft was also drawn up and discussed at the White House that afternoon. On this occasion, Mackenzie King suggested certain changes in the document, two of which were of particular importance. He argued that the reference to the appointment of a commission under the United Nations should follow the specific recommendations of the three signatories on immediate action. He also suggested that, at the end of the paragraph, "We are not convinced that the spreading of the specialized information regarding the practical application of atomic energy before it is possible to devise . . . safeguards . . . would contribute to a constructive solution of the problem of the atomic bomb," there should be added the following sentences: "On the contrary, we think it might have the opposite effect. We are, however, prepared to share on a reciprocal basis with other United Nations detailed information concerning the practical industrial application of atomic energy just as soon as effective and enforceable safeguards against its use for destructive purposes

---

[1] According to Messrs. Pickersgill and Forster, the King Diaries from Nov. 10 to Dec. 31, 1945 could not be located after his death. This entry which falls into that period, is based on his engagement sheets, *Hansard*, and then Canadian Ambassador to the U.S. Lester B. Pearson's notes of the meetings.

"Pearson's report to Ottawa on the Prime Minister's visit is reproduced in J.A. Munro and A.I. Inglis, "The Atomic Conference, 1945, and the Pearson Memoirs", *International Journal*, Vol. XXIX, No. 1 (Winter, 1973-74) pp. 90-109. See also *Mike, The Memoirs of L.B. Pearson* (Toronto: University of Toronto Press, 1972) I, pp. 258-63.

can be devised.'' Such a change made this crucial part of the statement positive rather than negative. Both these changes were warmly supported by the President and Prime Minister Attlee. Mackenzie King also suggested the removal of all words and phrases from the document which implied that, in accepting the agreement, the signatories were acting for their respective governments. As finally approved, the agreement was between heads of governments and not between the governments themselves.

Pearson considered that the general effect of the changes proposed by Mackenzie King removed the impression that the three conferees were shelving the problem by sending it to a commission and that they had no fixed ideas about it themselves. In Pearson's view there was a general understanding that referral of the problem to a commission of the United Nations meant that the world organization was being given a very severe test at the outset of its existence and that the three powers were now obligated more than ever to strengthen and develop the United Nations organization so that it could successfully meet this and other tests.

The British draft was also discussed and a drafting committee consisting of Pearson, Sir John Anderson and Dr. Vannevar Bush, subsequently chairman of the U.S. Atomic Energy Commission, was appointed to prepare a new draft. This committee met at 5:30 p.m. at the White House and again later in the evening. At 10:00 p.m., the President and the prime ministers met to go over the draft sentence by sentence, a task which was completed by midnight. The statement was signed by the three heads of government on Thursday morning (November 15) at 11:00 and immediately read to the White House press correspondents by the President.

2. *Joint Declaration of President Truman and Prime Ministers King and Attlee on Atomic Energy, as Read by President Truman at a News Conference with Prime Ministers King and Attlee, November 15, 1945*

(PP/Harry S. Truman, Vol. 1945, No. 191, pp. 472-75)

THE PRESIDENT. Will you please listen for just a moment. I am going to read to you the document which has been signed by the Prime Minister of Great Britain and the Prime Minister of Canada, and the President of the United States. Copies will be handed to you as you go out, as soon as I finish reading.

Questions on this document will have to come at a later time, when you are familiar with it.

This is headed ''The President of the United States, the Prime Minister of the United Kingdom, and the Prime Minister of Canada, have issued the following statement.

"1. We recognize that the application of recent scientific discoveries to the methods and practice of war has placed at the disposal of mankind means of destruction hitherto unknown, against which there can be no adequate military defense, and in the employment of which no single nation can in fact have a monopoly.

"2. We desire to emphasize that the responsibility for devising means to ensure that the new discoveries shall be used for the benefit of mankind, instead of as a means of destruction, rests not on our nations alone, but upon the whole civilized world. Nevertheless, the progress that we have made in the development and use of atomic energy demands that we take an initiative in the matter, and we have accordingly met together to consider the possibility of international action:

"(a) To prevent the use of atomic energy for destructive purposes.

"(b) To promote the use of recent and future advances in scientific knowledge, particularly in the utilization of atomic energy, for peaceful and humanitarian ends.

"3. We are aware that the only complete protection for the civilized world from the destructive use of scientific knowledge lies in the prevention of war. No system of safeguards that can be devised will of itself provide an effective guarantee against production of atomic weapons by a nation bent on aggression. Nor can we ignore the possibility of the development of other weapons, or of new methods of warfare, which may constitute as great a threat to civilization as the military use of atomic energy.

"4. Representing, as we do, the three countries which possess the knowledge essential to the use of atomic energy, we declare at the outset our willingness, as a first contribution, to proceed with the exchange of fundamental scientific information and the interchange of scientists and scientific literature for peaceful ends with any nation that will fully reciprocate.

"5. We believe that the fruits of scientific research should be made available to all nations, and that freedom of investigation and free interchange of ideas are essential to the progress of knowledge. In pursuance of this policy, the basic scientific information essential to the development of atomic energy for peaceful purposes has already been made available to the world. It is our intention that all further information of this character that may become available from time to time shall be similarly treated. We trust that other nations will adopt the same policy, thereby creating an atmosphere of reciprocal confidence in which political agreement and cooperation will flourish.

"6. We have considered the question of the disclosure of detailed information concerning the practical industrial application of atomic energy. The military exploitation of atomic energy depends, in large part, upon the same methods and processes as would be required for industrial uses.

"We are not convinced that the spreading of the specialized information regarding the practical application of atomic energy, before it is possible to devise effective, reciprocal, and enforceable safeguards acceptable to all nations, would contribute to a constructive solution of the problem of the atomic bomb. On the contrary we think it might have the opposite effect. We are, however, prepared to share, on a reciprocal basis with others of the United Nations, detailed information concerning the practical industrial application of atomic energy just as soon as effective enforceable safeguards against its use for destructive purposes can be devised.

"7. In order to attain the most effective means of entirely eliminating the use of atomic energy for destructive purposes and promoting its widest use for industrial and humanitarian purposes, we are of the opinion that at the earliest practicable date a Commission should be set up under the United Nations Organization to prepare recommendations for submission to the Organization.

"The Commission should be instructed to proceed with the utmost dispatch and should be authorized to submit recommendations from time to time dealing with separate phases of its work.

"In particular, the Commission should make specific proposals:

"(a) For extending between all nations the exchange of basic scientific information for peaceful ends,

"(b) For control of atomic energy to the extent necessary to ensure its use only for peaceful purposes,

"(c) For the elimination from national armaments of atomic weapons and of all other major weapons adaptable to mass destruction,

"(d) For effective safeguards by way of inspection and other means to protect complying states against the hazards of violations and evasions.

"8. The work of the Commission should proceed by separate stages, the successful completion of each one of which will develop the necessary confidence of the world before the next stage is undertaken. Specifically, it is considered that the Commission might well devote its attention first to the wide exchange of scientists and scientific information, and as a second stage to the development of full knowledge concerning natural resources of raw materials.

"9. Faced with the terrible realities of the application of science to destruction, every nation will realize more urgently than before the overwhelming need to maintain the rule of law among nations and to banish the scourge of war from the earth. This can only be brought about by giving wholehearted support to the United Nations Organization, and by consolidating and extending its authority, thus creating conditions of mutual trust in which all peoples will be free to devote themselves to the arts of peace. It is our firm resolve to work without reservation to achieve these ends."

And this document is signed by the three of us.
That's all.

C.   President Harry S. Truman and Prime Minister W. L. Mackenzie King, Washington, D.C., October 27-28, 1946

1. Memorandum and Oral Message from President Truman to Prime Minister King (Note: President Truman based his remarks to Prime Minister King on this Memorandum, although he did not read from it, and a copy was given to Mr. King.)

(*For/Rel*, 1946, Vol. v, 1969, pp. 58-61)

The Government of the United States is grateful to the Government of Canada for the favorable consideration which the latter has given to proposals relating to joint defense. In no case has any military project which this Government considered urgent been delayed by any lack of cooperation on the part of Canada.

Because of the extreme importance in an unsettled world of continuing and reinforcing measures of joint defense it is believed that the consideration of these matters, hitherto primarily in military hands, should also now be taken up directly by the governments. In suggesting this course, the Government of the United States is determined that the actions taken shall in no way be inconsistent with commitments under the Charter of the United Nations, full support of which is the cardinal point of United States policy. The decisions which the governments take and the further advancement of North American security through the recommendations of the Permanent Joint Board on Defense must always accord with the framework of the United Nations.

Early in 1946, pursuant to views expressed by the Joint Board, the two Governments decided to collaborate as partners in drawing up a basic security plan for the United States and Canada. A Joint Appreciation of the situation was prepared and planning has progressed satisfactorily. It may, however, not be practicable to proceed much further without assurances of support from the highest authorities of both Governments. Such assurances could take the form of concurrence in the Appreciation. Meanwhile, events at Paris and in the international field generally have not lessened the anxiety of those charged with assuring the security of the United States. Moreover, in the opinion of this Government, those events have demonstrated that decisions in the field of home defense should be taken now and implemented as rapidly as practicable. Only by being secure at home can Canada and the United States strengthen the United Nations and discharge their responsibility for contributing to world order and security.

Under these circumstances, it appears to the Government of the United States that close collaboration in defense matters with the Government of Canada must be carried forward actively. It believes this for the following reasons:

Two world wars have demonstrated that an aggressor must destroy the power of North America or be defeated.

Due to post-1945 technological advances, North America is no longer adequately protected by geography.

Canadian and United States military advisors agree that in five years North America must be prepared to meet major enemy capabilities.

While the peaceful foreign policies and intentions of Canada and the United States are clearly defined, there can be no guarantee that the governing officials of the U.S.S.R. will make decisions on the basis of a correct appraisal of the world beyond Soviet borders, or that the long term policy of the U.S.S.R. is not one of unlimited aggrandizement.

For the foregoing reasons North American nations henceforth must be prepared at home just as less fortunately placed nations have had to be in the past. Furthermore, under conditions of modern technology, defenses must be as far out from Canadian and American industrial centers as possible.

If within only five years another major power will be capable of jeopardizing North American security, action should be based on realization:

That Canada and the United States lag in cold weather knowledge and experience.

That, because of this lag and because of the expense involved, defense plans will take years to implement.

That, to be efficient in an emergency affecting North American territory, the Canadian and American forces should have the experience of working together, experience of the north, and increasing uniformity of equipment and methods.

The United States Government realizes that close collaboration with Canada in basic defense matters presents both governments with new problems of great complexity and difficulty. The responsible United States officials are aware of the special problems that face Canada, a member of the British Commonwealth of Nations. They have been instructed that the sole purpose of close military collaboration is defense, that every precaution must be taken to protect the traditional relations of the two countries and the position which each, respectively, enjoys.

The United States Government is also aware that the question of the financial cost of defensive measures is most serious for both Governments. It must not, however, be permitted to delay the planning of security at home, and should not delay the attainment thereof. While no final commitments can yet be made by either Government, it seems clear that the Joint Defense Board should recommend and the two Governments should negotiate some equitable means of sharing the financial burden of any defenses agreed to be necessary around the northern perimeter of the continent. Possibly the United States might agree to assume an equitable proportion of the cost of any facilities jointly found to be necessary on Canadian soil if the Canadian Government were to take into account that United States expenditures in Alaska and Greenland, for instance, contribute to Canadian as well as United States security.

Although many problems remain for future determination, the United States Government believes for the reasons set forth in this memorandum that decisions by the Canadian Government on the following existing problems would be timely and would enhance the security of the Canadian and American people:

1. Further Canadian Government endorsement of joint planning now in progress would assure the United States authorities of continuing Canadian cooperation and an adequate measure of joint action between Alaska on the west and Greenland on the east.

2. Approval of the 35th Recommendation of the Permanent Joint Board on Defense would help to define the relations between the armed forces of Canada and the United States and would provide authoritative guidance as to the nature and limits of the collaboration desired by both Governments.

3. It is hoped that the Canadian Government, with Newfoundland concurrence, will permit the stationing of certain United States Army Air Force units at the Canadian 99-year leased base at Goose Bay, Labrador. Reciprocally (as soon as the present congestion can be relieved), the United States authorities will be agreeable to a similar arrangement at United States bases in Newfoundland proper. While remaining an important feature of the defenses of the northeastern approaches to the continent, these latter bases are, however, too close to Canada and the United States to provide adequate protection against ultra-modern high speed aerial attack. Moreover, they do not afford as would Goose Bay, a highly favorable situation for the acquisition by United States and Canadian Air Force units of the experience of training together under cold weather conditions, of testing northern equipment and of coordinating their respective methods and tactics. Finally, arrangements of this kind at Goose Bay and the other bases would be consistent with the joint responsibilities which the two Governments have discharged in the past for the defense of Newfoundland.

In conclusion, the United States Government reiterates that it has been gratified by the cooperative attitude of the Canadian Government and by the informality, frankness and mutual trust which have prevailed during discussions of the delicate and momentous problems of joint defense. It believes that final decisions, not only on the three points just mentioned, but also on others in this field can be reached without necessity of any more formal documentation than has been customary since establishment of the Permanent Joint Board on Defense in 1940. There is no doubt that public opinion firmly supports effective collaboration with Canada and, in the view of the United States Government, this is a strong and satisfactory basis for joint action.

2. U.S. Account of Meeting Based on Canadian Governmental Sources

("Top Secret" Memorandum by the Assistant Chief of the U.S. State Department Division of British Commonwealth Affairs J. Graham Parsons, Washington, D.C., October 31, 1946, *Ibid.*, pp. 61-63)

Ambassador Atherton reported the substance of the conversation between the President and the Prime Minister as related to him by Mr. Pearson, Under Secretary of External Affairs in Ottawa. Mr. Pearson's account is based on a telegram from the new Canadian Ambassador, Mr. Wrong, with whom Prime Minister King talked immediately after leaving the White House.

Following an exchange of amenities and discussion of their respective domestic political problems, the gist of the conversation was as follows:

1. The President and the Prime Minister discussed the closest possible cooperation in defense matters in the interest of efficiency and economy. Under this heading was included full exchange of military information, not only between the United States and Canada but also with the United Kingdom. It was agreed by both that the closest cooperation was necessary.

2. The President mentioned the need for a strong air force and mentioned the possible stationing of United States units at Goose Bay. It was agreed that further discussion through the Cabinet Ministers concerned or through diplomatic channels should be held.

3. The Prime Minister stressed the need for the closest consultation on publicity relating to defense measures. This was agreed upon and the Prime Minister understood it would be a commitment binding on the United States.

4. The Prime Minister stated that he would wish to inform the United Kingdom of any agreements or arrangements of consequence on defense matters. The President raised no objection and referred in this connection to Field Marshal Montgomery's visit. He spoke with great approval of the latter's talks on standardization.

5. The President raised the question of the 35th Recommendation, Permanent Joint Board on Defense (which the Canadian Government has not yet approved), but it was not discussed in any concrete way.

Mr. Wrong's telegram stated that the President had been briefed on this matter by the State Department.

6. There was no discussion of any basic defense plan.

7. The President gave the Prime Minister a summary of Ambassador Bedell Smith's views as to the Soviet potential for offensive action. The Prime Minister stated that these views agreed with those of the Canadian Ambassador in Moscow.

8. The general effect of the conversation was to clear the way for further talks on joint defense at a high level but leaving in United States hands the initiative as to timing and channel.

9. The possibility of a visit by the President to Ottawa was discussed and both were enthusiastic. They agreed that a visit at some time late next spring when Parliament was in session would probably be most advantageous.

In regard to point 8 above, placing the initiative for further high level talks on joint defense in United States hands, it is suggested that after a suitable interval I be authorized to instruct Ambassador Atherton to ask Mr. Pearson, Under Secretary for External Affairs, for the reaction of the Canadian Government to the question raised by the President. The President, it will be recalled, read to the Prime Minister an oral message, copies of which, at the President's direction, were given to Ambassador Wrong here and Mr. Pearson in Ottawa. The oral message sets forth United States position on the joint defense matters mentioned above and on several others as well.

3. Prime Minister King's Account of Meeting

(Mackenzie King Record, University of Toronto Press, Vol. III, pp. 362-63)

Quite early in their conversation, President Truman "brought up the question of our common interests in Defence. He said he thought it was quite apparent about the U.S. and Canada that each depended in part on the other. There was need for co-ordinating our methods. He said that he had a visit from Field Marshal Montgomery—at first he referred to Alexander—but meant Montgomery of Alamein—and said that he had spoken about the British, themselves and Canada all having their similar standards of weapon. He himself approved of that. I said I also did. It was desirable they should operate together efficiently. The President said that anything in the nature of war between any of us was inconceivable and that war with any one of the three might certainly bring in the others. He then spoke of the United States Chief of Staff feeling that there was need for co-operation in defence and mentioned Goose Bay in particular. He had referred to Iceland and Greenland. He spoke of the U.S. planes having demonstrated that a flight we had in mind would be around the northern regions. He said there was need for meteorological studies so as to direct planes. The purpose would be helping civil aviation quite as much as military.

When he spoke of Goose Bay I mentioned that one consideration was that it belonged to the Labrador section which belonged to Newfoundland. We would have to work in full harmony with them which meant also working with full knowledge so far as the United Kingdom was concerned. The President said in all of these matters he agreed there should be a most complete understanding and agreement between all three. What he hoped for was agreement on defence matters. I said I hoped for agreement also and believe it should be possible to reach an agreement. We were a small country in population and wealth compared to the United States. They might wish to put in large numbers of men. I understood they were thinking of some 10,000 in Goose Bay. The President said he did not know the numbers or any details, that would have to be worked out with care and with agreement. He believed it could. I said we had to watch particularly the question of our sovereignty. Not that we entertained any fears on that score, but having regard to the years as they went by and to the view the people would take, large numbers of troops from other countries being stationed out of their own country, or would have to be arranged on the basis of agreement to protect national rights.

Truman spoke about meteorological stations to study the weather. He thought all we might wish to do could be done for several purposes without making any mention of boundaries. I said I thought what had to be most considered was the way in which the public became informed on these matters. The whole publicity should be agreed to in advance, steps to be taken very slowly and surely. Care would have to be taken not to give the Russians a chance to say we were trying to fight them. The President said there was no aggression in our mind at all. All that we were doing would be to make aggression impossible anywhere.

I spoke of the enormous expenditures the armed forces had made. I said I thought it would be well in regard to any statement we were making of our conversation to make clear that while we had touched on defence it had been with a view to discussing means of effecting economies and an effective co-operation between the forces. The President said he thought my judgment was right in referring to the matter in this way. I said that one could not take exception in seeking to effect economies in joint defence. The President mentioned that in working out plans he thought further steps should be taken up through Ministers and on a diplomatic level rather than by the services. With this I agreed. In fact a memorandum which I had been given, as well as the one he had been given, had expressed this view in common. It was clear that the purpose of the meeting was to give official sanction in both countries to go ahead and work toward an agreement as a result of which plans for defence would be co-ordinated and developed.

D. President Harry S. Truman and Prime Minister W.L. Mackenzie King, Washington, D.C., April 23, 1947.

1. Prime Minister King's Account of Meeting

(Mackenzie King Record, University of Toronto Press, Vol. IV, pp. 30-32)

"As I entered the President's Office," he wrote, "I noticed his Secretary in the outer room beckoned to Mr. Woodward to go in with me. This is something I did not altogether like. Wrong had asked me if he should come along and I had told him I thought I would prefer to see the President by myself. Some of the members of the American Government have a way of having a third person in the room. I do not think that as between the President and the Prime Minister that sort of thing is necessary. However, it made no difference in my conversation."

They first talked about the President's proposed visit to Ottawa on June 10, 11 and 12. Mackenzie King told Truman that "on the 10th of June, I would have fulfilled twenty years in the office of Prime Minister. He said that he would make every effort to come on that day. I said I thought if he did I could regard it as a crowning event and thereafter be prepared to part in peace. I expressed the hope he would be accompanied by Mrs. Truman and his daughter. He replied that Mrs. Truman was coming and he hoped his daughter might also come. He was writing to her to New York to see if she could come with them. Said we would make the announcement at both centres at the same time later on.

"I told him that the plain people wanted not only a chance to see him but to cheer for him. They thought he had been very courageous and fearless and carried out his convictions in a splendid way. His reply to that was: I only try to do what is right; not to trouble about anything else.

"He has a very happy smile which never leaves him.

"I spoke appreciatively of Marshall's attitude in seeking to get Canada her rightful place in the making of the peace; of what Marshall had said in London and in Moscow. I said it was something we had considered was due to our country having fought as she did from the start. Made sacrifices. The President said we had made sacrifices of men, money and material, etc., and certainly no country had, in proportion to its size, made a greater contribution. He said they would continue to press for Canada having her rightful opportunity. .

"I said we understood that some of the Latin-American countries had to be thought of. They had wished to enter the war and perhaps had to be promised they would have their share in peace-making, notwithstanding that they did not make any contribution in men or treasure. But I thought there should be a distinction between those countries like Mexico and Cuba, etc., and others that had made a real sacrifice. The President himself mentioned different countries of the British Empire and said he agreed very strongly. I said that the drafting [of the peace treaties] could be done by committees on some very important questions. Others forming other committees. I thought our country might be put on some of the larger committees. Others could be satisfied with lesser committees. The President agreed with this. . . .

Discussion then turned to trade policy, particularly the conference currently under way in Geneva. . . .

With Truman, Mackenzie King pointed out that "our people attached a great deal of importance to the Imperial preferences. That we would be prepared to lessen preferences, but only for some specific tariff reductions on the part of the United States. That long-term agreements with promises would not be enough. There would have to be specific things done. The President said he fully agreed with that point of view. That we should do all we could to make trade as general as possible. I spoke next of the depreciation of our currency and the need for American dollars. I said there would be a demand to restrict commodities coming in. I hoped we would not begin tariff restrictions if some other means could be found whereby we could get currencies more on a basis of par. Suggested the United States might wish to purchase some of our metal, aluminum, etc. The President said they had a pretty good supply of aluminum but he thought that zinc and lead and others were short. I spoke too of the policy on the part of the States which would help to relieve Europe in a way to enable some of the countries there to purchase our goods with American dollars. I said this was a subject the departments would have to be taking up themselves. He said he thought the State Department was giving consideration to this matter.

"I spoke about the Pan-American Union. I said I thought it was just as well not to have that pressed too strongly at present and hoped there would be no official invitations sent without a word with our Government first. That in debate in a large way there were those who seemed to think that Canada might be drawn aloof—away from the British Commonwealth into a Western hemisphere orbit. That some thought we ought to be consolidating our position more strongly in the British Empire. I thought it was best not to have unnecessary debate on that question at present. The truth was we wanted to be part of the British Commonwealth of Nations and also part of the Western hemisphere. . . . We had our interests with both and were in a position to be helpful in relations between both.

"The President said he understood that. I felt he was anxious to have us come into the Pan-American Union. . . .

"I was particularly impressed with the compact, healthy appearance of the President. He is now sixty-five years of age and was most friendly in his whole manner.

"I also spoke of the Defence matters that we had talked of the last time and said I thought the joint developments would work out fairly well and would continue to do so so long as there was not too much pressure or haste—or for the size of the undertakings. The President said he was very pleased in the way in which that relationship had worked out. He did not bring forward any subjects himself. . . .

E.   Prime Minister W.L. Mackenzie King and President Harry S. Truman, Ottawa, Ontario, June 10-12, 1947

1. Prime Minister King's Introduction of President Truman to Both Houses of the Canadian Parliament, June 11, 1947

(CHCD, Appendix A, June 11, 1947, Address of Harry S. Truman, pp. 4060-62)

We are indeed greatly honoured in having as our country's guest today the President of the United States of America. Your visit, Mr. President, is a welcome expression of friendship and good will, both personal and national. On behalf of the members of Canada's parliament here assembled, and of all whom we represent, I extend to you the warmest of welcomes.

In paying this neighbourly visit to our capital, we are delighted that you are accompanied by Mrs. Truman and Miss Truman. We are pleased that you have found it possible to make your stay of sufficient length to enable you to see something of Ottawa and its surroundings, and to give members of parliament and others the privilege of meeting you and Mrs. Truman, and your talented daughter. We know how greatly His Excellency the Governor General and Lady Alexander enjoyed their recent visit to Washington, and how very much they have been looking forward to having Mrs. Truman, Miss Truman and yourself as their guests at Rideau Hall. Nothing could be more symbolic of the happy relations between our two peoples than family visits between the White House in Washington and Government House in Ottawa.

I should like to add, Mr. President, how great a pleasure it is to me personally to be renewing today, in my own country, the deeply valued friendship formed with yourself on my visits to the United States from time to time. I shall always recall your wish, so generously expressed, almost immediately upon your assumption of office, that the relations between our two countries might continue to be as friendly as they had been at all times under President Roosevelt, and that you and I might come to share a personal friendship correspondingly close. You know how warmly both these wishes were and are reciprocated.

We are especially indebted to you, Mr. President, for your courtesy in consenting to speak to the members of our parliament in the course of your visit. To most men in high position, an escape from the ordeal of public addresses is a not unwelcome form of relaxation. To this doctrine, I am sure you will readily subscribe. Your willingness not only to speak but to allow your address to be broadcast will be warmly appreciated in all parts of Canada, as also in the United Kingdom, the United States, and elsewhere.

Your visit, Mr. President, vividly recalls the visit to Ottawa, in August 1943, of your illustrious predecessor. It was the first visit to Canada's capital of a President of the United States. That visit was at a time of war. At that time, the allied nations were still two years away from ultimate victory. Today, we are almost equidistant from the final battles which brought an end to hostilities in Europe and in Asia.

It was on the eve of the final battles that President Roosevelt was taken from his people. We do not forget it was without a moment's warning, and at that hour of world crisis, that the mighty burdens which he had borne so long and with such great fortitude were transferred from his shoulders to yours. Before final victory was won, you were called upon to take grave and historic decisions. Since the end of the war you have been faced with the baffling tasks of reconstruction, when the grim effects of world conflict are still more apparent than the foundations of peace. We are glad to have the opportunity, which your presence here today affords, to tell you, Mr. Truman, how greatly the Canadian people have admired the manner in which, under all these circumstances, you assumed and are now bearing the tremendous responsibilities of the office of President of the United States.

May I say how greatly we all admire the qualities of humour, sincerity and courage and the capacity for friendship which you possess in such large measure, and which, if I may say so, have been particularly evident since the last congressional elections. Far be it from me to introduce any note of party politics into words of official welcome, much less to say anything that, even to appearances, might be considered interference in the domestic affairs of another country. At the same time, I think that all of us in public life would agree that to be faced with a legislature of which the majority may be disinclined to accept the government's policies is not the most comfortable position in which to find oneself as head of an administration.

Because of a considerable experience in such matters, I may perhaps be allowed, in an aside to the President to express a personal word of sympathy and understanding. Many who are assembled in this chamber can tell you, Mr. President, that, as leader of a political party and as head of the government, there have been occasions when I too have had to face situations not wholly dissimilar. It may serve as a note of encouragement to you when I say I have yet to find that such embarrassments are necessarily a bar to many years of office.

May I conclude this word of welcome on a more serious note. You, Mr. President, have said: "If wars in the future are to be prevented, the peace-loving nations must be united in their determination to keep the peace under law. The breaking of the peace anywhere is the concern of peace-loving nations everywhere." This statement of American policy might equally be a statement of Canadian policy. In the solution of all world problems, effective co-operation between nations is a first essential. In effective co-operation, no finer example could be given to the world than that which has been developed between the United States and Canada over the years, and which was especially evident during the years of war.

The Ogdensburg agreement and the Hyde Park declaration are the two great landmarks of our wartime co-operation. During the war these agreements were the basis of joint action in defence, in production, and in finance. Over and over again we have heard it said that co-operation, which was so effective as one of the instruments of victory in war, should be continued as one of the means of achieving and maintaining security and prosperity in a time of peace. By continuing co-operation along similar lines, Canada and the United States will not only be furthering their mutual interests, they will be strengthening the foundation of a new world order, an order based on international understanding, on mutual aid, on friendship and good will.

2. *Address of President Truman to Both Houses of Parliament, June 11, 1947*

(*Ibid.*, pp. 4062-64)

This is my first visit to Canada as President of the United States, and I am happy that it affords me the opportunity to address this meeting of the members of both houses of the Canadian Parliament. Here is a body which exemplifies the self-government and freedom of the nations of the great British Commonwealth. The history of the Commonwealth proves that it is possible for many nations to work and live in harmony for the common good.

I wish to acknowledge the many courtesies extended to me on this visit by the Governor General, Viscount Alexander, who paid me the honour of a visit in Washington a few months ago. His career as a soldier and as a statesman eminently qualifies him to follow his illustrious predecessors.

For the courtesy of appearing before you, as for other courtesies, I am sure I am largely indebted to my good friend Prime Minister Mackenzie King. I was particularly happy to be present yesterday when he was honoured in the rotunda of this Parliament Building. It was a wonderful ceremony, and a tribute which I think he richly deserved. I also appreciate the political advice he gave me this morning. I have come to value and cherish his friendship and statesmanship. As our two nations have worked together in solving the difficult problems of the post-war period, I have developed greater and greater respect for his wisdom.

Americans who come to know Canada informally, such as our tourists, as well as those whose approach is more academic, learn that Canada is a broad land—broad in mind and in spirit as well as in physical expanse. They find that the composition of your population and the evolution of your political institutions hold a lesson for the other nations of the earth. Canada has achieved internal unity and material strength, and has grown in stature in the world community, by solving problems that might have hopelessly divided and weakened a less gifted people.

Canada's eminent position today is a tribute to the patience, tolerance, and strength of character of her people, of both French and British strains. For Canada is enriched by the heritage of France as well as of Britain, and Quebec has imparted the vitality and spirit of France itself to Canada. Canada's notable achievement of national unity and progress through accommodation, moderation, and forbearance can be studied with profit by her sister nations.

Much the same qualities have been employed, with like success, in your relations with the United States. Perhaps I should say "your foreign relations with the United States." But the word "foreign" seems strangely out of place. Canada and the United States have reached the point where we no longer think of each other as "foreign" countries. We think of each other as friends, as peaceful and co-operative neighbours on a spacious and fruitful continent.

We must go back a long way, nearly a century and a half, to find a time when we were not on good terms. In the war of 1812 there was fighting across our frontier. But permanent good came of that brief campaign. It shocked Canadians and Americans into a realization that continued antagonism would be costly and perilous. The first result of that realization was the Rush-Bagot agreement in 1817, which embodied a spirit and an attitude that have permeated our relations to this day. This agreement originally was intended to limit and to regulate the naval vessels of both countries on the great lakes. It has become one of the world's most effective disarmament agreements and is the basis for our much-hailed unfortified frontier.

I speak of that period of history to make the point that the friendship that has characterized Canadian-American relations for many years did not develop spontaneously. The example of accord provided by our two countries did not come about merely through the happy circumstance of geography. It is compounded of one part proximity and nine parts good will and common sense.

We have had a number of problems, but they have all been settled by adjustment, by compromise, and by negotiations inspired by a spirit of mutual respect and a desire for justice on both sides. This is the peaceful way, the sensible way, and the fair way to settle problems, whether between two nations that are close neighbours or among many nations widely separated.

This way is open to all. We in Canada and the United States are justifiably proud of our joint record, but we claim no monopoly on the formula.

Canada and the United States will gladly share the formula, which rejects distrust and suspicion in favour of common sense, mutual respect, and equal justice, with their fellow members of the United Nations. One of the most effective contributions which our two countries can make to the cause of the United Nations is the patient and diligent effort to apply on a global scale the principles and practices which we have tested with success on this continent.

Relations between Canada and the United States have emphasized the spirit of co-operation rather than the letter of protocol. The Rush-Bagot agreement was stated in less than 150 words. From time to time it has been revised by mutual agreement to meet changing conditions. It was amended as recently as last December.

The last war brought our countries into even closer collaboration. The Ogdensburg agreement of 1940 provided for the creation of the Permanent Joint Board on Defence. It was followed by the Hyde Park agreement of 1941, which enabled us to co-ordinate our economic resources with increased efficiency. Common interests, particularly after Pearl Harbor, required the creation of several joint agencies to co-ordinate our efforts in special fields. When victory ended the necessity for these agencies, they were quietly disbanded with a minimum disturbance of the national economies of the two countries—just common sense again.

The permanent Joint Board on Defence will continue to function. I wish to emphasize, in addition to the word "permanent," the other two parts of the title. The board is joint, being composed of representatives of each country. Canada and the United States participate on the basis of equality, and the sovereignty of each is carefully respected. This was true during the gravest days of the war and it will continue to be true, in keeping with the nature of all our joint undertakings.

The board was created, and will continue to exist, for the sole purpose of assuring the most effective defence of North America. The board, as you know, has no executive powers and can only make recommendations for action. The record of the board provides another example of the truly co-operative spirit that prevails between our two countries.

The spirit of common purpose and the impressive strength which we marshalled for action on all fronts are the surest safeguard of continental security in the future.

The people of the United States fully appreciate the magnificent contribution in men and resources that Canada made to the allied war effort. United States soldiers, sailors, and airmen in the heat of battle knew their Canadian comrades as valiant and daring warriors. We look back with pride on our association as staunch allies in two wars.

Today our two nations are called upon to make great contributions to world rehabilitation. This task requires broad vision and constant effort.

I am confident that we can overcome the difficulties involved, as we overcame the greater difficulties of the war. The national genius of our peoples finds its most satisfying expression in the creation of new values in peace.

The record proves that in peaceful commerce the combined efforts of our countries can produce outstanding results. Our trade with each other is far greater than that of any other two nations on earth.

Last year the flow of trade in both directions across the border reached the record peacetime total of two and a quarter billion dollars. We imported from Canada more than twice the value of goods we received from the United Kingdom, France, China and Russia combined. United States purchases from Canada were about six times our purchases from Great Britain, nearly ten times those from China, and eleven times those from France. We sold to Canada nearly as much as we sold to Britain and France together.

Gratifying as the volume of our trade now is, it is capable of even further expansion to our mutual benefit. Some of our greatest assets are still to be developed to the maximum. I am thinking of one particularly that holds tremendous possibilities, the magnificent St. Lawrence-Great Lakes system, which we share and which we must develop together.

The St. Lawrence project stirs the imagination of men long accustomed to majestic distances and epic undertakings. The proposal for taking electric power from the river and bringing ocean shipping 2,400 miles inland, to tap the fertile heart of our continent, is economically sound and strategically important.

When this programme is carried out, the waterway that is part of our boundary will more than ever unite our two countries. It will stimulate our economies to new growth and will speed the flow of trade.

There have been times when shortsighted tariff policies on both sides threatened to raise almost insurmountable barriers. But the need to exchange goods was so imperative that trade flourished despite artificial obstacles. The reciprocal trade agreements of 1936 and 1939 made possible a sensible reduction of tariff rates, and paved the way to our present phenomenal trade.

Something more than commercial agreements, however, is required to explain why Canada and the United States exchange more than two billion dollars worth of goods a year. Ambassador Atherton has aptly given the reason as not ''free trade,'' but ''the trade of free men.'' That record flow of goods and the high standard of living it indicates, on both sides of the border, provide a practical demonstration of the benefits of the democratic way of life and a free economy.

The benefits of our democratic governments and free economies operating side by side have spread beyond our countries to the advantage of the whole world. Both nations expanded their productivity enormously during the war and both escaped the physical damage that afflicted other countries. As a result, Canada and the United States emerged from the war as the only major sources of the industrial products and the food upon which much of the world depends for survival.

Canada has responded as nobly to the challenge of peace as she did to that of the war. Your wheat has fed millions who otherwise would have starved. Your loan has strengthened Britain in her valiant battle for recovery.

The United States is particularly gratified to find Canada at our side in the effort to develop the International Trade Organization. We attach great importance to this undertaking, because we believe it will provide the key to the welfare and prosperity of the world in the years immediately ahead.

In sponsoring the International Trade Organization, the United States, with the co-operation of Canada and other countries, is making a determined effort to see that the inevitable adjustments in world trade as a result of the war will result in an expanding volume of business for all nations.

Our goal is a vast expansion of agriculture and industry throughout the world, with freer access to raw materials and markets for all nations, and a wider distribution of the products of the earth's fields and factories among all peoples. Our hope is to multiply the fruitfulness of the earth and to diffuse its benefits among all mankind.

At this critical point in history, we of the United States are deeply conscious of our responsibilities to the world. We know that in this trying period, between a war that is over and a peace that is not yet secure, the destitute and the oppressed of the earth look chiefly to us for sustenance and support until they can again face life with self-confidence and self-reliance.

We are keenly aware that much depends upon the internal strength, the economic stability and the moral stamina of the United States. We face this challenge with determination and confidence.

Free men everywhere know that the purpose of the United States is to restore the world to health and to re-establish conditions in which the common people of the earth can work out their salvation by their own efforts.

We seek a peaceful world, a prosperous world, a free world, a world of good neighbours, living on terms of equality and mutual respect, as Canada and the United States have lived for generations.

We intend to expend our energies and to invest our substance in promoting world recovery by assisting those who are able and willing to make their maximum contribution to the same cause.

We intend to support those who are determined to govern themselves in their own way, and who honour the right of others to do likewise.

We intend to aid those who seek to live at peace with their neighbours, without coercing or being coerced, without intimidating or being intimidated.

We intend to uphold those who respect the dignity of the individual, who guarantee to him equal treatment under law, and who allow him the widest possible liberty to work out his own destiny and achieve success to the limit of his capacity.

We intend to co-operate actively and loyally with all who honestly seek, as we do, to build a better world in which mankind can live in peace and prosperity.

We count Canada in the forefront of those who share these objectives and ideals.

With such friends we face the future unafraid.

3. Toast of President Truman at a Parliamentary Luncheon, Chateau Laurier Hotel, June 11, 1947

(As quoted in P.J. Philip, ''Truman Grateful for Rousing Welcome,'' NYT, June 12, 1947, p. 2)

I would like to propose a somewhat peculiar toast. Never in my life have I received such a cordial welcome as I had from your Parliament this morning. You were kind to me.

I have heard of people receiving three cheers and a tiger, but it never happened to me before. I have seen pictures of rulers waving to their cheering people from balconies covered with rugs. I had some experience of that in Mexico.

I have heard of people walking on a red carpet, but I never did that until I came here.

I want to propose the toast of the Parliament of Canada.

4. Special News Conference of President Truman and Prime Minister King, June 12, 1947

(PP/Harry S. Truman, Vol. 1947, No. 112, pp. 276-77)

THE PRESIDENT: I want to say to you that this Canadian trip has been most interesting to me. I think it is an event in the history of the two countries. I think we understand each other better as a result of this visit, and I sincerely hope that the Canadians will pay us a visit. There isn't a chance in the world of our being able to give them the sort of reception that they have given me, but we do the best we can.

Our objective, of course, in the visit to Mexico and in the visit to Canada, is to solidify the friendship of the people who live on this continent. We want to do that for the whole Western Hemisphere, and then we want to do it for the whole world.

We have only one objective, and that is peace in the world for the benefit of all the peoples of the world. Unless we can do that, all the men who died in both our world wars died in vain. Unless we can do that, all the men who died in both the world wars died in vain. I repeat that. Because that is exactly what it means. The United States has but one objective in view, and that is peace in the world, and friendship with every nation in the world, and underline that *every*.

That's all I have to say, gentlemen.

Q. Thank you very much, sir.

THE PRESIDENT: Lovely place.

Q. Direct quotes?

THE PRESIDENT: You can say "the President said."

Q. No direct quotes, Mr. President?

THE PRESIDENT: I don't think you ought to make it direct quotes.

Q. Thank you so much for coming over.

THE PRIME MINISTER: I want to say, on behalf of the Canadian Government that every sentiment that the President expressed is re-echoed in the hearts of all of us who had the great pleasure of meeting him, seeing him, and talking to him on his delightful visit to our country.

THE PRESIDENT: I wasn't trying to put you on the record, but you went on record.

THE PRIME MINISTER: I am going to keep alongside you, as good neighbours.

F.   President Harry S. Truman and Prime Minister W.L. Mackenzie King, Williamsburg, Virginia, April 2, 1948

1. Address of Prime Minister King Upon Receiving an Honorary Law Degree, College of William and Mary, Williamsburg, Virginia, April 2, 1948

(The Alumni Gazette of The College of William and Mary in Virginia, Vol. xv, May 1948, No. 4, pp. 5, 29)

. . . "The college and Colonial Williamsburg have designated this day as Canadian-American Day. The citizens of Canada will be quick to recognize the signal honor thus being paid His Majesty's senior dominion in the present British Commonwealth of Nations. The international aspect of the occasion, and the national character of the welcome, could not find more gracious expression than they have in the presence, at the college this morning, of the President of the United States. I should like to convey to Mr. Truman and to his fellow citizens warmest thanks on behalf of Canada, for today's expression of friendship and good will on the part of our good neighbor, the United States. Is it too much to hope that, across the waters of the Atlantic and of the Pacific, this memorable day may shine forth as a beacon light of American hospitality and New World amity. . . .

"Settlement, self-government, free institutions, independence, all had their beginnings in Williamsburg or its vicinity. We are certainly near the foundations of freedom in the New World as we stand on the steps of the college with which are associated the names of the great patriot statesmen of Virginia.

"It is interesting today to recall that Canada enjoyed a like inheritance. This continent presents no more striking parallel than is to be found in the successive stages—from settlement and colony, through rebellion, to federation and nationhood—by which complete freedom in government has been achieved in our respective countries—freedom now shared with other countries of the British Commonwealth.

"The struggle to win and to maintain freedom is unending. Freedom, moreover, is one and indivisible. Twice in our generation, the peoples of the British Commonwealth and the people of the United States have found their freedom threatened through the loss of freedom by nations on the continent of Europe. Once again a like threat to our freedom looms large on the world's horizon.

"In some ways, the menace to freedom has never been graver or more insidious than it has become within the last three years. That menace arises no longer merely from armed aggression aimed at territorial expansion. While this is an ever-present danger, the menace to freedom comes as well from sinister plans to undermine the structure of free government within the borders of individual nations. Seeds of unrest and anarchy are being sown wherever, throughout the globe, the soil gives promise of their growth. In a word, freedom is threatened not only by military force but by an organized conspiracy to establish a tyranny over the human mind, to thwart the wills and destroy the souls of nations as well as of men.

"If against such an appalling menace, freedom—physical, mental, moral and spiritual freedom—is to be preserved, a way must be found, and that right speedily, to ensure that nations which are still free will not be suborned, defeated or destroyed one by one.

"In the preservation of freedom, the University and the State have each their tasks to perform. The supreme task of the University is to continue to be a citadel of freedom in its avowed opposition to any form of tyranny over the mind of man. Security remains the prime duty of the State. It is vital to the defence of freedom to maintain a preponderance of moral, economic and military strength on the side of freedom. Security for individual nations, including our own, can be assured only by the effective cooperation and united power of the nations that are still free. To achieve this great end is the supreme task of statesmanship today."

2. Address of President Truman Upon Receiving an Honorary Law Degree, College of William and Mary, Williamsburg, Virginia, April 2, 1948

(*Idem.*, pp. 3, 31)

"I can't tell you how much I appreciate the honor which this great college has conferred upon me. I appreciate most highly the cordial welcome of the governor and the citizens of this great State today. It is indeed an honor to receive this degree in such distinguished company.

"It was my privilege last year to pay a visit to Canada. I never was more cordially received in my life. I had that same privilege and the same treatment in Mexico and in Brazil. In fact, the Western Hemisphere believes in being good neighbors. I wish all the world could be good neighbors. There isn't any reason why they shouldn't.

"We run into the world wars in the defense of liberty. We still stand for liberty and for freedom of worship, freedom of conscience and freedom of the individual, things which were fundamental on this campus from its beginning.

"One great man who was chancellor of this school does not get enough credit for what he did for the United States of America and for the things for which we stand, our bill of rights. This is George Wythe, the greatest law teacher, I think, in the history of this hemisphere. Think of his graduates and his pupils, what they contributed to the welfare of the world and to the welfare of the United States of America.

"I hope that we can get those attributes in the whole world.

"Now we have today something to be proud of. There has been a unanimous agreement in the Security Council of the United Nations. I hope that is a portent of things to come.

"This great nation has never wanted anything but peace in the world. This great nation has never wanted to be anything but a good neighbor toward every other nation in the world. That is still her theory, that is still our policy.

"Again I want to thank you very much for this privilege. I can't tell you how much I appreciate it. I hope that when you young people take over the country, as you will some day, and the traditions of this school will be followed, that you will find peace in the world and the things for which the government and the people of the United States stand, along with this good neighbor on the North. Thank you very much."

3. Prime Minister King's Account of Meeting

(Mackenzie King Record, University of Toronto Press, Vol. IV, pp. 182-83)

    . . . Truman "looked remarkably well," he wrote. "Appears to be in very good condition physically. When we were standing in the corridor about to come into the building, there was a choir of men and women marching past. There were just the Governor General, Governor Tuck and the Bishop and myself and Mr. Pomfret all talking together. The President said: conditions at the moment were very serious. As serious he thought as in 1939. He was referring to what had happened in Berlin last night where Americans had to bring food and passengers into their own zone by air and where incidents may occur at any moment that would set the whole of Europe on fire. . . . I feel terribly concerned about it all. Indeed I have come to the conclusion that if we escape war before this month is over or next at the latest, it will be a miracle. If the Communists feel sure of winning Italy, they will probably wait until after that event and may even avoid open war, having captured another country. On the other hand, if they think they are going to fail in this, they may well precipitate a move into Europe before the election itself takes place. I think, too, the situation in Manchuria and Korea is equally dangerous and in China. I did not think it necessary to ask Truman whether he thought the situation was very dangerous, very critical, because he had openly expressed that view to me and to the others, as we were talking together. I did ask him when we were alone if there were any suggestions he would like to make to me. He said something to the effect that my judgment was sound in these matters. To just keep on as we were doing. He had in mind in this remark the negotiations re Atlantic Pact taking place in Washington just now. I was glad to hear him say before the others that he had seen my speech. This was before it was delivered. He was quite satisfied with it. I should be surprised if in his next pronouncement, he does not link up with what I said today. I told him that if, at any time, he wished to send a message to me personally or otherwise, to feel that he could do so with perfect confidence. He thanked me warmly.

"I saw him alone in his room with Mrs. Truman and their daughter just before the Governor General came in as well for us both to shake hands with him and I said I admired the way he was keeping on with his fight [in the election campaign]. He said he was going to fight for all he was worth and he would lick these other fellows yet. I notice the sympathies about here seem to be Republican. At the meeting today [the convocation ceremonies], he was much crowded for time and he was faced with a thunderstorm coming in. However, he did manage to have three and a half minutes and to say a good deal extemporaneously. He said if they got back to the White House, he hoped I would come and pay him a visit there. Mrs. Truman said something about not waiting until another term. I thought Mrs. Truman looked very tired. Indeed quite changed but was very pleasant. Margaret was exceedingly nice.". . .

IV. Prime Minister Louis S. St. Laurent (November 1948—June 1957) (Presidents Harry S. Truman and Dwight D. Eisenhower)

Louis St. Laurent became Prime Minister in November of 1948 and served until June of 1957. During this time, he had six meetings with U.S. Presidents—two with Harry S. Truman, and four with Dwight D. Eisenhower. All of these meetings are documented in this chapter. President Truman had assumed office in April of 1945, and served until January of 1953. He had met with Prime Minister King eight times, and was to have a total of ten meetings with Canadian Prime Ministers.

The first St. Laurent-Truman meeting, held in Washington from February 11-13, 1949 was in President Truman's words, "just a friendly visit." Prime Minister St. Laurent felt its purpose was to "renew our acquaintance."[1] (See Section A.) While such issues as Canadian-U.S. defence, the North Atlantic defence pact, and European recovery were discussed, the most important topic was the proposed St. Lawrence Seaway. The Seaway had by now become an enduring issue in Canadian-U.S. relations. Both President Truman and Prime Minister St. Laurent preferred the simultaneous digging of the Seaway for navigation and the construction of electric installation for power. However, given the fact that the U.S. Senate had rejected Seaway plans by both Presidents Hoover and Roosevelt, St. Laurent's position was that if both navigation and power were not approved soon, consideration should be given to the hydro scheme alone between Ontario and New York. However, nothing was resolved during the two leader's

---

[1]See "St. Laurent Begins Vital Truman Talk," NYT (February 13, 1949), pp. 1, 3; and "Truman Alert to PM's View on Seaway," TGM (February 14, 1949), p. 1.

ninety minutes of talks, and no communiqué was issued. The documentation for this meeting includes its initial announcement and rationale by the two leaders, and Prime Minister St. Laurent's summation of the meeting delivered a month later in a speech in Windsor, Ontario.

Prime Minister St. Laurent's second meeting with President Truman occurred on September 27-28, 1951. (See Section B.) The purpose of this hastily arranged meeting concerned the St. Lawrence Seaway.[2] The Canadian Cabinet had met on September 26, 1951 to plan the Speech from the Throne, and decided to proceed alone with an all-Canadian Seaway if necessary. However, the Cabinet wanted to include the announcement of this decision in the Speech from the Throne, and to do so, it was necessary to get President Truman's approval. The navigation project did not require U.S. approval, but the power development, concerning which Ontario had already concluded an agreement with Ottawa, involved New York State in the financing and construction of the International Rapids section. New York State's participation in turn necessitated Presidential approval. Prime Minister St. Laurent therefore telephoned President Truman, arranged a White House meeting which lasted for thirty minutes, and immediately returned to Ottawa. This meeting is substantively important on two counts: the Canadian Government officially made public its resolve to proceed with the Seaway without the U.S.; and there was a Canadian-U.S. agreement-in-principle to, this unilateral Canadian course of action, but with President Truman regarding it as "second best" to joint action. The documentation of this meeting includes President Truman's press conference preceeding their talks, the Joint Statement issued after the meeting, and the Canadian Speech from the Throne announcing the proposed St. Lawrence Seaway.

Prime Minister St. Laurent's third meeting with a U.S. President took place on May 7-8, 1953 in Washington. (See Section C.) Mr. Eisenhower had become President in January of 1953, and within one month of his inauguration, a White House Press Release announced that St. Laurent had accepted an invitation to a meeting whereby "matters of general interest to the U.S. and Canada will be considered."[3] Essentially a "goodwill call," the two leaders met for a total of one hour and forty-five minutes, during which they discussed such issues as: the Korean War, the situation in Laos, NATO, U.S. import restrictions, the St. Lawrence Seaway, joint defence, and the possibility of establishing a joint Canadian-U.S. economic com-

---

[2]See W.H. Lawrence, "Canada Offers to Build Seaway," NYT (September 29, 1951), p. 10; and "Seaway Decision Held Near," TGM (September 28, 1951), pp. 1-2.

[3]DSB (March 13, 1953), White House Press Release, April 6, 1953, p. 500.

mittee.[4] Although almost two years had passed since the hastily arranged St. Laurent-Truman meeting on the St. Lawrence Seaway, the project was still in hiatus given the U.S. Federal Power Commission's delay in authorizing the power project. Thus, Canadians, patient but firm in their resolve to proceed alone, were still waiting for the U.S. to appoint an authority to join with Ontario Hydro on the power works. Even more important was the increasing Canadian-U.S. friction over U.S. restrictions on the import of Canadian commodities, which Canadians held to be in contravention of the General Agreement on Tariffs and Trade (GATT). Canadian dairy products had been especially hard hit, and there were indications in Congress that these restrictions would be extended to other areas. No issues were resolved during the meeting, nor were there any precise indications of positions on bilateral issues. While there was an expression of hope for "an early favorable decision by the Federal Power Commission on the St. Lawrence Seaway" in the Joint Statement, there was no explicit mention of Canadian concern over Congressional efforts to increase tariffs. The documentation for this meeting includes Prime Minister St. Laurent's address to the National Press Club, which is significant given his assertion that the allies could not have military strength without economic strength; the Joint Statement issued by the two leaders subsequent to their meetings, and St. Laurent's report to the Canadian House of Commons.

Prime Minister St. Laurent's fourth meeting with a U.S. President occurred from November 13-15, 1953 when Eisenhower visited Ottawa. (See Section D.) Mr. Eisenhower was the third President to do so, with President Roosevelt having visited in September of 1944 and Truman in June of 1947. President Eisenhower was quite precise as to the nature of his visit, as expressed in a press conference of October 8—"There is no specific purpose other than social and a courtesy call . . ."[5] Indeed, according to confidential sources, "there was an agreement between Prime Minister St. Laurent and U.S. Ambassador Stuart that there need be no discussion of political and economic questions."[6] The most tangible results of this St. Laurent-Eisenhower meeting occurred in the form of two announcements made by the President prior to his departure; his approval of authorization to New York State to proceed with the St. Lawrence Power Project in coordination with the Province of Ontario; and the formation of a Cabinet level

---

[4]See George Bain, "St. Laurent, Eisenhower Will Review Trade, Seaway and NATO Problems," TGM (May 7, 1953), p. 19; and "St. Laurent Reports to Canadians On Trip," NYT (May 10, 1953), p. 72.

[5]PP/Dwight D. Eisenhower, Vol. 1953, #208, p. 208.

[6]Confidential.

trade committee that emerged from the proposal of the previous summit meeting.[7] Six issues were discussed in a very general sense during a one hour meeting Mr. Eisenhower had with the Canadian Cabinet: East-West tensions, world trade, joint Canadian-U.S. trade and economic committee, St. Lawrence Seaway, NATO and joint defence. No tangible outcome resulted from this Eisenhower visit; indeed, the informal Cabinet meeting was the only provision on the official agenda for the President to meet alone with St. Laurent or any of his Ministers. The documentation for this meeting includes St. Laurent's introduction of the President to the Canadian Parliament; Eisenhower's address to Parliament emphasizing the necessity of defence cooperation; and the Joint Statement issued by the two leaders.

Prime Minister St. Laurent's fifth meeting with a U.S. President, and his third meeting with President Eisenhower, took place from March 26-27, 1956 in the mountains of West Virginia at the Greenbrier Hotel near White Sulphur Springs. (See Section E.) This meeting, which was the personal idea of President Eisenhower, is unique in that it included the President of Mexico, Adolfo Ruiz Corintes.[8] The purpose of the meeting, the President declared, was to bring the "neighbors" of North America together for a "chat." While there was some discussion of multilateral and bilateral issues, nothing was resolved. The primary significance of this meeting lies in the fact that the informality heretofore characteristic of Canadian-U.S. summitry was multilateralized by President Eisenhower. Although the meeting was not especially successful in its attempt at tripartite camaraderie, St. Laurent did have an opportunity to discuss bilateral issues with the President. A session was held with the three leaders, which included a presentation by U.S. Secretary of State John Foster Dulles, during which the entire international situation was reviewed, including the rising tensions in the Middle East and Indochina. There was also a one-hour St. Laurent-Eisenhower conversation, which covered such international issues as The Republic of China on Taiwan, Quemoy and Matsu, and recognition of the People's Republic of China at Peking. Bilateral issues covered the dispute over the Columbia River, the Canadian twenty per cent tax on advertising revenues earned by U.S. publishers in Canada, and the Canadian-U.S. trade balance and U.S. investment in Canada. It is interesting to note that it was only in these bilateral conversations that problems of North America were brought

---

[7]See George Bain, "Forget Speeches, Just Act Natural," TGM (November 14, 1953), p. 1; and Raymond Daniell, "President Answers Canada on Seaway, Defence and Trade," NYT (November 15, 1953), p. 36.

[8]See George Bain, "Eisenhower Welcomes St. Laurent, Cortines at Goodwill Meeting," TGM (March 27, 1956), p. 1; James Reston, "Canadians Find Eisenhower Firm Against Peking," NYT (March 31, 1956), p. 1; and George Bain, "Conference Letter," TGM (March 28, 1956), p. 6.

up, and that for all the talk of neighbourliness, the leaders of Mexico and Canada did not meet by themselves. The documentation of this meeting includes President Eisenhower's press conference, and Prime Minister St. Laurent's report of the meeting to the House of Commons.

Prime Minister St. Laurent's last meeting with a U.S. President, and his fourth meeting with President Eisenhower, occurred on December 11, 1956 at Augusta, Georgia. (See Section F.) While on holiday in Florida, St. Laurent was invited by telephone to join President Eisenhower who was on a golf holiday in Georgia.[9] This four hour meeting captures with special clarity the mixture of informality and formality that characterizes Canadian-U.S. summitry. Americans and Canadians witnessed the curious spectacle of a Canadian Prime Minister being received with full military honours prior to a game of golf with a U.S. President.[10] Notwithstanding the nature of this meeting, three issues were discussed: tariffs on Canadian fish, Canadian-U.S. balance of trade, and the policies of Indian Prime Minister Nehru in the context of the Cold War. While nothing tangible resulted from the meeting, St. Laurent concluded that this sort of sportive diplomacy was highly effective, observing to the Canadian House of Commons that "a game of golf with one of those electric go-carts was about the best way to have an international conference . . ." The documentation for this meeting consists of the Prime Minister's report to the House of Commons.

A. President Harry S. Truman and Prime Minister Louis S. St. Laurent, Washington, D.C., February 11-13, 1949

1. Press Conference of President Truman, Washington, D.C., January 27, 1949

(PP/Harry S. Truman, Vol. 1949, No. 22, p. 118)

THE PRESIDENT: I have invited the Prime Minister of Canada to visit Washington on February 12. He has accepted the invitation, and it is expected that he will arrive in Washington on the evening of February 11, and will remain probably for 2 days.

The Prime Minister's acceptance of the invitation will permit us to renew his acquaintance—I became very well acquainted with him November 15, 1948—after having served first as Minister of Justice

---

[9]See W.H. Lawrence, "President Golfs with St. Laurent," NYT (December 12, 1956), p. 29.

[10]Appropriately, the nine hole match ended in a draw.

and then as Secretary of State for External Affairs since 1941. This will be the Prime Minister's first trip to the United States since he assumed his duties as Prime Minister. I meant to say that I am acquainted with him on my trip up—my visit to Canada.[1] That was the first time I had met him, and I am inviting him down here for the purpose of becoming better acquainted with the Prime Minister of our neighbor.

Q. For bulletin purposes, what's his name? (Laughter)

THE PRESIDENT: I very carefully was trying to avoid it, because I don't know how to pronounce it: Louis St. Laurent—L-a-u-r-e-n-t—I don't know how to pronounce it—that's a French pronunciation. I wouldn't attempt to pronounce it. Tony [Ernest B. Vaccaro of the Associated Press], you put me on the spot.

Q. I was myself on the spot.

Q. Mr. President, are there any specific questions you wish to take up with the Prime Minister of Canada?

THE PRESIDENT: No.

Q. Anything to do with the North Atlantic Security Pact, Mr. President?

THE PRESIDENT: None—nothing whatever. Just a friendly visit of the Prime Minister of Canada to the President of the United States. . . .

2. Prime Minister St. Laurent's Announcement of Meeting to the Canadian House of Commons, January 27, 1949

(CHCD, January 27, 1949, pp. 14-15)

I hope it will be of interest to hon. members to learn that the President of the United States announced today that he has invited me to visit Washington on February 12, 1949, and that I had accepted his invitation. The United States ambassador called on me yesterday morning to extend the invitation. I told Mr. Steinhardt I would naturally be pleased to accept it.

The President was kind enough to indicate that he would like to renew our acquaintance and to discuss the matters which are of common interest to our two countries as neighbours, and also the world situation as it affects our two countries.

Everyone knows that the friendly personal relations between the late President Roosevelt and our Prime Minister were of inestimable advantage to this continent and to the world. President Truman has expressed the desire, which I fully share, to maintain these friendly personal

[1] President Truman was momentarily confused. While Mr. St. Laurent became Prime Minister on November 15, 1948, Mr. Truman first met him in June of 1947 during the former's visit to Ottawa. Mr. St. Laurent was then Secretary of State for External Affairs.

relations between the leaders of the governments of our two countries. Hon. members will recall that President Truman visited Ottawa in June, 1947, at the invitation of my predecessor, and that his visit was both pleasant and beneficial.

3. Prime Minister St. Laurent's Account of Meeting, Windsor, Ontario March 12, 1949

(Address of Prime Minister St. Laurent, Kennedy Collegiate, Windsor, Ontario, March 12, 1949 (Mimeographed Copy, pp. 4-5))

. . . Four weeks ago I spent a weekend in Washington on the invitation of the President of the United States, who it had been my privilege to meet on rather intimate terms when I went down to the border a couple of years ago to meet him and accompany him up to Ottawa on the occasion of his official visit. Of course, my conversations with the President were of a confidential character and it would not, I suppose, be courteous to him to repeat in a public way any of the things he said to me but I can divulge what I said. I can tell you without divulging any confidences of his that I spoke to him about this great seaway project of the development of the St. Lawrence, and well, I came back with great encouragement and with the feeling that we would not have to do the things we might have to do if the two-fold development were not to proceed at an early date, that is to say, support the application of the State of New York and the Province of Ontario for the development separately of the waters of the St. Lawrence for hydro electric purposes. That will not be quite as costly, to develop the St. Lawrence for the two-fold purpose of transportation and hydro electric power but it will be very much more than the proportion for development for hydro electric will cost than if the two projects are proceeded with together. We are going to have to do it because Ontario needs that power so urgently now that it would be an economic proposition to develop it as a power project alone but I had high hopes after my visit to Washington that the two-fold purposes of the development are going to be approved and approved at an early date and we are going to have in that one of the great concrete demonstrations of the friendly and co-operative relations between these two countries.

I met the newspaper men, well, I suppose it is an hour ago now, and some of them asked me what were my impressions after my visit to Washington. Well, I told them quite frankly that it was difficult for a Canadian who goes down there and who was received as I was to realize that he was in a place which, according to law, was a foreign country and amongst foreign people because you have to make considerable effort to feel that you are not quite at home there and that you were not discussing problems in which those you were talking to evinced as great and as sympathetic interest as would any Canadian in any Canadian city. Well, I think that in this world where there has been much discord, so much talk about a cold war that it is very much greater and very much more powerful than the other, but still two peoples who can entertain friendly relations that happily exist between the American people and the Canadian people and to have those relations and all the discussions and the negotiations take place on the footing of absolute equality of sovereignty on both sides.

We have been negotiating many times with our American neighbours. We have been agreeing to do a great many things and they have been agreeing to do a great many things that we wanted but never have we been made to feel that we were obliged to agree to something because they were bigger and stronger than we were. Whenever anything was put before us for discussion and negotiation, it was always based with a view to the advantage of both the negotiating parties and I think that it is a very great thing for this American continent that that is the kind of relations that constitute the international relations of the two most important factors on this continent.

B.   President Harry S. Truman and Prime Minister Louis S. St. Laurent, Washington, D.C., September 27-28, 1951

1. Press Conference of President Truman, Washington, D.C., September 27, 1951

(PP/Harry S. Truman, Vol. 1951, No. 239, p. 546)

Q. Are you seeing the Canadian Prime Minister tomorrow, as I understand it?

THE PRESIDENT: Yes. On the St. Lawrence Seaway project . . .

Q. Is there any reason why the St. Lawrence and Niagara power projects should be linked together?

THE PRESIDENT: Yes, there is a very good reason—because we want to get them both constructed.

Q. But the Niagara power is ready to go now—as an independent proposition.

THE PRESIDENT: Yes, but I am not for it. I never have been in favor of taking them apart, for the very simple reason that I don't want to see one constructed without the other. I would like to see them both constructed. . . .

*2. Joint Statement of President Truman and Prime Minister St. Laurent
Following Discussions, September 28, 1951*

(PP/Harry S. Truman, Vol. 1951, No. 240, pp. 545-47)

The President and the Prime Minister discussed the St. Lawrence project. They agreed on the vital importance to the security and the economies of both countries of proceeding as rapidly as possible with both the seaway and the power phases of the project. They explored the matter of the next steps to be taken in achieving the early construction of the project. They both agreed that it would be most desirable to proceed along the lines of the 1941 Agreement between the United States and Canada.

The Prime Minister informed the President of the needs of Ontario for power and of the arrangement the Canadian Government could make with the government of that Province for its participation with the appropriate Federal or State authority in the United States for the power development. In these circumstances, the Prime Minister indicated the Canadian Government would be willing to construct the seaway as a Canadian project if it is not possible to have the joint development undertaken on the basis of the 1941 Agreement.

The President expressed his strong preference for joint action on the Seaway and his hope that the Congress would soon authorize such action, but stated he would support Canadian action as second best if an early commencement on the joint development does not prove possible.

3. Speech from the Throne Announcing Proposed St. Lawrence Seaway, Canadian House of Commons, October 9, 1951

(CHCD, October 9, 1951, p. 2)

. . . My Prime Minister has conferred recently with the President of the United States on the vital importance to the security and economies of both countries of proceeding as rapidly as possible with both the seaway and the power phases of the St. Lawrence project.

The President stated he would support Canadian action to construct the seaway as second best if an early commencement of the joint development does not prove possible. Terms have been arranged with the government of Ontario for the participation of the Ontario Hydro Electric Power Commission with the appropriate federal or state authority in the United States for the power development in the international section of the St. Lawrence, and with respect to the division of costs between power and navigation. You will be asked to enact legislation to provide for an appropriate agency of the federal government to deal with the construction of the St. Lawrence Seaway. The proposed agency would be empowered to proceed either with the Canadian share of an international undertaking or a solely Canadian development, as soon as satisfactory international arrangements can be made for the power phases of the project in both countries. . . .

C.   President Dwight D. Eisenhower and Prime Minister Louis S. St. Laurent, Washington, D.C., May 7-8, 1953

1. Address of Prime Minister St. Laurent to the National Press Club, May 8, 1953

(Transcript of Address, May 8, 1953, National Press Club, Washington, D.C.)

. . . I came to Washington at the cordial invitation of the President to discuss some of the many matters of common concern to two neighbouring households whose properties adjoin one another for some five thousand miles; and whose relations differ from those of any two other countries on earth. We are citizens of two neighbouring nations who have never looked on one another as foreigners.

That does not mean that, in these neighbourly relations between us there have not sometimes been complicated and even vexatious questions to settle; but, most of time, we have settled them like good neighbours who want to remain and, indeed, feel it is essential that they remain good neighbours.

This feeling of neighbourliness has been reflected in relations of the warmest friendliness which have existed for many years between the man who happens to be the President of the American Union and the man who happens to be Prime Minister of Canada.

I feel certain that this traditional personal relationship between the leaders of the government of our countries will be continued between General Eisenhower and myself or whosoever may be Prime Minister of Canada after we have had our next elections.

This is not, of course, the first time I have met General Eisenhower, though it is the first time that I have seen him since he became President of the United States.

In Canada, we have never forgotten his visit in 1946 as the victorious commander of the armed forces of many nations in the Second World War. On that occasion we named one of our greatest mountains in his honour. As I recall it, he pretended to find some reflection in the fact that the mountain was bald. It is, in fact, snow-capped and we in Canada are proud that one of our highest peaks will always bear the name "Eisenhower".

Then two years ago, when General Eisenhower was serving as supreme commander of the forces of the North Atlantic Treaty Organization, I had the honour of welcoming him to Ottawa. On that visit we discussed some of the great problems which were involved in the erection of the defences of the North Atlantic community to which he has made so indispensable a contribution, and which remains our strongest bulwark in the defence of peace.

On both sides of the boundary we have come to realize how much these personal contacts between heads of governments can supplement our normal diplomatic relationships. I hope and believe that for many years to come it will be possible for an American President to be greeted in Ottawa and a Canadian Prime Minister to be welcomed in Washington with the warmth which has been characteristic of such visits over the past thirty years.

This visit is giving me the opportunity of discussing a wide range of subjects with the President and his colleagues in your government; and I dare say you gentlemen in the press will speculate with a good deal of accuracy about the things we will have talked about; and that some of you may even venture to report both what we will have actually said and did not say to each other.

We Americans and Canadians occupy most of the area of this continent. As we look out on the rest of the world from our North American Homelands we are, all of us, very thankful that we live in lands that have been so favourably endowed by Providence and we want—Americans and Canadians alike—to do everything we can to preserve our heritage from aggression and from the threat of aggression.

In most respects, Canada is much the smaller of our two countries. We have only one-eleventh of your population and despite the rate at which we have been developing, our developed national wealth is proportionately even smaller. That means that in looking after our joint defences the United States inevitably has the bigger share; though we feel that between individual Canadians and Americans there is no similar contrast.

The one respect in which we are bigger than you are is that we have more square miles of territory. Because of our size, our colder climate and our relatively sparse population, we in Canada have to devote proportionately a much greater number of people and a larger share of our resources to maintaining our ''national overhead''.

The maintenance of communications over great distances and difficult terrain, the provision of essential services of government, both national and local, and the many problems of protecting our people from the rigours of the Canadian weather necessarily absorb the energies of a certain proportion of our population which in the United States would be available for more definitely productive effort. I mention these special problems we have in Canada because they do help to explain why our developed wealth per capita is not as great as yours.

They are circumstances also which we in Canada have to take into account in determining what proportion of our national energies and resources can be devoted to defence.

We all entertained high hopes of a peaceful world in 1945; but our disillusionment came with unhappy speed. The United Nations was not able to organize the police force envisaged in the Charter to provide adequate security for those of us who really wanted peace, and as a second best we were obliged, for our security, to enter into regional or limited arrangements for which the Charter provided.

One such regional arrangement, the North Atlantic alliance, has been in existence for four years; and there is no doubt that its existence has helped the free world muster its strength; and has thereby removed the temptation to easy aggression in Europe.

The North Atlantic alliance was not made in opposition to the United Nations, but, as I have just said, within the framework of the Charter. For us in the free world both have the same aim—the preservation of peace. The U.N. was true to that aim when it decreed and organized resistance to naked aggression in Korea, a resistance which thanks largely to the heroic and massive efforts of this country and the Republic of Korea has also reduced the dangers of a third world war.

In these enterprises for the achievement of a peaceful world Canada has been proud to march at the side of the United States, and to recognize the leadership this great country was providing for the free and independent nations. We are proud also that, so far, we have been able to meet our military and political commitments to the United Nations and the North Atlantic alliance.

Though our contribution and our sacrifices are not mathematically comparable with yours, we Canadians have the third largest force of the United Nations in Korea, aside from the courageous South Koreans themselves; we have a brigade group—I think you would call it a regimental combat team—in the integrated force in Germany; we have nine fighter squadrons equipped with the most up-to-date jet fighter aircraft already in Europe, and we plan to have our air division of twelve squadrons completed by the end of this year; we are adding considerably to our naval strength for the defence of the North Atlantic and the Atlantic sea lanes; and we are providing mutual aid to our North Atlantic partners at a rate which is comparable with yours when account is taken of our smaller national income. In fact our whole defence programme which was put in motion subsequent to the outbreak in Korea now takes up about 45% of our budget.

And I am certain that if the call should ever come again for Canadians to defend the free world against wholesale aggression, that call would be answered with the same response that was made in 1914 and 1939.

But, like the United States, Canada wants to prevent a third world war, not to fight one.

In building up our strength to prevent another war, there has been the closest and most continuous cooperation with our opposite numbers here in Washington at every level. We recognize that nothing is more essential to our national security than such co-operation.

But we want that co-operation to remain, as it has been, co-operation between two distinct countries. Much as we like you Americans, we want to remain Canadians.

We agree with you on most things that are fundamental—we have the same basic views on liberty and democracy—but there are differences between us, too, and we are stubborn enough often to prefer our own ways. Canada's decision to be a distinct and independent nation was made years ago and we can all take it as a fact now that we will continue to exist side by side as two separate nations, though moving along with other free nations to that closer and closer co-operation which is required by the facts of life in this second half of the twentieth century.

Americans and Canadians are proud of their close friendship based on mutual respect. We can be just as proud of the co-operation we have achieved in providing for our common defence. This co-operation is all the more effective because it is solidly based on respect for each other's rights, responsibilities and interests.

Despite what has been happening in recent weeks, the necessity for this defence co-operation remains. I do not think we can afford to act on the assumption that the so-called cold war will thaw out over night. Your President has wisely said that we must be prepared to examine all overtures in good faith, but he has also warned us that it would be very foolish to accept words in place of deeds and to decide that conciliatory gestures can by themselves remove the danger that threatens our security.

We can only afford to lessen the measures we have taken for our defence after positive proof by the Soviet Union that it has truly abandoned any aggressive or subversive designs.

There is however a danger in thinking that the free nations can make themselves secure through military strength alone. Military strength is indispensable, but we must also find the means to maintain and develop the measure of social justice and economic opportunity we have achieved in our own countries, and we must work for the extension beyond our countries of human well-being and of that basic human equality which is the hallmark of a genuinely free society.

If we are not willing to do that, how can we expect to convince others that our way of life has more to offer than Communism.

Therefore, while we are strengthening the free nations of Western Europe and halting aggression in Korea, we cannot afford to overlook those vast areas and populations in Asia and Africa and even in this hemisphere where mass poverty prevails. It is not very helpful to preach the abstract advantages of freedom to men and women who are suffering from misery and starvation.

And here may I say publicly what I have already said privately to President Eisenhower, and that is how impressed we were with the speech he delivered to the American Society of Newspaper Editors about the middle of last month. Then he set forth in clear and simple words the aspirations of freedom-loving men. Let us hope that the Communist leaders of the world will heed them and show by their deeds that they really want peace.

If the free world is to be strong and prosperous and therefore able to deal effectively with threats to its freedom, the economies of the free nations must be as strong and prosperous as they can be made. Free men will stand strong in defence of freedom, even in the face of great hardship; but it is too much to expect them to remain steadfast indefinitely if the future holds little for them and their families but austerity and the fear of depression. Unless the national economies of the free world can be made and kept healthy and productive, Communism could win a bloodless victory without any war, hot or cold. And most of us think that to keep the free nations economically sound there must be a high and expanding level of international trade.

We all know how great was the disruption of the economies of Europe after the last war. We know how shattered Germany and Japan were after their defeats. If all these nations and the nations of the Middle and Far East not now subject to Communist domination are to achieve political stability, it seems imperative for them to have stable markets in which they can sell a reasonable proportion of the goods they produce so they can buy the essentials they need. And for most countries of the world the United States appears to be the greatest potential market and source of supply.

What many of these countries would wish to sell you does not amount to very much in proportion to your total national wealth but it is often vital to them.

The United States would seem to have little to fear from wholesome competition with the other nations of the free world. Is your economy not too strong and are your industries not too productive to be in any serious danger from imports? American business has always proclaimed its faith in the wholesome effects of honest competition. Is it not then the part of wisdom to widen the area of competitive trade and see if more nations cannot make their own way into prosperity and strength?

Many of us feel that the United States has a very direct interest in seeing the countries of the free world earn more dollars. Since the last war billions of American dollars have been raised every year by taxes on United States citizens to be spent on mutual aid or defence support in other countries—to help in keeping the economies and defences of the free world strong. Canada does not receive such assistance; in fact we also contribute to it.

"Trade not aid" sounds like a good slogan and every North American should consider what it implies.

Every new dollar the free countries can earn through added trade with the United States or Canada will help diminish the burden of special assistance on the American and Canadian taxpayer. Would that not be better for the morale and relations of the free world?

If however real progress is to be made in freeing trade, the United States will have to give a bold lead. You have doubtless heard enough of the criticisms which other people—and many of your own people —have directed at the present level of your tariffs, the obstacles presented by your customs procedures and certain other features of your country's commercial policies. These criticisms do not reflect any lack of appreciation of the constructive efforts of the United States in many directions since the war. They reflect rather the recognition by all of us of the crucial importance of your position.

As between Canada and the United States there are special considerations. Over many years now we have built up the highest level of trade between two countries that the world has ever seen. This vast exchange of goods for the common advantage of our two peoples is a thing of utmost value. It is a fundamental part of the good relations between our countries; it underlies the welfare of our peoples and it is essential to the strength and prosperity of this continent—the bastion of the free world. It seems to us of the gravest importance that no retrograde steps be taken that would imperil this great structure and it must be seen as a whole or it can very easily be imperilled. We cannot nibble at this corner here and knock out that piece there to protect some special interest without weakening the entire fabric. That is why we in Canada, like the other free countries, so greatly hope that over the next few months your country will avoid taking any backward steps and will move rapidly as possible towards the kind of commercial policy which is required in your own interest and in that of the whole free world. Both the United States and Canada badly need strong friends and allies. To have them and to hold them requires trade policies that are those of good neighbours.

In addition to defence and trade I think I would be betraying no secrets if I intimated to you that the President and I have been talking about the St. Lawrence Seaway and Power Project. This of course is something mainly of North American concern and of perhaps even greater concern to Canadians than to Americans.

Although some of your compatriots may not agree with us, we are convinced that the completion of this undertaking will make a really significant contribution to the wealth and strength and hence to the security of our two countries.

All American administrations for the past 25 or 30 years have approved of the Seaway, and surely no one can justify opposition to the harnessing of the power which the bounty of Providence has placed in the St. Lawrence River.

In 1941 an agreement between our two governments was made for the joint development of the international section of the St. Lawrence Waterway. Your Congress did not see fit to approve the agreement, which of course was within its constitutional right and we Canadians do not complain of that.

But when it appeared to us in 1951 that eventual ratification was unlikely, the Canadian government decided that it would embark on this project of deepening the existing navigation channels on its own.

We Canadians are most conscious of the benefits that the United States as well as Canada will enjoy in the improvement of this international section of the St. Lawrence by admitting coastal and oceangoing vessels to our Great Lakes ports. We are most anxious to get on with the job, because of the increasing need for water-carried traffic and because of the interest of Ontario and New York in the hydro-electric potential which will be harnessed in conjunction with this development. Approval was quickly received from the International Joint Commission for the power project and, in Canada, the province of Ontario really needs this additional electrical energy and is able and ready and anxious to build its share of the power works, which, of course, require a dam extending from either side of the River and meeting in midstream. In the United States the New York State Power Authority is anxious to proceed with the American share of the undertaking as soon as it can get a licence from the Federal Power Commission to which it applied last October after the favourable decision of the International Joint Commission was announced. We in Canada are waiting anxiously for the results of that application because without the dam the development of the seaway itself cannot be started.

These then are some of the matters we have been discussing. Primarily, though, the purpose of my visit has been, as I said earlier, to continue that warm and friendly relationship which has long existed between the heads of the governments of our two countries.

That personal contact helps to maintain the unique relationship between Canada and the United States.

I had occasion to put our relationship in what I believe is its proper perspective two years ago when I had the honour of introducing Mr. Vincent Auriol, the President of the French Republic, to our Canadian Parliament. Since I was not then speaking to Americans, I can repeat my words without any fear of being charged with flattering you. President Auriol had just come to Canada after spending a few days in the United States and that was why I said: "Here in Canada you will not fail to note the close, friendly relations which bind us to our southern neighbours, and also the untrammelled independence we enjoy in our own land. If our frontiers bordered on those of some grasping imperialistic neighbouring state, we might not have this opportunity of welcoming you in a free parliament as the distinguished and respected head of a free France. Canada is, I think, the best evidence, permanent and historic evidence, of the peaceful purposes of the United States."

2. Joint Statement of President Eisenhower and Prime Minister St. Laurent Following Discussions, May 8, 1953

(PP/Dwight D. Eisenhower, Vol. 1953, No. 70, pp. 275-77)

The President of the United States, the Secretary of State, and other members of the Cabinet have held discussions during the last two days with the Canadian Prime Minister, Mr. Louis S. St. Laurent, and the Secretary of State for External Affairs, Mr. L. B. Pearson. The meeting continued a long standing practice of visits exchanged across the border between Prime Ministers of Canada and Presidents of the United States. The conversations consisted of a full and frank exchange of views on the world situation in general and on United States-Canadian relations in particular. They were conducted in that spirit of friendship and cooperation which has long been characteristic of official discussions between the two Governments and they revealed a far-reaching identity of objectives.

In a survey of the world situation today, the President and the Prime Minister gave particular emphasis to recent developments in the USSR and the Soviet orbit and their effects upon the free nations of the world. It was agreed that while every effort should be made to bring about a relaxation of current tensions, the free nations could not afford to diminish their efforts toward the achievement of united strength and ability to meet aggression. Acts, not words, would be proof of Communist intentions. Though recent developments in Korea where Canadian and United States troops are fighting side by side have seemed more hopeful, nevertheless, in Laos a new act of aggression has been committed which might have serious consequences for Thailand and the whole of Southeast Asia. These developments in Southeast Asia must cast doubt on Communist intentions.

In the discussions on the European area, emphasis was placed on the necessity of maintaining the momentum of vigorous support for NATO. The achievements of the recent NATO Ministerial meeting were noted with satisfaction. It was agreed that both countries must continue to do their full share to further NATO objectives.

Views were exchanged concerning progress made toward the expansion of world trade. It was recalled that trade between the United States and Canada is greater than that between any other two countries. The Prime Minister stressed the great importance attached by Canada to the liberation and expansion of world trade and expressed the hope that the United States would play a role of leadership in this field. The President stated that, as an interim step, the Administration has recommended to the Congress the one-year renewal of the Reciprocal Trade Act and intends to submit to the Congress shortly its proposals regarding Customs simplification. The President also pointed out that he has recommended to the Congress the establishment of a Commission to study all aspects of United States economic foreign policy so that future policies will be comprehensive, constructive and consistent.

The Prime Minister emphasized the importance to Canada of an early start on the St. Lawrence project and the especial urgency to Canada of the power development. The President assured the Prime Minister that the United States is fully aware of Canada's urgent need for St. Lawrence power. He said that he favored the development of the United States share of St. Lawrence power under the authority of New York State and that he hoped for an early favorable decision by the Federal Power Commission in this matter. The President in this connection referred to the decision of the Cabinet on this subject announced today. The Prime Minister said that the Canadian Government was still prepared to discuss United States participation in the international section, provided that arrangements for power construction are completed and provided the whole seaway would not be delayed. He stressed again Canada's readiness to proceed at once with the work under the Canadian St. Lawrence legislation of 1951.

Recognizing the importance to the free world of the adequate defense of the North American continent, the President and the Prime Minister emphasized the desirability and effectiveness of cooperation on the basis of the Ogdensburg Declaration of 1940, which established the Permanent Joint Board on Defense between Canada and the United States. Post-war arrangements for continental defense have continued in this framework. It was recognized by the Prime Minister and the President that joint defense facilities erected in Canada under these arrangements strengthen the defense and the security of both Canada and the United States. The President assured the Prime Minister that the United States, for its part in such joint actions, will continue scrupulously to respect Canadian sovereignty.

The Prime Minister and the President reaffirmed the importance of continuing the wholehearted cooperation between the two countries in the field of continental defense, and in the wider field of international action designed to preserve and strengthen peace.

3. Prime Minister St. Laurent's Report of Meeting to the Canadian House of Commons, May 9, 1953

(CHCD, May 9, 1953, pp. 5055-57, 5063)

Mr. Chairman, if you could be somewhat indulgent about the pertinency of the few remarks I wish to make to the item of the estimates under discussion, perhaps hon. members would be glad to have just a short report on the visit which the Secretary of State for External Affairs and I have just made to Washington. I can assure hon. members that it was most interesting and extremely pleasant, and I think we have some good reason to expect that it will bear some fruit. I found that the President, his cabinet ministers, the heads of departments and the leaders in the two houses of congress were anxious to give us a great deal of time in order to discuss with us the problems that were of mutual concern to us and to them; and in the course of those discussions they were most sympathetic and most anxious to ascertain all the possible implications of whatever might be contemplated or done on either side of our boundary.

I have just had time barely to glance at our Canadian newspapers but, from what I have been able to see in the less than an hour since I left the plane, there have been fairly full reports of what took place, although I have not seen in the papers the complete text of the communique that was issued last night after the second quite long interview in his own office with the President and several of his cabinet colleagues. Perhaps it might be convenient if I tabled a copy of that communique. (See previous entry.)

Hon. members will have noted the reference to a cabinet decision announced earlier before the communique was put out. In the headlines in the morning *Citizen* I see this: ''New Problem in Issue of Seaway''. It may create a new problem of express new urgency in connection with what will have to be done by our good friends in the United States, but it creates no new problem for us. Our position remains the same. At the present time the only thing that is under consideration officially is the application of the state of New York with respect to the power development. If there is an early and favourable decision, as the President has expressed the hope there will be, then we are in a position to go ahead right away with both the power development and our part of the undertaking to provide a seaway even in the international section; but we will still be disposed to listen to and discuss any proposal that might come from our United States friends, provided that it can be made and discussed and disposed of in such a manner as not to retard the completion of the project.

It is necessary in the United States that there be some legislation.

There is no legislation now under which any agency of the United States can act to take part in the development of the seaway, but there are preposals before congress. I felt quite satisfied that this cabinet decision was intended to intimate that the time was growing short. There was this application; but there was the hope of the President and the administration that the application would receive an early favourable decision and that therefore the way would be opened to act, and that if they were really anxious in wishing to have some part now in providing the seaway there ought to be action and speedy action. I take it that that was the purpose of this statement or this declaration by the cabinet.

I was asked by the press club yesterday when I expected there would be a decision. I had to say of course that while I was a lawyer I never ventured to predict when a decision in a case that had been taken under advisement would be handed down. But I am quite satisfied that the administration is doing everything that it would be proper for it to do to have the federal power commission realize that an early decision is desirable, and that the present administration feels that that decision should be in the form of granting the application of the state of New York.

There were of course quite lengthy discussions about trade. Perhaps hon. members will have noted the summary of the very encouraging speech made by the President in New York on Thursday evening. The headline is: "Ike calls world trade vital. Says policy is essential to American prosperity. Stand is opposed to that of some in party clamouring for high tariffs."

Well, I found that that was the attitude of the President and his cabinet colleagues. Of course they are not in a position to forecast what congress will do or may do; but I was speaking with several of the leaders, both of the Senate and of the House of Representatives, and those I had the opportunity of speaking to seemed to share the views of the President with respect to the interest of the United States in expansion of world trade. It emboldened me to say at the press club yesterday that we were very hopeful there would be nothing done in the United States that could be regarded as a retrograde step at this time instead of an advance toward the liberation and expansion of world trade.

On the whole I think the atmosphere that grows out of these personal contacts is of value, just as I thought was of value the atmosphere that prevailed and the form of relations that grew out of the conference of the commonwealth prime ministers in London last November and December. I am confident that we shall again find at the next conference the same sincere desire to co-operate, in spite of the difficulties which are serious and which exist in all our various areas. We shall find the same unanimity about objectives, and the same sincere desire to co-operate again in the manner that will be most apt to enable us all to achieve those objectives.

The President and his colleagues expressed the hope that there would be other opportunities for these personal contacts, and I told him that I was not speaking as the leader of a party. I left with him a copy of the unanimous resolution that had been passed by this house and I told him that the Secretary of State for External Affairs (Mr. Pearson) and I were there speaking for the people of Canada and not for any one party of the people of Canada. . . .

This morning before leaving Washington I met some of our Canadian newsmen and, in discussing with them what had taken place, I incidentally referred to the fact—as indicative of the genuine desire to find helpful ways of overcoming possible embarrassments—that a suggestion had been made that we might possibly have a joint committee that would look into possible sources of embarrassment and to try to suggest ways of relieving those sources of embarrassment without creating greater difficulties. The fact that we had a permanent joint board on defence was referred to in the discussions as a board that had been very helpful in removing possible causes of embarrassment.

The President asked the secretary of state and Mr. Pearson, who were there, to look into the matter and see if there could not be something suggested that would be a board or committee to which grievances could be referred. That committee or board could make suggestion as to how such matters could best be handled without creating any appearance of retrograde steps in the liberalism of trade policies—and that is to be looked into.

Hon. members know that we have that kind of committee with the United Kingdom which makes suggestions for the improvement of trade. I omitted mentioning this matter and I have heard since that it is going to be referred to in the reports of the conversation I had with our Canadian newsmen this morning. I would not want members of parliament to feel that I had intentionally withheld anything at all in respect of the discussions I had. I think that the Secretary of State for External Affairs (Mr. Pearson) and I took that as quite a strong indication of the president's sincere desire to avoid having things done that would be disturbing and remain disturbing. . . .

The matter did not go very far. It was just something that was incidentally referred to. The president turned and said to the secretary of state: ''I want you and Mr. Pearson to look into that and suggest something which you think could help us.'' It did not get beyond that.

The permanent joint board was referred to, and that is a board of appointees of the two governments who go into like matters, examine them carefully and make recommendations. The board does not make binding decisions; it makes recommendations to the government and its work has been extremely helpful and I think it is one of the contributing factors to this background, which enables the president to say: ''Whatever we do in your country, we are going to respect your sovereignty.''

D.   Prime Minister Louis S. St. Laurent And President Dwight D. Eisenhower, Ottawa, Ontario, November 13-15, 1953

1. Prime Minister St. Laurent's Introduction of President Eisenhower to Both Houses of the Canadian Parliament, November 14, 1953

(CHCD, Appendix, November 13, 1953, Address of Dwight D. Eisenhower, pp. 23-24)

Mr. President, members of the Parliament of Canada, we are greatly honoured by the presence here today of the President of the United States of America. I am sure that I speak not only for those who are seated in this chamber but for all of our fellow Canadians, Mr. President, when I say to you how pleased we are that you have been able to pay another visit to our capital city, this time as the first citizen of your great country.

My words in this chamber do not always meet with unanimous approval, but I know I can say, with absolutely no risk of dissent this time, that we are all most happy that the President is accompanied by his charming wife.

Your visit, sir, marks the third time that the chief of state of the United States has paid a visit to the capital city of Canada. Just ten years ago your great wartime president honoured us by coming to Ottawa after the first of those historic conferences in Quebec. Mr. Roosevelt set a precedent which I hope will continue to be followed in the future. There can surely be no more tangible evidence of the friendly relationship which exists between our two peoples than friendly visits of this kind between representatives of our two nations.

When I had the privilege of being your guest in Washington earlier this year, Mr. President, I found evidence among all those whom I was privileged to meet of a warm and friendly feeling for the people of Canada. That is only one reason why I hope—and all Canadians both in this chamber and outside will share that hope—that you will return to Washington with an increased consciousness of our high regard for the American people and for yourself. We would also like you to know that we are grateful for the leadership your nation is providing in the common effort of free men and women to make our world a safer and better place for future generations.

This leadership given by the United States is moreover untainted by any desire for national self-aggrandizement. By positive and unselfish actions, which are unique in history, the American people have recognized that threats to the safety and well-being of liberty-loving peoples anywhere are threats to all peoples everywhere who believe in the dignity and freedom of the individual. Your nation's contributions to the restoration of war-devastated lands have been generous to an extent unprecedented in international relations. Your example, as a member of the United Nations, of vigorous and immediate resistance to wanton aggression has revived the hopes of anxious peoples that, through collective action, international peace may be secured and maintained.

The characteristically energetic manner in which the United States has fulfilled the responsibilities it has voluntarily assumed has been interpreted by a few detractors as an indication that your country is seeking to impose its policies on or dominate the life of other free nations.

We Canadians are in the best position to know how false are such suspicions. Although your population and your economic and military strength are many times greater than ours, we have no fear that this strength will be used to threaten or overawe us. We are the more secure because you are a good as well as a strong neighbour. No guns have been fired in anger across our borders for almost a century and a half. The only invasions from the south are of the annual friendly variety when millions of your compatriots travel north to share in the enjoyment of our great natural recreational facilities and perhaps to feel the pulse of our growth. Canadians in their turn retaliate by moving in large numbers to experience the entertainment and cultural advantages of your great cities and to bask in the sun of your semi-tropical southlands.

Of course, there are many strong American influences on Canadian life, but these have not prevented the growth of a distinct Canadian feeling and culture, which flourishes and will continue to develop alongside the influences of your dynamic society. This is as it should be, for our own history teaches us that co-operation can be closer when differences are recognized. Likewise, the co-operation between our two countries is deep and close because it is free and desired, not something imposed upon a reluctant people by a powerful neighbour.

We in Canada also feel, Mr. President, that the powerful influence which your nation exerts in the world community is, in action as well as in aim, an influence for good, and we welcome it.

Together, the United States and Canada prove to the world that a great power and a lesser power can work in harmony without the smaller being submerged by his bigger neighbour. We Canadians know that in the interests of our mutual defence we can wisely and safely pool many of our military resources with yours in a security system which is genuinely collective. We know, too, that through the instruments of diplomacy and through direct negotiation we can solve amicably and justly the many problems which arise along our lengthy common border. Sometimes we may wish they could be solved more rapidly, but we know they can be solved in the end. And we also know that when the Canadian view on any matter is different from the American view, our opinions will be listened to with patience and respect.

That our two nations get along so well is due in no small part to the leaders whom the American people, in their wisdom, have chosen. It is particularly gratifying to Canadians to see in you, Mr. President, the Supreme Commander of the second world war, under whose inspiring leadership the fighting men and women of Canada made their contribution to victory, and to see in you also the first Supreme Commander in Europe of the North Atlantic alliance. In that capacity you received into your command the Canadian brigade group in Germany and laid the plans for the Canadian air division which is now in Europe.

As a supreme commander in war and in peace, and as the political head of your nation, you have justly earned a reputation for fair-mindedness and friendliness, sincerity and integrity. Those are noble qualities. They no doubt are the qualities which inspired the editorial writer of one of our leading newspapers on learning of your visit to this country to say:

> The President of the United States will be welcome to Canada, welcome not only as head of a great world power but as a man we have already met and liked, admired and respected.

Mr. President, in this country and in this house where there are two official languages, I wish also to tell you in the language of my French ancestors that all my fellow citizens of the same origin as mine are just as happy as our English-speaking Canadians to have this opportunity of wishing you and Mrs. Eisenhower the heartiest welcome and to assure you of our highest consideration.

2. Address of President Eisenhower to Both Houses of Parliament, November 14, 1953

(*Ibid.*, pp. 24-28)

. . . I also extend greetings to my French-speaking Canadian friends. I know that I am very foolhardy in even trying to express myself in this tongue. Therefore, I crave your indulgence for all the mistakes which I may make in personally and directly expressing to you my feelings of friendship and of high esteem.

I salute you also for the important part which you have played, in co-operation with your English-speaking fellow citizens, in the development of this great country.

Mr. Prime Minister, for the very great generosity of the personal welcome that you have expressed toward me I am humbly grateful; as well as for the reception that Mrs. Eisenhower and I have experienced here and throughout this city. We should like to extend to all your people our very deep appreciation, especially for the honour of being received before this body. I assure you that you have given us distinction that we shall never forget.

Since World War II I have now been privileged three times to visit this great country and this beautiful city.

On my first visit, more than seven years ago, I came to express to the Canadian people a field commander's appreciation of their memorable contribution in the liberation of the Mediterranean and European lands. On my second, I came to discuss with your governmental leaders your country's role in the building of Atlantic security. Both visits, in the warmth and spirit of a great people's welcome, were days that I shall remember all my life.

This day I again salute the men and women of Canada.

As I stand before you, my thoughts go back to the days of global war. In that conflict, and then through the more recent savage and grievous Korean battles, the Canadian people have been valorous champions of freedom for mankind. Within the framework of NATO, in the construction of new patterns of international security, in the lengthy and often toilsome exploration of a regional alliance, they have been patient and wise devisers of a stout defence for the western world. Canada, rich in natural gifts, far richer in human character and genius, has earned the gratitude and the affectionate respect of all who cherish freedom and seek peace.

I am highly honoured by the invitation of the parliament of Canada that I address it. For your invitation is rooted in the friendship and sense of partnership that for generations have been the hallmark of relations between Canada and the United States. Your country, my country —each is a better and stronger and more influential nation because each can rely upon every resource of the other in days of crisis. Beyond this each can work and grow and prosper with the other through years of quiet peace.

We of our country have long respected and admired Canada as a bulwark of the British commonwealth and a leader among nations. As no Soviet wile or lure can divide the commonwealth, nothing will corrupt the Canadian-American partnership.

We have a dramatic symbol of that partnership in the favoured topic of every speaker addressing an audience made up of both our peoples—our unfortified frontier. But though this subject has become shopworn and well-nigh exhausted as a feature of after-dinner oratory, it is still a fact that our common frontier grows stronger every year, defended only by friendship. Its strength wells from indestructible and enduring sources—identical ideals of family and school and church, and traditions which come to us from a common past.

Out of this partnership has evolved a progressive prosperity and a general well-being, mutually beneficial, that is without parallel on earth. In the years ahead, the pace of our mutual growth will surely be no less.

To strive, even dimly, to foresee the wonders of Canada's next generation is to summon the utmost powers of the imagination. This land is a mighty reservoir of resources. Across it, at this moment, there moves an extraordinary drama of enterprise and endeavour —Canadians, rapidly building basic industries, converting waters into hydoelectric energy, scrutinizing your soil for new wealth, pushing into the barrens of the north for minerals and oil. You of Canada are building a magnificent record of achievement, and my country rejoices in it.

More than friendship and partnership is signified in the relations between our countries. These relations that today enrich our peoples justify the faith of our fathers that men, given self-government, can dwell at peace among themselves, progressive in the development of their material wealth, quick to join in the defence of their spiritual community, ready to arbitrate differences that may rise to divide them. This parliament is an illustrious symbol of a human craving, a human search, a human right to self-government.

All the free legislatures of the world speak for the free peoples of the world. In their deliberations and enactments they mirror the ideas, the traditions, the fundamental philosophies of their respective nations.

On the other hand, every free nation, secure in its own economic and political stability, reflects the responsible leadership and the wise comprehension which its legislature has brought to the management of public affairs.

This continent uniquely has been a laboratory of self-government, in which free legislatures have been an indispensable force. What is the result? It is a mighty unity built of values essentially spiritual.

This continent, of course, is a single physical and geographical entity. But physical unity, however, broken by territorial lines, fortress chains and trade barriers, is a characteristic of every continent. Here, however, independent and sovereign peoples have built a stage on which all the world can see:

First, each country's patriotic dedication to its own enlightened self-interest, free from vicious nationalistic exploitation of grudge or ancient wrong.

Second, a joint recognition that neighbours, among nations as among individuals, prosper best in neighbourly co-operation, factually exemplified in daily life.

Third, an international will to cast out the bomb and the gun as arbiters and to exalt the joint search for truth and justice.

Here on this continent we present an example that other nations some day surely will recognize and apply in their relationships among themselves. My friends, may that day be close because the only alternative—the bankruptcy of armament races and the suicide of nuclear war—cannot for long, must not for long, be tolerated by the human race. Great has been our mutual progress. It foreshadows what we together can accomplish for our mutual good.

Before us of Canada and the United States lies an immense panorama of opportunity in every field of human endeavour. A host of jobs to be done together confront us. Many of them cry for immediate attention. As we examine them together in the work days ahead, we must never allow the practical difficulties that impede progress to blind our eyes to the objectives established by principle and logic.

With respect to some aspects of our future development I hope I may, without presumption, make three observations.

The first is: The free world must come to recognize that trade barriers, although intended to protect a country's economy, often in fact shackle its prosperity. In the United States there is a growing recognition that free nations cannot expand their productivity and economic strength without a high level of international trade.

In our case, our two economies are enmeshed intricately with the world economy. Obviously we cannot risk sudden dislocation in industry and agriculture and widespread unemployment and distress, by hasty decisions to accomplish suddenly what inevitably will come in an orderly economic evolution. "Make haste slowly" is a homely maxim with international validity.

Moreover, every common undertaking, however worth while it may be, must be understood in its origins, its application, its effects by the peoples of our two countries. Without this understanding it will have negligible chance of success. Canadians and citizens of the United States do not accept government by edict or decree. Informed and intelligent co-operation is, for us, the only source of enduring accomplishment.

To study further the whole subject of United States foreign economic policy, we have at home appointed a special commission with wide representation, including members of the congress as well as spokesmen for the general public. From the commission's studies will come, we hope, a policy which can command the support of the American people and which will be in the best interests of the United States and the free world.

Toward the strengthening of commercial ties between Canada and the United States, officials of our two governments have for some months been considering the establishment of a joint economic and trade committee. This committee, now approved, will consist of cabinet officers of both countries. They will meet periodically to discuss in broad terms economic and trade problems and the means for their equitable solution. I confidently believe that out of this process the best interests of both our countries will be more easily harmonized and advanced.

The second observation is this: Joint development and use of the St. Lawrence-Great Lakes waterway is inevitable, is sure and certain. With you, I consider this measure a vital addition to our economic and national security. Of course, no proposal yet made is entirely free from faults of some sort. But every one of them can be corrected, given patience and co-operation.

In the United States my principal security advisers, comprising the national security council, favour the undertaking for national defence reasons. The cabinet favours it on both security and economic grounds. A committee of the United States Senate has approved a measure authorizing it.

This measure provides for United States participation in a joint development by both countries. The proposal now awaits action by the United States Senate which, I am confident, will act favourably on it or some similar measure. The ways and means for assuring American co-operation in this great project will, I hope, be authorized and approved during the coming session of the congress.

I have noted with satisfaction the New York power authority's acceptance of the federal power commission's licence. With this act the stage is set for a start on the St. Lawrence power project which will add materially to the economic strength of both countries.

My third observation is this: You of Canada and we of the United States can and will devise ways to protect our North America from any surprise attack by air. And we shall achieve the defence of our continent without whittling our pledges to western Europe or forgetting our friends in the Pacific.

The basic threat of communist purpose still exists. Indeed the latest Soviet communication to the western world is truculent, if not arrogant, in tone. In any event our security plans must now take into account Soviet ability to employ atomic attack on North America as well as on countries, friendly to us, lying closer to the borders of the U.S.S.R. Their atomic stockpile will, of course, increase in size, and means of delivery will improve as time goes on.

Each of our two nations seeks a secure home for realization of its destiny. Defence of our soil presents a challenge to both our peoples. It is a common task. Defensively, as well as geographically, we are joined beyond any possibililty of separation. This element in our security problem is an accepted guide of service leaders, government officials and legislatures on both sides of the border.

In our approach to the problem, we both realize that purest patriotism demands and promotes effective partnership. Thus we evolve joint agreements on all those measures we must jointly undertake to improve the effectiveness of our defences, but every arrangement rests squarely on the sovereign nature of each of our two peoples.

Canada and the United States are equal partners and neither dares to waste time. There is a time to be alert and a time to rest. These days demand ceaseless vigilance. We must be ready and prepared. The threat is present. The measures of defence have been thoroughly studied by official bodies of both countries. The permanent joint board on defence has worked assiduously and effectively on mutual problems. Now is the time for action on all agreed measures.

Steps to defend our continent are of course but one part of the world-wide security program. The North Atlantic Treaty Organization, for example, is an essential defence for Ottawa, for Washington, and for our neighbours to the south, as well as for communities thousands of miles to the eastward. Implicit in the consultations and detailed studies which must continue and in the defences which we have already mounted is the need for world-wide vigilance and strength. But the purpose is defence. We have no other aim.

In common with others of the free world, the United States does not rely on military strength alone to win the peace. Our primary reliance is a unity among us forged of common adherence to moral principles. This reliance binds together in fellowship all those who believe in the spiritual nature of man, as the child of God.

Moreover, our country assuredly claims no monopoly on wisdom. We are willing, nay, anxious, to discuss with friends and with any others all possible paths to peace. We will use every means, from the normal diplomatic exchange to the forum of the United Nations, to further this search. We welcome ideas, expressions of honest difference, new proposals and new interpretations of old ones—anything and everything honestly offered for the advancement of man's oldest aspiration.

There are no insoluble problems. Differences can be resolved; tensions can be relieved. The free world, I deeply believe, holds firmly to this faith, striving earnestly towards what is just and equitable.

My friends, allow me to interpolate here an expression of my own personal faith. I call upon all of you who were in responsible positions, either in civil government or in the military world, in the dark days of 1940, 1941 and 1942. There seemed no place from which to start to conquer the enemy that bid fair to enslave us all. Already he had put most of Europe under his heel. I stop to think of the bewilderment of our people, the fears of our people in those days, and then of how in a few short years we were coming home to celebrate that great victory that we thought could at last mark the end of all wars. We see how fast human outlook can change from one of despondency, almost of despair in many quarters, to one of exultation. Today as we fail to understand the intransigence that we feel marks others, as we try to colour every proposal we make with what we believe to be reason, understanding, even sympathy, as we are nonplussed as to why these offers are never taken up, let us never despair that faith will win through.

The world that God has given us is of course material, intellectual and spiritual in its values. We have to hand over to those who come after us this balance of values, and particularly the certainty that they can enjoy the same kind of opportunity in this spiritual, intellectual and material world that we, who will then be their ancestors, enjoyed before them. That, it seems to me, is the real problem that Canada and the United States today face together. It is one reason I get such a thrill every time I come to this country, because here I sense in the very atmosphere your determination to work in that direction, not acknowledging defeat, certain that we can win, because there are values that man treasures above all things else in the world.

The free world believes that practical problems should be solved practically, that they should be solved by orderly procedure, step by step, so that the foundation for peace, which we are building in concert with other nations, will be solid and unshakeable. I deem it a high privilege to salute, through this their parliament, the Canadian people for the strength they have added to this faith and for the contribution they are making toward its realization.

Beyond the shadow of the atomic cloud, the horizon is bright with promise. No shadow can halt our advance together. For we, Canada and the United States, shall use carefully and wisely the God-given graces of faith and reason as we march together toward the horizon of a world where each man, each family, each nation, lives at peace in a climate of freedom.

3. *Joint Statement of Prime Minister St. Laurent and President Eisenhower Following Discussions, November 14, 1953*

(PP/Dwight D. Eisenhower, Vol. 1953, No. 247, pp. 776-77)

The following joint communique was issued by President Eisenhower and Prime Minister St. Laurent at the conclusion of the meeting of the Canadian Cabinet.

1. During the course of President Eisenhower's state visit to Canada, the Prime Minister of Canada and members of the Canadian Cabinet had an opportunity of having informal discussions with him on matters of mutual interest to the United States and Canada. The President and

the Prime Minister last reviewed some of these questions when the Prime Minister visited Washington last May.

2. Views were exchanged on recent developments in the world situation and on measures which might bring about a relaxation of current international tensions. It was agreed that all efforts for peace and improved world conditions being made by the United Nations or elsewhere should be supported and the necessity of maintaining the strength, unity and determination of the free world to resist aggression was fully recognized.

3. The President and the Prime Minister agreed on the importance to the free world of healthy national economies and of the expansion of world trade on a multilateral basis. Satisfaction was expressed at the recent establishment of a joint United States-Canadian Committee on Trade and Economic Affairs. The importance of the St. Lawrence Seaway and Power Project was emphasized, and there was full agreement on the urgency of initiating the first phase—construction of the Power Project in accordance with arrangements which already have been made between the two governments.

4. In discussing the means of strengthening the security of the free world, the importance of collective arrangements under the North Atlantic Treaty Organization was emphasized, including the special responsibility of the United States and Canada for building up the defenses of this continent. There was complete agreement on the vital importance of effective methods for joint defense, especially in the light of evidence of increasing technical capability of direct attack on both countries by weapons of great destructive power. Cooperation on joint defense matters had its origin in the Ogdensburg Agreement of 1940 which established the Permanent Joint Board on Defense. In 1947 the two countries issued a joint statement which set forth the principles and methods by which cooperation would be continued and strengthened. The full respect of each country for the sovereignty of the other is inherent in these principles. These principles are equally valid today when Canada and the United States, recognizing that the defense of North America must be considered as a whole, are undertaking further efforts for their joint security. The arrangements for collaboration which have proved satisfactory over the years provide a firm basis on which to carry forward the close relationship between Canada and the United States in matters of common defense.

E. President Dwight D. Eisenhower and Prime Minister Louis S. St. Laurent, White Sulphur Springs, West Virginia, also with President Adolfo Ruiz Cortines of Mexico, March 26-27, 1956

1. Press Conference of President Eisenhower, Washington, D.C., March 7, 1956

(PP/Dwight D. Eisenhower, Vol. 1956, No. 53, pp. 295-96)

. . . Q. William H. Lawrence, New York Times: Mr. President, could you tell us, sir, any of the specific purposes for which you are meeting with the Mexican President and the Canadian Premier at White Sulphur?

THE PRESIDENT: Well, one of the things is in recognition of the fact that the North American Continent is a continent that is bound together by geography; you can't get away from it and therefore we have common problems.

So far as we have common aspirations, common policies, international policies in the world, we have particular relationships with our two big neighbors. So we just want to meet for a chat—talk—with these two people.

You will recall that we meet one evening, we are there all through the next day, and the following day we leave. It is not one of these long international conferences. . . .

2. Prime Minister St. Laurent's Report of Meeting to the Canadian House of Commons, April 9, 1956

(CHCD, April 9, 1956, pp. 2727-28)

. . . This visit took place at White Sulphur Springs on March 26 and 27 between the heads of governments of the United States, Mexico and Canada. The host at this meeting was the President of the United States who in his invitation and subsequently emphasized that it would be of an informal character without agenda for the purpose of exchanging views on matters of mutual interest and of getting to know each other better.

In view of the character of the meeting, no decisions were reached and none was expected. It was, however, from my point of view, both helpful and agreeable to be in a position to discuss current international affairs with the presidents of the United States and Mexico in this informal way. There was also an opportunity to bring up one or two subjects of specific Canadian-United States concern with President Eisenhower and Mr. Dulles.

The general discussion centered largely upon the comprehensive report which Mr. Dulles made on his recent visit to Asia. It has been stated in the press that in the subsequent exchange of views there was an emphatic expression of policy difference between the United States and Canada in respect of coummunist China. The reports in that form are without foundation. It is quite true that both President Eisenhower and Mr. Dulles explained very frankly the reasons why recognition of the communist government at Peking could not be contemplated under present circumstances and why they felt their support should be continued to the government of Chang Kai-shek. However, there was nothing said about the Canadian position which would suggest any change whatsoever from that stated in the house by the Secretary of State for External Affairs (Mr. Pearson) on January 31 either in respect of recognition or of our attitude toward the islands of Quemoy and Matsu off the coast of China.

Each government is fully aware of the position of the other in these matters, as indeed they were before the meeting at White Sulphur Springs. It is true, however, and this was recognized at our recent meeting, that there are many countries which have recognized the Peking regime, and that this has created a problem as to which regime should represent China at the United Nations, a problem which may be expected to grow more acute as time goes on.

There was considerable discussion over the position in the Middle East, the seriousness of which, of course, everyone recognized. It was agreed that, while all possible steps to reduce immediate tension should be taken, peace could only be secured there by an agreed political settlement between Israel and its neighbours, In this connection, the three governments welcomed the expected intervention of the United Nations at this time, since formalized through the resolution which has just been passed unanimously by the security council. I am sure that the Secretary General of the United Nations has our best wishes for success in the very important mission on which he is now engaged in consequence of this resolution.

There was also general discussion of the possible consequences of recent communist party developments in Russia. I got the impression that it was felt that any firm conclusion in regard to the long-range importance of these changes would be premature but that, in any event, they would not warrant any relaxation of effort on our part, either in defence or diplomacy or negotiation.

Consideration was also given to the problems arising out of the emergence of new states in Asia and Africa, states which are as sensitive about their national independence as they are insistent on greater human welfare for their people. In this connection there was an exchange of views as to the desirability of continuing international economic assistance to materially underdeveloped countries, and especially as to the importance of removing any feeling that such assistance on the part of western countries had any ulterior motive or was inspired by any other spirit than good will and understanding. On the Canadian side, we expressed the view that it might help to remove any suspicions of ulterior motives if the United Nations were brought more into the picture than it had been, at least from the point of view of using the organization as a clearing house for plans and policies and information in regard to international assistance schemes. We felt that this had been done with good results in the annual meetings of the ministerial committee of the Colombo plan, and that possibly this practice could be usefully extended to the wider field of the United Nations, so that it would become clear to the whole world community what various countries were doing in this matter and why they were doing it.

In our bilateral talks, I emphasized once again to the President the importance of better-balanced trade between our two countries. I referred to the existing unfavourable balance in our visible trade, and I mentioned that the compensation or correction of this imbalance by capital movements occasionally was the cause of some concern in this country lest the control of our economic development, which should remain in Canadian hands, might be prejudiced thereby.

I also suggested to the President that the time seemed to have come when problems regarding the use of water power on rivers crossing the international boundary might well be studied at a conference between representatives of the two governments. Here I might perhaps extend this a little to answer a question of which notice was telephoned to my office by the hon. member for Kamloops (Mr. Fulton). There was no discussion of the problem, but merely the suggestion that it would probably be desirable at this time to have it studied by a joint conference representing the two governments, to try to get at something which would make for the possibility of expeditious use of these water powers to the best possible advantage of the people who might derive advantage from their use. It was left at that, with the understanding that the subject would be further pursued in discussions between our Department of External Affairs and the Secretary of State of the United States.

Needless to say, the President expressed a very warm feeling for this country and gratification at the way in which relations between our two peoples were based on mutual respect and friendship and frank statement of diverging views, when there were diverging views. He took advantage of the opportunity to mention some concern over the proposed 20 per cent advertising tax on Canadian editions of United States magazines. My explanation to him of the nature and purpose of this proposal will serve, I hope, to lessen his concern about it.

Having to make this statement, I would not want to end it without expressing once again my grateful thanks to the President and the government of the United States for the kindness and friendly hospitality which they showed us during our visit. I would also like to express my sincere appreciation of the opportunity thus afforded to me to become acquainted with the President of Mexico and to renew my acquaintance with the foreign minister of Mexico. It should be a source of real gratification to all Canadians that the relations between Canada and Mexico are developing in such an important and satisfactory way.

F. President Dwight D. Eisenhower and Prime Minister Louis S. St. Laurent, Augusta, Georgia, December 11, 1956

1. Prime Minister St. Laurent's Report of Meeting to the Canadian House of Commons, January 9, 1957

(CHCD, January 9, 1957, pp. 31-32)

. . . I was very happy when, toward the end of my short holiday in Florida, I received a telephone call from the White House that the president would be glad if I would drop off at Augusta, Georgia, on my way back, have lunch with him and have a game of golf. Well I found in fact, you know, that a game of golf with one of those electric go-carts was about the best way to have an international conference because you are getting off the go-cart quite frequently for only a couple of minutes but for time enough to reflect on what has been said up to that moment and to reflect on what is going to be said when you get back on the seat of the go-cart. I can assure the hon. gentlemen that the tone of our conversation and the character of the relationship was somewhat better than would have resulted from any blasting that might have occurred.

I can assure the hon. gentlemen first of all that I expressed some considerable gratification at the fact that he had been able to turn down the recommendation of the tariff board there that there be such an increase in tariff on fish from our Canadian fisheries as would seriously interfere with the continuance of that trade which is very vital to a substantial portion of the population of the Atlantic area. I was very glad to find that the President agreed with the suggestion that had been made to me that the difficulties of the New England fishermen were not due so much to the fact that there was fish coming in from Canada and there was also some coming in from Iceland but were due to the fact that they had rather exhausted their fisheries and therefore their costs of producing fish in their own boats had considerably increased and had got beyond what both the Icelandic fishermen and the Canadian fishermen could supply fish for in that market even with the tariff that was already in existence.

I was very glad to receive the impression that the President was quite conscious of the importance of the Canadian market to the United

States trading nation and I must confess that he was rather surprised when I said to him that in the course of the present year it looked as if we were going to import from the United States almost a billion dollars' worth of goods more than they were going to buy from us and that was a figure that seemed to astound him. I also told him I was not saying it in any plaintive way because we were getting that large volume of additional commodities because most of them were being built into productive facilities that were going up in our own country but that that was a situation which of course he realized could not continue. It was being balanced at the present time by the attractiveness of industrial development in Canada to United States capital; but that there was going to be, as a result of the investment of American capital in Canada, a very substantial increase in production and that we were buying more than we were selling at the present time just as it sometimes happens to a farmer that he buys more in the spring than he sells in the spring. But it is because he is going to use the fertilizer and seed which occasion the additional buying to have a crop that is going to be larger in the fall; and that we were going to have a crop of production in our country a portion of which was going to be the crop resulting from the investment of his own fellow citizens in the industries of our country and that there would have to be at that time a much fairer balance of trade because it could not be expected that trade with them—of course it is not a one-way street—would be so predominantly moving more northward than the volume that was moving southward.

Well, I came away with the impression that the golf game had been very enjoyable but also that there had been other aspects of the half day I spent with him that were quite more important in what I was going to remember than the golf score on the splendid golf links of Augusta.

There was another reason for which I was very happy to have this confidential chat with the President which occurred on the eve of Mr. Nehru's visit. I said to the President quite frankly that I believed he and Mr. Nehru at the present time were probably the two most influential statesmen in the world, the two statesmen whose influence radiated the most widely in the free world at this time. I said, "Of course, I am not saying anything about China because I have never been behind the bamboo curtain and I do not know Mr. Chou En-lai, but I do know, or at least I think I know from my own personal observation, that Mr. Nehru is a statesman of whom, whether or not they will admit it openly, all Asians are proud. They are proud of his stature in the world at this time, and his attitudes, even for those who will not state that they fully agree with them, are attitudes which have an influence on their thinking." I believe the same is true of the President of the United States. The personal attitudes of the President of the United States are attitudes that radiate throughout the free world, and whether or not we always agree with all of them our thinking is always influenced to a degree by the attitudes which are adopted by him.

I asserted with conviction that Mr. Nehru was just as anti-communist as Mr. Eisenhower was, although in India there was not the same fear of dangers imminent from communism that Senator McCarthy had in the United States; that there might not always be the same approaches to the proper methods of counteracting what influences might be exercised by communism; but that it should not be forgotten that the background of the United States or the North American continent was not the only background against which we should appraise the attitudes of other people throughout the world outside of the North American continent.

V. Prime Minister John G. Diefenbaker (June 1957-April 1963) (Presidents Dwight D. Eisenhower and John F. Kennedy)

Prime Minister John G. Diefenbaker assumed office in June, 1957, and served until April, 1963. During his tenure, he had ten meetings with U.S. Presidents—seven with Dwight D. Eisenhower and three with John F. Kennedy. Six of these ten meetings (three with Eisenhower and three with Kennedy) are documented. President Eisenhower took office in January of 1953 and served until January of 1961. He had met four times with Prime Minister St. Laurent, and was to have a total of eleven meetings with Canadian Prime Ministers.

After her visit to Canada, Queen Elizabeth II visited the United States in October of 1957. Prime Minister Diefenbaker accompanied Her Majesty as Minister-in-Attendance during the time she was in Washington. It was here that Diefenbaker first met President Eisenhower during the latter's incumbency. Ceremonial in nature, this meeting is not documented. Nor is the second Diefenbaker-Eisenhower meeting which occurred in December of 1957 in Paris at the NATO Heads of Government meeting. Fifteen NATO leaders had met to discuss general principles of agreement on the military, political, and economic questions facing the alliance. President Eisenhower held short bilateral meetings with other NATO leaders, as did Prime Minister Diefenbaker, and it was in this context that the two men met briefly.

The third Diefenbaker-Eisenhower meeting occurred in Ottawa from July 8-11, 1958. (See Section A.) The purpose of the meeting, to quote President Eisenhower, was "to talk together about our common problems." And problems there were, for U.S. Representatives Brooks Hays and Frank Coffin, members of the House Foreign Affairs Committee, had just issued a report citing several contentious issues. Meeting for a total of three hours, Messrs. Diefenbaker and Eisenhower discussed such international issues as the Soviet economic threat and disarmament, concentrating on the Soviet position on inspection; as well as such bilateral issues as North American defence and the two countries' NATO contributions, the control of foreign subsidiaries in Canada, boundary water issues and the implications for Canada of Alaskan statehood.[1] These concerns are evident in the five documents presented: President Eisenhower's press conference preceding the meeting; Prime Minister Diefenbaker's introduction of President Eisenhower to the Canadian Parliament; the President's address to Parliament which referred to specific issues confronting the two nations and constituted a rejection of Canada's grievances. The tangible results of this meeting are shown in the next documentary entry, which includes: a statement of their position on disarmament talks, a statement concerning "full consultations" with respect to United States and Canadian export laws and policies, and an announcement of the establishment of the Canada-United States Committee on Joint Defence. The final entry consists of Diefenbaker's report of the talks to the House of Commons.

The fourth meeting between Diefenbaker and Eisenhower, which is not documented, occurred in June of 1959 at the St. Lambert lock near Montreal. The two leaders met to open and dedicate the St. Lawrence Seaway, a project which had finally come to fruition. Queen Elizabeth II presided as the Canadian Head of State over seven-and-one-half hours of salutes and displays. Entirely ceremonial in nature, there are no indications that Diefenbaker and Eisenhower held substantive conversations.

The Prime Minister's fifth meeting with President Eisenhower occurred in Washington from June 3-4, 1960, within two weeks after the abortive Paris summit conference between President Eisenhower and Premier Khrushchev. (See Section B.) After Eisenhower's earlier admission that the U.S. U-2 plane downed deep in the U.S.S.R. was on a spy mission, Khrushchev had scuttled both the Paris meeting and the planned Eisenhower visit to the Soviet Union. Although the Canadian-United States summit meeting had been planned before the Paris Conference, in light of the worsening of Cold War tensions that resulted from it, Diefenbaker's visit was seen as part of a reevaluation of the international situation.[2] The purpose of the meeting, to quote

---

[1]See Raymond Daniell, "President Begins Talks in Ottawa," NYT (July 9, 1958), p. 1; Raymond Daniell, "President Backs Policy on Trade in Canadian Talk," NYT (July 10, 1958), p. 1; and TGM (July 10, 1958), p. 1.

[2]See "Where Do We Go From Here," TGM (May 31, 1960), p. 6; Phillip Deane, TGM (June 4, 1960); and "Mr. Diefenbaker In Washington," NYT (June 3, 1960), p. 30. A.D.P. Heeney, Canadian ambassador in Washington from 1959 to 1962, provides his account of the summit meetings of these years in *The Things That Are Caesar's, Memoirs of a Canadian Public Servant* (Toronto: University of Toronto Press, 1972), pp. 155-81.

from the White House Press Release, was "to provide the occasion for informal talks."[3] In contradistinction to the first Diefenbaker-Eisenhower summit meeting, bilateral economic points of contention had receded in importance, although Canada's trade deficit with the United States remained. Both nations were facing difficulties stemming from the trade arrangements of the European Economic Community. But international issues resulting from the Paris summit collapse were considered to be of major importance, especially as they affected North Atlantic and North American defence arrangements. One such issue was the continued U.S. development of the Bomarc missile. Despite test failures and the supercedure of missiles over manned aircraft as the principal form of the external threat, Canada had placed its primary air defence burden on Bomarc after cancelling its fighter-interceptor program. Secondly, Diefenbaker objected to General de Gaulle's proposal that NATO policy planning be more centralized through Big Three Cooperation (United States, United Kingdom, France) in the face of Soviet rigidity following the collapse of the Paris summit conference. Diefenbaker's brief Washington visit was therefore viewed as a Canadian quest for assurances from the President that Canada would retain its place in Western and North American defence planning.[4] During two hours of meetings, the two leaders discussed events surrounding the Paris summit conference, in addition to disarmament, NATO, the Bomarc and North American air defence. In addition, economic issues were discussed in a general sense, including the British entry into the Common Market and its impact on Commonwealth preferences, and bilateral economic relations. The documentation on this meeting includes the Joint Statement issued by the two leaders, their exchange of toasts, and Prime Minister Diefenbaker's report to the House of Commons.

The sixth Eisenhower-Diefenbaker meeting, which is not documented, occurred in September of 1960. A welter of government leaders addressed the General Assembly of the United Nations, and President Eisenhower spent several days in New York City meeting with such leaders as Nkrumah, Tito, Nasser, and Nehru. On September 27, Eisenhower met briefly with Prime Ministers Macmillan and Diefenbaker for general discussions, and returned to Washington that evening.

The seventh meeting between Diefenbaker and Eisenhower occurred on January 17, 1961, in Washington.[5] (See Section C.) The purpose of this very short and informal meeting was entirely ceremonial, consist-

---

[3]DSB (May 30, 1960), p. 858.

[4]"Diefenbaker Gets Assurance by U.S.," NYT (June 5, 1960), p. 21.

[5]See George Bain, "PM Eisenhower Signing Columbia River Project," TGM (January 18, 1961), p. 5; and "Canada and the United States of America," NYT (January 17, 1961), p. 36.

ing of the signing of the Columbia River Treaty by the two leaders. Approximately fifteen years earlier, the United States had suggested that the two countries might cooperate to control the Columbia River for both hydroelectric power and flood protection. The two countries referred the matter to the International Joint Commission in 1944, requesting an investigation and report. After years of sporadic negotiations, in 1959 the International Joint Commission came to an agreement and its suggestions were turned over to a team of negotiators, who spent most of 1960 working on the matter. The agreement was hurried along so that it could be signed as one of the last major acts of the Eisenhower Administration. However, the Canadian Federal Government had not yet reached agreement with British Columbia on several financial and jurisdictional aspects of the Treaty. Thus, with only three days left as President, Eisenhower was joined by Prime Minister Diefenbaker for this ceremonial event. The documentation on this meeting includes the two leaders exchange of remarks at the signing of the Treaty, and Prime Minister Diefenbaker's report of the meeting to the House of Commons.

Within one month of his last meeting with Eisenhower, Prime Minister Diefenbaker was back in Washington to hold his eighth meeting with a U.S. President—this time John F. Kennedy on February 20, 1961. (See Section D.) The purpose of the meeting, which essentially consisted of a business luncheon, was, to quote President Kennedy, to have "a discussion of matters of mutual interest."[6] The two leaders discussed joint defence, bilateral economic matters, Canada's relations with China and Cuba, and the deteriorating situation in the Belgian Congo.[7] The only tangible statements resulting from the meeting were the announcement that President Kennedy had accepted Prime Minister Diefenbaker's invitation to make his first State Visit to Canada, and that the Canadian-United States Joint Committee on Trade and Economic Affairs, which had last met in February of 1960, would meet in Washington on March 13. The documentation for this meeting includes the Joint Statement issued by the two leaders, and Prime Minister Diefenbaker's report of the meeting to the House of Commons.

The ninth meeting Prime Minister Diefenbaker had with a U.S. President occurred from May 16-18, 1961, when Kennedy paid a 42-hour State Visit, making it his first trip outside the United States as President. (See Section E.) Diefenbaker saw the meeting as an attempt "to achieve new strength with the understanding that each is necessary for the other."[8] During their first two-and-one-half-hour

---

[6]PP/John F. Kennedy, Vol. 1961, No. 25, p. 66.

[7]See John T. Saywell, ed., *Canadian Annual Review for 1961* (Toronto: The University of Toronto Press, 1962), pp. 111-12; and Harold Greer, "June Ottawa Visit Planned By Kennedy," TGM (February 21, 1961), p. 1.

[8]"The Hallmark of Freedom," IGM (May 19, 1961), p. 6.

session, the two leaders discussed a host of multilateral and bilateral topics, ranging from aid to developing countries to the problem of farm surpluses.[9] After a concluding breakfast meeting, they issued a Joint Statement listing in very general terms seven subjects they had discussed: the United Nations, disarmament, defence, Western Hemisphere, Laos, O.E.C.D., and trade. Nothing concrete emerged from this summit meeting; indeed, it has become something of a classic in Canadian-United States summitry due to the intangible and divisive effects it was seen to have generated. Reports flourished concerning such incidents as the working memo Kennedy inadvertently left behind listing "things to push for," and marginalia referring to the Prime Minister as an "S.O.B." In addition, the President seriously strained his back during the traditional planting of a ceremonial tree. Finally Kennedy solicited a greater Canadian involvement in the Western Hemisphere which some Canadians felt inappropriate given the President's status as an official guest in Canada. The documentation for this meeting includes Prime Minister Diefenbaker's introduction of President Kennedy to the House of Commons, the President's address, the Joint Statement issued by the two leaders subsequent to their talks, and the Prime Minister's report of the meeting to the House of Commons.

The tenth and last meeting Prime Minister Diefenbaker had with a U.S. President occurred on December 21-22, 1962, at Nassau in the Bahamas. (See Section F.) Despite the fact that Kennedy and Diefenbaker had not met for a year and a half, there were no plans to do so in December of 1962.[10] President Kennedy and British Prime Minister Harold Macmillan had scheduled a meeting in Nassau primarily to discuss their respective nuclear roles. Macmillan invited Diefenbaker to come to Nassau after President Kennedy had left, so the two Commonwealth leaders could themselves have an entire day of conversations. After meetings between Macmillan and Kennedy on December 19, it was announced that the talks between the two leaders had been extended. As this extension conflicted with Macmillan's plans to meet with Diefenbaker, it was announced that the Canadian leader would not arrive as planned, but would fly to the Bahamas in time for a luncheon meeting with both Kennedy and Macmillan. It was noted, however, that Diefenbaker would not participate in the additional Kennedy-

---

[9]See Raymond Daniell, "Kennedy Bids Canada Join U.S. in Hemisphere Role," NYT (May 18, 1961), p. 12; Raymond Daniell, "Kennedy In Ottawa," NYT (May 17, 1961), p. 1; and Bruce Macdonald, "Kennedy Asks Canada To Boost Foreign Aid," TGM (May 17, 1961).

[10]See *External Affairs* (April, 1957), pp. 129-32; George Bain, "Macmillan-Kennedy Talks Extended To Third Day," TGM (December 20, 1962), p. 1; and George Bain, "NATO To Get U.K.'s Polaris," TGM (December 22, 1962), p. 1.

Macmillan talks on that day. Prime Minister Diefenbaker's talks with Macmillan were then rescheduled for the next day. The luncheon of Kennedy, Macmillan and Diefenbaker was relatively brief and entirely social in nature.

The significance of this meeting concerns the difficulties Canada and the United States were experiencing regarding nuclear weapons. In conjunction with earlier NORAD and NATO commitments, the Canadian Government had embraced such weapons systems as the Bomarc missiles, CF-104 aircraft, and the "Honest John" rockets which were effective only when armed with nuclear warheads. However, Prime Minister Diefenbaker had for some time been equivocating as to whether Canada would or would not accept these warheads, and the political situation in Canada was becoming increasingly difficult with some Ministers reportedly being close to resigning over the issue. Thus, one month after returning to Canada from Nassau, Diefenbaker made his major statement on Canadian defence policy which he based on the Nassau talks. U.S. officials categorically took exception to this statement, issuing their own version of the talks five days later through a U.S. State Department Press Release. The fact that Diefenbaker had been at Nassau, first at a luncheon with the two leaders, and then alone with Prime Minister Macmillan, gave his subsequent statements, accurately or inaccurately, a greater authority than they would otherwise have had. The documentation for this meeting consists of Diefenbaker's account of the meeting as contained in his statement to the House of Commons, and the U.S. press release rebutting the Diefenbaker statement. A well-known sequence of events followed, culminating in a general election which Mr. Pearson's Liberals won, without a clear majority.

A. Prime Minister John G. Diefenbaker and President Dwight D. Eisenhower, Ottawa, Ontario, July 8-11, 1958

1. Press Conference of President Eisenhower, Washington, D. C., July 2, 1958,

(PP/Dwight D. Eisenhower, Vol. 1958, No. 153, pp. 516-17)

Q. Can you tell us what you hope to accomplish by your visit to Canada next week?

THE PRESIDENT: Well, I can't describe in detail everything that I expect to do, but I believe this:

First of all, with our two close neighbors, our relations should be just as close as we can possibly make them. I believe those relations cannot be close unless we have a chance to talk together about our common problems. There are problems involving the water of northwest United States and southwest Canada. There is the oil problem. There is lead and zinc. There is the surplus wheat. There are numbers of problems that I believe we should take right out on the table to see whether sensible men, people of good will on both sides, can find ways of handling so that there will not be too much damage occur to either.

Now, that is what I hope to bring back, a feeling that we can meet this.

You people may know there are, I think, two meetings a year between certain members of our Cabinet and certain members of theirs, in order to settle these things so far as possible. But occasionally I think heads of government can do a little bit more than can Cabinet officers to bring about an understanding; and that is it—to bring an honest agreement, and where there are things that don't seem soluble for the moment, to at least agree to attack them in a friendly way.

Q. Prime Minister Diefenbaker has suggested a Canadian-American wheat pool to get rid of our surplus. Will that be the start?

THE PRESIDENT: I haven't heard that. I will discuss anything he wants to because I like Mr. Diefenbaker and I think he is a very able man.

2. Prime Minister Diefenbaker's Introduction of President Eisenhower to Both Houses of the Canadian Parliament, July 9, 1958

(CHCD, Appendix, July 9, 1958, Address of Dwight D. Eisenhower, pp. 2081-82)

. . . President Eisenhower comes to us as the renowned leader of a mighty state, but what is more meaningful today is the fact that he comes to us as a good neighbour and friend. We are happy that he is accompanied by his gracious wife and helpmate, for Canadians are very fond of her, too.

I now wish to add a word of welcome in the French language, and to assure you, Mr. President, that the warmth of Canadian feeling toward you and our great neighbour is one that comes from the heart.

To you and to your gracious wife, I extend a most cordial welcome.

In visiting us unaccompanied by pomp and circumstance the president is following an old and precious precedent in the relations of our two nations. Although you come to us, sir, as the head of a powerful state, the intelligence service informs me after diligent inquiry that you come bearing no arms and carry no armour other than a brassie and a putter. May I, sir, as an aside express the wish that under clear skies and on fairways not too narrow you will be able, while here, to use this armour and add to your list of victories.

The communist world is waging an intensive economic global offensive of "aid and trade", an offensive which is not designed to secure profits in a bookkeeping sense in order to secure the ordinary values of trade for its peoples, but an offensive whose success will be measured by the degree to which the souls and hearts and the freedoms and aspirations of the recipients will be subverted under communist tyranny.

I think this is a very great occasion. We say what we have said on occasions in the past, that our countries are united in defence. I believe, sir, that the Soviet challenge demands that we can be no less in economic objectives. I believe that each of our nations, and each of the nations of the free world, in forming economic policies, while at all times looking primarily to the welfare of the individual nations, must as never before take into account, in the common interest and for survival itself, the effects of such policies on the economic welfare and interests of all other free nations. And I go even further and suggest that, to meet the ever-enlarging expansion of communist economic cold war, joint action is imperative to the end that world trade will be expanded and the financial base of liquid resources necessary for such expansion will be materially increased. I feel sure I speak for all Canadians when I say that Canada stands prepared to assume her full share and to make her full contribution to such a bold policy.

Mr. President, our two lands have a glory of their own, the glory of two peoples moving forward together, not complacently but with a humble pride, and joined in fraternal association that has extended through a century of tragedy and storm in different parts of the world.

We can on this occasion, in the simplicity of our faith, thank God that our nations know nothing of ancestral hatreds or animosities. Above all, we may hope that this spirit of peaceful and co-operative relations will in due course become the fortune of all mankind.

Sir, as you came into our city you drove by and crossed over a small canal. Few know today when or why it was built. It was built more than 100 years ago to help protect this country from yours. Today it is a museum piece; it represents a past that is past.

I would recall to you, sir, on this the occasion of your visit to our country one of the earliest visits by Canadian parliamentarians to Washington. When Abraham Lincoln went to Gettysburg to deliver his immortal and timeless address, one of those who accompanied him as his guest on the Gettysburg platform was the Hon. William McDougall, one of the fathers of the Canadian confederation. Mr. McDougall had been in Washington with Mr. Galt on a small matter regarding trade, and Mr. Lincoln, with that informality which has continued since to characterize our relations, invited Mr. McDougall to accompany him. It is of interest, too, sir, that when the next day Mr. McDougall wrote to his family in Canada his opinion, so different from many opinions uttered that day, was that the president's words would live in history.

In the years since there have been many comings and goings; there have been meetings, and not all brought satisfaction to both sides. But there has remained that glory to which I referred a moment ago, that we can discuss, that we have discussed, that we shall in the days ahead continue to discuss our problems and our differences with the candour of free men in friendship, understanding and manly frankness.

I have often been asked by other nations what is the secret of the dedication of these two nations to neighbourliness and mutual respect. The answer, we know, is this. We trust each other in a union of hearts based on common ideals and the abiding principles of freedom and the rights of men. Our peoples are North Americans. We are the children of our geography, products of the same hopes, faith and dreams, products as well of those forms of expression which have been nurtured and enriched in the traditions and common heritage of Magna Carta, the Bill of Rights and habeas corpus.

When, 13 years ago, you were given the freedom of the city of London another great warrior-statesman, Sir Winston Churchill, said of you that you had shown "the capacity for making great nations march together more truly united than they have been before." I take leave to quote your noble reply in which in part you said:

> Humility must always be the portion of any man who receives the acclaim earned in the blood of his followers and the sacrifices of his friends.

Mr. President, it is in your clear knowledge that it is only by constructive deeds of living men that the sacrifices of the dead can have their proper values that parliament, yes, the Canadian people as a whole, give you their warmest welcome and acclaim. I salute you, sir, as the wartime commander under whose leadership the legions of freedom marched when liberty was under siege and no man knew where salvation lay. I greet you, sir, as one whose wisdom, humanitarianism and prestige are once more humanity's major hope for freedom and for peace.

Members of the parliament of Canada, I have the high privilege of presenting to you a great and good tribune of freedom in war and in peace, the President of the United States.

3. Address of President Eisenhower to Both Houses of Parliament, July 9, 1958

(*Ibid.*, pp. 2082-86)

As I begin, may I be permitted to speak a few words in my halting French to my French friends of Canada. The Prime Minister did this with great courage. I assure you I do it in abject fear.

Here, in Canada, you have demonstrated that differences in speech and forms of speech need not impair communications between free peoples. So it must be among all nations of the free world. Though we may speak in different tongues and accents, that fact does not weaken our determination to work for a just and lasting peace. All of Canada has a great and rich tradition in the service of this high purpose. Her dedication to it has been staunch and persevering. Her example encourages free men everywhere.

Mr. Prime Minister, I want you to know of my deep personal appreciation of the warmth of the welcome you have extended to me and of the generosity of the remarks you have just delivered concerning me. Along that same line, I should like to express my very great appreciation of the warmth of the welcome that Mrs. Eisenhower and myself have experienced throughout the city, along its streets and in every meeting in which we have had a part. We are truly grateful.

This is my fourth visit to your beautiful capital. I recall so well that when your gracious Queen came to Washington from Ottawa we spoke together of the beauty of this city and of the greatness of Canada. It is good to return, to see old friends and to make new ones.

I came here first in 1946 to congratulate the Canadian people on the brilliant role played by the Canadian forces you placed under my command in the world war which had then recently ended in victory. My next visit was made as commander of NATO forces in Europe. In 1953 I returned as president, and talked in this house of some aspects of the relationship between our two countries.

I then spoke of the St. Lawrence seaway in prospective terms. Today it is near completion and next year it will be opened. This is truly a great joint accomplishment. It will open up important regions of both Canada and the United States to ocean traffic. It will ever stand as a monument to what can be achieved by the common effort of two sovereign nations.

On that same occasion I spoke of the need to devise ways to protect our North America from any surprise attack. Since then we have made great strides. The distant early warning or D.E.W. line has been built and placed in operation. In the process of its construction I am sure much has been learned which will contribute to the more rapid development of the northern reaches of Canada and our new state, Alaska.

Last month an agreement was concluded between our two governments to establish a combined air defence headquarters for this continent. We have also, both of us, striven, as we will continue to strive, for the Soviet Union's agreement to a system of inspection to protect against surprise attack through the Arctic. Recent Soviet communications have strengthened the hope that they will come to see that by such a system any basis for their professed fears of an attack across the pole will be removed. For Canada and the United States such a system in operation would add measurably to our security against a sudden attack. Possibly it might also pave the way for still further measures of arms control and permit some reduction of the burden and danger of modern armaments.

Both of these developments, the seaway, a broadened, deepened road for peaceful commerce, and the strengthening of our common defence of this continent, strikingly illustrate two things. The first is that change is the law of life and of relations between nations. When two great peoples such as ours, energetic and optimistic, live side by side in all the diversity that freedom offers, change is rapid and brings in its wake problems, sometimes frictions.

The second lesson I see in these common achievements in diverse fields is that by mutual respect, understanding and with good will we can find acceptable solutions to any problems which exist or may arise between us. It is important to remember this. Such differences as are from time to time expressed never affect the similarity of purpose which binds our two countries together.

Of course, each of us possesses a distinctive national character and history. You won your independence by evolution, and the United States by revolution. Our forms of government, though both cast in the democratic pattern, are greatly different. Indeed, sometimes it appears that many of our misunderstandings spring from an imperfect knowledge on the part of both of us of the dissimilarities in our forms of government. And yet, despite these dissimilarities in form, our two governments are developing and are increasingly using effective ways to consult and act together. This we do to meet the problems that confront us in our relations with each other, and in the relations of both with other nations of the world.

We share the basic belief that only under free institutions, with government the servant and not the master, can the individual secure his life, his liberty, and the pursuit of happiness. We are both determined to frame and follow policies which safeguard the lives and homes of our people, their peace of mind, their material well-being and, above all other things, their ideals. True to these ideals both of our countries, for example, are determined that the great decisions of peace and war will remain always under civilian control.

Moreover, we both recognize a design of aggressive communist imperialism which threatens every free nation. Both of us face a military threat and political attacks. Our system of free enterprise is challenged throughout the world by a state-directed, state-controlled economic system. Indeed, this could well be the area in which the competition will be most bitter and most decisive between the free world and communist imperialism. We must never allow ourselves to become so preoccupied with the differences between our two nations that we lose sight of the transcendent importance of free world co-operation in the winning of the global struggle.

Acting in accordance with our common dedication the two of us, with others, have drawn together in collective security arrangements. The most notable of these is the North Atlantic Treaty Organization in which both Canada and the United States are equal partners. We are both determined to maintain what George Washington described as "a respectable military posture." We are equally determined to maintain our institutions in good repair and to ensure that our own economies function well.

Thus we seek not only to meet the expanding needs of our people but also to set an example of free men's accomplishments which will encourage and attract those less fortunate. Finally, we are agreed that we shall never cease striving for a just and lasting peace to be achieved by negotiation with those who challenge us. We overlook no opportunity to settle the issues which divide the world and under safeguarded conditions to reduce the burden of armaments.

Now, against this background of similarity in basic factors and policy, let me now point to some of the matters which it seems to me are troublesome between us. Among these are the surplus wheat disposal policies of the United States, the imbalance of our mutual trade, certain aspects of United States private investment in Canada, and Canadian fears of a trend in the United States away from forward-looking policies in the field of trade.

I am sure you agree that we should talk frankly to each other. Frankness, in good spirit, is a measure of friendship. It should be the practice, I believe, on both sides so to speak, when either feels that important interests are adversely affected by actions contemplated or taken by the other. Happily, these instances are rare. In mentioning today specific problems on which we do not see eye to eye I am doing so, of course, as an American, expressing an American viewpoint. I can assure you that your Prime Minister, in discussing these problems with my associates and me, most loyally and eloquently expresses the viewpoint of Canada.

It is my conviction, in which I believe he fully concurs, that for all of our present problems and all of our future ones we will find acceptable solutions. It will take understanding, common sense and a willingness to give and take on both our parts. These qualities we have always found in our dealings with Canada. I hope you have not found them lacking in us.

First then, in some detail, I should like to comment briefly on our surplus wheat disposal policies. I think no one can quarrel with our purpose, though some of our methods may seem unorthodox by traditional standards. Simply stated, our wheat disposal program has three aspects. In times of local famine or disaster we give wheat away: We have also bartered it for strategic materials. Finally, we sell wheat for local currency to countries which cannot afford to purchase it commercially. In these cases our policy is to lend back to the government in question most of the proceeds for local economic development. Our intent is not to damage normal commercial markets, and in this I think we have been generally successful.

I know that in the past there was criticism of certain aspects of these programs, and particularly of our barter arrangements. I believe that the basis for these objections has been largely removed. Increasingly close consultation between officials of our two governments has ironed out many misunderstandings respecting our surplus disposals. Your government knows in detail what we are planning. I assure you that it is our desire and intention to keep the doors of consultation fully open. There must never be a final word between friends.

In several respects, despite inconvenience and even occasional damage in the past, Canada stands to benefit from our moving some surplus agricultural commodities into consumption overseas. First and most evident of all, many hungry people around the world have had food which they otherwise would not have had. Second, had these products remained in dead storage they would have had a depressing influence on the world market and world prices. Finally, the funds which we have been enabled to make available to recipient countries should in the long run help to raise standards of living and create enlarged markets for all of us.

I come next to the question of the imbalance of trade between our two countries. You buy more from the United States than you sell to us and this fact is of concern to many thoughtful Canadians. There are a few basic points which should be noted in this connection.

First of all, the United States and Canada are not state traders. All the products of industry manufactured in the United States and sold to customers abroad are sold through the enterprise of the private seller. These articles come to you in Canada only because of the desire of the individual Canadian consumer to buy a particular piece of merchandise. The United States government does not place goods in Canada as part of a state-directed program. This aspect of our trade with each other is the natural consequence of two private enterprise economies working side by side and trading with each other.

Then we should also remember that the free world represents a multilateral trading community. To try to balance our books once a month or once a year with every nation with which we trade would stifle rather than expand trade. I assume that Canada is as interested as we are in the expansion of world trade rather than in its artificial redirection. Both our peoples want to buy and sell in a climate of economic vigour and expansion. An imbalance in trade with one country, in such a climate, is usually balanced or largely offset by the state of the accounts with other trading nations.

This is the case with Canadian trade. Your export deficit to the United States is offset by export surpluses to other countries and by the flow of investments to Canada. The promotion of healthy multilateral trade, as opposed to artificial bilateral balancing, is an important objective of the international monetary fund and the general agreement on tariffs and trade, to which both Canada and the United States belong.

For a moment I want to address myself as well to the other side of the trade equation, namely your exports to the United States. Here you can rightly say that through quotas and tariffs our governmental policies can either expand or restrict your opportunities to sell to us. The same of course is true of actions taken by your government which can affect the volume of our exports to Canada.

Neither of our countries is a "free trader" in the classical economic sense. Each of us feels a responsibility to provide some protection to particular sectors of our economies which may be in distress or are for other reasons deserving of governmental assistance. We have taken some actions of this sort. So has Canada.

Oil imports into our country contribute a case in point. We believe that to ensure adequate supplies of oil in an emergency, it is necessary that exploration to develop oil reserves be carried forward with vigour. This means a healthy oil industry throughout the continent. A healthy domestic oil-producing industry is vital to our national security. We recognize that our security and yours are inseparable. We have been keenly sensitive to that fact in considering the nature of the voluntary restrictions on oil imports that have been put into effect by oil companies in the United States, and have minimized their impact on your economy.

Our restrictive action with respect to oil is not in any sense reflective of a change in the fundamental trade policy of the United States. Such actions must be viewed in perspective. For example, since the so-called escape clause was incorporated in our trade agreements legislation in 1951, there have come from industry in the United States a number of requests for the imposition of quotas or higher tariffs. In about a dozen cases presidential approval for some relief has been granted. In only one of these cases was Canada directly affected as an exporter. We have always conscientiously sought to take account of your interests as well as our own in seeking the best remedy to these intricate problems. I believe that a study of the record will bear out the truth of this statement.

Next, the flow of investment funds from the United States into Canada has led to expressions of concern on your part. These funds have been attracted to your country by the business opportunities Canada has offered. Though they may raise questions in specific cases respecting control of an industry by United States citizens, these industries are, of course, subject to Canadian law. Moreover, these investments have helped you to develop your resources and to expand your industrial plant at a far faster rate than would have been possible had you relied wholly on your own savings. They have thereby helped to provide employment, tax revenues and other direct benefits. These funds have also helped Canada to finance with ease its recent surplus of imports from the United States, a fact that is testified to by the premium of the Canadian dollar over the United States dollar.

I am confident that if there are some defects in this investment process, ways will be found to correct them because that is in the interests of both our countries.

One final word on the foreign trade policy of the United States. In 1934 the United States took an historic decision to embark on a positive policy of fostering trade with the launching of the reciprocal trade agreements program. This policy we continue to support and practice. The government of the United States, after a public searching of soul at times of renewal of the trade agreements act, has consistently reaffirmed this policy. Have no fear that the United States will abandon a policy so well established. The problems I have been discussing concern our economic lives. Our points of economic contact are varied and numerous, as they of necessity must be under our chosen system of private enterprise.

Our governments have a responsibility to help compose difficulties, but we must not forget that thousands of individual citizens of Canada and the United States must themselves find in their diversified activities the answers to many of these problems.

Finally, there is no cause to be surprised or disturbed to discover that occasionally differences arise between us. The distinguishing character of the peoples of the free world lies in the fact that differences between them can develop, can be expressed and then amicably resolved. We in the United States have no more desire than you have to seek in our relations with other nations the silent, sullen unity that elsewhere has been purchased or imposed. The hallmark of freedom is the right to differ as well as the right to agree.

I have spoken to you today in the knowledge that through you I address a nation strong in the tradition of freedom and vigilant in its defence. You and we are alike convinced, by our history, our religious faith and our common heritage of freedom that economic well-being and political liberty both depend upon the efforts of individuals and on their willingness to accept the responsibilities of freedom. Today I assure you once more of the pride and gratification that we of the United States feel in our long and friendly association with you, our sturdy northern neighbour.

We stand together at a pivotal point in history. All that we Canadians and Americans, and those who went before us, have built, all that we believe in, is challenged as it has never been challenged before. The new horizons of competition range from the polar areas, and extend to the infinity of outer space. It is for us, all of us, to bring to the challenge a response worthy of ourselves and of our two nations.

As we do, we shall know the satisfaction of having built, in friendship, a safer and ampler home here on the earth for this generation and those that shall come after us.

4. Three Joint Statements of Prime Minister Diefenbaker and President Eisenhower Following Discussions, July 9 and 10, 1958

(Ext/Aff. August 1958, pp. 172-73)

a) *Statement on Surprise Attack* (July 9, 1958)

The President and the Prime Minister discussed today questions concerning disarmament and in particular proposals for safeguards against surprise attack. This discussion reaffirmed the closeness of the views of the two governments on a suitable approach to these questions. Particularly, they emphasized the great importance which both countries attach to a system of control which would cover the Arctic and related areas.

The President and the Prime Minister exchanged views on the recent letter from Chairman Khrushchev to President Eisenhower with reference to expert examination of possible systems of supervision and control to prevent surprise attack. Although they recognized that certain aspects of Mr. Khrushchev's recent letter were unacceptable, they were nevertheless encouraged by certain elements of responsiveness to the earlier Western proposals on this matter. Mr. Diefenbaker indicated Canada's willingness to make a constructive contribution to study of control methods and it was agreed that the experts of both countries would work together and in co-operation with those of other free world countries concerned in study of this problem.

b) *Statement on Export Policies* (July 9, 1958)

The Canadian and United States Governments have given consideration to situations where the export policies and laws of the two countries may not be in complete harmony. It has been agreed that in these cases there will be full consultation between the two governments with a view to finding through appropriate procedures satisfactory solutions to concrete problems as they arise.

c) *Statement on Committee on Joint Defence* (July 10, 1958)

The Prime Minister and the President have taken note of the intimate co-operation which exists between their two governments in matters relating to continental defence. In furtherance of the policies of both governments that such matters shall be subject to civilian decision and guidance, they have agreed that there will be established a cabinet committee to be known as the Canada-United States Committee on Joint Defence. This committee will consist in Canada of the Secretary of State for External Affairs, the Minister of National Defence and the Minister of Finance, and for the United States, of the Secretary of State, the Secretary of Defence and the Secretary of the Treasury. Other Ministers may participate on an Ad Hoc basis as requested by the committee. The committee will consult on matters bearing upon the common defence of the North American Continent which lies within the North Atlantic Treaty area. It will in a supervisory capacity supplement and not supplant existing joint boards and committees. The committee will normally meet alternately in Washington and Ottawa. The Chairman of each meeting will be the Secretary of State of the country in whose capital the meeting is held.

5. *Prime Minister Diefenbaker's Report of Meeting to the Canadian House of Commons, July 11, 1958*

(CHCD, July 11, 1958, pp. 2139-42)

Mr. Speaker, yesterday the Leader of the Opposition asked whether I could make a statement regarding the discussions which took place as between the President and Secretary of State of the United States, various members of the government and myself. While I have not had an opportunity during the intervening hours to make very much preparation in this regard, I will outline in general the discussions which took place, leaving, however, detailed discussion until the debate on external affairs which is set for next week.

The members of this house and our fellow citizens in this city have shown very clearly how happy they were to welcome the President of the United States to Ottawa. A visit of this kind is an opportunity for us to demonstrate the ties of history and kinship which bind us together, and I know we were all very pleased to have the President address this house. He stated his views frankly and in a straightforward manner, as we have done for this government. We appreciated the opportunity to hear him explain the views of his country on those important issues which are of consequence to both our nations. Nothing better illustrates the strength of our relationship than that we can talk honestly to each other without endangering the association which holds us together.

The same spirit which was evidenced in this house was also apparent during the discussions between the President and the Secretary of State of the United States, the Secretary of State for External Affairs, other ministers and myself. We were aided by the presence of Mr. Dulles, who shared with us his broad experience and wide grasp of the problems of international relations. He had just returned from Paris and was able to give us a general idea as to the attitude of France respecting the great problems which particularly affect her and those which affect Canada jointly with France as members of NATO.

I think what has taken place illustrates the need of some continuing body to permit of a general discussion from time to time of our respective points of view. Respecting the earlier reference to the need for arrangements to permit of discussion from time to time between members of the congress of the United States and the parliament of Canada, while constitutionally as far as the President is concerned no decision in that regard could, of course, be achieved, the success of the meeting in general, as a meeting between the President and myself and the others to whom I have referred, indicates how very important it is that something in the nature of an exchange of opinions should take place from time to time as between the parliament of our country and the congress of the United States. My hope is that the recommendations which were made by the committee composed of Congressmen Hays and Coffin will be accepted; that a committee on Canadian-United States relations will be set up in the United States congress, and that we in our House of Commons will set up a similar committee, and that from time to time mutual exchanges will take place between members of these committees or between members of parliament and members of congress outside those committees, to the end that in general discussion the views of each nation may be ascertained and thereby, through discussions, causes of disagreement removed.

As far as the general discussions which took place are concerned, the President and I touched upon most of the pressing issues of the day as well as upon matters of more particular bilateral interest. There was very broad agreement on these fundamental issues, and whatever differences we may have on details there was never any question either before these meetings or during them—nor will there be, I know, in the days ahead—that either of our nations will lose sight of the fact that we must remain united in our objectives and in our determination if freedom is to be maintained.

The Secretary of State for External Affairs and I discussed with

President Eisenhower and Mr. Dulles such matters as progress toward disarmament and the changing nature of Soviet policy with reference to the economic challenge of the critical situation in the Middle East. The Minister of National Defence had an opportunity to talk over our mutual defence problems with Mr. Dulles. The Minister of Finance and the Minister of Agriculture discussed trade and economic questions, and the Minister of Public Works and the Minister of Northern Affairs and National Resources had a talk on the problem of boundary waters. In addition to these more formal talks there were, of course, opportunities for a less formal exchange of views in the atmosphere of the social occasions during which we met.

With respect to the international situation, members of the house are aware that discussions have taken place during the last year or so with regard to the providing of safeguards against the danger of surprise attack, and Canadians and Americans have a particular and special interest in these arrangements for the polar regions. These matters were discussed with reference to the recent letter which Mr. Khrushchev sent to the President signifying Soviet readiness in principle to enter into direct discussions on the technical aspects of the problem of preventing surprise attack.

Hon. members will not expect me to indicate even in general terms the contents of the President's contemplated reply, but that its broad purpose is to bring about such technical talks will be evident from our agreement that experts should work together on this problem. Studies have been under way for some time, and I understand that similar work has also been done in the United States. The meaning of our agreement is not only that there should be consultation between our officials; such exchanges of views on disarmament matters have long been a feature of our normal relations. It signifies rather that in the immediate future our collaboration should concentrate in a practical way on this particular and very important matter.

As to the general question of defence, it has been the aim and purpose of this government—and I think that view has been accepted by the Canadian people as a whole—that at all times in our joint defence efforts we must assure and maintain over and above every other consideration the political and civilian control with respect to military matters. During the course of the President's visit we reviewed the complex issues which arise from the joint efforts of our two governments in the field of continental defence. There was mutual recognition of the increased necessity for regular consultation between our two governments, both on the specific requirements with which the two governments may expect to be faced in providing for the security of North America and on international events which could lead to the necessity of activating the continental air defences. There was full realization that our joint efforts in the defence of North America must continue to serve the objectives of the NATO alliance in which we have banded together with other like-minded countries in the search for collective security in an uneasy world.

In these discussions we took note of the intimate co-operation of our two countries over the past two decades in matters relating to continental defence and of the machinery which had been established to provide for the consideration of defence problems of common concern. We recognized that these interdependent defence relationships must continue and, indeed, that they would become even more important and more complex in the face of the advanced weapon technology which is now available to potential aggressors. We agreed that while existing machinery in the defence field had served us well in the past and would undoubtedly continue to do so in the future, the need existed to supplement existing channels for consultation by providing for a periodic review at the ministerial level of problems which might be expected to arise. We recognized that decisions in this field would involve not only consideration of the military aspects of our common defence but also political and economic factors. We thought it particularly important as well that every step should be taken to maintain the principle and the fact of civilian control and guidance of these common military activities.

We agreed therefore that we should establish a joint ministerial committee to be known as the Canada-United States committee on joint defence, with scope to consider all matters bearing on the common defence of the North American continent. . . .

In regard to the question of defence production, we examined together the situation which arises in these days of mounting defence costs and the need for rationalizing whenever possible and consistently with national requirements the industrial base for our own defence needs. In anticipation of a meeting of the newly-announced committee at cabinet level on defence matters, some consideration has been given to the sort of items which might be placed upon the agenda. Further consideration, of course, will have to be given in consultation with our colleagues in each country to prepare ourselves to discuss in adequate detail many of these matters.

That in general represented the tenor of the discussions with respect to the subject of defence. So far as particulars are concerned, they will be available in committees; in the committee on defence, as an example, when the minister might be asked further questions with respect thereto.

I now come to the problem of economic questions. Consideration was given to the principal economic issues that are now facing the free world. It was agreed that some of those have become intensified by the Soviet economic offensive. It is more important now than ever before that measures be considered which might be expected to strengthen the economies of countries in the free world through the expansion of international trade and the promotion of programs of economic development. If progress can be made in these directions, as I believe it can, it may become easier to make fully convertible the main currencies in which world trade is conducted; but it would be quite wrong to suggest, as one newspaper did this morning, that any plans had been agreed upon, or been determined in part, with respect to convertibility of sterling since, of course, such action is entirely for decision by Her Majesty's government in the United Kingdom.

We received from the President and his Secretary of State reports concerning the prospects for the trade agreements legislation. We described the preparations being made for the commonwealth trade and economic conference. Within those limits various matters were discussed, all of which, of course, cannot be referred to at this time. However, there is one matter of particular interest and that is the necessity, as we see it in Canada, of revising the list of strategic materials which come under either prohibition or control for export to the Soviet bloc and to communist China. This matter is going to be considered at length at a conference that is about to take place in Paris of representatives of nations of the free world.

I raised with the President the question that some Canadian subsidiaries of United States companies may have been prevented from accepting orders from communist China, or from peoples in that country, by the application of United States foreign assets control regulations, even though acceptance of such orders would be permitted by the policy of the Canadian government. The President expressed the view that the United States regulations should not be applied in any way to the disadvantage of the Canadian economy. If cases arose in the future where the refusal of orders by companies operating in Canada might have any effect on Canadian economic activity, the United States government would consider favourably exempting the parent company in the United States from the application of the foreign assets control regulations with respect to such orders.

It was made perfectly clear, and I want to underline this fact, that there was no question at any time that, with respect to the operations of Canadian companies, Canadian law shall govern and Canadian wishes shall be respected. Further consideration of this question will naturally require some days. I go no further at this time except to re-underline what I have said to re-emphasize the stand taken by this government, that Canada as a sovereign nation has the right to the maintenance in its full amplitude of its legislative enactments, both dominion and provincial.

I think that in general is a summary of—not in particular—the discussions that took place. I must say that during the course of the three days I was more than ever impressed with the very reasonable and co-operative attitude that was taken to assure that at all times anything that takes place in the economic field which might conceivably cause difficulty to either of our countries will to the limit of our respective capacities be resolved to the end that our unity shall be maintained; that in whatever we do there will be a full realization on the part of each of us that in taking our individual courses as individual nations every regard and respect will be paid to the fullest consideration that nothing that is done shall detrimentally affect the other country; and that indeed we now approach an era internationally where it becomes more important than ever before that the nations of the free world must, in the interests of survival itself, bring about economic changes in unity that might 15 or 20 years ago have been regarded as impossible of achievement.

I conclude by saying in very simple words that this conference did represent a forward step. There was a spirit of mutual respect and forbearance and a common desire to arrive at decisions which will assure that the unity that we all desire to attain will be preserved, and that the sovereignty of each of our countries will not be impinged upon in any way.

B. President Dwight D. Eisenhower and Prime Minister John G. Diefenbaker, Washington, D.C., June 3-4, 1960

1. Joint Statement of President Eisenhower and Prime Minister Diefenbaker Following Discussions, June 4, 1960

(PP/Dwight D. Eisenhower, Vol. 1960-1961, No. 142, pp. 458-59)

The Prime Minister of Canada, the Right Honorable John G. Diefenbaker, and the President of the United States have consulted on a wide range of subjects of both an international and bilateral nature. The Canadian Ambassador at Washington and the Secretary to the Canadian Cabinet assisted in the discussions, together with the United States Secretary of State and the United States Ambassador at Ottawa.

The Prime Minister and the President were in agreement on measures which should be taken to maintain the security of the free world. They reaffirmed their determination to continue to work for peace with justice. Particular attention was paid to the importance of achieving, with effective international control, an end to nuclear testing and progress toward general disarmament.

The Prime Minister and the President reviewed the course of relations between their countries during recent years and noted with pleasure the extent to which the problems arising in such relations have yielded to the process of friendly and continuing consultation. They considered that satisfactory means of carrying on such consultation have been established in personal exchanges as well as by regular diplomatic arrangements and the various joint committees that have been created. They expressed their belief that there has been established between the two countries a model for the relationship between neighbors.

2. Exchange of Toasts Between President Eisenhower and Prime Minister Diefenbaker, June 3, 1960

(*Ibid.* No. 171, pp. 456-58)

THE PRESIDENT: Every member of this company feels a very definite sense of honor and distinction in the privilege of having with us tonight the Prime Minister of the great republic of Canada.

It would be a fitting occasion, since this is at least semiformal, to address you, sir, in sonorous phrases, telling about the history of our relations between our countries and expressing the admiration and respect we feel for you as the leader of that country.

Actually, we feel that here we are in the family. You are another of our best friends. You are the head not merely of a great republic that borders us on the north, you are the leader of a people that with us shares common ideals, common international purposes, and common culture and language.

So the sense of honor and distinction we have is more than that of an official character. It is extremely personal and cordial.

This afternoon the Prime Minister and I had a long talk, as we have in the past. I suppose it is two and a half years now and more that we have been discussing our common problems. And whether they would be of wheat or oil or any other difficult matter, they are dealt with as friends should deal with such problems: as a family deals with its own problems; and there emerges from these discussions the kind of compromise, the kind of composition of difficulties with which we can both live, and which can serve as guides for the future.

And the one thing that I want to take the privilege of repeating to you, that the Prime Minister said to me this afternoon, and in which it gives me the greatest pride and satisfaction, is this: "In the last two and a half years, Mr. President," he said, "the relations of Canada and the United States have reached the height of friendliness, cordiality, and true cooperation that has never before been attained so far as I know." "And," he said further, "to my mind those relations are a model for the world, if the world is truly seeking, through cooperation, to attain a just and permanent peace."

So you can understand how happy all of us are here, to say through me, that we are proud to have with us this great representative of Canada—and to ask all of you to join with me in a Toast to Her Majesty Queen Elizabeth the Second.

THE PRIME MINISTER: May I say how deeply grateful I am to you for the opportunity that you have given my wife and me today, to enjoy a day that will always be memorable to us.

You summarized a moment ago the views that I expressed this afternoon, and those views I reiterate now: during the last several years that I have held the position of Prime Minister, our relations and the relations between our two countries, outstanding as they have been in the past, have not been excelled in any other period in our history.

And we owe quite a bit to you in the United States. As a matter of fact, if it hadn't been for Benjamin Franklin—and that is going back a little before our time—if it hadn't been for Benjamin Franklin, we wouldn't have had a Canada, because in 1761 the government of Great Britain gave serious consideration to trading us for the Island of Guadalupe.

And then again, as you Toasted Her Majesty the Queen, we have had differences in the past between the British people and the people of the United States, but as to the Senators here present, you recall on another occasion the only reason that the British have a Commonwealth at all is because there were thirteen Colonies in North America who took a strong and a firm stand in 1775.

Sir, we recall too that we had quite interesting relationships with you during the 1860s and many of our people from Canada enlisted in the Northern army, and some loaned their money to the South; and when it was all over, they once more joined together and gave that reverence to the Union that has been characteristic of the people of this land and out of which the name of Lincoln earned eternal reverence everywhere where liberty is respected and regarded.

And we have had our relations over the years. We were together in two World Wars. We were together, particularly in the Second World War.

That unity which today was epitomized in the manner of the reception that began when you, Mr. Secretary [Herter], received my wife and me at the Airport, there is something about this relationship that I can't describe.

I come into your country. You come into mine. We don't always agree. We sometimes have our differences. But I will always look back on this day as one that represents, to me, the embodiment of those great and eternal principles of liberty. We get together. We discuss. We are not at all afraid. I did not look to see whether the coat of arms of the United States had any sound recording instruments in it. We speak freely. We understand each other.

I see the Chief Justice of the United States here this evening. I think of how your shrines of freedom are our shrines—our shrines are your shrines. And that is the spirit in which we have met again today, a spirit of deep attachment to our respective countries, and only with that recognition in unity can we be assured among the free countries of the world of the maintenance of those things in which we believe.

And I assure everyone here that I come here not to discuss the great election that is about to take place, because after all one of the greatest elements in statesmanship is to view what takes place in another country with detachment, although even with interest. But I say to you, sir, that now that you approach the end of your service to the United States, you have earned from all of us in the free world not only affection, not only the realization that a few short years ago you led the legions of freedom, but in the last 8 years—and I was present when you received your nomination in the City of Chicago—in the intervening 7-1/2 years you have become the embodiment of those principles to which each of us owes our common dedication to the United States of America; great in the opportunities that Providence has given it, magnificent in the manner in which it has discharged its responsibilities that today cover all the seven seas and all the continents.

To you, sir, as the leader of this Nation—this may be my last opportunity to do so, and not only on behalf of my own country but on behalf of the nations of the Commonwealth, which recognize the Queen either as the head of the Commonwealth or in the capacity of Queen of Canada—all of us owe to you, in these days of peace, the same debt of gratitude that we pay you for what you did in the days of war. I am not going to say any more than that.

Thank you, Mr. President, for what represents to me one of those occasions when idle sentiment and words do not convey the meaning I want to express.

To the people of the United States, may I say this: we live side by side, and the fact that we do, and have, in peace, for 150 years, is the greatest answer that can be given to the forces of communism everywhere in the world when they say that this Nation is a warlike and aggressive nation.

We give the people of the world the answer to that statement which has received at the hands of the Communists widespread circulation.

Sir, it has been a privilege to be here. My wife and I very much appreciate everything that has been done. Tomorrow, when I return to my own country, I shall tell the people of that country what they already know: that you and I recognize, and our countries recognize, that only in the maintenance of a unity of purpose and objective, and a common dedication, will the things for which we stand be finally successful.

I ask you, ladies and gentlemen, to rise and drink a Toast to the President of the United States.

3. Prime Minister Diefenbaker's Report of Meeting to the Canadian House of Commons, June 6, 1960

(s/s, No. 60/23)

With the permission of the House I should like to report in general on the visit which I made last Friday and Saturday to Washington at the invitation of President Eisenhower. As I pointed out on my arrival there, this was not a formal visit; it was the kind of call which one makes on a close neighbor with whom one is on friendly terms and with whom one is in the habit of talking over matters of mutual interest.

I particularly point out the warmth of the welcome extended to me because I represented Canada, both by the President himself, his Secretary of State and all the officials and members of the public with whom I came in contact. We are bound to have differences between our countries, as friends and neighbours will, but beneath the surface of whatever intermittent strains may arise in our relationship there is a vein of continued understanding and goodwill that springs not only from our heritage but also from the common sense of the importance of being united in safeguarding common values.

I am going to refer to one or two of the matters which were discussed, although I know the House will not expect me to go into any detail on the substance of those talks. We found ourselves in agreement with regard to the circumstances which led to the summit failure and also the position which the Western nations should now adopt individually and within the NATO alliance in their relations with the Soviet Union. The need is to establish and preserve an equilibrium between the maintenance of defensive preparedness on the one hand and on the other a continued readiness to retain existing contacts with the Soviet world and extend those contacts on the basis of mutual agreement whenever the opportunity arises.

I discussed with the President matters connected with the future policies in NATO. I expressed the view that the time had come for the NATO nations to re-examine the capacity of that alliance to deal with the problems which lie ahead. Hon. Members will recall that at the Ministerial Meeting of NATO last December the United States Secretary of State proposed that a study be made of long-range planning for the 1960's. My view, which I expressed to the President, was that recent international happenings had increased the urgency of undertaking this study.

The United States is already engaged in preliminary work along these lines. My view was that, after that study had been fully proceeded with, the NATO governments should give early and serious attention to the holding of a meeting at heads-of-government level in order that those who have the responsibilities of leadership may join in a collective effort to establish and sketch new lines of endeavour for NATO in the years ahead. All of us are fully conscious of the importance of thorough preliminary consultation, for unless we achieve the free interflow of ideas and suggestions in the future we cannot take advantage of the opportunity to open up new and secure paths of progress for the alliance.

I further stated that should it be agreed that a heads-of-government meeting of NATO should take place, Canada would be prepared to extend invitations to the NATO leaders to hold that meeting in Canada.

I discussed with the President the proposal which he put forward first in 1955, and to which he referred in recent public statements, that consideration should be given to a system of aerial inspection as a means of removing the threat of surprise attack. In that connection, he pointed out the views expressed by the Leader of the Opposition in support of action in that direction. The President confirmed that study was being given to the "open-skies" proposal. I said that such a proposal, if and when advanced in the United Nations, should have co-sponsors and that Canada would join in sponsoring an appropriate resolution in that regard.

Other subjects were generally of an international nature, the outlook for progress on disarmament and the ending of nuclear-weapons tests. There was agreement on the importance of pursuing negotiations on these matters which would serve at the moment as important and continuing points of contact with the Soviet Government. Information on the most recent Soviet disarmament plans as enunciated by Mr. Khrushchev was not available in comprehensive form and it was therefore not possible to discuss this development in any detail. However, as the Secretary of State for External Affairs said in the House last Friday, although the Soviet proposals are heavily weighted in propaganda aspects, the Western nations should demonstrate a readiness to examine them with serious intent, and the agency for that consideration exists in the 10-nation Committee on Disarmament which will resume its deliberations tomorrow in Geneva.

As for the bilateral relations between the United States and Canada, various aspects of policies affecting the two countries jointly were discussed, including continental defence and problems in the trade and economic fields. We spoke frankly about the concern that Canadians feel over recent United States wheat surplus disposal policies which could damage Canadian wheat export markets, particularly in Latin America and Africa. However, I think I can sum up the general feeling and the attitude that was shown during these discussions by reading the words of the communiqué and drawing particular attention to those in the concluding paragraph. [See entry 1 above for joint communiqué.]

Again, I repeat . . . that the unusual warmth of the welcome and the expressions not only of friendship but of a desire to co-operate in every way so as not to cause harm one to the other was most apparent, and I must publicly express my thanks and appreciation for everything that was done on the part of our great neighbour to show its feelings toward our country.

C. President Dwight D. Eisenhower and Prime Minister John G. Diefenbaker, Washington, D.C., January 17, 1961

1. Exchange of Remarks Between President Eisenhower and Prime Minister Diefenbaker at Signing of the Columbia River Basin Treaty, January 17, 1961

(PP/Dwight D. Eisenhower, Vol. 1960-1961, No. 416, pp. 1029-30)

THE PRESIDENT: The signing of this treaty marks the culmination of a long effort—indeed 16 years long—between Canada and the United States to reach a common ground of agreement on the development of the Upper Columbia.

I personally believe that the work which will now go ahead, when these treaties are properly approved, will be one of the great developments for the benefit of both our countries.

Moreover, in more intangible benefits, there is a tremendously important advance. That comes about because these two nations living so close together have to watch each other, probably, at times. Nevertheless, we are such great friends, as Mr. Diefenbaker has also said, that we serve as a model for other countries.

This is another step in cementing that friendship and making it more lasting and useful to the whole world.

So, for me to be able to sign this treaty, in the last 2 or 3 days of this administration, is indeed a great personal gratification and satisfaction. I thank you, Mr. Prime Minister, and your associates for the work you have done to facilitate this treaty and to be a part of this great step in the future cooperation of our countries.

THE PRIME MINISTER: This, I believe, is an historic milestone in Canadian-American relations. As you have said, this project is one of the greatest projects that has ever been undertaken. Indeed, it is the first occasion in history when two nations, side by side, have agreed to the distribution of power as between their two countries, and the sharing of the development of an international river to the same extent as will be the result in the years ahead.

And as you have said, this relationship between our countries is something that is a model for all mankind. Indeed, it would be difficult to understand the relationship between our two countries when placed alongside the relationships that prevail between other countries in the world today. My hope is that, in the years ahead, this day will be looked back on as one that represents the greatest advance that has ever been made in international relations between countries.

While we are joined in sentiment and in a common dedication to freedom, we are, under this project, joined as well in an economic development for the benefit of both our countries.

And I want to say this, Mr. President, as you approach the end of your term of office, and in deep sincerity, how much your friendship has meant to me. And I speak for all Canadians when I wish you good health, long years of service on behalf of peace. Indeed we think of you as the great leader of the legions of freedom in the darkest days of war. We think of you as well as the architect of international relationships. Your dedication to the achievement and the attainment of peace is something that has been an inspiration to all of us in the free world.

I think that this day is the culmination of your dedication to the assurance that each nation is indeed its brother's keeper and that only in the raising of the opportunities economically can there be a true foundation for peace.

We, in our cooperation, are building for the future. And if only the other nations could catch something of this relationship so that each of us would through economic endeavor and cooperation help others less enjoyably placed economically, a long step forward can be made.

This is a great day. I wish you well, and I know that in the days ahead your contribution everywhere in the world, with the prestige that is yours, will do much to bring about the attainment of peace in this generation.

2. Prime Minister Diefenbaker's Report of Meeting to the Canadian House of Commons, January 18, 1961

(CHCD, January 18, 1961, p. 1159)

Mr. Speaker, as the house knows the Columbia river treaty was signed in Washington yesterday. The President and Secretary of State and the under secretary of the interior signed for the United States of America. The treaty was signed for Canada by myself together with the Minister of Justice and the Canadian ambassador at Washington.

I indicated the other day that I would make at the earliest possible date copies of the treaty and also the statement I made outlining some of the features and particulars of that treaty. In view of the widespread interest in these documents I propose that with the consent of the house they be printed as an appendix to *Hansard*.

May I say that in the signing of this tremendous treaty the course followed was one that gave emphasis to the importance of the occasion. The fact is that it was the last major official discharge of responsibility on the part of the President of the United States. That fact gives it emphasis. During the course of our stay there the Minister of Justice, myself and several representatives from the two countries were entertained at luncheon at the White House, the last function of the kind that will take place during the presidency of Dwight D. Eisenhower.

I agree with the remarks that were made at the conclusion of this treaty, that it represents a major advance in co-operation by the two nations without the sacrifice of the rights, the sovereignty or otherwise of either country, and is indeed a landmark in responsible joint action by nations for their economic betterment. . . .

D. President John F. Kennedy and Prime Minister John G. Diefenbaker, Washington, D.C., February 20, 1961

1. Joint Statement of President Kennedy And Prime Minister Diefenbaker, February 20, 1961

(PP/John F. Kennedy, Vol. 1961, No. 45, pp. 106-7)

President Kennedy and Prime Minister Diefenbaker met today in Washington to discuss informally a wide range of international problems as well as bilateral questions of interest to the two countries. The Secretary of State, Mr. Dean Rusk, and the United States Ambassador-designate to Canada, Mr. Livingston Merchant, assisted in these discussions together with the Secretary of State for External Affairs, Mr. Howard Green, and the Canadian Ambassador to the United States, Mr. Arnold Heeney.

The President and the Prime Minister welcomed this early opportunity for a friendly exchange of views between neighbors, in a tradition consistent with the long and intimate association between the peoples of Canada and the United States.

The President and the Prime Minister reviewed defense and security problems in all their aspects. They reaffirmed their purpose to work together for peace and freedom in the world. They expressed their readiness to cooperate wholeheartedly with all countries which sincerely seek this objective whatever the differences in approach or outlook. They recognized the central importance of the United Nations, as well as the essential role of direct diplomatic negotiation, in the pursuit of peaceful settlements. They agreed on the need to work steadily toward effective agreements under international control in the field of disarmament.

In reviewing the bilateral problems between the two countries, emphasis was placed upon the various consultative arrangements of a formal and informal character which have been developed between the

United States and Canada as a valuable supplement to the traditionally close and friendly relations between the two governments. The President and the Prime Minister noted with satisfaction that joint meetings are about to take place in Canada between members of both houses of the federal legislatures of the two nations.

The President and the Prime Minister re-emphasized the importance of close consultation on economic matters. They announced that the joint United States-Canada Committee on Trade and Economic Affairs will meet in Washington, D.C. on March 13. This joint Committee at Cabinet level has been of great value over the years in furthering understanding between the two governments on questions affecting economic relations of the two countries.

2. Prime Minister Diefenbaker's Report of Meeting to the Canadian House of Commons, February 20, 1961

(CHCD, February 20, 1961, pp. 2220-21)

Mr. Speaker, I am deeply grateful to the house for giving me the opportunity to make a statement on the meeting which the Secretary of State for External Affairs (Mr. Green) and I had earlier today with President Kennedy and the Secretary of State of the United States, Mr. Dean Rusk.

I shall begin by reading the text of the communique which was issued at the conclusion of the meeting, for it sets forth in general the nature of the discussions which took place. [See previous entry.]

I wish now to elaborate on the text of the communique by giving the house something of the atmosphere and substance of the meeting. I would emphasize at once that I found on the part of the President and the Secretary of State not only an attitude of the utmost friendliness but an obvious desire to assure the maintenance and continuance of the good relations which prevail between the United States and Canada. For my part, having had this opportunity to sit down with President Kennedy in a common, informal examination of the issues which face our countries, I have returned to Ottawa reinforced in my conviction that with good will and constructive endeavour on both sides there is no problem which we cannot surmount.

Our discussion began with a general review of the international situation. Naturally, the house will realize that I cannot go into detail, but there are certain subjects that should be mentioned.

The problem uppermost was the situation in the Congo and in particular in proceedings which are now taking place in the United Nations. Canada and the United States share the same aims in this complicated and dangerous crisis. We are agreed on the importance of preserving the independence and the integrity of the Congo and on the vital necessity of avoiding civil war in that country. We are agreed that in order to keep the Congo out of the cold war it is imperative to support the United Nations fully. Only in this way will it be possible for the Congolese, in freedom and without violence, and without interference from the outside, to re-establish the internal stability of their country and to provide a new cement to the structure of their institutions so as to work out their political destiny.

We looked at the situation in Laos where Canada, as a member of the international supervisory commission, has had a direct interest for some years. There have been developments there over the week end. These and related developments were discussed, in general terms, with particular reference to the declaration of policy made yesterday by the King of Laos.

As to NATO, the President and I agreed that the United States and Canada, with all member nations, must collaborate in the work of building up the cohesion and unity of the alliance. I drew the President's attention to my continuing view that there are certain problems facing NATO which will require the attention of heads of government as soon as it is possible for them to be assembled.

In the field of joint defence on the North American continent we discussed a number of current questions, including in particular the Canada-United States defence production sharing program.

We also dealt in a general way with the economic field, not going into detail, however, because, as I mentioned earlier, there will be a meeting within the next three weeks of the joint committee on trade and economic affairs at cabinet level.

We discussed the problem of international surpluses and the food for peace program which is now also receiving the attention of the United Nations.

With regard to trade, I gave the President an explanation of Canada's view on trade between our countries and the importance which we attach to improving the trading position of Canada in relation to the United States.

We also discussed the organization for economic co-operation and development and I informed the President that the Canadian government would shortly be submitting the O.E.C.D. convention to parliament for approval. The President assured me that he shared the Canadian view regarding the importance of this convention which is now receiving congressional consideration.

Mr. Speaker, no one could meet with the President without being impressed by his broad and far-sighted view of international affairs. The President and his senior colleagues demonstrated in every way an understanding interest in the relations between our countries. The President revealed a ready desire to preserve the distinctive quality of the Canadian-United States partnership, with each nation discharging its responsibility toward the attainment of the common purpose and without the sacrifice of sovereignty by either country.

In the past we have had the privilege of hearing presidents of the United States speak to the Senate and members of the House of Commons. We have heard President Truman, and President Eisenhower, and I am happy at this time to announce that I extended an invitation—one with which I hope this house and the other place will agree—to President Kennedy on behalf of the Canadian government to visit Canada at some convenient time before the end of the current session of parliament. The President advised me that he would be glad to accept this invitation, subject to the determination of a time convenient to both our countries.

The arrangements for the visit will be proceeded with through diplomatic channels. In extending the invitation I expressed the hope that he would mark his first visit to our country as President by consenting to address a joint session of parliament.

To summarize my remarks, I am more than ever convinced of the value of these informal meetings. There is something about our relationship which might well be a model for other nations in the world, as exemplified in the manner which was so evident today when we met together annd discussed the problems which face our respective countries. Where there is disagreement we endeavour by mutual concession to arrive at a basis for amicable settlement, thereby epitomizing something which is so necessary in the world today.

This meeting should not be measured in terms of its duration or in the number of flags unfurled but in the opportunity it offered for better acquaintanceship, better understanding and also for making possible a discussion of common problems in a businesslike and informal manner appropriate to the closest of neighbours and friends.

To me this was a revealing and exhilarating experience. The President of the United States has the kind of personality that leaves upon one the impression of a person dedicated to peace, to the raising of economic standards not only in his own country but in all countries, and to the achievement in his day of disarmament among all the nations of the world.

E. Prime Minister John G. Diefenbaker and President John F. Kennedy, Ottawa, Ontario, May 16-18, 1961

1. Prime Minister Diefenbaker's Introduction of President Kennedy to Both Houses of the Canadian Parliament, May 17, 1961

(CHCD, Appendix, May 17, 1961. Address of John F. Kennedy. pp. 4961-62)

Today it is my honour to welcome here, on behalf of the Canadian parliament and people, one who comes to us not only as a new but as a renowned leader of the free world, and also as a good neighbour and friend.

Mr. President, the extraordinary welcome from the people which you have received is a demonstration of their admiration and affection not only for your country but for you and Mrs. Kennedy. As you passed through the streets yesterday and today, Mr. President, you must have been conscious of a divided attention, and all who had eyes to see could see why that was so.

This is an unusual gathering, Mr. President, bringing together as it does the members of the Senate and the House of Commons. I believe with your experience in both legislative branches of parliament you will feel particularly at home in the parliament of Canada, for I am told that on occasion the Senate of the United States and the House of Representatives are not always in agreement either with themselves or with the President. In that regard they seem at the moment to be similar in class and kind to what we have here.

In these houses of parliament, as with yours, we cherish our right to live under a system of government deriving its just powers from the consent of the governed, our right and our glory being that here in our institutions, opposing views are respected. Here, as in your country, views are not only uttered but are debated. Men who are free to speak are also compelled to answer, and it is our common right to live our lives according to our lights and without any dictation from any ruling clique. Today, sir, I bring to your attention the words of Robert Frost, the poet of your inauguration, who recently in the city of Jerusalem signed the guest book of the university there with these words:

> Something there is that does not love a wall
> —it is friendship.

When you spoke in New Brunswick to the university there four years ago you quoted from the same poet:

Good fences make good neighbours.

We in Canada believe that good fences are necessary. We are determined that as to our two countries, no one shall be permitted to build a wall between them. We have fences between us, but they are not hostile barriers; but rather, by way of co-operation, evidences of distinctiveness that each of our countries cherishes and of the independence and sovereignty that each must respect in the other.

Throughout the years there has been a movement of peoples between our countries. Hundreds of thousands, if not millions, have gone from Canada to the New England states, and great numbers from the United States have settled in Canada. Indeed, sir, Massachusetts holds a special place in my heart and sentiment, for two of my wife's ancestors, Brewster and Warren, were of the Mayflower company that laid the foundations of democracy in the new world in the British tradition.

I summarize the relations between our countries as represented in your presence here today by that inscription on the St. Lawrence seaway granite plaque which reads:

> This stone bears witness to the common purpose of two nations whose frontiers are the frontiers of friendship, whose ways are the ways of freedom, and whose works are the works of peace.

We have our problems in trade; we have them in defence. I am of those who believe this, that no nation in the world today by itself can provide for adequate defence. Canada cannot. I say to you, sir, that one of the abiding things of this gathering has been the fact that we realize this fact, that we together have a responsibility to each other to maintain jointly our defences for the benefit of freedom.

That brings me to the next question, and it is this; the need for unity in addition to security. Co-operation in defence and economically is a price that all freedom loving nations, great and small, not only in NATO but everywhere in the world, must pay; for the prize of co-operation may be freedom itself.

I think great benefit comes to us by your visit, sir, in that you again have the opportunity of stating some of the principles upon which the western world stands. I have felt that we have failed among the western nations to state in simple terms the things in which we believe so that all mankind may understand that those principles shall recognize the equality of all peoples, that each and all shall work for the benefit of the other.

Great responsibilities rest upon those such as yourself who are the leaders of the free world. Leaders will not always be right in their decisions. Sometimes they will be on the wrong side. That is of the essence of democracy; but as long as they are never on the side of wrong, freedom will not suffer.

You have a great responsibility as the leader of the world's most powerful nation; young in years, old in experience, scholar, veteran, author, statesman. When I was in Ireland a few weeks ago—and Ireland is the rock whence you were hewn, sir—I was told something of your ancestry, shown the arms of the O'Kennedys of Ormonde and of the Fitzgeralds, renowned in Irish history as the "Geraldines." And I was shown a poem about the Geraldines written by the poet-patriot Thomas Davis, who, incidentally, was the most famous Dublin associate of one of Canada's fathers of Confederation, Thomas D'Arcy McGee, one verse of which has significance today:

"These Geraldines! These Geraldines! rain
Wears away the rock
And time may wear away the tribe
That stood the battle's shock;
But ever, sure, while one is left of all
That honoured race,
In front of freedom's chivalry is that
Fitzgerald's place."

That is your place today, Mr. President. And I express the wish, not only on behalf of my fellow Canadians but of all people who love freedom everywhere that you may be richly endowed—in thought with faith, in words with wisdom, in deed with courage, and always in service.

In these qualities is greatness. These qualities I have in mind when I present to the Senate and the House of Commons the President of the United States.

2. Address of President Kennedy to Both Houses of Parliament, May 17, 1961

(*Ibid.*, pp. 4962-65)

I am grateful for the generous remarks and kind sentiments expressed toward my country and myself, Mr. Prime Minister. We in the United States have an impression that this country is made up of descendants of the English and the French, but I was glad to hear some applause coming from the very back benches when you mentioned Ireland. I am sure they are making progress forward.

I feel I am truly among friends.

It is a deeply felt honour to address this distinguished legislative body, yet may I say I feel very much at home with you here today, for one third of my life was spent in the parliament of my own country, the

United States congress. There are many differences between this body and mine. The most noticeable to me is the lofty appearance of statesmanship which is on the faces of the members of the Senate, who realize that they will never have to place their case before the people again. I feel at home here also because I remember in my own state of Massachusetts many friends and former constituents who are of Canadian descent. Among the voters of Massachusetts who were born outside the United States the largest group by far was born in Canada. Their vote is enough to determine the outcome of an election, even a presidential election. You can understand that having been elected president of the United States by less than 140,000 votes out of 60 million, I am very conscious of these statistics.

The warmth of your hospitality symbolizes more than the courtesy which may be accorded to an individual visitor. It symbolizes the enduring qualities of amity and honour which have characterized our countries' relations for so many decades. Nearly 40 years ago a distinguished prime minister of this country took the part of the United States at a disarmament conference. He said "They may not be angels, but they are at least our friends." I must say I do not think we have probably demonstrated in the 40 years since then that we are angels yet, but I hope we have demonstrated that we are at least friends.

I must say that in these days when hazard is our constant companion, I think friends are a very good thing to have. Your Prime Minister was the first of the leaders from other lands who was invited to call upon me shortly after I entered the White House, and this is my first trip as President—the first trip of my wife and myself—outside our own country's borders. It is just and fitting and appropriate and traditional that I should come here to Canada across a border which knows neither guns nor guerillas.

But we share more than a common border. We share a common heritage traced back to the early settlers who travelled from the beachheads of the maritime provinces and New England to the far reaches of the Pacific coast. Henry Thoreau spoke a common sentiment for them all: "Eastward I go only by force, westward I go free. And now I must walk towards Oregon and not towards Europe." We share common values from the past, a common defence line at present, and common aspirations for the future—our future, and indeed the future of all mankind.

Geography has made us neighbours. History has made us friends. Economics has made us partners. And necessity has made us allies. Those whom nature hath so joined together, let no man put asunder.

What unites us is far greater than what divides us. The issues and irritants that inevitably affect all neighbours are small indeed in comparison with the issues we face together, above all the sombre threat now posed to the whole neighbourhood of this continent and in fact to the whole community of nations. But our alliance is born not of fear but of hope. It is an alliance which advances what we are for, as well as opposing what we are against.

And so it is that when we speak of our mutual attitude and relationship, Canada and the United States speak in terms of unity. We do not seek the unanimity that comes to those who water down all issues to the lowest common denominator, or to those who conceal their differences behind fixed smiles, or to those who measure unity by standards of popularity and affection instead of trust and respect.

We are allies. This is a partnership, not an empire. We are bound to have differences and disappointments, and we are equally bound to bring them out into the open, to settle them when they can be settled, and to respect each other's views when they cannot be settled.

Thus ours is the unity of equal and independent nations, co-tenants of the same continent, heirs of the same legacy, and fully sovereign associates in the same historic endeavour; to preserve freedom for ourselves and all who wish it. To that endeavour we each must bring great material and human resources, the result of separate cultures and free economies. And, above all, that endeavour requires a free and full exchange of new and different ideas, a full and frank consultation on all issues and all undertakings. For it is clear that no free nation can stand alone to meet the threat of those who make themselves our adversaries, that no free nation can retain any illusions about the nature of that threat, and that no free nation can remain indifferent to the steady erosion of freedom around the globe.

It is equally clear that no western nation on its own can help those less developed lands fulfill their hopes for steady progress. And, finally, it is clear that, in an age when new forces are asserting their strength around the globe, when the political shape of the hemisphere is changing rapidly, nothing is more vital than the unity of your country and mine.

And so, my friends of Canada, whatever problems may exist or arise between us, I can assure you that my associates and I will be ever ready to discuss them with you and to take whatever steps we can to remove them. And whatever those problems may be, I can also assure you that they shrink in comparison with the great and awesome tasks that await us both as free and peace loving nations.

So let us fix our attention not on those matters that vex us as neighbours, but on those issues that face us as leaders. Let us look southward as part of the hemisphere with whose fate we are inextricably bound. Let us look eastward as part of the north Atlantic partnership upon whose strength and will so many depend. Let us look westward to Japan, to the newly emerging lands of Asia and, beyond Asia, to Africa and the Middle East where live the peoples upon whose fate and choice the struggle for freedom may ultimately turn. And let us look at the world in which we live and hope to go on living, and at the way of life for which Canadians and Americans alike have always been willing to give up their lives if necessary to defend and preserve it. I was reminded again of this on my visit to your war memorial.

First, if you will, let us consider our mutual hopes for this hemisphere. Stretching virtually from pole to pole, the nations of the western hemisphere are bound together by the laws of economics as well as geography, by a common dedication to freedom as well as a common history of fighting for it. To make this entire area more secure against aggression of all kinds; to defend it against the encroachment of international communism in this hemisphere; and to see our sister states fulfill their hopes and needs for economic and social reform and development, are surely all challenges confronting your nation and deserving of your talents and resources, as well as ours.

To be sure, it would mean an added responsibility, but yours is not a nation that shrinks from responsibility. The hemisphere is a family into which we were born, and we cannot turn our backs to it in time of trouble. Nor can we stand aside from its great adventure of development. I believe that all the free members of the organization of American states would be both heartened and strengthened by any increase in your hemispheric role. Your skills, your resources, your judicious perception at the council table—even when it differs from our own views—are all needed throughout the inter-American community. Your country and mine are partners in North American affairs; can we not become partners in inter-American affairs?

Second, let us consider our mutual hopes for the north Atlantic community. Our NATO alliance is still, as it was when it was founded, the world's greatest bulwark of freedom. But the military balance of power has been changing. Enemy tactics and weaponry have been changing. We can stand still only at our peril.

NATO force structures were originally devised to meet the threat of a massive conventional attack, in a period of western nuclear monopoly. Now, if we are to meet the defence requirements of the 1960's, the NATO countries must push forward simultaneously along two major lines.

First, we must strengthen the conventional capability of our alliance as a matter of the highest priority. To this end we in the United States are taking steps to increase the strength and mobility of our forces and to modernize their equipment. To the same end, we will maintain our forces now on the European continent, and will increase their conventional capabilities. We look to our NATO allies to assign an equally high priority to this same essential task.

Second, we must make certain that nuclear weapons will continue to be available for the defence of the entire treaty area, and that these weapons are at all times under close and flexible political control that meets the needs of all NATO countries. We are prepared to join our allies in working out suitable arrangements for this purpose.

To make clear our own intentions and commitment, to the defence of the western world, the United States will commit to the NATO command area five—and subsequently still more—Polaris atomic missile submarines, which are defensive weapons, subject to any agreed NATO guidelines on their control and use, and responsive to the needs of all members but still credible in an emergency. Beyond this, we look to the possibility of eventually establishing a NATO sea-borne force which would be truly multilateral in ownership and control, if this should be desired and found feasible by our allies once NATO's non-nuclear goals have been achieved.

Both of these measures—improved conventional forces and increased nuclear forces—are put forward in recognition of the fact that the defence of Europe, and the assurance that can be given to the people of Europe, and the defence of North America, are indivisible; in the hope that no aggressor will mistake our desire for peace with our determination to respond instantly to any attack with whatever force is appropriate, and in the conviction that the time has come for all members of the NATO community to further increase and integrate their respective forces in the NATO command area, co-ordinating and sharing in research, development, production, storage, defence, command and training at all levels of armaments. So let us begin. Our opponents are watching to see if we in the west are divided; they take courage when we are, and we must not let them be deceived or in doubt about our willingness to maintain our own freedom.

Third, let us turn to the less developed nations in the southern half of the globe, those whose struggle to escape the bonds of mass misery appeal to our hearts as well as to our hopes for a free and stable world community. Both your nation and mine have recognized our responsibilities to these new nations. Our people have given generously, though not always effectively. We could not do less, and now we must do more.

For our historic task in this embattled age is not merely to defend freedom. It is to extend its writ and to strengthen its covenant to peoples of different cultures and creeds and colours, whose policies or economic system may differ from our own but whose desire to be free is no less fervent than our own. Through the organization for economic co-operative development and the development assistance group we can pool our vast resources and skills and make available the kind of long term capital, planning and know-how without which these nations will never achieve independent and viable economies, and without which our efforts will be tragically wasted. I propose further that the O.E.C.D. establish a development centre, where citizens, officials, students and professional men of the Atlantic areas and the less developed countries can meet to study the problems of economic development.

If we in the Atlantic community can more closely co-ordinate our own economic policies—and certainly the O.E.C.D. provides the framework if we but use it, and I hope you will join us in doing so— then surely our potential economic resources are adequate to meet our responsibilities. Consider, for example, the unsurpassed productivity of our farms. Less than 8 per cent of the American working force is on our farms; less than 11 per cent of the Canadian working force is on yours. Fewer men on fewer acres than almost any nation on earth, but free men on free acres, can produce here in North America all the food a hungry world can use, while all the collective farms and forced labour of the communist system produce one shortage after another. This is a day to day miracle of our free societies, easy to forget at a time when our minds are caught up in the glamour of beginning the exploration of space.

As the new nations emerge into independence they face a choice, shall they develop by the method of consent or by turning their freedom over to a system of totalitarian control? In making that decision they should look long and hard at the tragedy now being played out in the villages of communist China.

If we can now work closely together to make our food surpluses a blessing instead of a curse, no man, woman or child need ever go hungry again. And if each of the more fortunate nations can bear its fair share of the effort to help all the less fortunate—not merely those with whom we have had traditional ties but all who are willing and able to achieve meaningful growth and dignity—then this decade will surely be a turning point in the history of the human family.

Finally let me say just a few words about the world in which we live. We should not misjudge the force of the challenge we face, a force that is powerful as well as insidious, that inspires dedication as well as fear, that uses means we cannot adopt to achieve ends we cannot permit.

Nor can we mistake the nature of the struggle. It is not for concessions or territory. It is not simply between different systems. It is the age old battle for the survival of liberty itself. And our great advantage, we must never forget, is that the irresistible tide that began 500 years before the birth of Christ, in ancient Greece, is for freedom, and against tyranny. That is the wave of the future, and the iron hand of totalitarianism can ultimately neither seize it nor turn it back. In the words of Macaulay, "A single breaker may recede, but the tide is coming in."

So we in the free world are not without hope. We are not without friends. And we are not without resources to defend ourselves and those who are associated with us. Believing in the peaceful settlement of disputes and in the defence of human rights, we are working through the United Nations, and through regional and other associations, to lessen the risks, the tensions and the means and opportunity for aggression that have been mounting so rapidly throughout the world. In these councils of peace—in the United Nations emergency force in the Middle East, in the Congo, in the international control commission in southeast Asia, in the ten nation commission on disarmament—Canada has played a leading, important and constructive role.

If we can contain the powerful struggle of ideologies and reduce it to manageable proportions, we can proceed with the transcendent tasks of disciplining the nuclear weapons which shadow our lives and of finding a widened range of common enterprises between ourselves and those who live under communist rule. For, in the end, we live on one planet and are part of one human family; and whatever the struggles that confront us we must lose no chance to move forward toward a world of law and a world of disarmament.

At the conference table and in the minds of men the free world's cause is strengthened because it is just. But it is strengthened even more by the dedicated efforts of free men and free nations. As that great parliamentarian, Edmund Burke, said, "The only thing necessary for the triumph of evil is for good men to do nothing." To do something is in essence why I am here today. This trip is more than a consultation, more than a good will visit. It is an act of faith, faith in your country and your leaders, faith in the capacity of two great neighbours to meet their common problems, and faith in the cause of freedom in which we are so intimately associated.

3. Joint Statement of Prime Minister Diefenbaker and President Kennedy Following Discussions, May 18, 1961

(PP/John F. Kennedy, Vol. 1961, No. 193, pp. 387-88)

President Kennedy and Prime Minister Diefenbaker stated that they had a welcome opportunity of renewing the personal contact they established during the Prime Minister's visit to Washington in February and of examining together questions of concern to both their governments. Their discussions covered broad international issues as well as specific Canadian-United States questions.

United Nations. The President and Prime Minister stated their confidence in the United Nations as an organization dedicated to the peaceful settlement of differences and the defense of national and human rights.

Disarmament. They reaffirmed that the goals sought by both countries is a secure world order in which there can be general disarmament under effective controls. They agreed, in particular, that the negotiation of a nuclear test ban treaty with effective provisions for inspection was a basic step in the process of moving towards disarmament.

Defense. The President and Prime Minister examined certain aspects of U.S.-Canadian defense arrangements and the international defense commitments which both countries have assumed, notably in NATO. They expressed the conviction that a strong defense must be maintained until such time as effective disarmament measures can be secured under proper safeguards. They agreed that it is more than ever necessary that the strength and unity of NATO be reinforced.

Western Hemisphere. The President and Prime Minister discussed the need for accelerating economic progress and social reform throughout the hemisphere, as well as the need to strengthen the strong hemispheric trend away from dictatorship and towards democracy. They recognized that these objectives are closely related. They were in accord that the alignment of a regime in the Western hemisphere with Communist leadership abroad was a matter for serious concern, threatening as it did the peaceful and democratic evolution of the Latin-American peoples. The Prime Minister assured the President of Canada's continued and increasing interest in inter-American affairs.

Laos. The President and Prime Minister examined the problem of Laos. They reaffirmed the objective of negotiating at Geneva a truly independent and neutral Laos. In this connection they examined the experience of the International Control and Supervisory Commission created by the Geneva Accords of 1954. They agreed that the development of and general support for effective control machinery represented a key element in a settlement of the Laos situation and an essential ingredient in achieving peace and stability in South East Asia.

O.E.C.D. Noting that both countries are now members of the Organization for Economic Cooperation and Development and are participating in the Development Assistance Group, the President and Prime Minister examined the continuing responsibility of their countries to assist under-developed nations. Both countries have had active programs of economic assistance to under-developed nations for many years. It was agreed that the new machinery would enable the policies and contributions of the two countries in this field to be more closely related than in the past.

Trade. The President and Prime Minister noted the efforts which their two governments had been making in the tariff negotiations in Geneva to work out satisfactory trading relations with the European Economic Community and exchanged views on how this broad objective of importance to both countries can best be achieved. They emphasized the interest of both countries in promoting employment and a general expansion of world trade.

To banish the scourge of war, to improve the human lot, to defend and to enlarge the area of freedom, to assist peoples less privileged than our own—these are aims that bind together Canada and the United States and which, with other allies and friends, our two countries will, jointly and steadfastly, pursue.

4. Prime Minister Diefenbaker's Report of Meeting to the Canadian House of Commons, June 6, 1960

(CHCD, May 19, 1961, pp. 5039-41)

Following the usual custom I intend to make a statement concerning some of the matters which were discussed between President Kennedy and myself, in order to amplify to some extent the terms of the communiqué which, as is the case with all communiqués—and I emphasize the comprehensiveness of that statement—did not cover in particular, or deal in detail with what has taken place, for reasons which will be obvious to most people.

The President placed before parliament his views on certain major issues before us, and what he said to me personally was, of course, consistent with what he said in parliament although amplified in considerable detail. The scope of the discussions was set forth in the communiqué. While the nature of some of the subjects discussed denies that they be given public utterance, I think I can properly report on some of the main topics of the discussion.

As far as the world situation in general is concerned, there is a continuing crisis as the Soviet Union wages its campaign for global domination, and the dust clouds of soft words and the periodic soft answers must not be allowed to delude anyone into believing that the Soviet challenge will not continue with unabated, or even increased, determination. However, today an announcement was made which all the world hopes will lead to an amelioration of relations between east and west. I refer, of course, to the prospective meeting between the President of the United States and Chairman Khrushchev. Immediately on his arrival, when we met together personally, the President gave me that information, and we both expressed the hope that out of that meeting in Vienna in consequence of the personal exchange of views might come, in the interests of humanity as a whole, that degree of agreement which has been the expectation and the hope of mankind since 1946.

As far as our relations with the United States and the western hemisphere are concerned, President Kennedy laid strong emphasis on them, both in his public and in his private discussions. We reviewed the problems facing all the countries of North and South America, and noted the situation, among a number of these countries, in connection with different ranges and stages of economic development, and the special situations in regard to their social and political structures which have such a bearing on both their development and stability.

The President would welcome Canada's participation in the organization of American states. This, of course, has been discussed and was recently discussed in this house by the Secretary of State for External

Affairs. So far as this question is concerned, which has been a continuing one throughout the year for the consideration of governments of Canada, it is still in that category and, of course, no commitments were made, or would be made, without parliament being made aware in advance of any such action.

I was much impressed with the emphasis which the President placed on the importance of the problems confronting our two countries' hemispheric affairs. I assured him that his views would be the subject of serious consideration. I referred to his reviews respecting membership in the organization of American states and the other problems that are incidental to that membership, and I should hope, that at an early date parliament will have the opportunity, if it so desires, of discussing this question.

With reference to Cuba, I made it clear to the President that the Canadian government has no intention of acting as mediator between the United States and Cuba. Indeed, as stated before, there was no foundation for the press report that such an offer had been put forward.

We discussed the affairs of southeast Asia, and particularly the situation in Laos and South Viet Nam. We are agreed on the objective of establishing a truly independent and neutral Laos, and of the necessity of securing general support for effective control machinery; because only if this is done will the Laos situation be resolved and peace and stability attained in southeast Asia. We discussed the experience of the international control and supervisory commissions, on which Canada has been serving, and the vital importance of the role of these commissions was emphasized.

It is natural that the question of Chinese representation in the United Nations at the next session of the general assembly should have been canvassed, and we agreed to consult together, therefore, in the next few months in respect of this subject, because it will not come up for consideration until September.

The policies and programs of our countries in relation to underdeveloped nations received attention. We recognize that we now have, in the development assistance group, a new forum for reviewing and co-ordinating our programs in this field. I placed before the President, with some degree of pride, the outstanding record of Canada in aiding other countries since the end of World War II, and I also pointed out the very substantial increase in Colombo aid and in the general scale of aid that has been given since 1958.

There was some considerable discussion in the field of economic affairs. I pointed out that Canada has a tremendous balance of payments deficit in commodity trade, and that this was a matter that had to be resolved. Each of our countries is by a wide margin the other's most important trading partner. With the great volume and complexity of our economic relations it is realized that problems will arise but what is of paramount important is that these problems be met through discussion, by regular consultation and free exchanges of views and the continuing spirit of good will.

The European economic community and the tariff relationships now being worked out were discussed at length. Both countries have been working actively to ensure that trading relationships with this community should favour the maintenance and development of a large volume of trade in each direction. The importance of trading relationships with Europe would be considerably enhanced if the United Kingdom government decided to join the Six in the common market.

The problem that is common to both of us, namely farm surpluses, especially wheat, was discussed. We agree to continue to work closely together in this field. I know the house will endorse the views expressed by the President on Wednesday about food surpluses and how to make constructive use of them. The food for peace program already embodies many of those ideas. I express my appreciation of the support which the United States has given to the Canadian suggestion for a food bank made at the U.N. and the F.A.O. My expectation is that some more specific proposals in this regard will be placed before the United Nations assembly in September.

Questions of defence were discussed mostly in connection with NATO. Emphasis was laid on the increase in the capability of the alliance to wage war defensively with conventional forces in order to reduce the likelihood of having to rely more extensively upon nuclear weapons for defence.

In so far as NATO is concerned, the views I expressed to the President were that with a population of about 400 million people and with a gross national product four times that of the Soviet union, the NATO nations possess great strength, but that the strengthening of unity in NATO is a continuing imperative and must not be neglected. I believe that the leaders of the NATO countries will have to advance further than the steps already taken to strengthen wider unity, not only in defence but economically and even politically.

The position of affairs in West Berlin was discussed. It is of great importance to Canada, and Canadians should realize this fact; for Canada has undertaken, along with its NATO allies, serious commitments in regard to West Berlin and the maintenance of the freedom of the people of that city.

The President told me of what was taking place in Geneva from the point of view of the United States, and of the endeavour in particular to reach agreement on a pact to end nuclear testing. I believe that as we endeavour to bring about disarmament, an effective treaty to end nuclear testing is a basic step before any disarmament of a more general character can be achieved. I believe we must continue to press for controlled disarmament and in particular, in the light of the progress of the last few years in the upper skies and the recent achievements of Commander Shepard and Major Gagarin, we face the stern fact that without international control of space the future will be even more perilous than the present.

In so far as our purposes are concerned, I am of those who have advocated not only to the President but on other occasions that we in the free world should explain our purposes, our ideals, our aims, to the noncommitted world to a degree that we have not done heretofore. I found in my trip to Asia some years ago that too often the interpretation of what we stand for has been left to the whims of the communists. Indeed, I believe that in 1918 when President Wilson made his declaration, and again in 1941 with the Atlantic charter, these declarations had a tremendous effect; and I feel that today the ideals of the free world should be restated in simple terms so that all mankind will know that we have joined in a declaration of principles, and that all will recognize in these principles the equality of races and will condemn discrimination in any form.

I think all of us were very pleased at the manner in which Canadians received the President and his wife. I want to say particularly how much I appreciated the fact that, while no arrangements had been made for him to meet the members of this house and the other place, as soon as I suggested it to him on the evening of his arrival he said he fully understood that this would be the proper course to follow and in keeping with the responsibility discharged by the parliamentarians of this country. We recognize President Kennedy as the courageous, inspiring leader of the free world. He bears a tremendous burden. His concern is great: his dedication is great. I think our meeting together was worthwhile in every sense of the word, for it underlined that spirit of co-operation between our nations that is a model for all mankind.

F. President John F. Kennedy and Prime Minister Harold Macmillan, Nassau, Bahamas, December 18-21, also with Prime Minister John G. Diefenbaker, December 21-22, 1962

1. *Prime Minister Diefenbaker's Report of Meeting to the Canadian House of Commons, January 25, 1963*

(s/s, No. 63/6, pp. 6-7, 11-12)

. . . I was in Nassau. I formed certain ideas. I read the communique that was issued there and I came to certain conclusions based on that communique. Those conclusions are as follows, and these are the views expressed also by the United States Under-Secretary of State, George W. Ball: that nuclear war is indivisible; that there should be no further development of new nuclear power anywhere in the world; that nuclear weapons as a universal deterrent are a dangerous solution. Today an attempt is being made by the United States to have the NATO nations increase their conventional arms. The Nassau agreement seemed to accept these three principles as basic, and to carry them out both countries agreed to assign to NATO part of their existing nuclear force as the nucleus of a multilateral force.

What was the plan? The "Skybolt", they said, had not been too successful—although it is ironical that the day after the communique the first one was successfully launched into space. The day is rapidly passing when we will have missile sites that are set, firm, on land. The new concept is the "Polaris" missile, which is delivered from a submarine. When the "Polaris" missiles are delivered to the United Kingdom as part of the multi-lateral force, Britain will not have her independent nuclear-deterrent power any more to the same extent, excepting to use these in a case of supra-national emergency.

. . . I am going to read the paragraphs in question from the communique. They illustrate in a most striking way the state of flux of the defence of the free world. The communique shows that changes are taking place, and I will read the various paragraphs that set this out:

> "The President informed the Prime Minister that for this reason—" (That was, that it was very complex, and so on) ". . . and because of the availability to the United States of alternative weapons systems, he had decided to cancel plans for the production of 'Skybolt' for use by the United States. Nevertheless, recognizing the importance of the 'Skybolt' programme for the United Kingdom and recalling that the purpose of the offer of 'Skybolt' to the United Kingdom in 1960 had been to assist in improving and extending the effective life of the British V-bombers, the President expressed his readiness to continue the development of the missile as a joint enterprise between the United States and the United Kingdom, with each country bearing equal shares of the future cost of completing development."

Then the Prime Minister of the United Kingdom, while recognizing the value of this offer, decided, after full consideration, not to avail himself of it because of doubts which had been expressed about the prospects of the success of the enterprise. As an alternative, the President offered the "Hound Dog" missile; but the "Hound Dog" missile cannot be used on British aircraft because it would put the bottom of the aircraft too close to the ground, causing danger to those operating the planes.

The statement continues:

"The Prime Minister then turned to the possibility of provision of the 'Polaris' missile to the United Kingdom by the United States. After careful review, the President and the Prime Minister agreed that a decision on 'Polaris' must be considered in the widest context both of the future defence of the Atlantic Alliance and of the safety of the whole free world. . . . The Prime Minister suggested and the President agreed, that for the immediate future a start could be made by subscribing to NATO some part of the forces already in existence. This could include allocations from United States strategic forces, from United Kingdom Bomber Command, and from tactical nuclear forces now held in Europe. Such forces would be assigned as part of a NATO nuclear force and targeted in accordance with NATO plans."

Finally, they came out in favour of this multilateral NATO nuclear force. Returning to the "Polaris," the President and the Prime Minister agreed that the purpose of their two governments with respect to the provision of the "Polaris" missiles should also be provided. These forces, and at least equal United States forces, would be made available for inclusion in a NATO multilateral nuclear force. At the same time, while they set up this multilateral force in embryo, the last paragraph points out that the President and the Prime Minister agreed that, in addition to having a nuclear shield, it was important to have a non-nuclear sword. For this reason, the communique concludes, they agreed on the importance of increasing the effectiveness of their conventional forces on a worldwide basis.

That is a tremendous step—a change in the philosophy of defence; a change in the views of NATO, if accepted by the NATO partners. Certainly it represents a change in the views of two nations which play such a large part in the NATO organization. They went further, as I understand it. They concluded that the day of the bomber is phasing out. Britain wanted a striking force of its own. Britain needed a delivery system produced at the lowest cost. Hence, the "Skybolt." With the advent of the "Polaris" missile, the United States believed there was no longer need for the "Skybolt," and this was agreed to by the Prime Minister of the United Kingdom. Who made the mistake? Are they to be condemned? No less than $600 million was spent on the development of the "Skybolt," which was believed to be the essence of defence measures for the United Kingdom itself. I point this out because everywhere in the world, as a result of Khrushchev's changing moods, and vast improvements in technology both with respect to defensive and offensive warfare, the decisions of today are often negatived tomorrow. . . .

To summarize our viewpoint, there is a will to peace, as the Secretary of State for External Affairs said yesterday. There is progress being made. We must maintain our defence. We shall not allow Canada to be placed in a subservient or unsovereign position. We shall follow the course that we have been following—one that has been consistent. It has been one of calm consideration of the matters as they arise.

We know . . . that the way to prevent nuclear war is to prevent it. What course should we take at this time? I emphasize what I have already stated, that we shall at all times carry out whatever our responsibilities are. I have said that strategic changes are taking place in the thinking of the Western world, and there is general recognition that the nuclear deterrent will not be strengthened by the expansion of the nuclear family. With these improvements in the international situation, this is no time for hardened decisions that cannot be altered. We must be flexible and fluid, for no one can anticipate what Khrushchev will do.

A meeting is about to take place in Ottawa of the NATO nations. They will meet here on May 21 to 23 and the very fact that they are meeting here indicates the attitude towards Canada and the feeling of the NATO nations towards her. . . .

What shall our attitude be? It will not be one of recklessness, not one of making final decisions in the face of a changing world. I mentioned Nassau a moment ago and, as one examines what took place there, he realizes that we are living in a new and changing world of defence realism. . . .

I have said earlier that all the nations made mistakes, $3 billion worth of mistakes and more, up to 1960, but the fact that a mistake may have been made, or may not have been made should not be a basis for the continuation of a policy just because to admit it would be wrong. Delivery of the F-104G has commenced, but the strike-reconnaissance role has been placed under doubt by the recent Nassau declaration concerning nuclear arms, as well as other developments both technical and political in the defence field. It will be necessary, therefore, at this meeting in May, for Canada to give consideration to this matter and we will, in co-operation with the nations of NATO, undertake a clarification of our role in NATO defence plans and disposition.

We are united in NATO. We have never and will never consent to Canada breaking any of her pledged words or undertakings. It is at that meeting, where there will be reviewed the entire collective defence policy, that we shall secure from the other member nations their views, and on the basis of that we will be in a position to make a decision, a consistent decision, first to maintain our undertakings and secondly to execute, if that be the view, the maintenance of our collective defence. In the meantime the training of Canadian forces in the use of these weapon systems can continue.

So far as NORAD is concerned I have said at the beginning of my remarks that Canada's sovereignty must be maintained. We shall continue our negotiations. They have been going on quite forcibly for two months or more. . . .

There was never any concealment of the fact. We will negotiate with the United States so that, as I said earlier, in case of need nuclear warheads will be made readily available. In other words, we will be in a position to determine finally, in the interests of Canada and our allies, the course to be followed in the light of changing circumstances in the disarmament field, which have become encouraging recently through Khrushchev's acceptance of even a minimum observation of nuclear testing. We will discuss with the nations of NATO the new concept of a nuclear force for NATO. If that concept at Nassau is carried into effect, much of our planning in the past will pass out of existence.

2. *U.S. Department of State Press Release, "Counter" Report of Meeting, January 30, 1963*

(U.S. Department of State, Press Release entitled "U.S. And Canadian Negotiations Regarding Nuclear Weapons," January 30, 1963)

. . . During the debate in the House of Commons various references were made to recent discussions at Nassau. The agreements made at Nassau have been fully published. They raise no question of the appropriateness of nuclear weapons for Canadian forces in fulfilling their NATO or NORAD obligations.

Reference was also made in the debate to the need of NATO for increased conventional forces. A flexible and balanced defense requires increased conventional forces, but conventional forces are not an alternative to effective NATO or NORAD defense arrangements using nuclear-capable weapons systems. NORAD is designed to defend the North American continent against air attack. The Soviet bomber fleet will remain at least throughout this decade a significant element in the Soviet strike force. An effective continental defense against this common threat is necessary. . . .

The provision of nuclear weapons to Canadian forces would not involve an expansion of independent nuclear capability, or an increase in the "nuclear club." As in the case of other allies, custody of U.S. nuclear weapons would remain with the United States. Joint control fully consistent with national sovereignty can be worked out to cover the use of such weapons by Canadian forces.

VI. Prime Minister Lester B. Pearson (April 1963-April 1968) (Presidents John F. Kennedy and Lyndon B. Johnson)

Prime Minister Lester B. Pearson took office in April, 1963, and served until April, 1968. During his tenure, Mr. Pearson met ten times with U.S. Presidents—once with John F. Kennedy before his November, 1963, assassination, and nine times with Kennedy's successor, Lyndon B. Johnson. Eight of these nine meetings (the one with Kennedy and seven with Johnson) are documented.

President Kennedy had met three times with Prime Minister Diefenbaker, and held one meeting with Mr. Pearson at Hyannis Port, Massachusetts, from May 10-11, 1963, in which an attempt was made to stabilize the Canadian-United States relationship. (See Section A.) The purpose of the meeting was to establish a working relationship between the two leaders, or, to quote their Joint Statement, to inaugurate "a period of particularly active and productive cooperation" including "more frequent consultation at all levels." Although there was no specified agenda, the two governments had exchanged notes on topics each would like to explore, and the two leaders covered these points during ten hours of talks.[1] The issues included mutual defence arrangements and the defence production sharing agreements, disarmament and the abolition of nuclear tests, the GATT talks scheduled for Geneva which would open the Kennedy round, and general proposals for the improvement of channels of communication and consultation between the two nations. However, the most pressing issue and the one

---

[1]See George Bain, "Seek To Repair Rift in the Old Channels," TGM (May 10, 1963), p. 1; George Bain, "Atom Aims Accord Expected," TGM (May 11, 1963), p. 1; and Tom Wicker, "Pearson Confers with President On Joint 'Defense'," NYT (May 11, 1963), pp. 1-3.

which had contributed to the fall of the government of Prime Minister Diefenbaker, was the question of the Canadian acquisition of nuclear warheads. Other important issues included a revision of the Columbia River Treaty and some response to the labor violence that erupted in dockyards of the Upper Great Lakes System.

Specific results of the meeting were stated in the communiqués, and they included the acceptance by the two governments of the Campobello Island, New Brunswick summer home of President Franklin D. Roosevelt, as an International Park, and the opening of what were to be successful discussions on the problem of Canadian nuclear weapons. However, disagreements were reflected over the Columbia River Treaty, territorial jurisdiction at sea, and a current balance of trade in favour of the United States. Documentation for the meeting includes the exchange of remarks at Mr. Pearson's arrival and the two concluding Joint Statements, one on Campobello and the other covering seventeen substantive points from the discussions.

Prime Minister Pearson's second meeting with a U.S. President, which is not documented, occurred when he attended the Kennedy State Funeral in Washington in November of 1963. In the context of a ceremonial event held at the State Department for the foreign dignitaries present at the funeral, Pearson met for about a half hour with the new President, Lyndon B. Johnson.

A third, more substantive meeting between the two leaders was held on January 21 and 22, 1964. (See Section B.) Topics of discussion included such bilateral issues as continuing labor strife within the Seafarers Union on the Great Lakes, the United States interest equalization tax and Canada's increase in the withholding tax on the repatriation of profits to foreign parent companies, and increasing Canadian sales of uranium to countries other than the United States, especially France.[2] The meeting was also the occasion for signing two formal agreements between Canada and the United States, including the revision of the Columbia River Treaty that was now acceptable to all parties, and an agreement on the establishment of an International Park at the Roosevelt home on Campobello Island. Less formally, the meeting resulted in the formation of the Merchant-Heeney working group that was to return the "Principles for Partnership" report, and an agreement-in-principle to start negotiations on a Canadian-United States airline division of routes. The documentation for this meeting includes the Joint Statements on the signing of the two formal agreements, an exchange of toasts at a luncheon held between the two

---

[2]See Bruce Macdonald, "Stronger Links With Johnson Aims of Pearson on 2-Day Visit," TGM (January 22, 1964); NYT (January 22, 1964), p. 64, and George Bain, "Johnson-Pearson Confer," TGM (January 22, 1964), p. 1.

signings, a Joint Statement on the two leaders' talks, and a press conference given by Prime Minister Pearson after his meetings with the President.

Prime Minister Pearson's fourth meeting with a U.S. President, which is not documented, occurred when he met briefly with President Johnson in February 1964 during the International Awards Dinner of the Joseph P. Kennedy, Jr., Foundation held in New York City. Pearson's fifth meeting, again with Johnson, took place in New York City on May 28, 1964. (See Section c.) Both leaders were in the city fulfilling separate speaking engagements, during which they held a brief, informal meeting devoted to the escalating U.S. war in Vietnam.[3] Simultaneously, Canadian-U.S. officials were meeting in Ottawa. The purpose of the meeting was the solicitation, by the President, of a "confidential and responsible interlocutor" between himself and Hanoi. The documentation for this meeting, which resulted in six unsuccessful missions by Canadian diplomat Blair Seaborn to Hanoi, is from the "Pentagon Papers." The first item documented is a U.S. diplomatic report of a high level visit to Ottawa a month before the New York meeting, in which officials "roughed out" the role of the Canadian intermediary. The second item is a telegram to the U.S. Embassy in Saigon recounting the meeting.

Pearson's sixth meeting, again with Johnson, was largely ceremonial as they proclaimed the finalized Columbia River Treaty on September 16, 1964, and viewed from a Tri-Star jet the sites in British Columbia and Washington State where major construction would take place. (See Section D.) The ceremonies began at a NORAD installation at Malmstrom Air Force Base, Great Falls, Montana, and concluded at the International Peace Arch at the border of British Columbia and Washington State. This marked the first time that Johnson had visited Canada.[4] There was only limited time for private talks between the two leaders, which included the two hour aerial survey, and the limousine ride from Vancouver to the border. Documentation for this meeting includes the exchange of welcoming remarks at the air force base in Montana, and the speech of Johnson at the International Peace Arch in which the President articulated his "four pillars" of the Canadian-United States relation. The Johnson speech, given the fact that it

---

[3] See John Saywell, (ed.), *Canadian Annual Review For 1964* (Toronto: University of Toronto Press, 1965), pp. 199-200. According to the PMO's Press Release of May 25, 1964, which gave Pearson's schedule from May 26-29, it stated that he was to be in New York City on May 28, arriving at 12:00 noon; that evening he was to address the American Iron and Steel Institute Dinner; and at 10:00 the next morning was to leave for London, Ontario.

[4] See "Canada and U.S. Implement Pact," NYT (September 17, 1964), p. 29; and Ruth Worth, "Canada Hard Bargainer," TGM (September 17, 1964), p. 1.

constitutes his basic statement on the relationship and that he did not
make a Parliamentary address, should be regarded as comparable to
other Presidential speeches before the Canadian Parliament.

The seventh summit meeting between Prime Minister Pearson and a
U.S. President was also a ceremonial confirmation by him and President Johnson of an agreement that was the result of a long series of
negotiations. The Agreement Concerning Automotive Products between the United States and Canada (Auto Pact) was signed at the LBJ
Ranch at Johnson City near Austin, Texas, during the visit of Mr.
Pearson on January 15 and 16, 1965.[5] (See Section E.) The Auto Pact
rationalized the production of automobiles and automotive parts for a
single North American market, while at the same time assuring a
certain level of Canadian production. Instead of a planned visit to
President Johnson in Washington, the Prime Minister flew from his
regular winter holiday in Florida to the LBJ Ranch. In addition to the
signing of the Pact in this informal setting, the President and Prime
Minister had substantive discussions on the continuing negotiations
over the sharing of commercial air routes, the financial crisis in the
United Nations, problems in NATO, and the war in Vietnam. Specifically, it was reported that President Johnson sought more Canadian
assistance to the U.S. ally, the Republic of Vietnam. However, other
than the signing of the Auto Pact, there were no major results of this
meeting. Documentation includes the exchange of remarks at the
signing of the agreement including a short press conference which
followed, and remarks irreverently reviewing the meeting delivered by
Mr. Pearson at the Rideau Club.

Prime Minister Pearson's eighth meeting with a U.S. President
occurred on April 3, 1965, at the Camp David Presidential retreat in
Maryland.[6] (See Section F.) The meeting occurred in the midst of
President Johnson's first large-scale U.S. build-up in South Vietnam,
the first major U.S. bombing of North Vietnam, and the first signs of
strong opposition to the President's policies in Southeast Asia. The
night before they were to meet, Prime Minister Pearson delivered a
speech at Temple University in Philadelphia in which he carefully
suggested that a bombing halt by the U.S. might be helpful in reaching
peace in Vietnam. The President was displeased with what he saw as
Pearson's interference, and while stating publicly that there was "no
conflict," their luncheon was reported quite chilly and the rapport

---

[5]See Bruce Macdonald, "Prime Minister at LBJ Ranch," TGM (January 16,
1965), p. 1; "U.S. and Canada To End Tariff For Auto Makers," NYT (January
16, 1965); and Bruce Macdonald "Pearson Says Agreement On Autos May
Lead To Other Trade Deals," TGM (January 18, 1965), p. 26.

[6]Cabell Phillips, "President Is Cool To Pearson Plan," NYT (April 4, 1965),
pp. 1, 4; George Bain, "A Significant Difference," TGM (April 7, 1965), p. 7,
and "Report Johnson Angry With Prime Minister," TGM (April 8, 1965).

between the two leaders can be said to have fallen off considerably after this meeting. Within a week of their meeting, President Johnson in a speech at Johns Hopkins University announced expanded economic aid to Vietnam, referring to "misguided friends and allies of the United States."[7] While there was no mention of Pearson's suggestion, the President defended his air attacks as a necessary component of "the surest road to peace" and emphasized that he was ready for "unconditional discussions."[8] In addition, the President promised a billion dollars for a United Nations expanded aid plan in the Mekong. In addition to Vietnam, it was reported that the two leaders talked about air routes, difficulties on the Great Lakes, and the general state of the world, as well as Mr. Johnson's social program, "The Great Society," and social welfare issues generally. The documentation for this meeting includes the Temple University speech, a brief meeting with members of the Press brought to Camp David for the summit meeting, and Prime Minister Pearson's report in the House of Commons.

Prime Minister Pearson's ninth meeting with a U.S. President consisted of a working luncheon before the ceremonial laying of the cornerstone of the Visitors Center at Campobello Island International Park on August 21, 1966.[9] (See Section G.) This visit was Johnson's second to Canada. The issues covered at this meeting included Vietnam, economic trends and trade matters, the problem of inflation, developments in Africa, and NATO problems. Documentation for the meeting includes the exchange of remarks by the President and Prime Minister at the laying of the cornerstone, and the Prime Minister's report in the House of Commons. Coming after the Temple University incident, Pearson's remarks are important in delineating his attitude toward the Canadian-United States relationship, while President Johnson's remarks concentrate on a justification of his Vietnam policy. Noteworthy in both speeches, especially Pearson's, is the perceived summit continuity from the Roosevelt-King years.

The tenth and last meeting between Prime Minister Pearson and a U.S. President took place on May 25, 1967. (See Section H.) This meeting was part of a quick trip to Canada which President Johnson made during the Canadian centennial year. It was anticipated that Johnson would follow the custom set by Franklin Roosevelt in 1943 and followed by all successive Presidents by visiting Ottawa and addressing the Canadian Parliament. However, Mr. Johnson con-

[7]"Johnson Cool To Pearson's Call," TGM (April 5, 1965), p. 1.

[8]John Saywell (ed.), *The Canadian Annual Review For 1965, op. cit.*, p. 222.

[9]On August 20, 1964, Mrs. Pearson and Mrs. Johnson had participated in the official opening and dedication of the Park. For the August 1966 meeting, see Robert Semple, "Johnson Meets Pearson," NYT (August 22, 1966), pp. 1, 12; and Anthony Westell, "To Lunch By Helicopter," TGM (August 22, 1966), p. 1.

stantly equivocated on the date and finally, on short notice, announced that he would visit only EXPO '67, and then talk with Prime Minister Pearson at Pearson's summer home in Harrington Lake, Quebec.[10] After a whirlwind tour of the Place des Nations and the United States Pavilion, the President helicoptered to the Prime Minister's summer home. At a two and one half hour working lunch session, Johnson and Pearson discussed the Middle East crisis occasioned by the Egyptian expulsion of the United Nations Emergency Force (UNEF), and the blockade of the Straits of Tiran to Israeli sea traffic. In these steps that would lead to the June, 1967 Middle East War, President Johnson was quoted as saying that he was going to seek Mr. Pearson's advice as "one of the leading experts."[11] Vietnam was also discussed, but no substantive results arose out of either topic, with the exception that President Nasser used Johnson's visit to denounce Pearson for his pro-Israeli stance. The documentation for this meeting includes President Johnson's remarks upon his arrival at EXPO '67, a press briefing given by the Prime Minister and President prior to Johnson's departure for Washington, and Pearson's report on the meeting in the House of Commons.

A. President John F. Kennedy and Prime Minister Lester B. Pearson, Hyannis, Massachusetts, May 10-11, 1963

1. Exchange of Welcoming Remarks of President Kennedy and Prime Minister Pearson, May 10, 1963

(PP/John F. Kennedy, Vol. 1963, No. 178, p. 394)

THE PRESIDENT: It is a great pleasure to welcome the Prime Minister of Canada to the United States and also to my native State of Massachusetts.

We share a neighbor's pride in the distinguished career which the Prime Minister has carved out in the service of his country and in the cause of peace, and we welcome him as an old friend of the United States. As a former Ambassador to this country in the difficult days of the Second War, as a distinguished international leader in the cause of amity between nations, as President of the General Assembly, and, in 1957, as the result of the culmination of his work for peace, the winner

---

[10]See Max Frankel, "Johnson Flies to EXPO '67," NYT (May 26, 1967), pp. 1, 17, and John Saywell, *Canadian Annual Review for 1967, op. cit.,* pp. 223-24.

[11]Anthony Westell, "Prime Minister, Johnson Discuss," TGM (May 26, 1967), pp. 1, 2.

of the Nobel Prize. We, therefore, are most happy, Prime Minister, that we have this opportunity to meet with you and to discuss those matters which concern our two great countries. We share more than geography—a history, a common commitment to freedom, and a common hope for the future, and it is my strong conviction and that of my fellow countrymen that in this great cause, Canada and the United States should stand side by side. So we are very glad to welcome you here, Prime Minister, as the leader of our neighbor and friend, and also as an old friend of the United States.

THE PRIME MINISTER: May I think you, Mr. President, for your words of welcome and tell you how happy I am that my first visit outside Canada as Prime Minister should have been to that State which has so many unique and historic ties with my own country— Massachusetts. I am looking forward, Mr. President, to my talks with you. In your own characteristic naval fashion, you referred to them as covering the waterfront, and I am sure we will have lots to talk about. We will be discussing matters of interest to our two countries in the context of world peace and better relations between all peoples, and we will be discussing problems of special interest to our two countries, and I am sure we will discuss them in that frank and friendly way which characterizes relations between two peoples who speak the same language, even when they differ, as they are bound to differ from time to time.

I am sure, Mr. President, that after our talks and my brief visit to your summer home in Massachusetts, that we will have a better understanding of each other's problems, and that we will set a course which will further strengthen the friendly and durable good neighborhood between our two peoples.

Thank you again, Mr. President. I am happy to be here. There is only one thing I enjoy more than a visit to the country where I spent so many happy years myself, and that is the return to my own home in Canada.

2. Joint Statement of President Kennedy and Prime Minister Pearson Concerning the Roosevelt Cottage on Campobello Island, May 11, 1963

(*Ibid.*, No. 180, p. 397)

The President and the Prime Minister received a very generous offer from the Hammer family to donate the Roosevelt cottage and surrounding grounds on Campobello Island to the two countries to be used for public purposes which would appropriately commemorate that great President and good friend of Canada. The Prime Minister and the President, after consulting Premier Robichaud of New Brunswick where the island is situated, have accepted the offer with deep appreciation.

3. Joint Statement of President Kennedy and Prime Minister Pearson
Following Discussions, May 11, 1963

(*Ibid.*, No. 179, pp. 394-96)

During the past two days the President and the Prime Minister have met together in this historic State where so many of the currents of the national life of the two countries have mingled from early times.

2. Mr. Pearson's visit to Mr. Kennedy's family home took place in the atmosphere of informality and friendliness which marks so many of the relations between the people of the United States and Canada. There was no agenda for the talks. It was taken for granted that any matter of mutual interest could be frankly discussed in a spirit of goodwill and understanding.

3. In this community on the Atlantic Seaboard, the Prime Minister and President reaffirmed their faith in the North Atlantic Alliance and their conviction that, building upon the present foundations, a true community of the Atlantic peoples will one day be realized. They noted that questions which would be under discussion at the forthcoming NATO Ministerial Meeting in Ottawa would give both countries an opportunity to demonstrate their belief in the Atlantic concept.

4. Their Governments will continue to do everything possible to eliminate causes of dangerous tensions and to bring about peaceful solutions. In this task, they will continue to support the role of the United Nations, and to make every effort to achieve progress in the negotiations on nuclear tests and disarmament.

5. In the face of continuing dangers, the President and Prime Minister emphasized the vital importance of continental security to the safety of the free world and affirmed their mutual interest in ensuring that bilateral defense arrangements are made as effective as possible and continually improved and adapted to suit changing circumstances and changing roles. The Prime Minister confirmed his government's intention to initiate discussions with the United States Government leading without delay towards the fulfilment of Canada's existing defense commitments in North America and Europe, consistent with Canadian parliamentary procedures.

6. President Kennedy and Prime Minister Pearson reaffirmed the desire of the two Governments to cooperate in a rational use of the continent's resources; oil, gas, electricity, strategic metals and minerals, and the use of each other's industrial capacity for defense purposes in the defense production-sharing programs. The two countries also stand to gain by sharing advances in science and technology which can add to the variety and richness of life in North America and in the larger world.

7. The President and the Prime Minister stressed the interest of

both countries in the balance of payments between them and with the rest of the world. The Prime Minister drew particular attention to the large United States surplus in the balance of current payments with Canada and noted the importance of allowing for this fact in determining the appropriate policies to be followed by each country. It was agreed that both Governments should always deal in a positive and cooperative manner with developments affecting their international trade and payments.

8. The Prime Minister and the President noted that encouraging discussions had recently taken place between Governor Herter and Canadian Ministers about the prospects for general trade negotiations and that these talks would be continuing with a large number of other countries in the General Agreement on Tariffs and Trade in Geneva next week. The two Governments will cooperate closely so that these negotiations can contribute to the general advantage of all countries.

9. While it is essential that there should be respect for the common border which symbolizes the independence and national identity of two countries, it is also important that this border should not be a barrier to cooperation which could benefit both of them. Wise cooperation across the border can enhance rather than diminish the sovereignty of each country by making it stronger and more prosperous than before.

10. In this connection the President and the Prime Minister noted especially the desirability of early progress on the cooperative development of the Columbia River. The Prime Minister indicated that if certain clarifications and adjustments in arrangements proposed earlier could be agreed on, to be included in a protocol to the treaty, the Canadian Government would consult at once with the provincial Government of British Columbia, the province in which the Canadian portion of the river is located, with a view to proceeding promptly with the further detailed negotiations required with the United States and with the necessary action for approval within Canada. The President agreed that both Governments should immediately undertake discussions on this subject looking to an early agreement.

11. The two Governments will also initiate discussions shortly on the suitability of present trans-border air travel arrangements from the point of view of the travelling public and of the airlines of the two countries.

12. On the great waters that separate and unite the two countries —the St. Lawrence River and the Great Lakes—it is essential that those who own and sail the ships should be free to go about their lawful business without impediment or harrassment. The Prime Minister and President shared a common concern at the consequences which could result from industrial strife on this central waterway. They urged those directly concerned to work strenuously for improvement in the situation, and to avoid incidents which could lead to further deterioration.

To help bring about more satisfactory conditions they have arranged for a meeting to take place in the near future between the Canadian Minister of Labour, Allan J. MacEachen, the United States Secretary of Labor, W. Willard Wirtz, the President of the AFL-CIO, George Meany, and the President of the Canadian Labour Congress, Claude Jodoin.

13. On the oceans that surround the two countries, while there has always been healthy competition, there has also been a substantial similarity of sentiment among those who harvest the sea. The need for some better definitions of the limits of each country's own fishing waters has long been recognized, particularly with respect to the most active fishing areas. The Prime Minister informed the President that the Canadian Government would shortly be taking decisions to establish a 12-mile fishing zone. The President reserved the long-standing American position in support of the 3-mile limit. He also called attention to the historic and treaty fishing rights of the United States. The Prime Minister assured him that these rights would be taken into account.

14. The President and the Prime Minister talked about various situations of common interest in this hemisphere. In particular they expressed a readiness to explore with other interested countries the possibility of a further cooperative effort to provide economic and technical aid to the countries in the Caribbean area which have recently become independent or which are approaching independence, many of which have long had close economic, educational and other relations with Canada and the United States. Such a program could provide a very useful supplement to the resources which those countries are able to raise themselves or to secure from the international agencies which the United States and Canada are already supporting.

15. Our two countries will inevitably have different views on international issues from time to time. The Prime Minister and the President stressed the importance of each country showing regard for the views of the other where attitudes differ. For this purpose they are arranging for more frequent consultation at all levels in order that the intentions of each Government may be fully appreciated by the other, and misunderstandings may be avoided.

16. These preliminary discussions between the President and the Prime Minister will lead to a good deal of additional activity for the two Governments over the next few months. It is expected that there will be almost continuous exchanges of views during that period as work progresses in resolving many matters of concern to the two countries. Then, in the latter part of the year, meetings will be held of the Joint Cabinet-level Committee on Trade and Economic Affairs and on Defense.

17. The Prime Minister and the President look forward to a period of

particularly active and productive cooperation between the two countries.

B. President Lyndon B. Johnson and Prime Minister Lester B. Pearson, Washington, D.C., January 21-22, 1964

1. Joint Statement of President Johnson and Prime Minister Pearson at Signing of the Columbia River Agreement, January 22, 1964.

(PP/Lyndon B. Johnson, Vol. 1963-1964, Book I, No. 135, pp. 205-6)

President Johnson and Prime Minister Pearson presided today at the White House at the signing of further important agreements between the two governments regarding the cooperative development of the water resources of the Columbia River Basin. Mr. Rusk, Secretary of State, signed for the United States, and Mr. Martin, Secretary of State for External Affairs, signed for Canada.

The arrangements which are now being made will be of great benefit to both countries, particularly to the province of British Columbia in Canada and to the states of Washington, Idaho, Montana, and Oregon in the United States. Today's signing took place in the presence of representatives of the area on both sides of the border.

The downstream power benefits resulting from increased generation in the United States are to be shared by the two countries, and the United States is to compensate Canada for the flood protection which it receives. Effective storage amounting to 15,500,000 acre-feet will be provided in Canada from two dams on the main stem of the Columbia at Mica Creek and Arrow Lakes, and from one dam near Duncan Lake, all in British Columbia. The additional storage approximately doubles that presently available for regulation of the flows of the Columbia River.

Under the terms of the treaty, the United States has the option to commence construction of the Libby project on the Kootenai River in northern Montana with 5,000,000 acre-feet of usable storage. Canada and the United States each will retain all of the benefits from the Libby project which accrue in their respective countries.

At the Hyannis Port meeting in May 1963 President Kennedy and Prime Minister Pearson "noted especially the desirability of early progress on the cooperative development of the Columbia River. The Prime Minister indicated that if certain clarifications and adjustments in arrangements proposed earlier could be agreed on, to be included in a protocol to the treaty, the Canadian Government would consult at once with the provincial Government of British Columbia, the province in which the Canadian portion of the river is located, with a view to proceeding promptly with the further detailed negotiations required with the United States and with the necessary action for approval within Canada. The President agreed that both Governments should immediately undertake discussions on this subject, looking to an early agreement.''

These things have now been done. The way has been cleared for the completion of the necessary financial and related arrangements in the United States and the ratification of the treaty by Canada.

The primary purpose of the first set of documents signed today was to agree now on the clarifications and adjustments that would eliminate possible sources of controversy between the two countries in later years. These documents contain important, if rather technical, provisions regarding such varied matters as conditions governing flood control; the intention to complete arrangements for the initial sale of Canada's share of the downstream power benefits at the time when ratifications of the treaty are exchanged; the avoidance by Canada of standby transmission charges in the event of sales of downstream benefits in the United States; provision for cooperation in connection with the operation of the Libby Dam in the light of the Canadian benefits from it; clarification regarding water diversions; the procedures relating to hydroelectric operating plans; the adoption of a longer stream flow period as a basis for calculating downstream power benefits; various matters relating to power load calculations; adjustments to be considered in the event of the provision of flood control by Canada ahead of schedule; the avoidance of any precedent regarding waters other than those of the Columbia River Basin; and clarification regarding the position of the boundary waters treaty of 1909.

The other set of documents relates to the arrangement to be made for the sale of the Canadian entitlement to downstream power benefits for a period limited to 30 years. The arrangements which the two governments have agreed upon will be beneficial to the United States in facilitating the coming into force of the treaty and thereby removing uncertainty about the availability of power and flood control protection for the northwestern part of the United States for a considerable period of time. Equally, they will benefit Canada by removing uncertainty about the return to be received by Canada from the Columbia River development during the first 30 years after the completion of each dam.

The treaty, together with the arrangements now being made, represents an important step in achieving optimum development of the water resources of the Columbia River Basin as a whole, from which the United States and Canada will each receive benefits materially larger than either could obtain independently.

The arrangements fully respect the sovereignty and the interests of the two countries. As was said in the Hyannis Port Communique,

"Close cooperation across the border can enhance rather than diminish the sovereignty of each country by making it stronger and more prosperous than before."

2. Exchange of Toasts between President Johnson and Prime Minister Pearson, January 22, 1964.

(*Ibid.*, No. 136, pp. 202-8)

THE PRESIDENT: The Prime Minister asked me if I was going to make a speech and I told him I was going to attempt to, not over 3 minutes in length, but I would expect loud and vociferous applause.

I choose to feel that this is not just a meeting today between two heads of government, but rather a reunion of neighbors who meet around the dining table in friendship and with affection. Mr. Prime Minister, we in this country are proud of your achievements and we are joined in your purpose. We have applauded your craftsmanship and approved of your leadership from your major role in the creation of the United Nations to your winning of the Nobel Peace Prize and even your performance as defense man on the Oxford hockey team.

I attended a delightful dinner last evening at the Canadian Embassy and found myself greatly outnumbered. That is not a unique experience for me. Having been in political life as long as I have, I frequently find myself in a minority. But this is such a minority that I thought I should do something about it. We had seven men from Oxford, one from Cambridge, and one from the San Marcos Teachers College. So, not to be outdone, I invited my friends from the Congress to come join us today for lunch.

Mr. Prime Minister, I remember so well the largest American hero of his time, Franklin D. Roosevelt loved so warmly the greatest Canadian of his era, MacKenzie King and, indeed, you may have been present on the occasion in Quebec in 1943 when President Roosevelt said to Prime Minister MacKenzie King, "My old friend, your course and mine have run so closely and affectionately during these many long years that this meeting adds just another link to the chain."

Mr. Prime Minister, may I take the liberty and may I be presumptuous enough to suggest that our friendship may run this same cheerful course that was so stoutly started by our great predecessors and so cordially continued by ourselves. I believe, Mr. Prime Minister, that we have built here on your first visit the intimacy and the candor that belong to two good and old friends. As I suggested this morning, as we walked out on the porch to observe this beautiful sunny day, that whenever we have anything to say to each other, let us just pick up the telephone and say it, whether it be to discuss a problem or simply to ask, "How are you getting along up there?"

So if you would join me now, I would like to ask you to rise and raise your glass, and let us toast at this high moment Lester B. Pearson, "Mike" Pearson, the Prime Minister of Canada, a loyal neighbor, a durable ally, hockey star, and a good and most understanding friend.

THE PRIME MINISTER: May I thank you very warmly, sir, for your kindness in proposing this toast and you, gentlemen, for the friendly way in which you acknowledged it.

You, Mr. President, said how outnumbered you were last night at the Canadian Embassy when you honored us by dining at our Embassy. You were outnumbered, I think, nine to one, Oxford and Cambridge versus the Teachers College. But I would remind you, Mr. President, that those of us who went to Oxford and Cambridge went there because we had done so well beforehand at our teachers colleges. Now if you had worked as hard as we did and if you had been as good an athlete as Dean Rusk was, you might have got to Oxford, too. But if you had, you probably wouldn't have become President of the United States.

I am very grateful to you, sir, for your generous and friendly hospitality and particularly, if I may say so, for giving me the opportunity of meeting so many members of the Congress. I used to be a diplomat: I used to be Ambassador in Washington. And in those days the State Department would never let me talk to members of the Congress. No doubt they were right, because if diplomats started establishing contacts, too close contacts, with members of the Congress, it wouldn't have any great effect on the Congress, but I don't know what it would do to diplomacy and the State Department.

But I am grateful, sir, for the opportunity of meeting so many old friends from the Congress. And I am very conscious of the fact that in the relations between our two countries, which are of such continuing importance, that while it is of vital importance for our governments to keep in close touch, and they will, it is I think of equal importance for our legislatures to keep in close touch. And I am very grateful, indeed, that during the last years we have built up this kind of congressional and parliamentary contact.

And I believe we had a very good example of its importance last week. I don't like to single out anyone in particular, but perhaps, Mr. President, you might let me mention a senator from a State so near Canada, who had so much to do with that development, Senator Aiken. We are very happy, Mr. President, to be here today, also, because we are signing a very important treaty for the developments, in the interests of both our countries, of the Columbia River, a treaty which will be of such great importance to the Northwestern part of the United States. Senator Magnuson will forget about lumber difficulties, perhaps, and Senator Morse. And, also, we are to sign this afternoon an agreement which hasn't the tangible importance that the Columbia treaty has, but has a very great sentimental and symbolic significance.

In setting aside Campobello as a sort of international tribute to a very, very great American, I want to thank those who have been good enough to make that possible. We have had very good talks in our short, short visit—the kind of discussion that you expect between representatives of the United States and Canada. They have been frank, they have been friendly, and they have covered a great variety of subjects. There have been no inhibitions of any kind. Why the President and I, in the midst of more important matters, took some time off to argue whether the greatest quarterback in American football history was Sam Baugh from Texas or Y.A. Tittle from San Francisco. We didn't agree on that.

We have, I think, not solved problems, but we have established a good and friendly relationship between ourselves and strengthened that relationship which existed already between our governments, which will make it easier for us to solve these problems. Our relations, the relations between our two countries, are so close and so friendly, so intimate, and our peoples are so close together, that this in a sense is our problem, because it is taken for granted, I think perhaps more on our side of the border than on your side of the border, that we are so much alike that we will never have any difficulties.

The particular triumph of the Canadian-American relationship is that we have had difficulties and that we have solved them and we are going to have more in the future, but we are going to solve them, too.

It is easy to keep the peace when you have nothing to row about. But rows without wars, that means something. That is the symbol of our relationship. I remember saying some years ago in Toronto—and I got a great deal of criticism, and I was Secretary of State for External Affairs at that time—that the days of easy and automatic relations between our countries are over. So they are. I don't know how easy or automatic they used to be, but I know that in the future we are going to have problems and difficulties.

There are no two countries where the relations are more important to each other economically and in every other way than those between our two countries, but I am not frightened about this kind of thing because I have absolute confidence that with the kind friendly understanding which we have, we will be able to face these problems and we will be able to solve them.

We in Canada are very, very sensitive, indeed, about the development of our own Canadian identity building up in the northern half of this continent, a nation which stands on its own feet as much as any nation, any nation anywhere, can stand on its own feet these days.

You may at times think we are perhaps a little too sensitive, but we do appreciate, we do realize, that in our relations with the United States, why, we will have our bilateral difficulties, we do realize that in this country you are bearing the greatest burden that any country at any time ever had to bear, the burden of maintaining peace and establishing security and enduring progress in a nuclear outer space atomic age.

I was talking—and I don't know whether I perhaps should say this—but I was talking last week to General de Gaulle in Paris'. We had a very happy visit there and we were very warmly received by the country which, after all, is the other mother country of Canada. Sometimes down here in the United States they forget that one-third of our people in Canada are French-speaking. I mentioned this to the President last night. General de Gaulle said, ''You are always boasting, you Canadians, that you know the Americans better than anyone else.'' Which is true. We really should. ''What do you really think of them?''

I was trying to find words to express at the same time my admiration and anxiety about the United States, and I said, ''Well, General de Gaulle, as I have often put it in speeches in Canada, my feeling about the United States is this: To live alongside this great country is like living with your wife. At times it is difficult to live with her. At all times it is impossible to live without her.''

3. Joint Statement of President Johnson and Prime Minister Pearson on the Campobello Park Agreement, January 22, 1964

(*Ibid.*, No. 138, pp. 210-11)

President Johnson and Prime Minister Pearson signed today in the Treaty Room of the White House an intergovernmental agreement providing for the establishment of the Roosevelt Campobello International Park at the house formerly belonging to President Franklin Delano Roosevelt on Campobello Island, New Brunswick. The President and the Prime Minister recalled the generous offer of the Hammer family, made to President Kennedy and Prime Minister Pearson at Hyannis Port in May 1963, to donate the property to the Governments of Canada and the United States as a memorial to President Roosevelt. President Johnson and Prime Minister Pearson have welcomed the opportunity on this occasion to sign the intergovernmental agreement under which the Roosevelt estate will become an International Park jointly owned and operated by the United States and Canada as a memorial open to the peoples of the countries and of all the world.

The establishment of the Roosevelt Campobello International Park represents a unique example of international cooperation. The Park will stand forever as an expression of the close relationship between Canada and the United States as well as a fitting memorial to the President of the United States who so greatly strengthened that relationship and who himself spent so many happy days of rest and relaxation on Canadian soil and in Canadian waters. The memorial will celebrate President Roosevelt's love of Campobello Island and of sailing in the deep waters of the Bay of Fundy; his deep sense of the abiding values of conservation and recreation; and the old and friendly relations between the people of the Maritime Provinces of Canada and the people of New England and New York. When Canadians and Americans visit the International Park, they will see a living expression of the historic collaboration between their two countries; while visitors from other parts of the world may find it an inspiration for similar cooperative arrangements along many frontiers across the world.

This intergovernmental agreement has, of course, been drawn up in close consultation with the government of the Province of New Brunswick where the property is located. The agreement will require legislative action in both countries. The President and the Prime Minister hope for speedy enactment of such legislation in order to open the Roosevelt Campobello International Park to the people of both countries at the earliest moment.

4. Joint Statement of President Johnson and Prime Minister Pearson Following Discussions, January 22, 1964

(*Ibid.*, No. 140, pp. 215-16)

Useful discussions on many matters have been held during the past two days while Prime Minister Pearson has been visiting Washington as the guest of President Johnson. The Prime Minister was accompanied by Mr. Paul Martin, Secretary of State for External Affairs. Mr. Dean Rusk, Secretary of State, was with the President.

The President and the Prime Minister had a wide-ranging discussion about the international situation. In their view of world affairs they discussed the NATO alliance and the Atlantic Community, the prospects for easing East-West tensions, the importance of practical specific initiative toward disarmament, and the current problems in Asia, Africa, and the Western Hemisphere. They will continue to cooperate fully in helping the countries of these areas move toward economic development, political stability, and peace along their borders.

The Prime Minister and the President noted with satisfaction the progress made towards the cessation of nuclear testing. They affirmed their desire to promote additional measures to ease international tensions and to support further advances towards effective disarmament. The steady development of the peacekeeping capacity of the United Nations remains for both a goal essential to the preservation of world peace.

The President and the Prime Minister examined various bilateral defense questions and noted with satisfaction that appropriate agreements have lately been concluded between their two Governments. They agreed to plan for a meeting of the Joint Ministerial Committee on Defense during the first half of this year. They reaffirmed the support of both Governments for the developing defense production sharing program, which is of mutual benefit.

The Prime Minister and the President referred to the balance of payments problems of their respective countries. They reviewed outstanding economic problems between the two countries, including certain trade and tax measures. They agreed on the urgency of successful GATT negotiations to achieve a substantial reduction of trade barriers in order to meet the goal of expanded world trade.

The President and the Prime Minister reviewed the work of the joint Cabinet level Committee on trade and economic affairs at its meeting last September and agreed that it should meet again around the end of April.

The Prime Minister and the President discussed at some length the practicability and desirability of working out acceptable principles which would make it easier to avoid divergences in economic and other policies of interest to each other. They appreciated that any such principles would have to take full account of the interests of other countries and of existing international arrangements. The President and the Prime Minister considered that it would be worthwhile to have the possibilities examined. Accordingly; they are arranging to establish a Working Group, at a senior level, to study the matter and to submit a progress report to the April meeting of the Joint Committee.

The Prime Minister and the President agreed that negotiations on the bilateral air agreement should be undertaken almost immediately, with a view to working out satisfactory arrangements on a North American basis.

The President and the Prime Minister noted the importance of shipping on the Great Lakes and the St. Lawrence Seaway and agreed to cooperate with each other and with labor and management in each country to avoid industrial strife along these waters.

Final agreement was reached on the use of the resources of the Columbia River Basin, and this agreement was embodied in an exchange of notes between Secretary of State Rusk and the Secretary of State for External Affairs for Canada, Mr. Paul Martin. The Columbia River Treaty signed in 1961, was ratified that year by the United States; the agreements reached today pave the way for Canadian ratification and make possible the further development of the resources of this great Basin.

At the same time, the President and the Prime Minister have joined in arrangements to establish on the East Coast the Roosevelt International Park at Campobello, New Brunswick, in memory of a President who took a keen interest in both countries and in the good relations between them.

In recognition of the breadth and importance of their mutual interests, the President and the Prime Minister have determined to maintain close and continuous contact, on a personal and confidential basis and in the spirit of candor and friendship that has characterized these meetings.

5. Prime Minister Pearson's Press Conference Following Discussions, Blair House, Washington, D.C., January 22, 1964

(PMO, Transcript of Press Conference)

Q. Were you and President Johnson in accord on what the consequences of such a move (recognition of Mainland China) by France might be?

A. I found myself in very general accord with the President on practically everything that came up in our discussions except one matter where we found ourselves in rather violent disagreement. We were discussing which was the greatest quarterback in U.S. football history and he said Sammy Baugh of Texas and I said Y.A. Tittle of New York and San Francisco. Otherwise we were in general agreement.

Q. Mr. Prime Minister, what, in your opinion, is the major unresolved issue or controversy, if you will, in relations between Canada and the United States?

A. Well, we have a good many issues and we will continue to have a good many issues and I would like to say this, as I said after the Hyannis Port meeting, that while the atmosphere of this conference, if you can call it that, could not have been more friendly and no delegation, no prime minister coming to Washington could have been given a warmer welcome, nor could a conversation have been carried on in a friendlier atmosphere, nevertheless atmosphere is one thing and specific problems and difficulties are something else. The atmosphere, if it's right, makes it easier for you to deal with your difficulties, but we have difficulties, we had after Hyannis Port, goodness knows, and we will continue to have, and you ask me what are the most important. That's not an easy question to answer. I suppose our most important problem between the two countries in the bilateral sense, is the problem of our financial and economic relations. That covers a lot of ground. We have to do something in Canada to reduce our unfavourable balance of payments, which has been over a billion dollars a year for a good many years and that unfavourable balance is made up largely of our unfavourable balance with the United States. In the efforts which we make in Canada to reduce that—we must do that—we occasionally have to take steps which seem to affect United States interests and this causes a problem. We also have a very serious and as yet unresolved problem of shipping on the Great Lakes. You don't hear very much about it now because the Great Lakes are frozen. I don't know whether they are frozen now, they were a week ago. But when shipping resumes on the Great Lakes, if there is a further outbreak of harassment against Canadian ships in American ports on the Great Lakes, there will be a lot of trouble in Canada, and we talked about that. That's one reason we've had to take over the Seaman's Union in Canada and put it under government trusteeship, and this is not accepted in certain union quarters in the United States and had caused us a lot of trouble, far more trouble up there than you realize down here. That is another difficulty. We have difficulties in regard to co-ordinating our policy whenever we can on export of agricultural products. Oh, we have lots of problems, but I must say I feel that while we will have problems, with the kind of understanding and friendship that was exhibited at this meeting and which has persisted for many years, we'll be able to solve them all right.

Q. Mr. Prime Minister, could you spell out in more detail the objectives of this exploration for possible acceptable principles?

A. Well, I wouldn't like to spell it out in too much detail otherwise there wouldn't be any need for a working party which we are setting up, but George, you remember, it's a joint initiative. During the war we really worked together, the two countries in the war effort, in the economic and industrial side of the war effort, very, very closely and we had joint machinery for that purpose. Much easier to do these things some time in war time than it is in peace time. After the war, we laid down certain principles that would govern our economic relationship in very general terms. These relationships since that time have grown so in complexity and importance to an extent not equalled by the relationships between any two countries in the world, I think. All you have to do is look at the figures. If we think the time has come to see if there should not be now some sort of guidelines, some principles which would—on which both governments would act—and before each government took any steps which affected economically the other, they would relate that particular policy to the principles agreed on, if we can agree on them. Now that's what we are going to try to work out and this is not going to be an easy thing to do and it will take a little time, but I am very glad that we are setting up this working group to see whether this special relationship, because it is, can be recognized by some kind of agreed principles which would govern the operation of our economic and financial policies toward each other.

Q. Will this lead to a government international economic commission?

A. I don't know what it would, I have no idea what it would lead to, but it is a recognition that we ought to do something about it, to see if we can't anticipate some of these problems before they become matters of political and public dispute.

Q. Well, Mr. Pearson, wasn't that the idea of that ministerial committee meeting we had on trade?

A. That's right, but that only meets once a year, once every six months and perhaps the machinery would be further use of ministerial committees. But then this study would be a study of the principles which would govern the operation of these committees and I don't want to be very specific about it because we are not specific in our own minds, but I think this is very much worth doing and I hope something worthwhile will arise out of it.

Q. Would you regard this, Sir, in any way as the beginning of admission that some day an economic union might be inevitable?

A. No, I haven't that in mind at all and we weren't considering that. We have now, for instance—and this is an analogy which should be accepted with some caution—we've got an International Joint Board on Defence which meets regularly in sort of . . . we have the International Joint Commission which meets regularly to decide border problems and the Columbia Treaty we signed today is partly due to the work of that commission. I don't know whether you could work out something like that on economic and financial relationships or not, but this is what they will be looking into.

Q. Did you discuss the differences between the two governments on the question of pricing wheat for export?

A. I didn't with the President. It may have been discussed in the meeting between the officials but we didn't discuss it. The President and I were alone for about an hour and a half this morning while the other meeting was going on and we discussed in very general terms the necessity of co-ordinating our agricultural export policy including pricing policies and that the machine which is already in existence for that purpose between the two governments should be used, but they haven't met for some time, I believe.

Q. They haven't met since last September.

A. No.

Q Could you, by referring to the war time experience, give us any better idea of what sort of principles we're talking about here?

A. No, I just used that illustration because I was concerned with that down here during the war. We had the Permanent Material Board, we had the Joint Industrial Production Board, we had all this kind of thing where we allocated our resources sort of jointly to the common objective of winning the war. It's not going to be quite so easy to do that in peace time. . . .

Q. Mr. Prime Minister, did you and the President have any discussion of increased Canadian participation in inter-American affairs. . . ?

A. Sure, the President asked me when we were going to join OAS.

Q. Well, what did you answer him?

A. I said we were giving the matter careful consideration. And he was unkind enough, well maybe it was somebody else, to remind me that I said some pretty interesting things about this when I was in Opposition.

Q. Mr. Prime Minister, did you invite the President to Canada?

A. What I said to him was that if he found it possible to go to Canada he would get a very warm welcome and we would be delighted to see him, but I didn't extend any formal invitation for any particular time. I know he's pretty heavily occupied here at the moment, but he knows what a warm welcome he would get if he found it possible to come to Canada. He's never been to Canada. . . .

Q. Mr. Prime Minister, there was a story published in Canada yesterday which said that you might offer your services as a broker and have Johnson and de Gaulle meet in Ottawa?

A. I saw that story and that was attributed to our Paris visit. The matter never arose in Paris, I assure you and I would be very reluctant indeed to act as a broker in that particular connection at this time. I don't think these two men need a broker. . . .

Q. Was there any talk about the withholding tax?

A. There was indeed. We had quite a discussion of both the Canadian withholding tax and the United States tax equalization law. . . .

Q. Mr. Pearson, could you give us a little explanation of that bilateral agreement on air that is mentioned in the communique?

A. Well, as a result of our meeting at Hyannis Port the President asked Professor Galbraith to go into the question from the American point of view of air relations between the two countries. He seemed well qualified to do that, not only because of his own ability, but because he had been a Canadian and travelled back and forward by air, I suppose, between the two countries. He made a report. It was a very interesting report and we had a chance to look at the report although it was a report to the President, and on the basis of that report we are now beginning discussions which may, and I hope will, bring about new air arrangements between the two countries making travel more convenient and giving the Canadian airlines an equitable share of transborder traffic.

Q. Does the U.S. position on that, Mr. Pearson, generally follow the Galbraith thesis?

A. I wouldn't like to hold them to any particular position now that the governmental negotiations are beginning, but I gather they thought the Galbraith report was a reasonable basis—in fact, they did think it was a reasonable basis for negotiations, and I think that they were quite impressed by it.

Q. What's your assessment of President Johnson?

A. He's a very good host, believe me, and a very easy man to talk to and to dine with and to get along with. I have never been a member of Congress.

Q. Mr. Prime Minister, was there any discussion of possible Canadian uranium sales. . . ?

A. No, not by me, it wasn't mentioned. But it may have been mentioned by the officials as one way in which we can increase our exports and thereby reduce our unbalance. It didn't seem to be a very practicable matter for me to take up with the President at a time when they are cutting down their uranium production in this country, but no one would be more pleased than I would be if uranium sales to this country could be increased because you know where they come from. The constituency of Algoma-East.

Q. Was there any discussion of the proposed sale of Canadian uranium to France?

A. No, because there is no proposal to that effect and there was a good deal of, I tried to explain that in Ottawa and I can understand how some misunderstanding might have arisen, but there was no discussion of that here nor was there any discussion of it in Paris as far as I was concerned.

Q. Could you give us a little explanation about this withholding tax for equalization? Was there any agreement about modifying it on either side?

A. No. I don't know. We discussed it from every point of view but I don't want to go beyond that. It is a difficult problem and one of immediate importance between us. Thank you gentlemen. I understand it is the custom of Blair House, but certainly not the custom in Ottawa, that the press stay and have a drink.

C. President Lyndon B. Johnson and Prime Minister Lester B. Pearson, New York City, N. Y., May 28, 1964

1. U.S. State Department Telegram (Sullivan/Rusk) to U.S. Ambassador Lodge (Saigon) Concerning the Seaborn "Interlocutor" Mission (Dated May 1, 1964, #1821)

("Canada in the Pentagon Papers: Unpublished Documents on the Seaborn Mission to Hanoi," *The Canadian Forum*, Volume LIII, No. 632 (September, 1973), p. 9)

I flew up to Ottawa yesterday to talk with Mike Pearson and Martin concerning the Canadian presence in Hanoi. . . .

They readily agreed that Seaborn should plan to spend much more time in Hanoi than have his predecessors in this assignment. They also accept as part of his mission an effort to establish ready access to and close contact with senior authorities in Hanoi, beginning with Ho Chi Minh. . . .

Following are some of the matters which we roughed out in Ottawa and which I will have further developed here. . . .

1. Seaborn should start out by checking as closely as he can what is on Ho Chi Minh's mind. We want to know whether he considers himself over-extended and exposed, or whether he feels confident that his Chinese allies will back him to the hilt. We want to know whether his current zeal is being forced upon him by pro-Chinese elements in his own camp, or whether he is impelled by his own ambitions.

2. Seaborn should get across to Ho and his colleagues the full measure of U.S. determination to see this thing through. He should draw upon examples in other parts of the world to convince them that if it becomes necessary to enlarge the military action, this is the most probable course that the U.S. would follow.

3. Seaborn should spread the word that he is puzzled by Hanoi's intentions. The North Vietnamese should understand that the U.S. wants no military bases or other footholds in South Viet Nam or Laos. If Hanoi would leave its neighbours alone, the U.S. presence in the area would diminish sharply.

4. The North Vietnamese should understand that there are many examples in which the Free World has demonstrated its willingness to live in peace with communist neighbors and to permit the establishment of normal economic relations between these two different systems. We recognize North Viet Nam's need for trade, and especially food, and consider that such needs could be fulfilled if peaceful conditions were to prevail.

Pearson also agreed to instruct Seaborn and his people in general to work more actively on trying to break the Poles off from constant and active espousal of North Vietnamese aggression. He felt, however, that the Poles are playing something of a middle role in Sino-Soviet matters these days and doubted that there would be much profit in this.

2. U.S. State Department Telegram (Ball) to U.S. Ambassador Lodge (Saigon) Recounting the Pearson-Johnson New York Meeting (Dated May 30, 1964, #2133)

(*Ibid.*, p. 10)

President and Mac Bundy met May 28 in New York with Canadian Prime Minister Pearson. Simultaneously Sullivan met in Ottawa with Foreign Minister Martin, Deputy Under Secretary Smith, and ICC Commissioner-Designate Seaborn.

President told Pearson that he wishes Hanoi to know, that while he is a man of peace, he does not intend to permit the North Vietnamese to take over Southeast Asia. He needs a confidential and responsible interlocutor to carry the message of U.S. attitudes to Hanoi. In outlining the U.S. position there was some discussion of QTE [quote] carrots and sticks UNQUTE.

Pearson, after expressing willingness to lend Canadian good offices to this endeavour, indicated some concern about this nature of QTE sticks UNQTE [unquote]. He stipulated that he would have great reservations about the use of nuclear weapons, but indicated that the punitive striking of discriminate targets by careful iron bomb attacks would be QTE a different thing UNQTE. He said he would personally understand our resort to such measures if the messages transmitted through the Canadian channel failed to produce any alleviation of North Vietnamese aggression, and that Canada would transmit messages around this framework.

In Ottawa Sullivan found much the same disposition among Canadian officials. While Foreign Minister Martin seemed a little nervous about the prospect of QTE expanding the war UNQTE, External Affairs officials readily assented to the use of Seaborn as an interlocutor. . . .

Seaborn, who struck Sullivan as an alert, intelligent and steady officer, readily agreed to these conditions and has made immediate plans for an accelerated departure. . . .

D. Prime Minister Lester B. Pearson and President Lyndon B. Johnson, Great Falls, Montana, and Vancouver, British Columbia, September 16, 1964

1. Exchange of Welcoming Remarks Between President Johnson and Prime Minister Pearson, Great Falls, Montana, September 16, 1964

(PP/Lyndon B. Johnson, Vol. 1963-1964 Book II, No. 574, pp. 1072-73)

THE PRESIDENT: Welcome to the United States, Mr. Prime Minister. And welcome to Montana whose majesty and western warmth should remind you of your own great country.

In 1963, Mr. Prime Minister, you said of Canada: "We are so friendly that we feel we can criticize the United States like a Texan does—and in the same idiom." This Texan hopes that you still feel that freedom, for we welcome the comments and the counsel which spring, as yours do, from friendship and understanding. Although I doubt that even with your grasp of languages you will be able to match the Texas idiom.

Twenty-one years ago President Franklin D. Roosevelt and Prime

Minister Mackenzie King met in Hyde Park. They agreed to work together to defend this hemisphere and to defend democracy everywhere.

From that day to this we have followed the same path of partnership. Free peoples everywhere are more secure because of our cooperation in NORAD, in NATO, and in the United Nations.

The freedom and richness of our lands, the hopes of the people it serves, depend upon the peace of the world that we live in. It is a symbol of our time that beneath the magnificence of this Montana stand weapons that are powerful enough to devastate much of a continent.

Those of us who seek peace know that only wisdom and patience, and the fortitude of long effort, can bring us near to that goal. But we will always pursue that goal.

You, Mr. Prime Minister, are a symbol of that effort. You have never wavered in the defense of freedom. But you also have given much of your life so that free men might live in peace.

You have done much for your people. You have carried the influence of Canada to the highest councils and to the most hazardous crises of the world.

But we greet you not only as a great Canadian today. We welcome you as a man whose home is found wherever man seeks fulfillment amid the peace that you, Mr. Prime Minister, have labored so long and so hard to build.

THE PRIME MINISTER: It gives me a very great pleasure to be on American soil once more and to receive such a kind and generous welcome from you, Mr. President, and from your distinguished colleagues.

This is a very brief visit, but it gives me time and opportunity to bring to you the warm good wishes of the Canadian people toward their American friends. You know, I feel like a neighbor dropping in to make a friendly visit. Indeed, that is what I am doing, because I just dropped in to pick up the President and take him back to Canada.

This is the kind of relationship which exists between our two peoples. It is close, it is informal, it is important, and it is neighborly. Like leaning over a back fence to talk to your neighbor, but a back fence which neither neighbor wishes to pull down and which both are anxious to keep in good repair. Of course, there are differences of opinion and, at times, frustrations between even the best of neighbors, and we have them between our two countries, but they do not prevent a warm underlying friendship and understanding.

Mr. President, you and I will be setting forth today on a fascinating and historic journey to explore from the air—I hope we will be able to see it—the mighty Columbia River and the region of a great cooperative development, a development which agreement between our two governments made possible.

To me the Columbia River project is the kind of enterprise which best demonstrates the partnership between the United States and Canada. This is what our two countries are uniquely fitted to do, to join together in the constructive development of our continent's resources for the benefit of present and future generations, in a world in which I hope we will be at peace.

The Columbia River Treaty is not only an achievement in itself, but an earnest for the future. We must follow it up with other fruitful joint endeavors which will give substance to our friendship which I am so proud to acknowledge this morning, and meaning to our good neighborhood, of which this happy meeting is a witness.

2. Remarks of President Johnson on Proclaiming the Columbia River Treaty, International Peace Arch, U.S.-Canadian Border, September 16, 1964

(*Ibid.*, No. 576, pp. 1075-77)

THE PRESIDENT: There are many reasons why my first trip abroad as President should be to Canada. In 1839 J. Pinckney Henderson, the Representative of the Republic of Texas to France and to England wrote that Great Britain might delay its recognition of the new republic for fear of the impact in Canada. But Canada remained loyal. Great Britain recognized Texas, and that recognition helped open the door to American union for Texas.

Had that not happened, Mr. Prime Minister, had Texas stayed independent, classical diplomacy suggests that we might very well today be concluding a treaty of mutual defense against the American influence. As a Texan, I can sympathize with the problems of living beside a wealthy and powerful and pervasive neighbor. That is just how the rest of the United States feels about Texas.

More than 3 years ago President Kennedy came to Canada. He told your Parliament his trip was "an act of faith." He said it was faith in our capacity to meet common problems, and in our common cause of freedom.

Well, my trip today is a fulfillment and a renewal of that act of faith. It is both a resolution of a common problem, and a strengthening of freedom's cause.

Lord Durham, in the famous report that laid the foundation for modern Canada, spoke of the possibility of establishing "partners in a new industry, the creation of happy human beings."

That partnership is the purpose of this treaty that we have signed today.

It will supply new electric power to millions of my countrymen. It will supply revenues to Canada, although I was somewhat shocked when I heard you read that cable about receiving $253,999,884, and then to show you what the Canadians really went for, they went for that last 25 cents.

It joins common purpose to common interest in pursuit of the welfare of the free people who share our continent.

My country is grateful for the spacious spirit with which this generous design was conceived and with the way it was carried out, even down to the last quarter. It is another landmark in the history of one of the oldest and one of the most successful associations of sovereign governments anywhere in the world.

What is the secret of this success? It begins with a truth: The only justifiable object of government is the welfare of individual men and women. It is a simple truth. But had others shared it with us, the world would have been spared many dark years.

With this as the animating design, our partnership has been built on four pillars. And the success of that structure might well serve as a model to the world.

The first pillar is peace.

The second pillar is freedom.

The third pillar is respect. One of my predecessors, Woodrow Wilson, said "You cannot be friends upon any other basis than upon terms of equality."

We maintain with each other the relationship that we seek for all the world: cooperation amid diversity.

Pericles said of a state that was much smaller than yours, "we have forced every sea and land to be the highway of our daring."

In the founding of the United Nations, in the Middle East, in the Congo, in southeast Asia, the world has responded to Canadian daring. You have followed not the highway of empire which helped destroy Athens, but you have followed the more difficult path to peace which can save the world.

And you have been a principal architect, Mr. Prime Minister, of that profound achievement.

The fourth pillar is cooperation. This agreement is the latest in an impressive list. We have disarmed our border; we have shared the costs of defense; we have divided power at Niagara; we have built the St. Lawrence Seaway; we have resolved scores of other problems.

Difficulties that divide others have united us. The reason is plain. We share interest and we share purpose. We come to the council table advised by reason, aware of each other's problems, anxious to find final agreement. You told us, Mr. Prime Minister, "As good neighbors we must be able to sit down and discuss problems realizing that solutions will not be found without hard work and without give-and-take on both sides."

We both have problems we must solve within our borders. My

country has a war to win on poverty. We must find justice for men of all races. We must crush the forces of division which gnaw at the fabric of our union.

You have your own difficulties. We watch, with friendly confidence in your capacity to merge differences in the grand dream of Canadian design.

But there is also much, Mr. Prime Minister, which we share.

In the world we seek peace, and mounting fulfillment for man. Here we work together, from ocean to ocean, in resources and science, to enrich the life of our two peoples to elevate the quality of our two societies.

Franklin D. Roosevelt once said, ''Democracy is the form of government which guarantees to every generation of men the right to imagine and to attempt to bring to pass a better world.''

That has been the story of your life, Mr. Prime Minister. It is also the strength of our two countries.

And I believe that future generations will have cause for gratitude that two great democracies—Canada and the United States—shared the most generous continent which God has ever granted to man.

E. President Lyndon B. Johnson and Prime Minister Lester B. Pearson, LBJ Ranch, Johnson City, Texas, January 15-16, 1965

1. Exchange of Remarks Between President Johnson and Prime Minister Pearson Upon Signing the U.S.-Canadian Trade Agreement on Automotive Products, January 16, 1965

(WHPS, Press Release, Exchange of Remarks, 10:16 a.m. CST)

THE PRESIDENT: The Prime Minister and I, with Secretary Martin and Secretary Rusk, are about to sign a historic agreement, an agreement for free trade on automotive products between Canada and the United States.

Two years ago it appeared that our two countries might have grave differences in this great field of trade. We faced a choice between the road of stroke and counterstroke and the road of understanding and cooperation. We have taken the road of understanding.

This agreement is the result of hard work on both sides all along that road. I am sure that the Prime Minister joins me in expressing our hearty thanks to the negotiators on both sides and to their chiefs, Mr. Rusk and Mr. Martin.

Mr. Prime Minister, would you like to say a word before we sign?

THE PRIME MINISTER: Mr. President, I share completely your satisfaction as we are able today to sign this automotive agreement, and our expression of thanks to those, including the Secretary of State and the Secretary of State for External Affairs, who conducted the negotiations.

This is one of the most important accords ever signed between our two countries in the trade field. As you say, we faced a very difficult situation in this particular area of industry, and through hard work and patient negotiation we have concluded an agreement which is of benefit to both countries. In effect, we have agreed to rationalize the production of our respective industries and to expand our production and trade through a dismantling of tariff and other barriers in the automotive field. This wasn't accomplished easily, and it could not have been accomplished at all if there had not been that mutual understanding, good will, and confidence which has grown up between our two countries over the years.

A measure of the significance of this agreement is basically this: Canada and the United States trade more with each other than any other two countries. Indeed, about one-fifth of your exports go to Canada, and automobiles and parts constitute the largest single category in that trade.

I am confident that this agreement will result in an even greater flow of two-way trade, and eventually the consumers on both sides of the border will share in its benefits.

Mr. President, I have said to you many times and you have said to me many times, that there are no problems between our two countries which can't be solved if we work at them hard enough and in the right spirit. This is what we have done in this agreement which we are about to sign.

FOLLOWING THE SIGNING CEREMONY THERE WAS A BRIEF QUESTION AND ANSWER PERIOD.

THE PRESIDENT: Mr. Prime Minister, would you like to make some observations and answer questions before you leave?

THE PRIME MINISTER: If there are any questions about the agreement or anything related to the agreement that you would like to ask, I would be glad to deal with them.

We are leaving here immediately after the signing, Mr. Martin and I, for Washington, and then later going home.

We have had a wonderful visit to the ranch. It was very considerate on the part of the President to provide the kind of climate this morning we are accustomed to. I notice some of your people seem to be taking it very hard. This has been a short but very, very happy visit. We had some interesting discussions last night in a homey and friendly atmosphere.

I had the pleasure and privilege of being taken around the country by the President immediately on arrival. I wasn't able to take my hat into the house before I was put on a jeep. It was wonderful. I saw a lot of deer. They were very small deer. They were very friendly. Up in Canada they are bigger and wilder.

Q. Mr. Prime Minister, why could not this agreement be used as a basis for other agreements in other industries?

THE PRIME MINISTER: Well, as far as we are concerned we would like to explore that possibility. This agreement may be important not only in itself but it could be important from that point of view. But the automotive industry, the organization of it on this continent, lends itself to this kind of agreement more easily than other industries. But we will certainly be anxious to have a look at the other situations to see if we can apply this. Anyway, we made a start.

Q. Could you run over briefly the other subjects you discussed?

THE PRIME MINISTER: Well, we had a chance to look at some of the other problems—bilateral problems—between our two countries that we are working on, economic and financial problems, the problem of air traffic between our two countries. I hope we will reach an agreement before long.

Then we have been looking at the U.N. problem. There is some difficulty there, as you know, facing the U.N. on financing and the proposed withdrawal of Indonesia. And the President has been discussing with me some of the problems of southeast Asia and difficulties there. International problems—we have of course in Canada a great responsibility, as the United States has, which is important for us to know about and see what we can do to help cooperate in it.

Q. Mr. Prime Minister, was the question of trade with Communist China discussed?

THE PRIME MINISTER: No, except in a casual way. We have been selling wheat and grains to China now for some time, and there was no particular discussion about that. Of course, we don't send anything to China on an agreed prohibitive list.

Q. Mr. Prime Minister, were there any other bilateral matters under discussion?

THE PRIME MINISTER: No. We mentioned the air negotiations as one that is most active at the moment and hope there will be an agreement before long.

Q. What does this involve?

THE PRIME MINISTER: We have had a problem between the two countries and we tried to bring that up to date in the light of new conditions, new developments in air traffic.

Q. Inaudible

THE PRIME MINISTER: We have an interest in these matters, but then under our aid agreement to countries in southeast Asia we are trying to be as helpful as we can in that part of the world.

2. Prime Minister Pearson's Account of Meeting Before the Canadian Periodical Press Association Dinner, Rideau Club, Ottawa, January 20, 1965

(Source: Confidential)

. . . I remember very well . . . the last time I spoke to you in this intimidating room—the dining room of the Rideau Club. As you said, I had just returned from Russia and I was full of Khrushchev. I have just returned from Texas with Mr. Martin, and we're full of L.B.J.! There was a startling contrast between the two visits so far as I was concerned. Mr. Khrushchev received us at a grand marble palace, Czar's Palace on the Black Sea with a great deal of pomp and formality and ceremony. L.B.J. received us in a ranch house in Texas with a maximum of goodwill but, I must say, a minimum of formality.

We had a very interesting and exciting and unique experience. Now that we're off the record, I can tell you, and I'm sure Mr. Martin will agree with me, that it was completely unforgettable. We arrived properly dressed "East Block" costume and we were met at the airstrip, which is a two mile long airstrip recently built which ends at the ranch house door, by the President and his wife suitably clad for Texas. We had been on the plane for some time and I expected, and my wife certainly expected, to go to our rooms and I wanted to get rid of my black hat and put on my sporting clothes. "Not at all," said Mr. Johnson, "but now, Mr. Wilson, I want to show you Texas!"

So, he put us first in a golf cart because it was 50 yards between the plane and a helicopter and we couldn't walk that distance, and then from the golf cart to a helicopter. We got in a helicopter because we had to go about 15 miles because he wanted to show us some ranch country where there were wild animals, tiny little Texan deer, about that big. So we got in the helicopter, we flew for about 15 minutes because there was another helicopter for our wives; there was another helicopter for the security people; there was another helicopter for the photographers; there was another helicopter for the liquor—the United States is a great power!

We had been travelling for about five minutes when Mr. Johnson said, "It's four thirty, we'll have a bourbon and branchwater." I rose to that challenge, but not Mr. Martin. It wasn't made in Windsor! Then we got off the helicopter and we had a parade of cars while we went through the Texas countryside, and Mr. Johnson saying to us the unbelievable beauty of the Texas landscape, which was nothing at all. He stopped about every 20 minutes to show us the countryside and to have a drink. It was nippy. And behind us in other cars were our wives, security, liquor, guns, cameras.

Mr. Johnson, I'm attempting to be factitious but I'm dealing with a powerful and a very great man and I hope that I won't be misunderstood when I tell these anecdotes about him because he is a great man. But, he is a compulsive telephone talker, like other people, but perhaps even more so because he has more opportunity and more facilities. And we had telephone communications not only with the cars behind with Lady Bird, but we had telephone communications with the capital of Texas, with Washington, with Vietnam, with the Congo, practically every place but Ottawa. We're a trouble up here except when it comes to periodical literature.

He was passing back to the ladies in the third car interesting sights as he saw them in the front car. This went on for some time. And then in the evening when we got back two and a half hours later in the dark, we were allowed to go up to our rooms. We had dinner. I couldn't help, but contrast this dinner with that which we had with Mr. Khrushchev some years before when we were dined in the most magnificent marble palace, one of the most magnificent in the world, with a great deal of pomp and ceremony; and a great deal of vodka. Dining with Mr. and Mrs. Johnson at the ranch in Texas was like dining in the old farmhouse in Shingcousi Township north of Toronto and the atmosphere is the same, and talk more or less the same. There were all sorts of people going around wandering in and out with telegrams, with important messages, and as I said to Mr. Martin, you can never tell whether a man who comes in is a valet or an Assistant Secretary of State except that the Assistant Secretary of State looked more like the valet and the valet looked more like an Assistant Secretary of State.

Then, in the evening we had, with the women still present because they don't segregate the sexes, they may segregate the people by colour in the south but not by sex, and we talked with the ladies there about some pretty important subjects. This may seem a little strange, this way of conducting international business and it was strange, it was unique. I don't think there's anything like it in the world and I don't think it would ever be done, even at the ranch, with anybody but Canadians. This was a great compliment to us. It was a reflection of the special relationship we have with the United States and the very friendly relationship we have established with the President and his wife. In that respect, it's a great asset and a great advantage. But it's also very dangerous because there's always a possibility that you are taken pretty much for granted because you are so close-treated almost like the Governor of Texas.

But it was a fascinating and unforgettable experience to have these messages being brought in, as they were to the President every few minutes, and dealing with some very important things that had de-veloped especially out in Vietnam—a very dangerous development and to have him say, "Let's have a look at this"—"Let's *have* a look at this." It was Mr. Martin and me to have a look at it too with him and Mr. Rusk who was there. This is quite unlike, I think, anything that could have happened at any other place in any other meeting between the leaders of any other government. We had an opportunity then in this kind of informal way to discuss some of our problems and to get more from the President in regard to his real views about things than if we'd sat around a table formally in the White House, because a man in these circumstances is likely to express exactly what he feels.

The next morning I got up early, because I get up early, but I went downstairs and found Mr. Martin already looking for a cup of coffee in the kitchen where he found the President of the United States. And then we saw some more messages and we went over some more telegrams with the American Government and told them where they were doing wrong in one or two respects. And then we had breakfast. We weren't asked what we were going to have for breakfast, we were *told* what we were going to have for breakfast. And we started off with hominy grits, this was quite an ordeal, but I said to myself—if, for Canada I can drink Vodka with Khrushchev, for Canada I could eat hominy grits with Johnson. And that's the way it went.

This may sound funny, and it was funny, it was unique. But I think Mr. Martin would probably agree with me when I say that we got through as much business in this informal way, and perhaps more usefully than if we had more formal meetings in Washington. We certainly managed to sign, in very informal and uncomfortable surroundings—we signed outside on a picnic table with a temperature of about 15 above zero—a treaty, an agreement between our two countries which really breaks new ground between our two countries. It is an experiment, this automotive agreement. I think it's going to work out very well, but it is an experiment and it took a good deal—well we worried whether we would proceed along this road. It's the first time we've ever tried to do it and we hope the results will be good. I believe it will. If it is good it may be the beginning of a new procedure in the negotiation of international trade agreements. It's a new approach, it's a continental approach, it's a rationalization of continental business in respect of one industry which perhaps—perhaps if it works out, can be extended. This may be the beginning of something pretty big and pretty important. I don't know whether we can extend this rationalization, this continental free trade to periodicals or not. I suspect that we should try the opposite path in regard to periodicals and parts.

Anyway, this was the real reason for our visit to Texas to sign this treaty. The President wanted it to be done there, and we were glad to go down there and do it and this is my official, off the record, report to you of what happened in Texas. . . .

F. President Lyndon B. Johnson and Prime Minister Lester B. Pearson, Camp David Presidential Retreat, Catoctin Mountains of Maryland, April 3, 1965

1. Address of Prime Minister Pearson at Temple University's Founder's Dinner of the General Alumni Association (On Receiving The University's Second World Peace Award), Philadelphia, Pennsylvania, April 2, 1965

(Source: The General Alumni Association of Temple University in Philadelphia, Pennsylvania.)

. . . In this tragic conflict, the U.S. intervened to help South Vietnam defend itself against aggression and at the request of the government of the country that was under attack.

Its motives were honourable; neither mean nor imperialistic. Its sacrifices have been great and they were not made to advance any selfish American interest. U.S. civilians doing peaceful work have been wantonly murdered in this conflict. . . .

The universal concern which is being expressed about the tragedy of Vietnam is a reflection both of this fearful possibility and of that sense of world community to which I have referred. All nations watch with deep anxiety the quickening march of events in Vietnam toward a climax which is unknown but menacing. All are seeking solutions to the dilemma confronting us, because all would be involved in the spread of this war.

The dilemma is acute and it seems to be intractable. On the one hand, no nation—particularly no newly-independent nation—could ever feel secure if capitulation in Vietnam led to the sanctification of aggression through subversion or spurious "wars of national liberation," which are really wars of Communist domination.

On the other hand, the progressive application of military sanctions can encourage stubborn resistance; rather than a willingness to negotiate. So continued and stepped-up intensification of hostilities in Vietnam could lead to uncontrollable escalation. Things would get out of hand.

A settlement is very hard to envisage in the heat of battle, but as the battle grows fiercer, it becomes even more imperative to seek and to find one.

What are the conditions for such a settlement? First, there must be a ceasefire; they must stop fighting.

Aggressive action by North Vietnam to bring about a communist "liberation," (which means communist rule) of the South must end. Only then can there be negotiation with any chance of success. In this connection, continued bombing action against North Vietnam beyond a certain point may not have this desired result. Instead of inducing authorities in Hanoi to halt their attacks on the South, it may only harden their determination to pursue, and even intensify, their present course of action. Modern history has shown that this is often the result and one that we don't intend when we take massive retaliatory action.

The retaliatory strikes against North Vietnamese military targets, for which there has been great provocation, aim at making it clear that the maintenance of aggressive policies toward the South will become increasingly costly to the Northern regime.

After about two months of air strikes, the message should now have been received "loud and clear." The authorities in Hanoi must know that the United States, with its massive military power, can mete out even greater punishment. They must also know that, for this reason, the cost of their continued aggression against South Vietnam could be incalculable.

If, however, the desired political response from Hanoi has not been forthcoming, and it hasn't yet, the response which would indicate a change in policy, this may result from a desire to avoid what would appear to Hanoi to be the public humiliation of backing down under duress. And the Northern communist regime is probably also under pressure from another direction to avoid the public abandonment of a policy which fits the Communist Chinese doctrine of "wars of national liberation."

If, then, a series of increasingly powerful retaliatory strikes against North Vietnam does not bring about this preliminary condition of a cease-fire, surely we must give serious consideration to every other way by which a cease-fire might be brought about.

There are many factors in this situation which I am not in a position to weigh or even know. But there does appear to be at least a possibility, in my view, that a suspension of air strikes against North Vietnam *at the right time* [1] might provide the Hanoi authorities with an opportunity, if they wish to take it, to inject some flexibility into their policy without appearing to do so as the direct result of military pressure.

If such a suspension took place for a limited time, then the rate of incidents in South Vietnam would provide a fairly accurate way of measuring its usefulness and the desirability of continuing it. I am not, of course—I would not dare—propose any compromise on points of principle, nor any weakening of resistance to aggression in South Vietnam. Indeed resistance may require increased military strength to be used against the armed and attacking communists. I merely suggest that a measured and announced pause in one field of military action at the right time might facilitate the development of diplomatic resources which cannot easily be applied to the problem under the existing

---

[1] Italics indicate underlined words in Mr. Pearson's draft.

circumstances. It could at least, at the very least, expose the intransigence of the North Vietnam government if they remained intransigent.

Obviously, the objectives of any lasting settlement cannot be defined in detail at this stage. But I think that few would quarrel with President Johnson's view which he expressed the other day—that an honourable peace should be based on "a reliable arrangement to guarantee the independence and security of all in Southeast Asia." Both sides should examine the substance of a possible, rather than a perfect, settlement.

In doing so, we should realize that the crisis in Vietnam is, in part at least, a reflection of a far broader conflict, and that a lasting resolution of the specific problem may be possible only within the framework of a much broader settlement. But one thing is certain: without a settlement guaranteeing the independence, neutrality and territorial integrity of North Vietnam's neighbours in Southeast Asia and without a willingness by all parties to respect and protect these, a continuation of the present fear and instability will be inescapable. I don't know where it will lead us all to.

The problem, therefore, remains the responsibility, not only of the U.S. which is bearing the brunt of the conflict there, but the responsibility of the whole international community. The members of that community will be obliged to make available the means of supervising any settlement in guaranteeing the fulfillment of its terms in spirit and in letter. The world community will also be obliged to assist in establishing the economic, as well as the political, foundations of future understanding and security . In this connection, I was encouraged by President Johnson's expression of the willingness of the United States once again to help in promoting economic and social co-operation in this. And that is very important.

There is at present a U.N. project for social and economic enterprise going on in this part of the world: the Mekong River Basin Project.

The Mekong River Basin embraces most of Indo-China, as well as Thailand and a part of Southern Communist China. In this U.N. project there are now twenty-one states participating. And they have been working on this project while the fighting has been going on and they have not been disturbed by either side. They have merely scratched the surface of a development which could go far to lift up the standards of life of these people from deprivation, distress and hunger, towards comfort and decent living. It *could* do this, *if* it were given the opportunity and the resources. The amount now being spent in armed conflict in Vietnam and Laos over a few weeks could do the job and could help millions of people to a better life for many years.

So I propose that the U.N. should try to enlarge this project in a spectacular way, even while the political and military conflict is going on—that the United Nations step in in this way; that for this purpose, the U.N. call a conference of the states concerned—whatever their political relations—including both Vietnam governments—in order to make this part of Southeast Asia a centre of international, social and economic development. That is the best way, not only to stop fighting, but to prevent it from starting again in the future. Finally, I would like to see the U.N. Secretary-General, a man of objectivity and dedication, without delay visit the countries in question to pave the way for such a conference. I would like to see it held as soon as possible. Because China is not a member of the United Nations, but must be at this Conference, if possible, a special development agency could be set up by the Conference to extend, enlarge, deepen and broaden the work now being done for these people.

With that kind of great international development project, with a cease-fire followed by political negotiations, with the countries in the area given an international guarantee of neutrality and an assurance of continued aid for peaceful development, then the danger, destruction and distress of the present hour might be replaced by peace, hope and progress.

I know this may seem unrealistic idealism in the light of what is going on there now, but perhaps we might find that if we take . . . idealism of this kind that it would be the most realistic policy we could follow, because it might prevent a war.

I know—I am very conscious of the fact—that the policy and the effort of the government of the U.S.A. is directed to this end and its effort deserves and should receive the support of all peace loving people.

We in North America have a special duty and a special opportunity in this struggle for peace. We enjoy a very high standard of material well-being and security with freedom. But our good fortune carried with it a corresponding obligation.

At the moment, the most immediate obligation facing the international community—not merely the United States—is to restore peace, freedom and security to the people of Vietnam.

If we fail here, the tragic consequences may extend far beyond the area directly concerned. If we succeed, it could make possible new and greater progress toward a better world. Thank you.

2. *Joint Press Conference of President Johnson and Prime Minister Pearson, Camp David, Maryland, April 3, 1965*

(PP/Lyndon B. Johnson, Vol. 1965, Book I, No. 162, pp. 378-79)

THE PRESIDENT: The Prime Minister was in Pennsylvania and I was going to be here and I asked him to come over and have lunch with me. He is returning shortly. We have no news for you but George indicated yesterday evening that we would see you today and so I told him to bring whatever group he felt was necessary up here.

The Prime Minister and I have talked about various problems that affect our respective countries. We talked about the problems in the Great Lakes, and aviation agreement, and our relations with other countries, and problems in Viet-Nam, Europe. We had a general discussion, a friendly one. He is returning.

I may have two or three announcements for you a little later regarding my schedule next week and regarding some appointments perhaps, but I'll still be working on them and by the time you get back to town I may finish them. If so, George will give them to you. If not, I'll give them to you on Monday.

That is all I have to say. If the Prime Minister has got anything to say I'll be glad.

THE PRIME MINISTER: I haven't much to say except it has been a very pleasant couple of hours and I am grateful to the President for giving me the chance to come to Camp David while I was in Philadelphia and having an exchange of views with him.

There were one or two things on the Canadian-American front we were concerned with. One was to try to remove the remaining difficulties in the way of an air agreement between our two countries, which we have been working on for some time and which is a difficult and complicated matter. A good many interests are affected. We hope to have that cleared up before long. I think I said that when I was down here about a year ago. I still hope.

Then we discussed the possibility of working out an agreement between our two Governments on Great Lakes problems—pollution, water levels. This can't be done by one side alone, and this requires also on our side provincial cooperation and we are going into that and see if we can work out an agreement to see if it will help.

Then, as the President said, we talked about the state of the world, which isn't as happy in some places as it should be.

I think that is about all that I have to say.

THE PRESIDENT: The Prime Minister will be leaving very shortly and I expect to stay here until Monday—unless Mrs. Johnson changes my mind.

Q. Mr. President, a couple of us will be over in the motel if you need us.

Q. Mr. Prime Minister, did you take up the question of Viet-Nam about which you talked in Philadelphia last night?

THE PRIME MINISTER: We talked about Viet-Nam and a view that I expressed last night. I don't want to say anything about that except to reiterate in our government we have tried to understand the position of the United States in Viet-Nam as I underlined last night and support that position. I have said before, and I don't mind repeating, it is the responsibility of the international community—not only of the United States which is bearing the responsibility at the moment. We wish to continue that support.

Q. Do you see any obstacle to continuing that, Mr. Prime Minister?

THE PRIME MINISTER: No, I would just want to say we would want to continue supporting the United States' effort to bring peace to the people of Viet-Nam which is the only thing that concerns the United States in this matter. As I said last night, the intervention of the United States in Viet-Nam was at the request of the Government of the country. It was an honorable intervention, we should remember this, not inspired by any mean or nationalistic motive or imperialistic motive. That was the spirit of the intervention and that is the kind of intervention we think ourselves and other countries should support. It is designed to bring peace and freedom to the country, and we support that.

Q. Is that satisfactory to you, Mr. President?

THE PRESIDENT: It is not a matter for me to pass judgment on what other governments do. It is his expression and he has expressed it very well.

Q. Mr. President, since the subject has been raised here about the Prime Minister's speech last night, is what he said figured in your talks today?

THE PRIME MINISTER: We were talking about the situation generally. I only made this speech last night. The President has other things to do than read my speech. Believe me, I would have been very glad to come down here and have a talk with the President about the state of the world.

THE PRESIDENT: His visit has nothing to do with Viet-Nam. That wasn't the purpose of it or anything else or anything you could blow up and make look big or dramatic.

He has told you about all he knows and I have too and we are glad to have seen you.

3. *Prime Minister Pearson's Report of Meeting to the Canadian House of Commons, June 6, 1960*

(CHCD, April 6, 1965, pp. 11, 34-36)

RIGHT HON. J.G. DIEFENBAKER (Leader of the Opposition): Mr. Speaker, I would like to direct a question to the Prime Minister, but first I want to congratulate him on the honour bestowed upon him on Friday evening by the presentation of the peace award at Temple University.

I wish to ask him whether the enunciation of his views regarding the Vietnam crisis represented a cabinet decision. I ask this because of the fact that on Friday afternoon the Secretary of State for External Affairs, in his version of the situation and Canada's views, expressed a somewhat dissimilar attitude to that of the Prime Minister in his extramural speech.

RIGHT HON. L.B. PEARSON (Prime Minister): When I spoke, Mr. Speaker, I was of course speaking as the leader of the government, with the knowledge and approval of my colleagues. What I said did not in my view contradict in any way what was said by the Secretary of State for External Affairs, but may have gone a little further than he went on Friday afternoon.

MR. DIEFENBAKER: Would the Prime Minister say whether the reaction of the President of the United States indicated that the suggestion of a pause, measured or otherwise, was refreshing to him?

MR. PEARSON: He was very interested in it, Mr. Speaker.

MR. DIEFENBAKER: Before the Prime Minister made his speech had he discussed the matter in any way with the officials of the Department of External Affairs, and had there been any exchange of views in this respect with the United States administration before the speech was delivered?

MR. PEARSON: Mr. Speaker, statements on external affairs are normally discussed with the Secretary of State for External Affairs who takes the responsibility for discussions in his department. The particular statement on Friday night was not taken up with the United States government or any United States authority before it was delivered, although our views in general in regard to Vietnam were well known to them.

MR. T.C. DOUGLAS (Leader of the NDP): My question is addressed to the Prime Minister, and it has to do with a press conference which he and President Johnson held at Camp David. Reports indicate that Mr. James Minifie asked the Prime Minister to express his views and those of the government, and the Prime Minister is quoted as having said that the Canadian government both supported and approved of United States policy and Vietnam. I wish to ask the Prime Minister if this is an accurate report of his comments at that press conference.

MR. PEARSON: I will be glad to send the text of what I said to the hon. gentleman. I do not have that text with me, as it was taken down, but subject to correction in detail I said this government had supported the policy of the United States in Vietnam and wished to be able to continue that support. . . .

I was invited by the President of the United States to fly over to see him at Camp David, when he heard that I was to speak in Philadelphia on Friday night, to discuss with him some aspects of our bilateral relations and world affairs. I was delighted to do that. It was a very interesting and, for me, a very useful couple of hours.

The right hon. gentleman seems a little worried about what went on.

I find it very difficult to please him in these and in other matters. Perhaps that is an objective which I would never be able to achieve; but if I do not talk about these things in public, in the House of Commons or outside the house, about these matters of immediate international danger and concern—if the government does not express itself on these matters—we are criticized as being a satellite, a mouthpiece of the United States of America.

But if we do speak out publicly, as we should on occasion, and only when the occasion seems to require it, then, Mr. Speaker, we should do that with responsibility and restraint and we should not, I suggest, be accused of interference in the affairs of another country; because what is going on in Vietnam at this time is the concern and the affair of every country in the world, and particularly of the neighbours and allies of the United States of America.

So that there may not be any misunderstanding of what I did actually say, I will put on the record just a few paragraphs, and I do not think they need any interpretation. . . .

I hope, Mr. Speaker, that was an appropriate message to take to the United States at this time, and an appropriate proposal to discuss with the President of that country.

G. Prime Minister Lester B. Pearson and President Lyndon B. Johnson, Campobello Island, New Brunswick, August 21, 1966

1. Exchange of Remarks Between Prime Minister Pearson and President Johnson at the Laying of the Cornerstone of the Visitor's Pavilion, Roosevelt Campobello International Park, August 21, 1966

(PMO, Transcript of Prime Minister Pearson's Address; and PP/Lyndon B. Johnson, Vol. 1966, Book II, No. 400, pp. 875-76)

THE PRIME MINISTER: Mr. President, when we signed the agreement in the White House on behalf of our two governments establishing the Roosevelt-Campobello International Park, we were providing for the kind of memorial to Franklin Delano Roosevelt he would have best appreciated.

I had not seen Campobello when the idea was first broached. I do not think President Johnson had either. But we both recognized, as President Kennedy had before us and as the Hammer family had done, when they so generously offered the property to the Canadian and United States Governments, what a happy and significant symbol it would be of that special relationship that has developed between our two countries and our two peoples over the years.

Why, Mr. President, that relationship even includes the influence of

Canada on the history of your own State of Texas. I do not think it is generally known that one of the signers of the Declaration of Independence of Texas in 1836 was a Canadian, Michel Menard, who was born in 1805 in the then village of Laprairie near Montreal. His memory is commemorated in the name of the town and county of Menard which is, I understand, 100 miles or so from Johnson City.

We are proud of this Canadian contribution to Texas independence; long before Texas took over the U.S.A.

In his first inaugural address, Franklin Roosevelt spoke words which had a very special meaning for Canadians as the first Presidential expression of his "good-neighbour policy." But neighbours, however good, particularly those that have long common fences, are bound to have their differences. So it is with us. The significance of our relationship is that we have learned to resolve our differences in the way good neighbours should always resolve them, in a spirit of moderation and conciliation, with mutual understanding and common sense.

This good-neighbourhood did not just happen. Indeed, it was not always so. Why, even peaceful and beautiful Campobello Island itself, now a symbol of our friendship, in the early years of the Nineteenth Century was the object of some controversy as to whether it should be a part of the United States or of Canada. . . .

Campobello contributed much to Franklin Delano Roosevelt and, through him, to the world. And he, in his turn, made Campobello a symbol of the special relationship between Canadians and Americans.

President Johnson and I have again discussed that relationship in the short and very pleasant visit we have had today. We have talked together in much the same, friendly way as President Roosevelt and Prime Minister Mackenzie King used to do. Perhaps our discussion has been even a little more informal than the conversations of those days. I don't know about that, but I do know how very greatly I appreciate an opportunity like this to speak to the President of the United States as a friend, and with the frankness that friendship makes possible.

I believe this is the eighth time, Mr. President, that you and I have talked in person since you assumed the heaviest responsibilities that can be carried today by a human being. In between, we have had our many phone discussions and written exchanges. I hope—and I know you share that hope—that this close contact will continue—I was going to say for many, many more years, but that might be interpreted, however remotely, as a political wish.

This afternoon—if we didn't cover—we at least touched on many matters of special interest to our two countries; as well as others of farther reaching international concern. Speaking for myself, I can only say that our few hours together have been most worthwhile. We need this kind of contact on every level.

There are no two countries in the world whose relationships are closer than ours; in trade, in finance, in the development of our resources, in the flow and contact of peoples.

The interdependence of our destinies is as inevitable as the complexity and difficulty of many of the problems that flow from that interdependence. We looked at some of those problems today. My view was confirmed that they can be solved in the future, as they have been in the past, by goodwill, tolerance and understanding.

On the broader international scene, I expressed my appreciation, which I know is felt by the vast majority of Canadians, of the courage, the patient strength and largeness of spirit being shown by the American people, as they bear so much of the burden of responsibility for peace and progress and freedom in the world.

The friends of the U.S.A.—and there is no closer friend than Canada—may not always agree with all the expressions of American policy and power. But they must all acknowledge that that policy has no design against the freedom or welfare of any other people; and that power, whether exercised in Vietnam or any other place, has no aggressive or imperialist purpose behind it. Today, with nuclear platforms circling our planet, if power is used for any other purpose than establishing and securing the peace, there is little hope for man's survival and perhaps not much reason for it.

As we meet this sunny Sunday afternoon under a blue sky on this lovely and tranquil island, hallowed by the memory of a great man, war and woe, conflict and cruelty may seem far away. But they are as close as the heart-beat of a neighbour and now we all are neighbours. So I hope that the guns of Vietnam and all the guns everywhere—may soon cease to fire; that the bombs may cease to fall;[1] that discussion, negotiation and agreement, the processes in which F.D.R., the Captain of Campobello, so passionately believed and so skillfully practised, that these healing processes may soon replace the fighting and the killing.

I know, Mr. President, that this is your own most cherished and longed for goal.

May God help you—and help us all—to achieve it.

THE PRESIDENT: I am very proud to be on this historic island with the distinguished Prime Minister of our neighbor and our close friend, Canada.

If Campobello had not been located between our two nations, I think President Roosevelt would have moved it here. He had a reverence for the island just as he had a deep affection, Mr. Prime Minister, for your country and for your people.

---

[1]While this phrase appeared in the Prime Minister's text, it was omitted in his oral presentation because Mr. Pearson did not want to imply he was suggesting a bombing halt.

When I first came to Washington 35 years ago, President Franklin Roosevelt was only a few months away from the Presidency.

Before his death 14 years later, he was to help change forever America's course in the affairs of the world. And he was to leave on a very young Congressman an enduring awareness of both the limits as well as the obligations of power.

I saw President Roosevelt on occasion during those years of intense debate over America's response to aggression in Asia and Europe. I saw his concern grow as one test after another gave the belligerent powers increasing confidence that they could get away with aggression.

And here, at Campobello—where the memory of Franklin Roosevelt is strong—I am reminded today of how those years have shaped the realities of our own time.

First, we know that our alternatives are sometimes determined more by what others do than by our own desires.

We do not choose to use force, but aggression narrows the alternatives—either we do nothing and let aggression succeed, or we take our stand to resist it.

We would always choose peace, but when other men choose peace at the expense of someone else's freedom, the alternative is unacceptable.

Second, we know that a great power can influence events just as much by withdrawing its power as it can by using its power.

Third, we have learned that unrest and instability in one part of the world are a real danger to other areas in the world and to other peoples who live in those areas. If hostilities in strategic areas can be contained, they will be less likely to threaten world peace with a confrontation of nations that possess unlimited power.

Fourth, we know that if a safe world order depends as much on a large power's word and its will as it does on weapons, for the world to be secure our friends must trust our treaties and our adversaries must respect our resolve.

Fifth, we know that power carries with it a mandate for restraint and patience; restraint because nuclear weapons have raised the stakes of unmeasured force; and patience, because we are concerned with more than just tomorrow.

No man loved peace more than Franklin D. Roosevelt. It was in the marrow of his soul and I never saw him more grieved than when reports came from the War Department of American casualties in a major battle.

But he led my Nation and he led it courageously in conflict—not for war's sake, because he knew that beyond war lay the larger hopes of man.

And so it is today. The history of mankind is the history of conflict and agony—of wars and of rumors of wars. Still today, we must contend with the cruel reality that some men still believe in using force and seek by aggression to impose their will on others. And that is not the kind of world that America wants, but it is the kind of world that we have.

The day is coming when those men will realize that aggression against their neighbors does not pay. It will be hastened if every nation that abhors war will apply all the influence at their command to persuade the aggressors from their chosen course.

For this is the real limit of power: We have the means of unlimited destruction, but we do not have the power alone to make peace in the world. Only when those who promote aggression will agree to come and reason together will the world finally know, again, the blessings of peace. That day, I do not doubt, will come, and once men realize that aggression really bears no rewards, it may be that the deepest hopes of Franklin Roosevelt—hopes for a genuine peace and an end to war of every kind—will finally be realized.

So it is good to be here with a man to whom peace has been a lifelong pursuit. American Presidents and Canadian Prime Ministers have always had a very close and informal arrangement reflecting the ties that bind our two countries together.

On this occasion, may we all remember the courage and the strength of a man whose name grows even larger with each passing year: Franklin Delano Roosevelt.

2. Prime Minister Pearson's Report of Meeting to the Canadian House of Commons, August 30, 1966

(CHCD, August 30, 1966, p. 7792)

MR. REAL CAOUETTE (Leader of Creditistes): The right hon. Prime Minister had a recent meeting with the President of the United States in New Brunswick. Did any agreement come out of that meeting or those talks, with regard to Viet Nam or American involvement in Viet Nam or was there any discussion about inflation, which seems to be taking a permanent hold?

RIGHT HON. L.B. PEARSON (Prime Minister): Mr. Speaker, there was no occasion to reach any particular understanding at these meetings in regard to our position on Viet Nam and the United States position, because our position is well known to the United States and I think we understand their position. We did discuss many other subjects within the limited time available, some two and one-half hours, and one of these was inflationary dangers and pressures in both countries; because this is more than a national problem.

H. Prime Minister Lester B. Pearson and President Lyndon B. Johnson, Harrington Lake, P. Q., May 25, 1967

1. Remarks of President Johnson Upon Visiting EXPO '67, Place des Nations, Montreal, P.Q., May 25, 1967

(PP/Lyndon B. Johnson, Vol. 1967, No. 237, p. 574)

It is always a great pleasure for me to visit Canada. Your magnificent EXPO '67—and knowledge that this is your centennial anniversary —serves to heighten my interest.

My first trip outside of the United States after I became President was to visit Canada. That was to Vancouver, where we met with Prime Minister Pearson to proclaim the Columbia River Treaty.

We came to conserve the water resources of our great continent —and so naturally that day it was pouring down rain.

It rained so hard, in fact, that I never delivered the speech that I had prepared for that occasion. But I hope you won't worry. While the temptation is hard to resist, I'm not going to deliver that speech here today.

I well recall some words your Prime Minister spoke to me on that rainy day in Vancouver, more than 2 years ago. He told me then:

"... I assure you, Mr. President, that had you landed at our most eastern airport in Newfoundland, 5,000 or more miles away, or at any place between, our welcome to you would have been equally warm both for yourself and as President of the United States. . . ."

You have focused the eyes of the world on the theme of your exhibition: "Man and His World." We hope that, among other lessons to be learned here, will be this: that proud and independent peoples can live peacefully side by side, can live in peace and partnership as good neighbors, that they need not waste their substance and destroy their dreams with useless quarrels and senseless, unconstructive conflict.

We of the United States of America consider ourselves blessed. We have much to give thanks for. But the gift of providence that we really cherish is that we were given as our neighbors on this great, wonderful continent, the people and the nation of Canada.

So we are very delighted to be here. We are so glad that you invited us. We thank you very much for your courtesy.

2. Press Briefing by President Johnson and Prime Minister Pearson, Uplands R.C.A.F. Base, Ottawa, May 25, 1967

(*Ibid.*, No. 239, pp. 576-77)

THE PRESIDENT: I want to tell you about our visit here today and to thank the people of Canada, the distinguished Prime Minister, and the other officials of the Canadian Government for their hospitality.

We had a delightful visit at EXPO. We were thrilled to see what you people had done there in the way of permitting other nations to come here and demonstrate their friendship for your great country and to exchange exhibits and ideas with our neighbors.

I imposed on the Prime Minister by going with him to lunch and counseling with him on the problems that confront the peoples of the world today. We, of course, discussed the situation that exists in the Middle East, the discussions that took place yesterday in the Security Council of the United Nations, and the likely discussions that will take place there in the days ahead.

As you know, we in the United States have a very high regard for Prime Minister Pearson. He has worked with our people over a long period. He has served in our Capital. He has distinguished himself as a citizen of the world. And he is one of the great living experts on the particular area of the world which greatly concerns us now.

The Prime Minister and I exchanged ideas. Our visit was a very agreeable one. We not only talked about the Middle East, but we talked about our respective countries, our problems with each other, the problems that good neighbors do have.

We also talked about the situation in Vietnam, as we have on other occasions. I brought him up to date on the reports that we have from there—our viewpoint. I am returning to Washington very shortly where I will meet Lord Casey from Australia, who is due there at 5:30.

I would summarize our visit by saying my talk with the Prime Minister and others was quite constructive and very agreeable. I would hope that in the days ahead I might have the opportunity to come here for a somewhat more extended stay than the situation today would permit.

I have been President a little over 3 years; and I have had a chance to visit Canada three times. I would like to have some other visits in the future.

Q. Mr. President, would you care to entertain questions?

THE PRESIDENT: No, I don't plan to have a press conference.

Q. How about the Prime Minister?

THE PRIME MINISTER: The President is due in Washington at 5:30 to meet with the Governor-General of Australia, so I hope he won't be detained.

I think the President, whom I was so happy to have as my guest at Harrington Lake, has said all that can be said about our talks.

We covered a lot of ground. From my point of view, they were very helpful, indeed, and I am very grateful to the President for getting his viewpoint on some of the very dangerous and difficult international situations that face us today.

I just want to express my gratitude for the President taking time to come here and, as he has indicated, he hopes to get back in our centennial year to Canada for a little longer visit.

So, I think if you will excuse us, I will go to the plane with the President and wave him goodby to Washington.

3. Prime Minister Pearson's Report of Meeting to the Canadian House of Commons, May 26, 1967

(CHCD, May 26, 1967, pp. 601-2)

MR. T.C. DOUGLAS (Leader of the NDP): Mr. Speaker, I should like to ask the right hon. Prime Minister whether he can give the house any information arising out of his discussions with the President of the United States in respect of whether any agreement has been reached between United States and Canada as to the position they will take vis-à-vis the situation in the Middle East, and particularly with reference to the right of access of the state of Israel and all other nations to the gulf of Aqaba?

RIGHT HON. L.B. PEARSON (Prime Minister): Mr. Speaker, I am very glad indeed to deal with that question as best I can, within the limitations of the fact that our conversations yesterday were of course confidential, as they were bound to be in the circumstances.

I do not think, however, I am betraying any confidence when I say there was complete agreement between the president and myself as to the special importance of two things in connection with the Middle East crisis. The first was the importance of maintaining the right of access to and innocent passage through the gulf of Aqaba, and that everything possible should be done through the United Nations to see if this can be arranged so that this danger spot can be removed.

The other danger spot, if I may call it that, about which we talked and where we agreed on certain ideas as a means of helping to remove the danger, is in the confrontation of the two forces on the Israeli-U.A.R. border, and the grave and great importance of placing on that border a United Nations presence. This would not be the United Nations Emergency Force, which has been disbanded, but in some appropriate way there must be a United Nations presence there which will operate on both sides of the border.

MR. DOUGLAS: Was there any discussion of the proposal of General de Gaulle, the President of the French republic, with reference to the possibility of a meeting of the four great powers to see whether within the framework of the United Nations these powers might agree on some course of action which would prevent the outbreak of hostilities in the Middle East?

MR. PEARSON: Mr. Speaker, this matter was discussed at some

length. It was felt that as the question is now before the Security Council nothing should be done to weaken its position in this connection, and that a meeting of the permanent members of that body—the four powers that have been mentioned—within the context of the Security Council might be a very useful procedure at this time.

My own view, as I expressed it, was that if this could not be done by a meeting of the permanent members of the Security Council, then the proposal that they should meet outside the U.N. should not be rejected; but it would be better if they could meet as permanent members of the Security Council. I understand that General de Gaulle's proposal was that they should meet simply as four great powers. If that procedure were adopted and would bring the U.S.S.R. into the discussions, it might be useful. But I understand there are some difficulties in bringing about that meeting.

VII. Prime Minister Pierre E. Trudeau (April 1968-   ) (Presidents Lyndon B. Johnson And Richard M. Nixon)

Prime Minister Pierre E. Trudeau assumed office in April of 1968, while Richard Nixon became President in January of 1969. Although Lyndon B. Johnson was President during the first nine months of the Trudeau incumbency, the two leaders did not meet. Trudeau and Nixon have met a total of five times to 1974, of which three are documented in this chapter.

The first Trudeau-Nixon meeting occurred in Washington from March 24-25, 1969. (See Section A.) Constituting the first state visit of a foreign leader during the Nixon Administration, the goal of the meeting was, to quote the Trudeau-Nixon Joint Statement, to inaugurate "a new era of consultation between Canada and the U.S." During this "get acquainted" visit, the two leaders spent two hours and forty-five minutes together, discussing in a general sense a gauntlet of issues: disarmament, the future of NATO, Latin America, trade problems, wheat, oil, the Safeguard Anti-Ballistic Missile System, a Canadian domestic communications satellite, student unrest and race problems, and bilateral consultation procedures.[1] The most important issue was the implications for Canada of the ABM proposal of President Nixon. The first phase of the proposal involved the deployment of missiles at sites in Montana and North Dakota, which had provoked

---

[1]See Jay Waltz, "Trudeau Goes to Washington Today for Get-Acquainted Talks With Nixon," NYT (March 24, 1969), p. 10; James F. Clarity, "Trudeau Confers With President," NYT (March 25, 1969), pp. 1, 11; and Gerald Waring, "President, Trudeau to Meet Here," *Washington Post* (March 24, 1969), p. 1, A10.

demands from the Opposition in Canada that the Prime Minister state his position on the ABM. The other bilateral issues of great concern to Canadians were oil and wheat. President Nixon had announced his decision to review U.S. oil policy, and Canadians were fearful that this might dampen the increasing U.S. market for western Canadian oil. There was also Canadian concern about the collapse of international pricing agreements on wheat, with producing countries attempting to underprice each other to gain sales advantages in the international wheat market. By way of background, the Trudeau foreign policy review which had been in process for several months, had also generated issues of a multilateral nature that could affect Canadian-U.S. relations, such as Canadian recognition of the People's Republic of China and the Canadian role in NATO. Three tangible initiatives emerged from this summit meeting. First, it was announced that the Joint Cabinet Committee on Trade and Economic Policy, which had not met since June of 1967, would meet from June 25-27. Secondly, it was announced that meetings would be initiated on April 2 between Canadian-U.S. Senior officials to study common interests in energy matters; and finally, the President agreed "in principle" to provide launch services for Canada's planned domestic communications satellite. The documentation for this meeting includes the Trudeau-Nixon exchange of welcoming remarks; their Joint Statement following their meeting, the address of Trudeau at the National Press Club during which he enunciated the "elephant" analogy, and Trudeau's report of the meeting to the House of Commons.

Although not documented, the second Trudeau-Nixon meeting occurred within a week of their first meeting, when Trudeau returned to Washington in March of 1969 for one day to attend the State Funeral of former President Dwight D. Eisenhower. Although Trudeau attended a White House reception hosted by President Nixon for the visiting dignitaries, at which the President held private talks with several foreign leaders, there is no indication he had any conversation with Trudeau other than an exchange of pleasantries.

The third Trudeau-Nixon meeting, also not documented, occurred in June of 1969 at ceremonies in Massena, New York, and the Place des Nations in Montreal. Entirely ceremonial in nature, and constituting the President's first visit to Canada, the purpose of the meeting was to mark the tenth anniversary of the St. Lawrence Seaway. Although such issues as the anti-ballistic missile system, the Canadian NATO force reduction, and the export of Canadian oil to the United States were still active from the Trudeau-Nixon March meeting, no references were made to them in the speeches and there are no indications that the Prime Minister and President discussed any issues.

The fourth Trudeau-Nixon meeting occurred in Washington on December 6-7, 1971, and is one of the more unique exercises in

Canadian-U.S. Summitry.[2] (See Section B.) Concerned with the "lack of reassurances as to the American disposition towards Canada," to quote Mr. Trudeau at his December 7 Washington press conference, "the purpose of (the) visit was to come down here and see if all this was true." The most compelling issue was the U.S. import surcharge which had been declared by President Nixon on August 15, 1971 in an attempt to deal with the U.S. foreign exchange deficit. Heretofore exempted from such major U.S. foreign exchange programmes, Canada received no exemption this time, notwithstanding the serious impact of the 1971 U.S. measures. This called into question not only the "special relationship," but raised such issues as the Canadian-U.S. Auto Pact, the defence production sharing agreements, and their role in contributing to the United States balance-of-payments problems. Although Trudeau desired to discuss bilateral issues in his meeting with President Nixon, most of the time during their two hour talk was spent discussing such multilateral issues as summit meetings with Soviet and Chinese leaders, NATO's forthcoming Ministerial Meeting, the Indo-Pakistani War, the Middle East, the European Security Conference and mutual balance force reduction. The two leaders also discussed economic relations between Canada and the United States in general terms that went beyond the ten per cent surcharge, but left specifics to Cabinet members who were also meeting. The Trudeau-Nixon discussions of international economic matters consisted essentially of the latter explaining the context of the U.S. desire to work out a recasting of the international monetary system. The President himself made no public statements concerning his meeting with the Prime Minister. Indeed, ceremonies had been kept to a minimum, and there were no formal welcoming remarks, toasts, or exchanges upon Trudeau's departure. The documentation for this meeting includes the Prime Minister explaining the rationale for his meeting in an exchange in the House of Commons, the press conference held by Trudeau in a Washington hotel during which he issued his "fantastic assurance" statement that the United States would respect the integrity of Canada, and the Prime Minister's report of the meeting to the House of Commons.

The fifth meeting between Trudeau and Nixon took place from April 13-15, 1972, in Ottawa.[3] (See Section C.) This was the sixth time a

---

[2]See "Nixon and Friends," NYT (December 12, 1971); George Bain, "Not Part of the Series," TGM (November 20, 1971), p. 6; John Rolfe and Ross H. Munro, "PMs Meeting With Nixon Is Described As Success," TGM (December 7, 1971), p. 1; and N. John Adams, "PM Returns With Pledge of U.S. Non-Interference," TGM (December 8, 1971), p. 1.

[3]See Ross H. Munro, "Nixon, Trudeau Break Impasse in Trade Talks," TGM (April 15, 1971), p. 1; George Bain, "Politically Useful," TGM (April 18, 1972), p. 6; and Anthony Astrachan, "Canada Gets U.S. Pledge," Washington Post (April 15, 1972).

U.S. President visited Ottawa and addressed the Canadian Parliament; the last President to have done so was John F. Kennedy eleven years earlier. The purpose of the forty-hour Nixon State Visit was "symbolic," to quote the President, and while there were no attempts at negotiations, views on Canadian-U.S. problems were exchanged. During their one hour and forty-five minute conversation, the two leaders discussed such multilateral issues as the President's trip to the People's Republic of China and his anticipations of the forthcoming trip to the Soviet Union; Southeast Asia; the Middle East; NATO; Strategic Arms Limitation Talks (SALT); and the reduction of troop levels in Europe. Concerning bilateral issues, two tangible results were forthcoming. First, the two leaders agreed to have their officials review negotiations on the auto pact and current trade issues, which had broken down in February. Secondly, there was agreement that both nations would explore the possibility of authorizing the International Joint Commission to regulate coastal waters, in light of particular concern about oil spills by ocean-going tankers. In addition, general discussions were held on the various plans for the transfer of Alaska oil to the United States, including the basic choice of an Alaskan route with tanker connections or a pipeline Canadian route; cooperative efforts in marine science; Canadian cooperation in reducing the importation of illegal narcotics into the United States; and the possibility of developing adjacent national parks in Alaska and southern Yukon. However, the most concrete accomplishment of the visit was the signing of the Canadian-U.S. Great Lakes Water Quality Agreement, which established both specific and general objectives for reducing pollution in the Great Lakes. The documentation for this meeting includes Prime Minister Trudeau's introduction of President Nixon to the Canadian Parliament; President Nixon's twenty-minute address during which he appeared to sound the call for Canadian political, strategic, and economic independence by restating the premises of the Nixon Doctrine; the Exchange of Remarks between the two leaders at the signing of the Great Lakes Water Quality Agreement, and Mr. Trudeau's responses to questions about the meeting in the House of Commons.

A. President Richard M. Nixon and Prime Minister Pierre E. Trudeau, Washington, D.C., March 24-25, 1969

1. Exchange of Welcoming Remarks Between President Nixon and Prime Minister Trudeau, March 24, 1969

(WHPS, Press Release, Exchange of Welcoming Remarks, 10:04 a.m. EST, March 24, 1969)

THE PRESIDENT: As most of you are aware, the Prime Minister is the first official visitor since the new Administration assumed office.

In welcoming him personally today and also in welcoming him representing his country, I do so saying first that it is altogether appropriate that he should be the first official visitor to this country. Because, as we look at the relations between your country and my country, Mr. Prime Minister, we recognize many factors that are often spoken of in the classroom and in the press and on television.

We share the longest common border of all nations. We share the common law. We share a common language. We share many common characteristics with regard to our history. And, in addition to that, we share a very precious asset, the asset of friendship.

In describing that friendship, however, I should emphasize a characteristic about it that sometimes we forget. That characteristic is that the friendship that Canada and the United States have enjoyed for so many years is not characterized by that total unanimity of view which destroys creativity, but it is characterized by a lively diversity and through that diversity we have the hallmark of freedom.

As the Prime Minister and I will be talking, and as his associates will be talking with the Secretary of State and their opposite numbers, we will find most areas in which we are in agreement. We will find other areas in which we find that we have differences. But those differences are ones that, between friends, we will be able to discuss and find, in most instances, a common ground which is perhaps superior to the position that either of us had before.

This is the mark of true friendship. And it is why, in speaking to you today, Mr. Prime Minister, I welcome you in behalf of all of the American people, so many of us of whom have known and enjoyed your country.

I can only add this: I only hope we can make you feel as much at home here in the United States as my wife and I, and so many hundreds of thousands of Americans, who have been welcomed in your country when we have visited there as private citizens.

THE PRIME MINISTER: On behalf of my colleagues and myself, I want to thank you for your very cordial welcome.

I am very happy to be here. I feel very honoured that you should have extended your welcome to me, sir, so early in the days of your new Administration.

We have, as you say, very many ties which link us, ties of friendship and ties of common interest. And, especially, we have a common outlook on the world. We have the same values and we tend to face the issues in a common way.

It is because of this, Mr. President, that I am looking forward to our discussions, discussions of matters of mutual interest. And I am looking forward to listening to your views on world problems, on the information and the wisdom that you will want to impart upon me in your talks.

For these reasons, I am very glad to be here. Like so many Canadians, I always look forward to a visit to the United States with great pleasure. I have great pleasure in being here and I am looking forward to my stay with great anticipation.

2. Joint Summary of Discussions of President Nixon and Prime Minister Trudeau, March 25, 1969

(Ext/Aff, XXI, No. 6, June 1969, pp. 231-34)

The President of the U.S.A. and the Prime Minister of Canada exchanged views on a wide range of international and bilateral matters. They seek a close, confident relationship between the two countries. The Prime Minister's visit has put the foundations in place for a continuing discussion on a number of questions.

The President has stated that he values the views and the outlook which the Prime Minister has imparted to him. The President said: "The viewpoint of the Canadian Government has always weighed heavily in the formation of United States policy. No other ally influences us more." The Prime Minister of Canada stressed that his Government is anxious to maintain and develop Canada's already close and friendly relations with the United States.

The President and the Prime Minister discussed the future of NATO. The President expressed the U.S. commitment to NATO. The President also emphasized the interest of the U.S.A. in negotiations with the Soviet Union rather than in confrontations.

The President of the United States and the Prime Minister of Canada have discussed the recent decision of the United States to proceed with the Safeguard System and its possible implications for Canada.

The President of the United States informed the Prime Minister of Canada of the reasons which led the United States to make this decision and of the United States' expectations as to its effects on East-West relations and on possible arms-control measures.

Over the years, the United States has regularly informed Canada of plans and developments in the ABM field; it has been agreed that this practice will be continued.

The Prime Minister will report to his Cabinet colleagues on his discussions with the United States Administration and a full assessment will be made of the implications for Canada of the Safeguard System.

The two countries share an intimate and valued trading relationship, unique in amount and diversity. They also share a commitment to further the expansion and freeing-up of world trade for the benefit of developing and developed countries alike.

As the next step in high-level consultation, a meeting of the Joint Cabinet Committee on Trade and Economic Policy will be held on June 25-27. The meeting will provide an opportunity to discuss the full range of economic and financial questions, including balance of payments, investment, energy, and trade.

In the context of the common interest of the two countries in the expansion of cross-border movement of energy, United States-Canadian developments in the matter of oil were discussed at length. Senior officials of the two Governments will, on April 2, initiate meetings to identify and study areas of common interest in energy matters and to work out constructive solutions to current problems against the background of long-standing arrangements.

The President and the Prime Minister agreed to work closely together with other exporting and importing countries to find positive solutions to current problems of the world wheat market within the framework of the International Grains Arrangement. Both countries will be working to overcome present market instability and to strengthen prices consistent with the provisions of the Agreement.

The two discussed Canada's plans for a domestic communications satellite, and the possibility of its launching by the U.S. The President stated that the U.S. is prepared, in principle, to provide launch services for this satellite, subject to appropriate arrangements which it is hoped will be worked out in the next few weeks.

The Prime Minister's visit marks a first step in a new era of consultation between Canada and the United States. We have done much together in the past; we can do more. Problems between us can be settled in ways that promote the interests and the identities of both nations.

The Prime Minister invited the President and Mrs. Nixon to visit Canada. The President has indicated that he wishes to accept the invitation.

3. Address of Prime Minister Trudeau to the National Press Club,
March 25, 1969

(Transcript of Proceedings, March 25, 1969, National Press Club,
Washington, D.C.)

There must be few countries in the world where individuals on either
side of a border feel so much at home on the other. I hasten to add,
however, that at times in our history we have paused to wonder whether
your friendly invitations ''to come and stay awhile'' have not been
aimed at Canada as a political unit rather than at Canadians as individuals.

Many of you will recall, I am sure, that your Articles of Confederation, as ratified in 1781, contained a clause which was an open invitation, and an exclusive one to Canada. And I read Article IV:

> ''Canada acceding to this confederation, and joining in the meas-
> ures of the United States, shall be admitted into, and entitled to all
> the advantages of this union; but no other colony shall be admitted
> into the same unless such admission be agreed to by nine states.''

So, we have always had a favored position. In any event, we did not
join, and history has recorded our differences.

Two hundred years later, the results of our separate and distinct
political existence are evident for all the world to see: professional
hockey is a major spectator sport from New York to Los Angeles, and
''Peanuts'' is one of the most popular comic strips from Halifax to
Vancouver.

But Americans should never underestimate the constant pressure on
Canada which the mere presence of the United States has produced. We
are a different people from you. We are a different people partly
because of you.

Our two countries have pushed against one another from time to
time, perhaps more courteously in recent years than previously, when
your invitation and your republicanism appeared more intimidating to
us.

Canadians still smart when they recall President Theodore
Roosevelt's tough instructions to Oliver Wendell Holmes, Jr., on the
occasion of the Alaska-Yukon boundary arbitration. But how many of
your historians have ever noted what Canada's first Prime Minister Sir
John A. Macdonald was at one time contemplating as your fate?

In 1867 that gentleman wrote to a correspondent in Calcutta:

> ''War will come some day between England and the United
> States, and India can do us yeoman's service by sending an army

of Sikhs, Ghoorkas and Beluchees across the Pacific to San Francisco, and holding that beautiful and immoral city with the surrounding California as security for Montreal and Canada.''

You see, Mr. Chairman, that although Canadians may not always be able to follow through, we should never be sold short on imaginative proposals.

Indeed, a question which some of your Canadian newspaper colleagues are now beginning to ask about my government is whether our ideas are capable of implementation. It's a valid question.

Imaginative and original approaches to problem solving are always welcome, but they must be practical and, even more important, they must be effective.

Some of our policies may be of interest to this audience, and with your permission, I should like to speak about several of them in a few minutes.

But first, let me say that it should not be surprising if these policies in many instances either reflect or take into account the proximity of the United States. Living next to you is in some ways like sleeping with an elephant: No matter how friendly and even-tempered is the beast, one is affected by every twitch and grunt.

There is in Canada at the present time a growing sense of unease that in a nation as rich as ours there is a problem of widespread poverty; that among people as dispassionate and understanding as are Canadians there is linguistic apprehensiveness and inequality; that in a world possessed of the technological means to journey to the planets, there exist terrifying threats to our environment and to our very existence.

Canada, by itself, cannot solve all these problems, and perhaps not even some of them. But we firmly believe that we can and must apply our talents and our resources in such a fashion as to seek solutions and, where appropriate, to persuade other states to cooperate with us in seeking these solutions. We have some qualifications for these tasks, and we have had considerable valuable experience which might prove to be of assistance to other states afflicted with similar problems. This is so partly because these qualifications, this experience, and the conditions which have spawned them, are similar in many respects to the differences and the difficulties which are found in the larger world community. And I wish to list some of them.

Canada is a federal state, the same as the U.S.A. Yet, two of our Provinces—Ontario and Quebec—are so populous in comparison with the other eight as to give to them an immensely influential position.

Nor is wealth in our country any more equitably distributed. The per capita income of the richest Province is about twice that of the poorest, and we have elaborate arrangements for redistribution of tax revenues among the Provinces of Canada.

Only one-third of all Canadians are of a stock that had English as its mother tongue, although two-thirds of the population live and work in English; the other third speak French daily as their normal means of communication—socially, in commerce and with government.

Within Canada there are French-speaking universities, radio and television networks, newspapers and labor unions. There is a complete language community.

Another item: Our economy is founded largely upon foreign trade. In this respect I should pause to point out that we sell more to the United States, and buy more from the United States, than any other country in the world. The immense size of this trade bears out this emphasis. Canada's purchases from the United States each year exceed in value the total purchases of your four next largest trading partners: Japan, Britain, Germany, and France combined—more than your total sales to all of Latin America.

So it is this pattern of uneven economic development, this heritage of linguistic diversity, and this dependence upon continued international intercourse that leads us to think that perhaps by way of some example we may be of benefit to a world which is so desperately seeking solutions to pressing problems.

As I say this, I hope that we Canadians do not have an exaggerated view of our own importance. We prefer to think that our place in the world is such that we can occasionally experiment with good ideas without risking a complete upset of the whole international order.

We are as pleased as is any country when our views are sought or our assistance requested. But we may be excused, I hope, if we fail to take too seriously the suggestion of some of our friends from time to time that our acts—or our failure to act—this or that way will have profound international consequences or will lead to widescale undesirable results.

But as an example to others we hope that we are able on occasion to serve a beneficial purpose. Our close relationship with the United States is an important illustration of what I mean. The fact that Canada has lived and flourished for more than a century as the closest neighbor to what is now the greatest economic and military power in the history of the world is evidence to all countries of the basic decency of United States foreign policy.

And I add in all seriousness that every occasion on which our policies differ from yours in an important fashion, that difference—if of course it is founded on good faith and sound evidence, as we hope is always the case—contributes to your international reputation as a good citizen as much as it does to ours.

When Canada continues to trade in non-strategic goods with Cuba, or proposes the recognition of the Peoples' Republic of China, or—as sometimes happens—finds itself supporting a point of view different from yours in the United Nations, the world is given evidence of your basic qualities of understanding and tolerance.

Because a state's foreign policies are in substantial part a reflection of its domestic scene, I wish to mention to you some of our basic programs.

What we are trying to do in Canada is to ensure to every individual the dignity to which he as a human being is entitled. Much of the unrest and turbulence now becoming evident in Western societies originates in the belief by the young, by the poor, by the minorities, that the massive socio-economic machines that we have developed in our countries are incapable of recognizing them as persons, and of catering to their individual needs. . . .

Most of our advanced societies are now in the position where they practically have to reassure their citizens and demonstrate palpably that these crises can be met, that government, in short, can govern; and we have to do this by steering a mid-course between too much authority and too much liberty, and it is a great challenge for all of us.

It should not therefore be expected that this kind of nation—this Canada that I am describing—should project itself onto the international scene as a mirror image of the United States. Much as our two countries are alike, much as they have in common—both with one another and towards other nations—we are different. And each of us is healthier as a result of that difference.

It cannot be expected that a country which is so deeply involved in social changes within its own boundaries should not be examining as well its foreign policies. Canada is, as you know, now reaching the conclusion of the first methodical and total review of our foreign policy and our defense policy since the end of World War II. We have gone back to first principles in doing so, and we are questioning the continuing validity of many assumptions.

Some policies will, without question, be found wanting for the conditions of today and be changed. Others will be retained. I want to emphasize that this review is not an excuse to prove our independence; that independence needs no proving. Nor is it an exercise intended to illustrate to the United States our potential for irritation. We have no desire, and no surplus energy, for that kind of activity.

We are building a new society in Canada. It should not be surprising that the external manifestations of this society may be somewhat different than has been the case in the past. But just as one of the invariable principles of that domestic society is the primacy of the individual, so is one of the invariables of our foreign policy genuine friendship with the United States.

The usual way of stating this fact is to refer in somewhat grandiloquent terms to our 4,000-mile unguarded border, to our lengthy history of amity and harmony, and to the many projects in which we are jointly engaged. It could also be illustrated by proving how interdependent our two nations are in economic, in resource, in geographic, and in environmental terms.

I prefer, however, to express all this more on the level of hockey and Charlie Brown, however. One of our better known humorists, Stephen Leacock, put things in their proper perspective. Writing as an English-speaking person in a bilingual society, he said:

> "In Canada we have enough to do keeping up with two spoken languages without trying to invent slang, so we just go right ahead and use English for literature, Scotch for sermons, and American for conversation."

So long as we continue to behave like this, I think the warmth with which Canadians and Americans regard each other will protect us all from any sins our governments might in error commit. . . .

[QUESTIONS AND ANSWERS FOLLOWING ADDRESS:]

Q. After hearing Mr. Nixon's argument, are you now in favor of an ABM system?

A. Well, you know, in Canada we have a Cabinet system of government. We do not have the Presidential system. This really means, in effect, that all I can do now is go back to my Cabinet colleagues, report to them the new information we have received, report to them the new technological information that has been imparted to us, and we will have to assess the impact of this on our own approach to foreign affairs, and we will have to announce a decision. I could not say, therefore, if Mr. Nixon's arguments have changed my mind, because I don't believe any of you or anyone knows what my mind was before. . . .

Q. Why doesn't Canada join the Organization of American States?

A. Well, as you know, we have been considering this for a long while. I think what has held us back most in the past is, as in the present, the sense that if we join the Organization of American States, we would be a pale reflection of the American image, and we did not find this useful.

To be quite blunt, we have never evolved a very coherent and organic policy towards Latin America. We have been turned towards Europe, other parts of the world, much more than we have towards South America and Central America. And, not having a clear, coherent policy, had we entered the OAS, I am afraid we would have brought no new knowledge and no new resolve, and the danger of that would have been that either we would have reflected the State Department's views in all matters, and this would have been, I believe, not only detrimental to ourselves, but it would have been detrimental to the kind of relationship that we hoped to establish with Latin American countries. Or, on the other hand, we would have necessarily felt obliged in many cases to disagree with the State Department just to prove our independence, but without any logical or consistent background or policy toward it.

So what we have done in this new administration is to send a high-level delegation to South America, a ministerial level, which toured most of the countries of Latin America and Central America, and which is now embarked upon defining for ourselves a policy as regards these nations.

The question of the OAS is really only secondary . . .

. . . we want to increase our relations with South America and with Central America. We want to do it in the areas of trade, in the areas of culture, of exchanges of many kinds—of people, of students, of ideas. And as a next step we will consider the OAS.

I would say that our inclination is towards asking admittance, but with the timing to be determined . . .

Q. Why does Canada support Cuban intervention in Latin America by trading with Cuba?

And along with it:

What should Uncle Sam do about Fidel Castro?

A. Well, I suppose a long dissertation on Cuba would be repetition of one that you have heard and read many times.

I would perhaps reject the premises of the question that we do support Castro's activities in South America merely because we are trading with them. Because if that were the principle on which we were to base ourselves, we could argue that the United States does trade with a lot of governments—most countries in the world trade with a lot of governments with policies of which they do not approve. And I believe that one of the best vehicles of understanding and closer relationships between countries is trade. The missionaries come first, and the traders come next.

I think that the Canadian approach to these problems—and it has not been an original one—is that in our relations with other countries we should not try and intermingle the two types of issues. Short of being at the state of war with another nation, we do not believe that curtailment of trade is in any sense conducive to a lessening of tensions between countries. On the contrary. We trade with Communist China. We trade with Cuba. The United States trades with many countries, the policies of which I am sure your people disagree.

Therefore, what should the United States do with Fidel Castro? I suppose anyone in this room now would say the thing you shouldn't do is ask the FBI.

I think it is important to realize that the force of nationalism, the force of independence, the feelings of independence of a nation are pretty hard to stifle, and that in international relations—as in domestic relations—the catchword, the key word is communication. The key word is dialogue, in the same sense that we are beginning to discover within our societies that you cannot repress sources of discontent and hope that you will have a peaceful society. But the only way is to talk about the values which the discontented groups feel. Talk about bridging this gap, whether it be a generation gap or color gap or geographical gap within a society or a rich-poor gap. The only way to prevent two societies developing within the nation, each with its own set of values which reflects the other person's set of values, is to discuss these values, to meet, to exchange, as you try to do in your politics—as we try to do in ours. And if this is true within societies where tensions are mounting, it is certainly true in international society. And that is why we have the United Nations. That is why we have forums where we discuss the other person's values.

And we think that in the case of Cuba this applies just as much as it applies in the case of Red China. It is once again only by discussion and communication that you can perhaps not convince the other person that your values are the right ones, but convince him that he has had a chance to make his point, and that the discussion is based on reason and appeal to thought rather than to emotion.

Q. On oil, Prime Minister, what is your position for or against the continental oil policy for the United States and Canada? Are you here to discuss it now?

A. Yes, we are. We did discuss it, both the President and myself, and then our Ministers and officials. We have a continental oil policy of sorts. It was set up in the past, and it worked reasonably well.

The technical details of it are perhaps a bit elaborate, but essentially it means that Canadian oil producers sell to Western Canada and sell to the United States an amount roughly equivalent to the amount of oil that Eastern Canada purchases overseas and, notably, from the Venezuelan producers. It is a deal between the American Government and the Canadian Government which is cost-saving for both parties.

The new oil discoveries and the implementation of this past policy is creating problems. We did discuss them and we are announcing in a press release that there will be further meetings on the 2nd of April with a view to looking at this continental oil policy and discovering the new avenues that might want to be followed.

I think we have arguments for the United States in the sense that our oil is not only cheaper, but it is more secure in terms of defense in any future conflict. It is continental oil. It is more easy of access. And if we do not continue exploring and discovering new sources of oil, there might come a time when there will be an oil gap that we won't be able to fill on this continent.

Discoveries at Prudhoe Bay perhaps retarded for some years the development of such a gap, but I think it is very present in our mind, both the American and Canadian Government, and we will now be seeking to establish new guidelines for a policy which will be in the mutual interests of both countries to permit the encouragement and development of oil resources in Canada, and at the same time not disrupting your internal markets.

We find that the discussions went very well, that there was a great deal of understanding between our governments on the over-all aims, and we are very optimistic that there will be emerging a renewed oil policy which will be satisfactory to both governments. . . .

Q. What is the attitude of your government in regard to Americans who travel to Canada to evade the draft? Has their entry noticeably affected the thoughts or policy of Canadians? And is there a limit to the number you will admit?

A. When a question is restricted to draft-dodgers, the answer is a very simple one. The status of being a draft-dodger does not enter at all into our immigration policy. You can have your draft card in your pocket. If you are dodging the draft, you are not even asked about it and you are admitted to the Canadian border.

It is an irrelevant question from the point of view of our policy, and because it is not a relevant question, we do not have statistics on it. We do not know how many draft-dodgers have been admitted to Canada and have stayed there. I believe it is a policy which is similar to that practiced by the United States as regards draft-dodgers. We do know that a number of Americans come to Canada to evade the draft. We also know that a number, perhaps a superior number, of Canadians come to the United States to join the United States Army. We do not have statistics. Some of them are even fighting in Vietnam.

But what effect these draft-dodgers have on our students is a question which, of course, I am no more informed on than you might be, sir. Their presence has been felt. They have aroused a great deal of sympathy on the Canadian campuses. By and large they have proved to be good students, orderly students, and much of their attitude, I believe, is dictated by reasons of conscience rather than by any desire to upset a particular order of things.

If the question were to go on and ask about deserters, I might be in a more delicate situation. Our policy as to deserters is not as clear as that regarding draft evaders. In general, we do have statistics on this and, in general, Canadian policy has been, shall we say, a little less free towards deserters than to draft evaders, on the basis that immigration does consider whether a prospective immigrant has any moral or legal commitment in the country of origin. And this applies, of course, not only to American immigrants but to immigrants from all countries. We do have statistics on this. I believe that we admitted 56 deserters in

Canada last year and this, as you see, is a very small number. There may be others in Canada but who have not asked for immigrant status and, therefore, on which we cannot report . . .

Q. Did you and President Nixon have a meeting of the minds on the future of an international grains agreement; and more specifically, the world price of wheat; and do you think that price is too high?

A. Well, we did have a meeting of the minds at least on our approach to it. We did feel that this international agreement, which was drafted after considerable pain by producing, exporting and importing nations, it would be desirable if it could be respected.

We realize that beyond this pious wish there is much work to be done. One of the large and important exporters is, of course, the Government of Australia. The Prime Minister of Australia will be in this country and in our country in some days' time, and we have agreed that we should try and involve the Government of Australia in our approach to re-establishing respect for the international grains agreement. To this extent there has been a meeting of the minds.

We have not found out how we could get the world community to accept our point of view, but there has been called a meeting early in April of the exporting nations. They are to examine this problem. They will then examine the problem that was asked, sir, about whether the price has been set too high.

Our Canadian answer to this is that the price was set after a great deal of discussion and debate. It is perhaps easy or tempting now to say the price was too high because of the current situation of the producing nations and the surpluses in grain. But this is the basis of all commodity agreements. If we didn't have an agreement, we might be able to probably say the price is too high now; but in years of shortage, then the price would probably appear too low to us and we would be tempted, all of us exporters, to up the price considerably to the consuming nations. And that is why a balance must be established in all these international commodities, commodities which are internationally traded, and that is why we have this approach.

. It is no longer the individual farmer who is selling his wheat or his sugar or his cocoa or whatever the other commodity is which is covered or should be covered by international agreements. It is the state itself which is involved. And we know that all of these policies, if they are not guided by an agreement, will tend to beggar each other, and the result will not be favorable.

In times of overproduction, it will be advantageous to the consuming nation; but in times of underproduction, it will be disastrous to them. And it is to average this out, sir, that we have these agreements. And on these general principles the President and his Administration agree very much with ours. . . . .

Q. One final question . . . When is General de Gaulle coming for a return visit?

A. I believe you have invited him to visit your country. We will see what he does if he goes to Louisiana, and then we will report.

4. Prime Minister Trudeau's Report of Meeting to the Canadian House of Commons, March 26, 1969

(CHCD, March 26, 1969, p. 7127)

Mr. Speaker, I wish to report briefly to the house on my recent meeting with the President of the United States.

If I were asked what has been the most significant result of the events of the last two days, I would say without hesitation that it is the fact that the groundwork has been laid for co-operation and consultation between our two governments, which will allow for the holding of consultations at all levels, the official level, the ministerial one and that of the leaders of governments.

I should report as well the significance, in my view, of the fact that President Nixon set aside some time so early in his new administration to receive the Prime Minister of Canada. No other country is as important to Canada as the United States; it is therefore reassuring to know that we have at this early date established the contacts and fortified the channels of communication so necessary to the effective conduct of our relations.

A number of matters were discussed by the President and myself, by the Secretary of State for External Affairs and his counterpart Mr. Rogers, and by other officials. These discussions led to a confirmation of the Canadian-United States commitment to the continued expansion and freedom of world trade, to agreement with respect to our community of interest in the expansion of energy movements across our border, and a confirmation of the importance of an early solution to the current wheat marketing problems.

I wish to add that we were given a very full explanation of the reasons which led President Nixon to initiate the Safeguard anti-ballistic missile program, and these I intend to convey to cabinet at the earliest opportunity so that Canada's attitude may be determined.

It was further agreed that a meeting of the joint cabinet committee on trade and economic policy will be held on June 25, 26 and 27.

I do not wish to sit down without saying that I found in President Nixon a warm and understanding friend of Canada, a man with whom I shall be able to speak on behalf of Canadians in a frank yet genial fashion. For this I am very thankful. To further this good beginning I extended to the President and to Mrs. Nixon a warm invitation to visit Canada at their earliest convenience.

B. President Richard M. Nixon and Prime Minister Pierre E. Trudeau, Washington, D.C., December 6-7, 1971

1. Prime Minister Trudeau's Response to Questions Concerning his Forthcoming Meeting With President Nixon, Ottawa, House of Commons, November 29, 1971

(CHCD, November 29, 1971, pp. 9955-56)

HON. ROBERT L. STANFIELD (Leader of the Opposition): Mr. Speaker, I wish to direct a question to the Prime Minister who I was interested and pleased to see has requested a meeting with the President of the United States. In view of the fact the Prime Minister has rejected suggestions over the past three months that it would be a good idea for him to meet with the President of the United States, can he tell the House what specific factors now make it desirable for him to have a meeting with the President?

RIGHT HON. P. E. TRUDEAU (Prime Minister): Mr. Speaker, I have never rejected the idea of a meeting with the President. On the contrary, I said he was to visit Canada in the spring some time. The question was one of timing. The timing is more appropriate now and that is why the meeting will happen now.

MR. STANFIELD: As I understand it, the meeting is taking place at the request of the Prime Minister. Can the right hon. gentleman say what specific matters he wishes to discuss with the President—what specific matters form the basis of his request for a meeting with the President at this time?

MR. TRUDEAU: It seems to me rather apparent from the news media that the President is meeting with a number of leaders at this time, friends of his, allies of the United States, and it does seem appropriate that at this point Canada should be meeting with the President of the United States to discuss multilateral and bilateral questions.

MR. STANFIELD: I had hoped the Prime Minister was doing more than just getting into line with the other distinguished visitors. . . .

MR. DAVID LEWIS (Leader of the NDP): My supplementary arises from one of the answers the Prime Minister gave. May I ask whether it was he who asked for the meeting with the President of the United States or whether an invitation was extended to him by the President in the first place?

MR. TRUDEAU: The approach was made by my office to the President of the United States in the first place.

MR. LEWIS: Would the Prime Minister be good enough to inform us how long ago this approach was made by his office and also whether in making this approach any specific matters were mentioned as a proposed agenda for the discussions?

MR. TRUDEAU: The approach was made some time last week. At that time the decision had been made for the Secretary of State for External Affairs to meet with Mr. Rogers in Washington and it was hoped that my meeting would follow that one as soon as possible so that I might be able to follow up some matters which the Secretary of State for External Affairs had discussed with Mr. Rogers. As to subjects on the agenda, there has not yet been an agreement as to the agenda. With regard to the particular question asked by the hon. member, I know of no specific subject which was mentioned; it was just that it would be good for us to get together to discuss multilateral and bilateral questions.

2. Press Conference of Prime Minister Trudeau, Statler-Hilton Hotel, Washington, D.C., December 7, 1971

(Transcript of Proceedings, ACE-Féderal Reporters, Inc., Washington, D.C., CR 4558, MBB1)

Q. Mr. Prime Minister, your staff have suggested to us that you found great significance in an assurance by the President that he was aware of the intense desire of Canadians that their identity be respected, that they be permitted an economic future and be allowed to determine it themselves, which is so much of a motherhood proposition, one wonders why you see great significance in it. Could you explain?

THE PRIME MINISTER: I think I agree with my staff, and, therefore, I can't evade the question.

Simply put: I think it has to do with the general atmosphere and perhaps even with the lack of confidence. There are a lot of questions being asked: Have the Americans stopped loving us? What are they going to do? Are they going to gobble us up? Are they going to leave us out in the cold?

There certainly have been a lack of reassurances as to the American disposition towards Canada, and I think this is particularly accentuated since mid-August when President Nixon announced his new economic policy, and it was aggravated, I suppose, by a series of circumstances, such as Mr. Kosygin's and Mr. Tito's visit in rapid succession, and so on. It is a fact that this atmosphere had at least an appearance, in Canada, of a lack of confidence expressed—not expressed—there was a motion of lack of confidence moved in Canada against the government because it had not established good relations with the Americans. And I suppose it could be said that the purpose of my visit was to come down here and see if all this was true, if there was any fence-mending needed. In fact, there was an extremely, not only great cordiality, but a true expression of friendship and every desire to respect in every way Canada's identity and its search for its own future. This was reassuring, perhaps not as much to myself as to the Canadian public.

Q. Mr. Prime Minister, we are also told you were invited, with a couple of your dinner guests, to give their views of Canadian-U.S. relations. I am wondering if you could describe, for instance, how the Vice President answered, or Secretary Connally?

A. Well, in truth, it wasn't my invitation nor my initiative. It was the President himself who, after the dinner and the toasts, the formal toasts to the Queen and to the President, he suggested that we, rather than go and spread out in the various salons of the White House, sit around the table and have this expression of views.

I wouldn't like to attempt to give in any detail the views which were expressed.

Perhaps briefly I could say that Secretary Connally repeated many of the things that he had been saying in the past. Perhaps the most significant phrase that I drew from him was that the United States were going, had been going through a temporary economic difficulty; that they had to take strong measures directed against no one, but meant to seek their own self-interests, to come out of these difficulties, and that the long-term aim of the United States as he saw it was that they establish themselves in a trade balance with the world which would be neutral. In other words, they didn't think they had to have a positive balance of commercial trade every year, but just thought that they should be in deficit with some and in surplus with others, so that their overall position in the world was one of balance. And I thought this very significant.

There are all kinds of supplementary questions which could come from it which I didn't have occasion to ask. Because if they are in balance, how are the invisibles paid for, I take it, foreign aid or Marshall Plans or help for underdeveloped countries? I think this is a very exciting view of the world by Secretary Connally, and one that certainly we would accept. . . .

Q. Mr. Prime Minister, if I may, I would like to refer to the first question.

I would like to ask you what will have been the use of your talks with President Nixon?

A. It's fairly simple. We wanted to insure that Canada and the United States would improve their relationships. We would like to know their intentions towards us are friendly; that they have no wish to intervene in our internal affairs, to orient our future in any other way contrary to our own wishes. They have every respect for the wish of Canadians to be masters of their own economic and social future and political future. They recognize the fact that it is important for us to determine our own future freely.

In our negotiations each of us is attempting to gain as much advantage for ourselves as possible, with every respect for the interests of others.

Q. Last week you said there might be breakthroughs as a result of the talks. Can you say what the breakthroughs are or if they occurred?

A. If one had to talk of breakthroughs, I think it is the answer to the first question which would closer describe it. It is the establishment in a way which is certainly satisfying to me that the United States not only wants to respect our political identity but our economic identity, and the breakthrough is almost—I wouldn't say philosophical, but expressed in terms of destinies of two countries.

The President said some things to me which, to me, are unequalled by any other President in speaking about Canada. Perhaps many of them thought the same thing. I don't know if the questions had been put to them.

But on the precise question, "Do you think that Canada is a place where you will always want to have a surplus trade balance in order that you will be able to export capital to Canada?" The answer was "No." "We, the Americans, we were in that position before the First World War. We depended on European capital and we wanted to free ourselves of that dependence, and we understand perfectly that Canadians are in the same position, and we will do nothing to prevent them from not feeling in any way that they are a colony of the United States of America."

This to me was a fantastically new statement in the mouth of the President of the United States, and it was said with utmost simplicity and not at all in a grudging way, you know, "If you don't want our capital, then you won't get it, and look after yourselves."

He said, "Just take what you want, and if we can help, we will. If you want less, take less."

For Canadians, I think this is the ideal position.

We want to be—and I said so to the President—we want to be in a good relationship with the American people. There are certainly many cases where we would welcome their capital and the technology that goes with it. There are other cases where we will prefer to go our own way. And the President's statement was, in my mind, a real breakthrough in that it recognized the entire freedom to Canada to do that.

Q. Mr. Prime Minister, you had applied the word "breakthrough" specifically to the list of so-called grievances, energy, the auto pact, defense sharing, and I wonder whether you see any breakthrough in those areas?

And also I would like to ask whether you conceive of President

Nixon saying anything other than, "But of course, do your own thing?"

A. Well, I had applied it there because the press is so concerned with minutiae and individual things and particular instances.

But to me the overall relationship between the two countries is more important.

On these particular things—well, to finish the third part of your question, "Could he say anything else but that?"—of course, he could have. He could have even not understood the question or refused to have answered it in such clear terms, or he could have, as I gave the example a moment ago, said, "Well, if you don't want foreign capital, we won't send any and you look after yourselves." He could have said, "You can take all kinds of measures against us if you don't want our capital. It is up to you to keep it out." There are many, many things he could have said, and he didn't.

On the particular items that you mentioned, no, I am afraid there will be no headlines this morning that there was any final conclusion reached in the three examples that you mentioned. . . .

Q. Mr. Prime Minister, you said recently in Canada that the United States neither knows nor cares much about Canada. Can we assume by what you have said this morning that you have changed your mind about this?

A. Yes, I think that certainly I have changed my mind. I wouldn't guarantee that in some weeks or months or years we wouldn't have to go through this kind of operation again. I think nobody really believes that the Americans are antagonistic to Canadians. What we really sometimes think is that the Americans take us for granted, very much as we take them for granted. And in that sense they don't care for us and we don't care for them, as has been pointed out by many of you when we wrote our white paper on foreign relations. We didn't talk hardly about the Americans. And when they wrote their foreign policy, they hardly talked about Canada.

It could be either because we take each other for granted or because the problem is so large and omnipresent that it can't be dealt with in the context of a white paper which deals with all countries. Therefore, I am not guaranteeing that I won't have to, or Canadians won't have to, again at some point in the future say the Americans have forgotten about us again.

But it will be a very simple thing, I am sure, so long as President Nixon is there for myself, or for any other Prime Minister, to come down and ask him and be reassured, if that is what we need.

Q. If it was the Nixon measures in August that led us to feel, in your words, that they perhaps wanted to "gobble us up," how can you be so reassured by what the President said, if he hasn't agreed with you to do something to lighten the burden on Canada of the August measures?

And did you put to the President your question that the United States might be acting in an imperialistic—economic imperialism, as you have said in Canada?

A. Yes, I put the question. And the latter part of your question is closer to what I was meaning in August about "gobbling up." I was asking aloud whether this new economic policy was a turn towards protectionism by the Americans and the statement of a policy whereby they would always want to be in a surplus trade balance with Canada in order that they be able to make us pay by, as I put it then, giving up parts of our country, of our industry.

It is in this sense that I said, "Have the Americans thought this through? Is this a policy which is indicative of a long-term trend? Or is it just something temporary?" And none of us knew the answers.

I think as time goes on it is becoming obvious, not only to us but to most of the world, that the 10 per cent surcharge is temporary, as Secretary Connally has said from the beginning; that on the longer term answer President Nixon has said that basically he is a believer in free trade. And Secretary Connally repeated the same thing last night: that the present difficulties of the United States are the reasons why they took these present protectionist measures; that they wanted to shake the rest of the world into a realization that we would all have to do some realigning of currency and reestablishment of good trade relations.

The United States, as Secretary Connally expressed again, didn't have too many tools whereby it could get everyone else to align. It can't float like the rest of the countries can float. It has to get the whole system to readjust.

So the answer to all these questions was not only, "These measures are temporary. The United States will want to go back to a world which believes in free trade as soon as possible. But specifically as regards Canada, we don't want to gobble you up. We don't necessarily feel that we have to have a surplus trade balance with you. We want both our countries to have free relationships with one another. And it is not our"—borrowing the phrase from Justice Holmes—"it is not our unstated major premise to keep Canada as a place where we can safely export capital and buy up the country gradually."

So this to me was a total answer to those concerns I then expressed. It doesn't mean we don't have to make sure our policies are developed; that our industrial policies are pursued in a way which will be to the advantage of Canada. In other words, we can't just rely on the American government and businessmen to treat Canada so nicely.

If we continue to, as we did in some past decades, if we continue to want to live beyond our means and buy more from the Americans than we can sell to them, of course, we will have to make this up by selling off parts of our industries and resources. But if we want to live within our means, the Americans have no expressed desire to buy us out.

Q. What kind of encouragement did you get for the removal of the surcharge as far as Canada itself is concerned?

And what kind of reciprocal trade concessions did the U.S. ask for, if any?

A. On the first question, there was no bilateral attempt to get this surcharge removed. We realize, as well as anyone else, as well as the Americans, that what is important is a restabilization of the currencies of the world; and that if there were just to be a special deal with Canada on the surcharge or on anything else, it would be of no value to the Americans and of no value to ourselves. If they remained in disequilibrium with the rest of the world, we would just arrive at some situation and be pushed away from it. So it is important that the solution be found in the group of ten. It is important that Canada not seek to, once again, to get concessions which, though they might look to be useful to us in the short run, would only be very temporary in results in that the Americans would have to begin all over with the other countries of the world.

In other words, I think Secretary Connally was using very tough means to shake all countries, including Canada, into looking at the negotiating positions as regards the currencies, as regards their trade barriers, as regards unsatisfactory barriers of relationships between themselves.

In the areas which were looked at between us, I suppose it is no indiscretion to say what has been said, even in the question this morning, that they did talk about the auto pact, they did talk about the defense production agreements. The President didn't talk to me about tourists or allowances, but I know it was discussed between officials and ministers. It is this type of question. And we raised the question with him of free uranium sales, of the anti-dumping practices, of the restrictions in trade of agricultural and aeronautic instruments with the United States, and so on. This is the kind of discussion, and I have said in Canada, that has been going on for a long while between Canadians and Americans.

The surcharge perhaps had the effect of really shaking us and saying, "Gosh, if there is anything we can do along these lines to settle those questions, well, so much the better."

We know that the European Common Market is making certain concessions; that the Japanese are making certain concessions; we will make certain concessions. But we used the occasion to get the Americans to make certain concessions to us.

Q. A Gallup poll published last week in Canada would indicate that Canadians appear to wish on the one hand to serve their own interests by attracting American capital to their country. At the same time, they appear to wish to assert their own independence to an increasing degree. Do you not think this is a paradox? In your discussions with President Nixon, did you look into the solution of this paradox?

A. This paradox is always present in the minds of Canadians. As I said to President Nixon, we Canadians do like to have American capital entering Canada in order to insure our progress. But we want to be free to choose. We want to be free to put American capital into geographic or economic areas where it is most needed; whereas, on the other hand, we would like, if we could, to prevent American capital from entering some geographic or economic area where we feel it is not needed.

We realize that our economies cannot be kept completely separate. But, recognizing this interdependency we would still like to be free to choose. This is the way in which we think the paradox can be solved.

Q. Mr. Prime Minister, I wonder if these talks will have any effect whatsoever on Canada's foreign investment policy? In other words, do you plan to rework the policy that you now have—

A. I don't plan to rework it at this time, as I told Parliament just last week. Our foreign policy, our foreign investment policy was decided and it will be announced as soon as we can publish the background material, which I expect will be very soon.

I think perhaps Canadians will now be prepared to discuss that policy and those background documents with greater freedom, less apprehension, and less of an inferiority complex. . . .

Q. My question is against the background of your statement on the Icebreaker Lenin, to the effect that Canada was worried about the cultural, economic, and military impact of our relationship. On account of that statement, some other things have happened. Did the President of the United States seek any reassurance from you as to the caliber and quality of Canadian relationships with the United States?

A. None whatsoever. I don't know if the President was good enough to even notice that I made such a statement. Whether it was on the Lenin, or in the Moscow press conference, I don't remember. But if he had noticed it, it hasn't fazed him in any sense, because he talked somewhat about his own denouche in going to Moscow and Peking. He volunteered to me a lot of information on why he was doing this and why, before doing that, he was seeking out the advice and was consulting with various friendly countries beginning with Canada, and then including some European and Japanese statesmen.

So I am very much afraid that my own little forays into the Soviet Union have not been noticed by the President.

Q. Did your step in concessions include suspension or offer to suspend some of the demands that Canada has been making in re-negotiating the automobile pact?

And, secondly, the Canadian Government figures would seem to indicate that the impact of the surcharge has been somewhat less than the alarms that had been originally created in Canada.

Could you address yourself to both of those, please?

A. The first question you asked was if he let up a little bit on concessions we were asking of the Americans on the auto pact?

Q. Yes, sir.

A. I didn't press any requests from the Americans on new concessions to us.

Q. Did the Canadians offer to make any concessions of their own?

A. We didn't volunteer any concessions either, but that is what the whole talks are about. They have been going on for many, many months now. We are trying to find a way of preserving the auto pact, which is useful to both countries, indeed, very beneficial to both countries, and we are going to do it in a way which insures the best bargain for both of us. And that is how we have been negotiating, and that is how the Americans have been negotiating.

The President and myself only talked about it in general terms. We let the slugging go on in the other rooms between the ministers. We only know there is lots of that. We will only know the results when they are announced. And I don't know when that will be.

And your second point had to do with the lesser effects than apprehended of the surcharge?

No, we did tell Parliament—I think Mr. Pepin gave the figures a few weeks ago—that the effect was less than apprehended, and explained that the impact had been calculated by phoning all the industries that we thought would be affected and asking them to estimate, "Did they have layoffs to follow?" And so on and so on. And it does appear the total we added up to, after all these consultations, was probably a bit high if the surcharge is only going to be a short-run affair. In other words, that more companies have decided to carry the extra costs on themselves, because they are figuring that, I take it, the surcharge will be of short duration.

Of course, all this does not stand if the surcharge turns out to be of long duration. Then they will cease to be able to carry these surcharges, these effects themselves, and then I am afraid the consequences might follow and there will be more use of our employment support legislation which, as you know, was introduced early this fall. . . .

Q. Mr. Prime Minister, my question might relate to one which was put earlier. In what way can these discussions, which were very friendly and comprehensive, be said to have any influence on this automobile pact which is of concern to Canadians? Canadians felt that the meetings in this regard were very important.

A. The main result would be psychological. One of the reasons why Mr. Benson introduced his budgetary measures a few weeks ago was to counteract the uncertainty surrounding the Canadian economy. We had heard Americans wished to repatriate all their industries in Canada to the United States.

Did they want to export unemployment to Canada? Were they attempting to orient our own economic destinies in line with their own interests? These were the questions which were being put currently in Parliament, the press, and by business people.

Once again, through this budget of $1 billion, we indicated our confidence in the economy and we asked the Americans to express confidence in ours and not to add to the uncertainty.

He said that the Americans did not wish to affect our economy negatively; that Americans were ready to cooperate in every possible way, in the interests of both countries. He had no wish to hurt us by repatriating our factories or other machinery and so on.

That was the main result of our talk. It was to reassure us, to show that Americans had confidence in us. . . .

Our whole argument with the Americans, and indeed with our other partners in the Ten, has been that we did it even before we were compelled to do so by the American measures. We floated as early as June 1970, and we have been engaged in a clean float ever since, and therefore don't ask us to realign unless you want us to artificially do something to worsen the position of our dollar. Just recognize that we did, in anticipation, what the Americans said that other countries should be doing.

Therefore, that's been our argument all along with the Americans; and they haven't—at least, the President has not in conversation with me, sort of said, "Well, you know, that doesn't count; we want you to do something more."

Obviously the Americans are trying to get the best possible float and repegging from everyone. Not best for the American advantage, I take it, but best so that the currencies re-enter a period of stability. Because, as once again President Nixon said quite clearly, if we use a big stick in order to get an advantage in terms of currencies or in terms of trade, it won't last because you can't drive a hard bargain and hope to stick for a long while. If it's too hard a bargain, we will be knocked off and we will be back to instability. . . .

Q. Mr. Prime Minister, did you and the President discuss any further steps that might be taken towards ending the war in Indochina?

A. No. The President gave me the figures of the de-escalation there, and he made some remarks on that, again, at our working dinner last night. He told me the record of the performance since we last met; but there was no talk of Canadian assistance in any way with the process.

We didn't even—as I think we did at my last meeting—discuss the question of whether Canada would be prepared to have some kind of a peace-keeping force if it was requested.

*3. Prime Minister Trudeau's Report of Meeting to the Canadian House
of Commons, December 7, 1971*

(CHCD, May 7, 1971, pp. 10205-6)

Mr. Speaker, as hon. members are aware, I spent several hours yesterday with President Nixon in Washington. I should like to take a few moments of the time of the House to report on those meetings and on the discussions which took place concurrently between the Ministers of Finance and Industry, Trade and Commerce, with their officials, and the United States Secretaries of the Treasury and of Commerce and their officials.

One of the purposes of my visit was to seek reassurance from the President, and it can only come from him, that it is neither the intention nor the desire of the United States that the economy of Canada become so dependent upon the United States in terms of a deficit trading pattern that Canadians will inevitably lose independence of economic decisions. I stated to the President as candidly as I was able the concern which had been expressed in Canada, and indeed by some hon. members, with respect to the character of the U.S.-Canadian relationship. That concern was precipitated, of course, by the introduction on August 15 of the new United States economic policies, but it has been reflected increasingly in recent years by the continuing flow to Canada of American investment with its inherent advantages and disadvantages.

I cannot emphasize too strongly the warmth and the understanding with which President Nixon responded to my questions and the candid attitude which he revealed. He assured me that it was in the clear interests of the United States to have a Canadian neighbour not only independent both politically and economically but also one which was confident that the decisions and policies in each of these sectors would be taken by Canadians in their own interests, in defence of their own values, and in pursuit of their own goals.

The century-old desire of Canadians to benefit from our North American neighbourhood and to profit from our relations with the United States, while at the same time remaining Canadian to the degree and extent that we choose, was put to the President by me and accepted by him without hesitation or qualification.

We are a distinct country, we are a distinct people, and our remaining as such is, I was assured, in the interests of the United States and is a fundamental tenet of the foreign policies of that country as expressed by the Nixon administration.

I should add that the President was sensitive to the suggestion that his August 15 policies could be interpreted as evidence that the United States was unable to accept a Canada with a strong trading and current account position vis-à-vis the United States. This interpretation he could understand, but he stated to me forcefully that it was incorrect. I have not the slightest doubt, having spoken to him, that his interpretation is the correct one and will be borne out by events.

If I may turn for a moment to the specific question of reforms in the monetary and trading practices of the world, the President and I agreed that no benefit would be gained by any short-sighted attempt on the part of any single country—the United States included—to gain immediate advantage. If the world trading nations and the international monetary community are unable to support with confidence whatever agreements are reached, then no progress will have been made. The same inherent instability and uncertainty which precipitated the August crisis will return, but with a viciousness not so far present because governments and the private sector will have lost confidence in their ability to come to grips with problems of this importance and this magnitude.

In short, Mr. Speaker, while the state of negotiations on specific points does not permit me to reveal to the House the precise state of play on any of the items which are understandably of interest to all hon. members, I am able to say that I have not the slightest doubt that those negotiations will be culminated soon, that the economic issues outstanding between Canada and the United States will be resolved, and that Canada will emerge in a healthier state. Much of the credit for progress in the process is due to the Secretary of State for External Affairs (Mr. Sharp), to the Minister of Finance (Mr. Benson), and to the Minister of Industry, Trade and Commerce (Mr. Pepin) for the skillful, tough and professional manner in which they have led the Canadian team of negotiators.

I have emphasized in these remarks those parts of my discussion with the President which were directed to economic issues and to Canadian-American relations. I hasten to add, however, that we spent a good deal of time on broader international matters—on the tragedy which is now unfolding on the Indian subcontinent, on the steps which are being pursued in the United Nations to arrest the hostilities and create a measure of confidence that the grievances in that area can be redressed, and on East-West relations generally. In keeping with the President's desire to inform the major allies of the United States about his pending visits to the People's Republic of China and the Soviet Union, we talked of the initiatives taken by both Canada and the United States to lessen tension and contribute positively to an orderly international climate.

Finally, Mr. Speaker, I am pleased to inform hon. members that the President told me with what pleasure he and Mrs. Nixon were looking forward to their visit to Canada this spring. I assured him that the warmth of the reception which I knew awaited them would be a clear indication of the friendship between the peoples of our two countries.

C. Prime Minister Pierre E. Trudeau and President Richard M. Nixon, Ottawa, Ontario, April 13-15, 1972

1. Prime Minister Trudeau's Introduction of President Nixon to Both Houses of the Canadian Parliament, April 14, 1972

(CHCD, Appendix, April 14, 1972, Address of Richard M. Nixon, p. 3)

On behalf of the people of Canada, and of their parliamentary representatives gathered in this chamber, I extend to you, Mr. President, and to Mrs. Nixon, a warm welcome to Ottawa.

You, sir, are the fifth holder of your office to honour a joint session of the Parliament of Canada. Because your colleague President Eisenhower visited this place twice, your address will be the sixth such to be heard here.

You see before you, Mr. President, Canadians from every corner of this far-flung land we call Canada. They reflect not just the geography of the country but as well the great mixture of peoples which adds such richness and variety to our national life. The different origins of many of these men and women, and the languages they speak, illustrate the diversity of Canada. Their presence in the Chamber symbolizes our unity of purpose and our devotion to our parliamentary heritage. Part of that tradition was carried from France to England by the Norman conqueror nine centuries ago. It blossomed there and found its way naturally to Canada where it serves us admirably, and distinguishes us from the many countries elsewhere in the hemisphere.

Your presence here today, Mr. President, is striking evidence of the flexible yet harmonious relationship which has evolved over the years between the United States and Canada. Our two countries and our two peoples have much in common, but they are not identical in their moods nor in their interests, and it is a disservice to a proper understanding of one another if we overlook these distinctions. Our friendship is more dynamic because of our differences, and our relationship deeper and wider. Those differences stem from a past which, parallel to yours, is distinctive; and from governmental institutions which preserve like values but by different means.

In our meetings this morning we spoke a common language, employing familiar idioms, recalling an entwined history, and discussing problems and boundless promise, and from that time to this, generation after generation of Canadians and Americans have looked upon the Great Lakes as great highways to the future for both of our countries.

But in recent years, as we know, the quality of the Great Lakes' waters has been declining, with ominous implication for 30 million Americans and 7 million Canadians who live near their shores.

The signing today of the Great Lakes Water Quality Agreement represents a significant step toward reversing that decline. This agreement extends the great tradition of cooperation between the United States and Canada. Just as the St. Lawrence Seaway transformed the Great Lakes into highways of peaceful commerce among nations, so the Great Lakes Water Quality Agreement can make them great symbols of international cooperation as man makes his peace with nature.

This Agreement represents an important beginning, one which has been made possible by the cooperation of our two national governments and of state and provincial governments as well. And now we must all follow through on the beginning. Under the Agreement, the International Joint Commission will provide important leadership in this effort.

But it is also essential that governments of all levels, in both of our countries, and private industry as well, work within their own constitutional frameworks to achieve the objectives the Agreement defines.

It is with very great pride and pleasure that I have signed the Great Lakes Water Quality Agreement between Canada and the United States, for this Agreement bears witness to all the world of great concerns which unite our two countries; our common appreciation for the natural heritage which undergirds our national strengths; our common recognition that problems which cross international boundaries require international solutions, and our common confidence that our traditional relationship can grow to meet new demands identifiable to each in terms of values we share and respect. What other two countries in the world can offer to their peoples and leaders such a contribution to understanding?

What is the effect on Canada and Canadians of the existence next door to us of the great country of America? Certainly, it is one of stimulation. There is little that the United States does that is not felt or noticed in Canada. Your lofty goals, your good natured hospitality, your successes and your failures, your accomplishments and your shortcomings, your throbbing vitality, are all deeply imprinted in the collective conscience of Canadians. Understandably, there is little that Canadians do which they do not compare with similar activity in the United States.

Our relationship with you is too complex to be described, too involved to be understood fully, too deeply entrenched to be disregarded. We are no more capable of living in isolation from you than we are desirous of doing so. For those reasons, the basic friendship of Canada in the past several decades has been taken for granted by the United States, as we have accepted yours. I assure you that the friendship will continue for it is a permanent feature of our relationship with you. It will adjust to circumstance and be made more articulate in the process, but it is not regarded by us as negotiable.

It is that friendship that has contributed immeasurably to the high degree of economic well-being, physical security and general happiness enjoyed by the peoples of both countries.

It is as an expression of that friendship that we welcome you, Sir, to this special session of the Parliament of Canada.

2. Address of President Nixon to Both Houses of Parliament, April 14, 1972

(Ibid., pp. 4-6)

To all of you who have welcomed Mrs. Nixon and me so warmly on this occasion, I trust you will make allowance for my attempt to speak in the language I studied 37 years ago. When I tried it today, before I came, on our top linguist in the American government, General Walters, he said, "Go ahead, you speak French with a Canadian accent."

I will have to admit that I am not very much at home in the French language but, as a former parliamentarian in my own country, I feel very much at home in this Chamber. I am grateful for the high privilege which your invitation represents. I am grateful, too, for this chance to return to Canada, and for the opportunity of signing here an historic agreement to restore and protect forever the quality of our Great Lakes which we share together. That agreement testifies to the continuing vitality of our unique relationship which has been described so eloquently by the Prime Minister. In discussing that relationship today, I wish to do so in a way that has not always been customary when leaders of our two countries have met. Through the years our speeches on such occasions have often centered on the decades of unbroken friendship we have enjoyed and our four thousand miles of unfortified frontier. In focusing on our peaceful borders and our peaceful history, they have tended to gloss over the fact that there are real problems between us. They have tended to create the false impression that our countries are essentially alike. It is time for Canadians and Americans to move beyond the sentimental rhetoric of the past. It is time for us to recognize that we have very separate identities; that we have significant differences; and that nobody's interests are furthered when these realities are obscured.

Our peaceful borders and our peaceful history are important symbols, to be sure. What they symbolize, however, is the spirit of respect and restraint which allows us to co-operate despite our differences in ways which help us both. American policy toward Canada is rooted in that spirit. Our policy toward Canada reflects the new approach we are taking in all of our foreign relations, an approach which has been called the Nixon Doctrine. That doctrine rests on the premise that mature partners must have autonomous independent policies; each nation must define the nature of its own interests; each nation must decide the requirements of its own security; each nation must determine the path of its own progress. What we seek is a policy which enables us to share international responsibilities in a spirit of international partnership. We believe that the spirit of partnership is strongest when partners are self-reliant. For among nations, as within nations, the soundest unity is that which respects diversity, and the strongest cohesion is that which rejects coercion.

Over the years, the people of Canada have come to understand these concepts particularly well. Within your own borders, you have been working to bring a wide variety of peoples and provinces and points of view into a great national union, a union which honors the integrity of its constituent elements. It was Prime Minister Laurier who said of Canada's differing components: "I want the marble to remain the marble; I want the granite to remain the granite; I want the oak to remain the oak." This has been the Canadian way. As a result, Canadians have helped to teach the world, as Governor General Massey once said, that the "toleration of differences is the measure of civilization."

Today, more than ever before, we need to apply that understanding to the whole range of world affairs. To begin with, we must apply it in our dealings with one another. We must realize that we are friends, not because there have been no problems between us, but because we have trusted one another enough to be candid about our problems and because our candour has nourished our co-operation.

Last December your Prime Minister and I met in Washington and he asked me if I thought the United States would always want a surplus trade balance with Canada so that we could always export capital here. My answer then, and my answer now, is no. As I said to him at that time, we in the United States saw this same problem from the other side before World War I. We then depended on European capital for our development and we wanted to free ourselves from that dependence. So, we fully understand that Canada is in that same position today.

Canada is the largest trading partner of the United States.

It is very important that that be noted in Japan, too![1]

Our economies have become highly interdependent. But the fact of our mutual interdependence and our mutual desire for independence need not be inconsistent traits. No self-respecting nation can or should accept the proposition that it should always be economically dependent upon any other nation. Let us recognize once and for all that the only basis for a sound and healthy relationship between our two proud

---

[1] The President, sometime before, incorrectly stated in response to a reporter that Japan was the United States' best customer.

peoples is to find a pattern of economic interaction which is beneficial to both our countries and which respects Canada's right to chart its own economic course. We must also build a new spirit of partnership within the western hemisphere that we share together. It has been said that Canada is bounded "on the north by gold, on the west by the East, on the east by history, and on the south by friends."

We hope that will always be the case. We hope it will be the case not only with respect to the United States, your immediate neighbour on the south, but with respect to all your southern neighbours, and ours, who are bound by the great forces of geography and history which are distinctive to the New World. But geography and history alone do not make a community. a true community must be a living entity in which the individuality of each member is a source of pride to all members, in which the unity of all is a source of strength to each. And the great community of the Americas cannot be complete without the participation of Canada. That is why we have been encouraged by the recent decisions of Canada to upgrade its participation as an observer in the Organization of American States to ambassadorial status and to apply for membership in the Inter-American Development Bank. For both of these institutions made the abstract concept of community within the Americas a living reality.

A sound concept of community is also important in another international area that we share, the Atlantic Alliance. Just one month after my inauguration as President of the United States, I observed that a new spirit of co-operation within that alliance was essential as we began a new search for co-operation between East and West. The recent agreements concerning Berlin, and the fact, for example, that thousands of families were reunited this Easter for the first time in many years, are among the first fruits of a new era of East-West negotiation.

But, as we seek better relations with our adversaries, it becomes all the more important to strengthen the alliances with our friends. We must never forget that the strength and the unity of the West have been an indispensable element in helping to bring about the new era of negotiation with the East. That is why we began our round of summit talks last December by meeting with the Prime Minister of Canada, and then with the leaders of other close allies. This is why our East-West conversations will always be accompanied by full and genuine consultations within the Atlantic Alliance.

This alliance began as a way of pooling military resources. Today, it is a way of pooling our intellectual and our diplomatic resources as well. Like our federal approaches to nationhood, like our Canadian-American brotherhood, like our inter-American neighbourhood, the Atlantic Alliance has achieved a creative unity in which the individuality of its members is respected and advanced.

Let us now turn to the world as a whole, for this is where the challenge of building a true community will be most difficult and most important. We, in Canada and the United States, have always been proud to live in what is called the New World. Today there is a new world coming for everyone who lives on this globe. It is our responsibility to make this new world a better world than the world we have known. Canadians and Americans have fought and died together in two world wars in this century. We live now in what has been called a post-war era. But mankind has known a long succession of post-war eras. And each one of them has turned out to be a pre-war era as well. The challenge we face today is to build a permanent post-war era, an era of lasting peace.

My visit to Ottawa comes midway between my visits to Peking and Moscow. In many respects these journeys are very different. In the People's Republic of China, we opened a new dialogue after 22 years of virtually no communication. In the Soviet Union, there is an opportunity to bring a continuing dialogue to productive conclusions. But in their central aim these journeys to Peking and Moscow are alike. Neither visit is directed against anyone, adversary or ally. Both are for the betterment of everyone, for the peace of all mankind. However, we must not allow the fact of summit meetings to create any unrealistic euphoria.

The responsibility for building peace rests with special weight upon the great powers. Whether the great powers fulfill that responsibility depends not on the atmospherics of their diplomacy but on the realities of their behavior. Great powers must not treat a period of detente as an interlude between periods of tension. Better relations among all nations require restraint by great nations, both in dealing with each other and in dealing with the rest of the world. We can agree to limit arms. We can declare our peaceful purposes. But neither the limitation of arms nor the declaration of peaceful purposes will bring peace if, directly or indirectly, the aggressive use of existing weapons is encouraged. The great powers have a responsibility for the aggressive actions of those to whom they give the means of embarking on such action. The great powers must use their influence to halt aggression, not to encourage it. The structure of world peace cannot be built unless the great powers join together to build it. Its strength will grow only as all nations, of all political and social systems, come to accept its validity and sustain its vitality. This does not mean the great powers must always agree.

We expect to continue to have profound philosophical and diplomatic differences with the Soviet Union and with the People's Republic of China in a number of areas. But, through opening new lines of communication, we hope to increase the chance that in the future we shall talk about our differences and not fight about them. As we have prepared for both these journeys the experience of Canada has been most helpful. I am grateful to both the Prime Minister and to the

Opposition Leader, Mr. Stanfield, for sharing their insights with us as we embarked on these endeavours. As we continue together our common quest for a better world order, let us apply the lessons we have learned so well on this continent: that we can walk our own road in our own way without moving farther apart; that we can grow closer together without growing more alike; that peaceful competition can produce winners without producing losers; that success for some need not mean setbacks for the rest; that a rising tide will lift all of our boats; that to go forward at all is to go forward together; that the enemy of peace is not independence but isolation; that the way to peace is an open world.

And let us remember too, these truths that we have found together, that variety can mean vitality; that diversity can be a force for progress; and that our ultimate destiny is indivisible.

When I spoke at the St. Lawrence seaway ceremonies in 1969, I borrowed some words from the monument there which I had joined Queen Elizabeth in dedicating just ten years before. That monument, as its inscription puts it:

> bears witness to the common purpose of two nations whose frontiers are the frontiers of friendship, whose ways are the ways of freedom, whose works are the works of peace.

The truth to which the inscription testifies is of profound importance to people everywhere in this world.

For the ability of our two nations, Canada and the United States, to preserve the frontiers of friendship, to walk in the ways of freedom, and to pursue the works of peace provides example and encouragement to all who seek these same objectives, wherever they may live.

There is nothing more exciting than a time of new beginnings. A member of this body caught that spirit when he spoke in Parliament about the beginnings of Canadian nationhood 100 years ago. Listen to him:

> Blood pulsed in our veins, new hopes fired our hearts, new horizons lifted and widened, new visions came to us in the night watches.

May that same sense of excitement inspire our two nations as we help lead the world to new beginnings today.

3. Exchange of Remarks Between Prime Minister Trudeau and President Nixon Following the Signing of the Great Lakes Water Quality Agreement, April 15, 1972

(U.S. Information Service, Ottawa, "Visit to Canada Of The President." pp. 20-22)

THE PRIME MINISTER: The importance of what we have done this morning cannot be described or measured by conventional means for this agreement does not fall within the normal categories of international activity. It will not contribute materially to the economies of either of our countries; it makes neither of us more secure in our relations with one another or the world beyond; it does little to diminish or remove any of the social problems which worry Americans and Canadians alike.

Yet while doing none of these things it accomplishes much more. For it marks our recognition of the fragility of our planet and the delicacy of the biosphere on which all life is dependent. This agreement deals with the most vital of all issues—the process of life itself. And in doing so it contributes to the well-being of millions of North Americans for it promises to restore to a wholesome condition an immense area which, through greed and indifference, has been permitted to deteriorate disgracefully.

Any catalogue of the distinctive features of this continent surely includes the far-flung water system we know as the Great Lakes. In them is contained the world's largest reservoir of fresh water. Out of them flows one of the world's mightiest and most important rivers.

The beauty and the utility of these waters have proved attractive to men for centuries. That attractiveness has led to extraordinary changes. The birch bark canoes of the Indians and the coureurs-de-bois have given way to giant ocean-going vessels; the handful of explorers who earlier stood in awe at the beauty of Niagara Falls or the Thousand Islands has been replaced by millions of tourists; the first few settlements and factories have burgeoned into sprawling cities and giant industrial complexes. In the process the lakes have suffered.

We now have the opportunity and the responsibility to ease that suffering and to restore to the Great Lakes a large measure of the purity which once was theirs. That task is being shared by those provinces and states that border the lakes and whose governments have encouraged this agreement and contributed to its success. The presence here this morning of the Premier of Ontario and the Minister of the Environment of Quebec as well as the members of the International Joint Commission is proof of the solid foundation of support which our acts enjoy. The tireless dedication of the Canadian Minister of the Environment, Mr. Jack Davis, is recognized in what we are doing, as is the fine level of cooperation which he enjoys with his American colleagues present this morning, Mr. Train and Mr. Ruckelshaus. This treaty is an example to the world of the interdependence of all men and women and of the advantages which flow from cooperative measures.

Indeed, Mr. President, your visit to Canada this week offers an opportunity to all nations to note the high standards which Canadians and Americans have achieved in their neighbourhood, of the benefits which flow from their friendly competition, of the room which exists for their individuality. In our talks yesterday each of us assured himself that he understood the other; each of us dedicated himself to the continuation of a relationship which has few parallels in history and which owes as much to the willingness of the American people to accept on their northern border an independent state with all the differences that that entails, as it does to the desire of Canadians to pursue their own destiny.

Canadians are happy that you came, Mr. President. We hope you will come again. We wish you and Mrs. Nixon a safe journey home and wisdom and stamina in the important days ahead.

THE PRESIDENT: In response to the remarks of the Prime Minister, I particularly wish to express at this occasion our great appreciation for the warm reception we have received here, and after having been here for the first time on a State Visit, I can only say that we hope that we can return, either on that kind of visit or another kind of visit. Of course, I do not have control of which kind of visit it will be.

When the first European explorers sailed the Great Lakes three centuries ago, they were deeply moved by the lakes' striking beauty and boundless promise, and from that time to this, generation after generation of Canadians and Americans have looked upon the Great Lakes as great highways to the future for both of our countries.

But in recent years, as we know, the quality of the Great Lakes' waters has been declining, with ominous implication for 30 million Americans and 7 million Canadians who live near their shores.

The signing today of the Great Lakes Water Quality Agreement represents a significant step toward reversing that decline. This agreement extends the great tradition of cooperation between the United States and Canada. Just as the St. Lawrence Seaway transformed the Great Lakes into highways of peaceful commerce among nations, so the Great Lakes Water Quality Agreement can make them great symbols of international cooperation as man makes his peace with nature.

This Agreement represents an important beginning, one which has been made possible by the cooperation of our two national governments and of state and provincial governments as well. And now we must all follow through on the beginning. Under the Agreement, the International Joint Commission will provide important leadership in this effort.

But it is also essential that governments of all levels, in both of our countries, and private industry as well, work within their own constitutional frameworks to achieve the objectives the Agreement defines.

It is with very great pride and pleasure that I have signed the Great Lakes Water Quality Agreement between Canada and the United States, for this Agreement bears witness to all the world of great concerns which unite our two countries; our common appreciation for the natural heritage which undergirds our national strengths; our common recognition that problems which cross international boundaries require international solutions; and our common confidence that our traditional relationship can grow to meet new demands.

4. Prime Minister Trudeau's Report of Meeting to the Canadian House of Commons, April 17, 1972

(CHCD, April 17, 1972, pp. 1344-48)

HON. ROBERT L. STANFIELD (Leader of the Opposition): Mr. Speaker, I should like to direct a question to the right hon. Prime Minister about the government's policy on foreign investment which was decided upon some months ago, although it has not yet been announced. Was the specific policy discussed by the Prime Minister and the President of the United States during his recent visit, or was it discussed at some less exalted level during the visit of the delegation? If it was discussed, will the Prime Minister very briefly indicate the results of such discussions?

RIGHT HON. P. E. TRUDEAU (Prime Minister): No, Mr. Speaker, there were no discussions whatsoever on the policy. . . .

MR. DAVID LEWIS (Leader of the NDP): Mr. Speaker, with regard to the meeting of the Prime Minister with the President of the United States may I ask the right hon. gentleman whether there was any discussion of the trade negotiations in view of the statement made by Mr. Ziegler, I believe, that the President and the Prime Minister had agreed to review their positions. Was that statement the result of a discussion between the two heads of government on the specific matters in the trade negotiations?

RIGHT HON. P. E. TRUDEAU (Prime Minister): Yes, Mr. Speaker, the President and I did discuss trade matters and the matter of imbalance of trade. The President stated publicly his position on a long-term imbalance. He stated to me that he felt the present deadlock between the two countries should be broken out of and both of us agreed to review our positions with a view to resuming negotiations, if possible.

MR. LEWIS: Does the agreement to resume negotiations to break out of the deadlock mean that the Prime Minister informed the President of the United States that the government of Canada is prepared to grant some of the concessions or parts of some of the concessions that the

United States negotiators are demanding, and did the President continue to demand that the present imbalance between Canada and the United States must be corrected, disregarding his general statement about the future which of course anyone would have to grant to any country in the world?

MR. TRUDEAU: In the short-term, Mr. Speaker, the President did spell out the type of problem the United States is meeting at the present time with its balance of payments and expressed the hope which has been there since last August that various countries would help or would contribute to the United States in its effort to improve its present economic situation. I repeated that it was Canada's intention to contribute in any way we could to the improvement of their position, knowing full well that a healthy economy in the United States is pretty important to Canada. But as to the concrete aspects of what this meant on his side and on our side, we did not enter into any great details. The President showed no desire to go into the details of the negotiations, nor did I. We both agreed it would be important to prevent this nonresolution of the situation from hardening. We both agreed, as I said, that we should each review our own position.

HON. GEORGE HEES: Mr. Speaker, I have a supplementary for the Prime Minister. During President Nixon's visit did the President advise the Canadian government that the position of the United States government as outlined by Secretary Connally on February 9 in the following words, that "the United States will seek appropriate means of reducing imbalances of trade with Canada," has changed in any way and, if so, in what way has the United States position changed?

MR. TRUDEAU: Mr. Speaker, the President did not refer to this statement by Secretary Connally. As I just said to the leader of the New Democratic Party, we talked of the desire on both sides to resume negotiations. We thought that the best way of doing it was for each of us to tell our people—I assume President Nixon will tell Mr. Connally that he should review the package—that we should review the package, which we will do.

MR. HEES: Did President Nixon assure the Canadian government that the American government does not intend to take unilateral action to correct the imbalance of trade, such as adding a 7 per cent tax on new Canadian cars entering the United States or cancelling the exemption from the interest equalization tax which Canada now enjoys, as has been widely rumoured?

MR. TRUDEAU: The President of the United States made no threats to Canada, Mr. Speaker, nor did I make any threats to the United States.

MR. HEES: Did the Prime Minister not bring up these very important matters with the President, or did he just indulge in pleasantries meaning nothing but I hope my people will vote for me and I hope I can help you get elected?

MR. S. PERRY RYAN: As a result of the talks with President Nixon, is the government now reviewing its position on the auto pact and, if so, can the Prime Minister say when a new position will be defined and made public?

RIGHT HON. P. E. TRUDEAU (Prime Minister): Mr. Speaker, I did undertake to look at everything that was in our package to see if it could be changed or modified in some way which would be more acceptable to the United States and no more damaging to Canada. There was no timing set on that and there was no specific mention of what aspects of the package we would look at. I repeat, the agreement was as general as I said in my first answer. It is that we would look at our negotiating positions, and neither the President nor I went into any great detail as to what this meant other than to see if it could be possible to renew negotiations fruitfully.

MR. RYAN: Has the Prime Minister given any direction to the relevant departments in this respect with regard to the auto pact?

MR. TRUDEAU: Mr. Speaker, the relevant ministers were informed of the substance of my talks with the President and I assume that this work is being done.

MR. J. EDWARD BROADBENT: The Prime Minister has suggested that the total packages are going to be reviewed. Was there an agreed upon date or a tentative date that the discussions should, hopefully, be resumed, or was a date arranged between the Prime Minister and the President at which time they would be able to convey to each other whether or not negotiations would be able to begin again soon?

RIGHT HON. P. E. TRUDEAU (Prime Minister): No, Mr. Speaker, no date was discussed. . . .

MR. DAVID MACDONALD: Can the Prime Minister indicate whether these important issues having to do with trading with the enemy and anti-trust laws that from time to time affect Canada's economic position were raised and whether there will be a vehicle for the resolution of these important problems?

MR. TRUDEAU: Mr. Speaker, I believe the hon. member is distinguishing between important problems, and they are indeed, which are very frequently discussed between our officials and ministers both in Washington and Ottawa, but I repeat that they were not raised at the level of talks between the President and myself on Thursday or Friday.

RIGHT HON. J. G. DIEFENBAKER: Mr. Speaker, we hear a great deal about packages. I wonder whether it would be possible for the Prime Minister to let the House of Commons know what matters were included in the Canadian package, because up to now it has been as silent as Pandora's box until opened?

RIGHT HON. P. E. TRUDEAU (Prime Minister): Mr. Speaker, the right hon. member is asking me for more than the President asked me. There was no discussion of the detailed contents of the package. However, I think that through a process of questioning certain answers have been obtained from the Minister of Industry, Trade and Commerce as to so-called irritants, both on the American side and on our side. I am afraid I would have to refer the right hon. member to his answers in *Hansard* with regard to what those were.

MR. DIEFENBAKER: Mr. Speaker, I follow *Hansard* very carefully, I have been in the House, and this has never been revealed. The Prime Minister was talking about exchanging packages and diminishing one claim or another in return for something else, a *quid pro quo*. Could he not summarize—1, 2, 3, 4, 5—what these items were in this package so that Canadians as a whole would know what kind of package it really is?

MR. TRUDEAU: Mr. Speaker, I think some Canadians have been astute enough to assume, for instance, that the auto pact was one of the items discussed in the package. Perhaps with a further degree of astuteness and a re-reading once again of *Hansard*, the right hon. member will observe other elements in the package that were mentioned by the minister.

MR. DIEFENBAKER: Mr. Speaker, I am no mind reader-even though the Prime Minister assumes I am.

MRS. GRACE MACINNIS: Mr. Speaker, I wish to ask about another aspect of the talks. In view of the recent bombing of Haiphong and other events escalating the war in Viet Nam, was there any discussion between the Prime Minister and the President of the United States of the war in Viet Nam and the possibility of bringing it to a conclusion quickly?

RIGHT HON. P. E. TRUDEAU (Prime Minister): Yes, Mr. Speaker, the President did discuss the position of his government as regards Viet Nam and he did repeat to me what is public knowledge, that he was committed to a policy of a negotiated settlement in Viet Nam with continued withdrawal of United States troops.

HON. D. S. HARKNESS: In view of the fact that western Canada, particularly Calgary and Edmonton, is badly in need of more air routes, and as the renegotiation of the bilateral air treaty with the United States which was supposed to take place in 1969 has not been concluded, was this question discussed with President Nixon when he was here last week?

MR. TRUDEAU: It was not discussed with me. I do know that officials have been discussing this problem, but I do not know whether they discussed it at this recent meeting. . . .

MR. ELDON M. WOOLLIAMS: Mr. Speaker, in light of the Prime Minister's answer to me on Thursday and in light of his answer today to the right hon. member for Prince Albert I would like to ask the Prime Minister whether there were any discussions with the President, or between officials when the President was visiting Ottawa, in reference to pipelines—I will not refer to the two routes because the Prime Minister knows what routes I am talking about—and in particular was there discussion of any policies to accelerate trade in energy products, namely, crude petroleum and natural gas?

MR. TRUDEAU: Mr. Speaker, in a very general sense, yes, the problem was raised. I did raise, in front of the President, the important question of energy and the Canadian policy on energy as we would be trying to develop it. The President also raised the pollution aspect of the transportation of oil and told me that he was well aware of the situation, but at our level we did not go into the problem in any great detail. I do know that the Secretary of State for External Affairs at his level was raising this problem with Secretary Rogers.

MR. WOOLLIAMS: Did the Prime Minister make the Canadian position clear on the question of danger of pollution to the west coast and set out, from the study that the Minister of Energy, Mines and Resources mentioned on Thursday, that if there is to be a transport route Canada prefers a pipeline down the Mackenzie? Was that position made clear to the Americans at that time?

MR. TRUDEAU: Mr. Speaker, the danger of pollution was indeed made very clear to the Americans by the government. I might add that, apart from the Secretary of State for External Affairs, the Minister of Energy, Mines and Resources was also present at the meeting with Secretary Rogers where this subject was discussed.

MR. STANFIELD: I have a further question for the Prime Minister, Mr. Speaker, in connection with his talks with President Nixon and arising out of reports from Washington that consideration is being given there to negotiating a deal with Russia whereby the United States would take oil or gas in exchange for U.S. feed or other grains. Can the Prime Minister tell the House whether this subject, which is of great importance to Canada, was discussed by himself and the President or at any level during the visit?

HON. MITCHELL SHARP (Secretary of State for External Affairs): Mr. Speaker, if I might be permitted to reply to that question, I did raise the subject with Secretary Rogers and I was informed that there was no sort of barter deal contemplated and that if oil or gas were to be purchased from the Soviet Union it would be part of the ordinary trade carried on between the two countries.

MR. LEWIS: I should like to ask a supplementary question of the Prime Minister, Mr. Speaker, with regard to the war in Viet Nam. In his answer to the hon. member for Vancouver-Kingsway the Prime Minister informed us that the President had made his position clear, which I need not repeat. Did the Prime Minister raise any protest to the President of the United States about the accelerated bombing of North Viet Nam, particularly that which has gone so deeply into North Viet Nam at Hanoi and Haiphong? Was any opinion expressed by the President of the United States to end the bombings so that meaningful negotiations for peace can resume?

MR. TRUDEAU: No, Mr. Speaker, I did not make any such comments to the President of the United States but I do know that his government and indeed other governments are aware of Canada's well stated position in this regard.

Appendix

First Visit of a U.S. President to Canada: President Warren G. Harding to Vancouver, British Columbia, July 26, 1923 (Address at Stanley Park)

(James W. Murphy (ed. Official Reporter, US Senate) Speeches And Addresses of Warren G. Harding, President of the United States Delivered During the Course of his Tour From Washington, D.C. to Alaska and Return to San Francisco, June 20 to August 2, 1923. Limited Edition, No. 318, 1923, (Published under the Patronage of President Calvin Coolidge et al.) pp. 327-32.)

I may as well confess to you at the outset a certain perplexity as to how I should address you. The truth of the matter is that this is the first time I have ever spoken as President in any country other than my own. Indeed, so far as I can recall, I am, with the single exception of my immediate predecessor, the first President in office even to set foot on politically-foreign soil (sic).

True, there is no definite inhibition upon one doing so, such as prevents any but a natural born citizen from becoming President, but an early prepossession soon developed into a tradition and for more than a hundred years held the effect of unwritten law. I am not prepared to say that the custom was not desirable, perhaps even needful, in the early days, when time was the chief requisite of travel. Assuredly, too, at present, the Chief Magistrate of a great Republic ought not to cultivate the habit or make a hobby of wandering over all the continents of the earth.

But exceptions are required to prove rules. And Canada is an exception, a most notable exception, from every viewpoint of the United States. You are not only our neighbor, but a very good neighbor, and we rejoice in your advancement and admire your independence, no less sincerely than we value your friendship.

I need not depict the points of similarity that make this attitude of the one toward the other irresistible. We think the same thoughts, live the same lives and cherish the same aspirations of service to each other in

311

times of need. Thousands of your brave lads perished in gallant and generous action for the preservation of our Union. Many of our young men followed Canadian colors to the battlefields of France before we entered the war and left their proportion of killed to share the graves of your intrepid sons. This statement is brought very intimately home to me, for one of the brave lads in my own newspaper office felt the call of service to the colors of the sons of Canada. He went to the front, and gave his life with your boys for the preservation of the American and Canadian concept of civilization.

When my mind reverts and my heart beats low to recollection of those faithful and noble companionships, I may not address you, to be sure, as "fellow citizens," as I am accustomed to designate assemblages at home, but I may and do, with respect and pride, salute you as "fellow men," in mutual striving for common good.

What an object lesson of peace is shown today by our two countries to all the world! No grimfaced fortifications mark our frontiers, no huge battleships patrol our dividing waters, no stealthy spies lurk in our tranquil border hamlets. Only a scrap of paper, recording hardly more than a simple understanding, safeguards lives and properties on the Great Lakes, and only humble mileposts mark the inviolable boundary line for thousands of miles through farm and forest.

Our protection is in our fraternity, our armor is our faith; the tie that binds more firmly year by year is ever-increasing acquaintance and comradeship through interchange of citizens; and the compact is not of perishable parchment, but of fair and honorable dealing which, God grant, shall continue for all time.

An interesting and significant symptom of our growing mutuality appears in the fact that the voluntary interchange of residents to which I have referred, is wholly free from restrictions. Our National and industrial exigencies have made it necessary for us, greatly to our regret, to fix limits to immigration from foreign countries. But there is no quota for Canada. We gladly welcome all of your sturdy, steady stock who care to come, as a strengthening ingredient and influence. We none the less bid Godspeed and happy days to the thousands of our own folk, who are swarming constantly over your land and participating in its remarkable development. Wherever in either of our countries any inhabitant of the one or the other can best serve the interests of himself and his family is the place for him to be.

A further evidence of our increasing interdependence appears in the shifting of capital. Since the armistice, I am informed, approximately $2,500,000,000 has found its way from the United States into Canada for investment. That is a huge sum of money, and I have no doubt is employed safely for us and helpfully for you. Most gratifying to you, moreover, should be the circumstance that one-half of that great sum has gone for purchase of your state and municipal bonds,—a tribute, indeed, to the scrupulous maintenance of your credit, to a degree equalled only by your mother country across the sea and your sister country across the hardly visible border.

These are simple facts which quickly resolve into history for guidance of mankind in the seeking of human happiness. "History, history!" ejaculated Lord Overton to his old friend, Lindsay, himself an historian; "what is the use of history? It only keeps people apart by reviving recollections of enmity."

As we look forth today upon the nations of Europe, with their armed camps of nearly a million more men in 1923 than in 1913, we can not deny the grain of truth in this observation. But not so here! A hundred years of tranquil relationships, throughout vicissitudes which elsewhere would have evoked armed conflict rather than arbitration, affords, truly declared James Bryce, "the finest example ever seen in history of an undefended frontier, whose very absence of armaments itself helped to prevent hostile demonstrations"; thus proving beyond question that "peace can always be kept, whatever be the grounds of controversy, between peoples that wish to keep it."

There is a great and highly pertinent truth, my friends, in that simple assertion. It is public will, not public force, that makes for enduring peace. And is it not a gratifying circumstance that it has fallen to the lot of us North Americans, living amicably for more than a century, under different flags, to present the most striking example yet produced of that basic fact? If only European countries would heed the lesson conveyed by Canada and the United States, they would strike at the root of their own continuing disagreements and, in their own prosperity, forget to inveigh constantly at ours.

Not that we would reproach them for resentment or envy, which after all is but a manifestation of human nature. Rather should we sympathize with their seeming inability to break the shackles of age-long methods, and rejoice in our own relative freedom from the stultifying effect of Old World customs and practices. Our natural advantages are manifold and obvious. We are not palsied by the habits of a thousand years. We live in the power and glory of youth. Others derive justifiable satisfaction from contemplation of their resplendent pasts. We have relatively only our present to regard, and that, with eager eyes fixed chiefly and confidently upon our future.

Therein lies our best estate. We profit both mentally and materially from the fact that we have no "departed greatness" to recover, no "lost provinces" to regain, no new territory to covet, no ancient grudges to gnaw eternally at the heart of our National consciousness. Not only are we happily exempt from these handicaps of vengeance and prejudice, but we are animated correspondingly and most helpfully by our better knowledge, derived from longer experience, of the blessings of liberty. These advantages we may not appreciate to the full at all times, but we know that we possess them, and the day is far distant when, if ever, we shall fail to cherish and defend them against any conceivable assault from without or from within our borders.

I find that, quite unconsciously, I am speaking of our two countries almost in the singular when perhaps I should be more painstaking to keep them where they belong, in the plural. But I feel no need to apologize. You understand as well as I that I speak in no political sense. The ancient bugaboo of the United States scheming to annex Canada disappeared from all our minds years and years ago. Heaven knows we have all we can manage now, and room enough to spare for another hundred millions, before approaching the intensive stage of existence of many European states.

And if I might be so bold as to offer a word of advice to you, it would be this: Do not encourage any enterprise looking to Canada's annexation of the United States. You are one of the most capable governing peoples in the world, but I entreat you, for your own sakes, to think twice before undertaking management of the territory which lies between the Great Lakes and the Rio Grande.

No, let us go our own gaits along parallel roads, you helping us and we helping you. So long as each country maintains its independence, and both recognize their interdependence, those paths can not fail to be highways of progress and prosperity. Nationality continues to be a supreme factor in modern existence; make no mistake about that; but the day of the Chinese wall, inclosing a hermit nation, has passed forever. Even though space itself were not in process of annihilation by airplane, submarine, wireless and broadcasting, our very propinquity enjoins that most effective cooperation which comes only from clasping of hands in true faith and good fellowship.

It is in precisely that spirit, men and women of Canada, that I have stopped on my way home from a visit to our pioneers in Alaska to make a passing call upon my very good neighbor of the fascinating Iroquois name, "Kanada," to whom, glorious in her youth and strength and beauty, on behalf of my own beloved country, I stretch forth both my arms in the most cordial fraternal greeting, with gratefulness for your splendid welcome in my heart, and from my lips the whispered prayer of our famed Rip Van Winkle: "May you all live long and prosper!"